MW01245337

# JEANNE D'ARC

## MAID OF ORLEANS
## DELIVERER OF FRANCE

Being the Story of her Life, her Achievements,
and her Death, as attested on Oath and Set forth
in the Original Documents

EDITED BY
T. DOUGLAS MURRAY

WITH ILLUSTRATIONS AND A MAP

## NATAL PUBLISHING LLC
*ARS LONGA, VITA BREVIS*

Copyright© 2024 Natal Publishing

All rights reserved

Cover art by Mauricio A. on Pixabay

# PREFACE

The following Document concerning the story of the life and death of Jeanne d'Arc, Maid of Orleans, is probably the only known instance in which a complete biographical record, of historical importance, has been elicited by evidence taken on oath. These depositions cover the childhood of the Maid; the series of her military exploits as Commander-in-Chief of the armies of France; her capture, imprisonment, and death at the stake in the market-place of Rouen.

The official Latin text of the Trial and Rehabilitation of Jeanne d'Arc, rescued from oblivion among the archives of France, and published in the forties by Quicherat, has been faithfully, and now for the first time, rendered into English. This account, given by numerous contemporary witnesses, of an episode which profoundly affected the history of Europe and determined the destinies of England and France must appeal to the general reader no less than to the student.

# INTRODUCTION

By the order of Pope Calixtus in 1455, the Trial of Jeanne d'Arc at Rouen, which had taken place twenty-four years before, was reconsidered by a great court of lawyers and churchmen, and the condemnation of Jeanne was solemnly annulled and declared wicked and unjust. By this re-trial posterity has been allowed to see the whole life of the village maiden of Domremy, as she was known first to her kinsfolk and her neighbours, and afterwards to warriors, nobles and churchmen who followed her extraordinary career. The evidence so given is unique in its minute and faith-worthy narration of a great and noble life; as indeed that life is itself unique in all human history. After all that can be done by the rationalising process, the mystery remains of an untutored and unlettered girl of eighteen years old, not only imposing her will upon captains and courtiers, but showing a skill and judgment worthy, as General Dragomiroff says, of the greatest commanders, indeed of Napoleon himself. While we must give due weight and consideration to the age in which this marvel showed itself on the stage of history, an age of portents and prophecies, of thaumaturgists and saints, yet when all allowance is made there remains this sane, strong, solid girl leaving her humble home, and in two short months accomplishing more than Cæsar or Alexander accomplished in so much time, and at an age when even Alexander had as yet achieved nothing.

The story is best given by the witnesses, and only indications or, so to speak, sign-posts are needed to point out the way. Before the work of Jeanne can be even vaguely apprehended something must be known of how France stood at her coming. A century of misfortune and sorrow, broken only by a parenthesis of comparative prosperity from 1380 to 1407, had left her an easy prey to the hereditary enemy. Torn asunder by factions which distracted Church and State alike, she was in no condition of health and courage to recover from the shock of the crushing disaster of Agincourt. For although the English were unable at the moment to follow up the victory they had gained, and Henry V. returned to England the bearer of barren glory, still the breathing time was not put to good account by the French, whose domestic jars made combined national action impossible. At Henry's second coming, regular resistance was hardly offered. His fleets and armies held the Channel and the ports and fortresses on both sides. The King of France was insane. His wife, Isabel of Bavaria, came to terms with the English King, and by the treaty of Troyes (1420) the Crown of France was to pass away from the Dauphin, whom his wretched mother would fain bastardise, to the issue of Henry and the Princess Catherine, the ready instrument of her mother's purpose. When Henry V. died the son born of this unhallowed marriage was declared King of France and England under the title of Henry VI. The poor child was less than a year old. His able and resolute uncle John, Duke of Bedford, ruled France as Regent, and carried the arms of England in triumph against all who dared to dispute his nephew's title. The Dauphin fled to the south, and abandoned to Bedford all territory north of the Loire. Paris was occupied and held by the English. The braver members of the Parliament and the University joined the Dauphin at Poitiers, but the accommodating and timid members did homage to Bedford and duly attorned to Henry VI. as to their lawful King. Orleans alone remained, of the strong places of France, in the hands of the patriot party. If Orleans fell, all organised opposition to Bedford would melt away.

As Orleans was the key of the military, so was Rheims the key of the political, situation. Rheims was the old city where for many centuries the Kings of France had been crowned and consecrated. Such a ceremony brought with it in an especial manner the sacrosanct divinity which in the middle ages hedged a King.

It is noteworthy that Jeanne's mission, as now defined and traced by French scholars, was the double one of rescuing beleaguered Orleans and crowning the Dauphin at Rheims.

Orleans had withstood a stubborn siege of many

months, but its fate seemed sealed. The Dauphin had almost given up the struggle. He had made futile appeals for help to the King of Scotland, whose infant daughter was betrothed to young Louis, afterwards the terrible Louis XI. To Naples also he made appeals, but no succour or hope came, and in despair he shut himself up at Chinon, giving up the cause of France as lost unless aid came from on high. Jeanne came as the messenger of glad tidings, and announced herself as one sent by God to aid France in her extreme need.

She came from Lorraine, out of which no good thing could come, as proverbs taught; for Lorraine had ever been branded as false to God and false to man. Ambiguous in its relations to France and to the Empire, it had, like most borderlands, the unstableness of character which comes of social and political insecurity. Jeanne's native town of Domremy was one of a cluster of hamlets on the verge of France, in the smiling valley through which a winding river made its way. Her father and mother were in a very humble station, having a little patch of land with rights of commonage on the village pastures, and were, from the evidence of their neighbours, frugal, hard-working, and "well thought of."

Jeanne herself was in no way marked out from her girl friends by any special accomplishments or ambition. She prided herself solely on her domestic usefulness and her skill in household work. She was intensely pious, but in no way introspective or morbid. God and His angels and saints were as real to her, more real indeed, than the men and women of her native village. The thoughts of sacred things subdued her soul to an unconsciousness of self, which marks her off even from such beautiful spiritual natures as Teresa and Bridget of Sweden and Catherine of Sienna, whose habit of mind was less simple and less humble than hers. She seems to have grieved long and deeply on the misfortunes of France, which was to her the only country claiming her allegiance. For, although geographically in Lorraine, Domremy was part of the French Kingdom, and its people were devotedly on the side of the Dauphin and the national party. The Duke of

Burgundy, who had sided with the English, had only one adherent in Domremy, and he was treated, after the manner of good-natured peasants, with a certain humorous toleration by the patriots of the village.

Growing up in this atmosphere, Jeanne, who was born on the feast of the Epiphany 1412, heard in her earlier girlhood of the sad state of her country torn asunder by faction and treason, and presenting a very broken front to the redoubtable armies of England, which had in the course of a century carried the banner of St. George over all the lands from Calais to Cadiz without once meeting an enemy strong enough to look them in the face on a pitched field of battle.

Agincourt, and the carnage after Agincourt, revived in French minds the humiliation of Poitiers and the horrors of Limoges, so that dread and hatred of the English were the burden of every household story. Nor must we forget that in Europe then, as in Asia and Africa now, news spread apace, and unlettered folk got to know in some strange way the doings of camps and courts.

Old prophecies too were on every lip. That weird unrest which Shakespeare shadows forth in Peter of Pomfret and his sayings, shaking the throne of Richard II. by their very vagueness, was nowhere felt more intensely than in Lorraine, with its blending of old Celtic myths, German romances, and tales of Provençal minstrelsy in all hearts and memories.

Sublime above all these loomed the Church and its tremendous message. And so, from current history and fable and folk-lore, Jeanne's imagination was fed, while her soul was ready to receive any mandate which the Lord of all things might deign to signify. She was thirteen years old when the first message came to her. The Archangel Michael, as she states, appeared, and she was struck with great fear; but afterwards she longed for his coming and his words. He admonished her to be pure and holy and religious, and she determined to be so. Later on St. Catherine (the Virgin) and St. Margaret appeared to her, and told her that the Lord ordered her to go into France and relieve Orleans. In her examination she tells these things with great particularity, meeting all questions as to age, size, voice, dress, language, and surroundings of the angels, with a simple directness which carries conviction of her absolute truthfulness.

Her doubts and misgivings as to her own unfitness she put aside as impertinences, when assured of her divine mission. No shadow of spiritual inflation or egotism is to be seen in all these things. Rather she held by the belief that her very unworthiness in the world's eye was the cause of her being chosen as a simple instrument in the hands of the Lord.

Her uncle led her to Vaucouleurs in 1428; Robert de Baudricourt, whom she believed she was told to see, declined to give ear to her stories; but Jean de Metz, whose evidence is of absorbing interest, tells us how he was overcome and won over to her by her compelling earnestness and faith. She came to Chinon with a small escort, and she and her guard had to travel mostly by night to avoid the Burgundians. "At Chinon," says Jean de Metz, "she had to submit to long inquiries."

The Dauphin was naturally loath to take a step so full of peril, and indeed so fraught with the danger of ridiculous failure, without grave, anxious, and searching investigation. He wished Jeanne to appear at Poitiers before the prelates and lawyers of Parliament. At Poitiers she was subjected to the closest examination, and in the end convinced the lawyers and churchmen of her good faith and the reality of her visions and voices. The Archbishop of Rheims, following "Gamaliel in the Council of the Jews," advised the Dauphin not to spurn the proffered help; and Charles, who had been already impressed by the "revelations," took the Archbishop's advice, and placed his forces and his fortune in her hands, trusting to divine help and succour. The armies of France were in marked contrast to those of England. French nobles had quasi-regal power in their dominions, and only fitfully followed the royal arms. In England, from the Conquest, the King was supreme lord of all, and every one owed direct and immediate allegiance to him. The English armies, unlike the French feudal array, were made up of peasants and artisans and adventurous young men seeking a career, and, in the last resort, as we know from Falstaff, of losels and waifs and ne'er-do-wells. Whether Lord Melville's famous saying that "the worst men make the best soldiers" be or be not accepted, it seems true enough that for aggressive wars at any rate the reckless bravery of adventurers goes very far. And Henry's army, composed as it was of English, Welsh, and Irish, was in truth an army of intrepid *condottieri*, intrepid to a fault, but lacking the chivalrous feelings which with all their drawbacks the feudal system and the knightly organisations tended to evolve.

Hardened and seasoned by years of warfare, the English in 1429 were without serious opposition or check in their movements and attacks. No French army kept the field. The King's authority was flouted. The Duke of Burgundy was openly for the English cause. The Duke of Brittany and Lorraine wavered from side to side. Money had run out, and the last chance of success was staked in a bold throw on the strange promises of the young country girl.

The evidence given by competent witnesses shows us clearly the magnitude of her achievements during the months of May, June, and July, 1429: the relief of Orleans; the victory of Patay; the capture of Troyes; and the triumphal march to Rheims, completing her work by the consecration of Charles in the old Cathedral, which had seen so many of his predecessors anointed and crowned within its walls.

But the marvel is that these stupendous achievements were not the results of mere enthusiasm, great and potent though that was, but of settled, farseeing skill and prudence on the part of Jeanne, joined to a strength of soul and purpose which multiplied the strength of the army tenfold.

Like Cromwell she "new-modelled" the army. The licentious gaiety of the feudal warrior had to give way to the sobriety and seemliness which became a Christian camp. The voluptuary and the blasphemer had to amend their lives. To revels succeeded prayers and fasts and vigils. Yet never for a moment did this great amendment degenerate into formalism or hypocrisy. Like all great souls she awakened latent good and drove vice abashed from her presence without any conscious spiritual superiority in herself. Men were ashamed to be base in such a presence. Nor did she ever become a law unto herself, as the "illuminated" are so apt to be; rather she was more than ever observant of all the duties and claims and observances of ordinary religious obligation, being ever in heart the simple maid whom the Lord for His own mysterious purpose, and without any merit of hers, had chosen for a mighty task.

These great qualities won for her the ready submission of the soldiers, while her name and fame brought levies of ardent volunteers, from all sides, eagerly contending for the glory of serving under such a leader. Her frame was hardy and enduring. She wore armour night and day for a week at a time. She ate sparingly and drank hardly at all, moistening a crust in wine, or, greatly fatigued, tasting a little as a restorative. While her woman's nature showed itself in her burst of tears when dishonouring names were flung at her by some brutal English soldiers, or when she screamed at the sharp and sudden pain of the wound she received, still there always came a quick moral reinforcement which restored her serene fortitude in the midst of indignities and perils.

Writers have differed and must go on differing with regard to the scope of her mission and the waning of her powers after the coronation of Rheims. If she dictated the letter to Henry VI. in which the words occur, "body for body you will be driven out of France," we may, by connecting this saying with her famous letter to the Hussites—in which she threatened to chastise them, "Saracens" that they were, when her work was done and France cleared of her enemies—and from other scattered phrases as well, come to the conclusion that in her belief France was to be wholly freed, and freed by her as agent of the Lord. But the letter to Henry VI. is of doubtful authority, and her appeal to Charles after the coronation to be allowed to return to her father and mother, supported by contemporary authority, seems to show that she looked upon her work as done, and the great outburst of weeping in the Cathedral was in all likelihood the sob of satisfied piety and patriotism, whose cares were at an end and whose task was fulfilled even to fruition.

This seems the true view, with which also the latest French students agree. Yielding to entreaty she threw herself further into the national struggle. She was still brave, still magnetic and inspiring, but no longer to herself or to others the sword in the hand of God.

But if in the campaign of May and June she showed the wonderful military genius to which so many competent witnesses bear testimony, in the weary winter of the same year she shows a clearness and depth of statesmanship scarcely less astonishing. In moments of national peril there are always "wise" men who think that further resistance is foolish and even criminal. Alfred had to deal with such time-servers. So had Bruce, and so later on had Washington. Jeanne with a sore heart found herself clogged and impeded by these prudent men. Foremost amongst them was the Archbishop of Rheims, Regnault de Chartres. His programme was one of reconciliation. The Duke of Burgundy was to become the ally of France, and as such was to act as negotiator and intermediary for a lasting peace between Henry VI. and Charles VII. Poor Charles was weary of the war, and lent a ready ear to the accommodator. In vain Jeanne warned him of the folly of these plans. To strike, and strike quickly, at Paris was her advice. Halting and hesitating, Charles consented. An army was placed at her disposal, but, just as victory seemed sure, she was ordered to desist, and Burgundy so duped the French King that he was allowed to go through the French lines into Paris, ostensibly to treat for peace, but in reality, as the event proved, to put himself under Bedford's orders, and to hold Paris as lieutenant for the Regent and ally of the King of England. Had Jeanne's advice been followed this shameful treason could never have come about. She had known and felt that the hatred of the Duke of Burgundy and his house against Charles VII. was too deep and too rooted to be pulled up in a moment. For twenty years France had been distracted by the factions of Burgundy and Orleans struggling for control. Fire and water were not more opposed. Burgundy looked to England, and Orleans to France. We must not too hastily condemn these factions. Nations in the modern sense had not fully arisen. The State was everything. Whether a great Anglo-French monarchy sitting in Paris ruled over France, England, Ireland, and Wales, or a more domestic French line only ruled over France itself, was a question on which upright men might well take opposite sides. Jeanne's special merit was that she saw the possibility of a great French nation, self-centred, self-sufficient, and she so stamped this message on the French heart that its characters have never faded. Ecclesiastics, on the other hand, with their conception of a Universal Empire and a Universal Church, thought little of National aspirations or claims. To them, anything which would allay the bitter rivalries of France and England naturally appealed, seeing, as they did, in such a change the promise of a return to the days before the Babylonian captivity at Avignon, and the bringing of all peoples into ready submission to Peter's chair. Jeanne's greatness is nowhere more manifest than in her willing loyalty to the Church and "our lord the Pope," while claiming for France absolute national independence. Herein she stands alone. Dante's two swords (wielded by Pope and Emperor) were lethal to national life. To the spiritual sword Jeanne bowed, but to no Emperor or King other than the anointed King of France could the loyalty of a French heart be due.

The winter of 1429 was spent in controversies of which the opposing principles of imperialism and nationality are the true keys. In the early spring, Jeanne, who had bravely stood by the national cause, and heartened all who withstood the party of compromise and surrender, saw only too clearly that for the time the French hopes of success had given way. That brave night ride to relieve Compiègne was in many respects a meeting of fate half way. No doubt, she defied augury, but signs of impending disaster multiplied; and when she fell into the hands of the Burgundians, she must have felt that while her own agony began, the cause of France might well gather more strength from her example as a sufferer, than from her futile struggle against cowardice and treason. Into one short year her whole astounding public career is crowded; Orleans, Patay, Troyes, Rheims, Paris, Compiègne; glory, exaltation, wreckage, and captivity. But France was at the end of it a conscious nation with an anointed King, and the work of deliverance was assured.

### The Trial and Rehabilitation.

The English had felt sorely the humiliations of the year 1429. In Bedford's report to the King's Council in London he told of those who were struck with fear by the incantations of this "limb of the fiend" who had startled them from their security; and proclamations were issued against those who in terror of the Maid deserted the army. Now that she, who had worked such mischief to them, was in their hands, betrayed by her own countrymen,[1] they wreaked vengeance upon her without stint.

---

[1] Had there been any desire on the part of the French King to rescue Jeanne from captivity, a 'King's ransom,' which was later paid for her by Cauchon, could scarcely have been refused in those days for a prisoner of war, however renowned. Unhappily for the memory of Charles, she was left to the tender mercies of the English without any offer being made for her release, or any attempt at rescue. There existed a bitter feeling of jealousy towards Jeanne in consequence of her great successes in the field. This was notably shown during her attack upon Paris, where she was thwarted in every direction, and all possibility of victory was taken from her by the conduct of the King. Whether or not Flavy, the Governor of Compiègne, who was completely under the control of the King, betrayed Jeanne at Compiègne, by shutting the gates and closing the drawbridge at her approach, will never be known, but suspicion has always pointed to his betrayal of the Maid.

Alain Bouchard states that, in the year 1488, he heard from two aged men of Compiègne, who had themselves been present, that a few days before her capture, the Maid was attending Mass in the Church of St. Jacques. After communicating and spending some time in devotion, she turned to the assembled congregation, and, leaning against a pillar, uttered this prediction: "My good friends, my dear little children, I am sold and betrayed. Soon I shall be given up to death. Pray to God for me, for I can no longer serve the King and the Kingdom of France."— *Grandes Annales de Bretagne*, also *Miroir des Femmes Vertueuses*.

The story of her prison life is a record of shame to her gaolers. Chained, mocked at, threatened, and insulted, her serenity never failed. She was in God's hand, and she bowed to His will.

Months of suffering and anxiety passed over her before her captors made up their minds as to the course they would take to bring about her death under the semblance of legal execution. If she could be convicted by an ecclesiastical court of crimes against the faith, her condemnation would redound to the fair fame of England and the pious[2] House of Lancaster, while covering the French and their sovereign with confusion as the allies and associates of a minister of hell.

Pliant churchmen were at hand to give countenance and help in this undertaking—bishops full of zeal and loyalty for our sovereign lord Henry VI., by the grace of God King of France and England.

The worst of these servile churchmen was the wretched Bishop of Beauvais, Pierre Cauchon. Many other prelates were Cæsar's friends, but he sits exalted in solitary infamy. He came to the Burgundian camp and claimed his victim in the name of Bedford, Regent of France for the English King. Had Jeanne been detained by the Burgundians, it is impossible to believe that Charles VII. would not have procured her release. Had she been held as a prisoner of war by the English, it is very likely that the shame of holding a woman captive in their hands would have made it possible to arrange for her ransom. But once charged with heresy and taken out of the hands of the Burgundians such hopes and chances were closed. Still, as an ecclesiastical prisoner she would have been entitled to counsel and guidance by religious persons, the Church offering admonition before preferring grave charges of rebellion against any of her children. But this would render her punishment uncertain. Grave doctors of

---

[2] The House of Lancaster was fervidly orthodox. Persecution of heretics begins with Henry IV. The "Cardinal of England" (Beaufort Bishop of Winchester) was the *malleus hereticorum* at home and abroad. He spoke against the Hussites at the Council of Basle, and he planned Crusades against both heretics and "Saracens."

the law and eminent churchmen had at Poitiers, after long inquiry, declared her worthy of trust and they might do so again.

Therefore it was determined that she should be held in a lay prison though charged with an ecclesiastical offence. Cut off in this way from all spiritual help and instruction, she was to be brought, when the process was ripe, before a well-chosen court bent on her destruction, and ready to entangle her in questions which might entrap her into erroneous or heretical statements.

And once more we are confronted, if we try to rationalise her life and put away all belief in inspiration, with the amazing problem as to where and how this untutored girl drew her stores of logic, law, and theology.

The trial took place in Rouen Castle,[3] the seat of Bedford's government in France. The choosing of her judges was committed to Cauchon, who selected the most sturdy adherents of the English. No formal charge was preferred, but Jeanne was interrogated. This course was severely condemned by a distinguished lawyer named Lohier, who puts clearly before us the procedure and principles that should govern such a hearing.

There should be in the first place in all such trials a definite indictment of the charges advanced against the accused, who in turn ought to have due time to answer all the allegations with the assistance of counsel.

In Jeanne's particular case, seeing that she had been already practically tried and acquitted at Poitiers at a trial

---

[3] The court before which Jeanne was brought to trial at Rouen was not a court of the Holy Office or Inquisition, neither was it, as the English courts for the trial of heresy were in Lancastrian times, a statutable court of ecclesiastical jurisdiction on whose decision, certified by the bishop, the sheriff was bound to act. It was a composite tribunal. The Bishop of Beauvais claimed and exercised jurisdiction as Ordinary. But the Deputy Inquisitor was joined with him as co-ordinate judge with officers of his own.

The Inquisition arose out of the troubles in Spain and South France, where heresy was to some extent necessarily a kind of treason to the polity of Christian Europe. Men were punished for heretical opinions, but these heretical opinions were in most cases lapses from allegiance at a time of national peril. The later Inquisition has no such excuse.

presided over by the Archbishop of Rheims, the metropolitan of the Bishop of Beauvais, it was putting her twice in peril for the same offence, and on the second occasion before an inferior court, a thing contrary to law and reason. Moreover the venue was wrong. She had been captured in one diocese as an ecclesiastical prisoner, and she was to be tried in another, and no assent of the chapter of Rouen could give jurisdiction in such a case.

Finally she was in a lay prison, held there by her political enemies, which made it impossible for her to have the liberty and spiritual assistance necessary to meet ecclesiastical charges. The trial ought to have been held in an ordinary court and not in the Castle.

All these objections are of great substance and go to the very root of the inquiry. But more vital than all was Jeanne's own expostulation against trial before Cauchon, who was her declared and bitter enemy, and the mere instrument of her foes and gaolers.

Gross however as the injustice was, there were certain barriers within which even Cauchon and his accomplices had to work their wicked wills. As there were fearless canonists like Lohier, who, as members of a great international Bar, were independent of any King or bishop, so the notaries, being apostolic and imperial officers, were in no way amenable to Cauchon or his crew. Every word spoken in court is duly and faithfully recorded, and this record formed the basis for the petition subsequently presented to the Pope by Jeanne's mother and brother when seeking amendment of Cauchon's judgment.

The trial is one of the most enthralling dramas in all history. The caution, the skill, the simplicity withal, shown by Jeanne in her answers to bewildering and entrapping questions, well earned the praise bestowed twenty years later by the accomplished lawyers who wrote on the case, sustaining the appeal for a new hearing.

The report gives all the details of the inquiry with fulness and accuracy, and when we carefully examine its course, we must agree with the canonists who said that the forms of law were indeed adhered to, but its spirit was grossly violated. The judges in Jeanne's case fortified themselves with the decision of the University of Paris, but that decision was procured by laying before the University what purported to be the statements of Jeanne, but what were in truth selected passages from her statements torn from qualifying contexts and often with the suppression of governing words.

Still this précis was also part of the record of the Court, although attempts were made to suppress it, and at the re-hearing Cauchon and his fellow hirelings were vehemently condemned for this nefarious proceeding.

By a sentence, so obtained and so buttressed, Jeanne d'Arc was done to death. The story of the execution is one of the most heart-rending incidents in history. No comment can deepen or add to the pathos of the narrative given by the bystanders.

In 1450 King Charles VII. empowered Guillaume Bouillé, Rector of the University of Paris, to inquire into the circumstances of Jeanne's trial, condemnation, and death, and to report the result of his investigation.

Great lawyers gave their opinions, and declared the trial void, as having been bad in substance as well as in form. But no regular judgment was pronounced.

Again in 1452 Pope Nicholas V., on appeal by Jeanne's mother, Isabel d'Arc, ordered inquiry, which duly took place, but without formal issue.

It is fortunate for truth and human interest that these inquiries were abortive. Had they on general grounds annulled the proceedings under Cauchon, how much would have been lost to us!

We should never have had that delightful picture of Domremy given by the simple people of the place. Nor should we have, as we have now, a sworn narrative of Jeanne's private and public life laying bare her very soul.

When Pope Calixtus ordered a full inquiry, he seemed to think, as Newman thought when writing the "Apologia," that the less argument and the more narrative and evidence that could be given the better; and so, instead of discussing the nature of angels, the limits of

Catholic obedience, the Great Schism,[4] and the assurances of salvation of the just, he and his deputies put aside such questions with patient contempt until they first made sure of the human side of the story. How Jeanne impressed her neighbours, her priest, and her kin; what kind of girl she was; what were her employments; was she restive and ambitious or quiet and satisfied; was her life pure; was she given to foolish imaginings, or was she a sane, modest, unpretending country maiden? Into all these things Cauchon had made inquiries, but as the answers were all favourable to the accused he suppressed the evidence.

The decree of Pope Calixtus has added a true romance to human story. In all that we know of the world's great ones we can find no parallel for the Maid of Domremy. Perhaps only in Catholic France was such a heroine possible. Certainly Teutonic Protestantism has as yet given to the world none of the exalted types of radiant and holy women such as those that illuminate Latin Christianity. Whether as a saint or a nation-maker, Jeanne's place in world-history is assured.

---

[4] The Great Schism arose out of the Babylonian captivity at Avignon (1306–1376). Popes and anti-Popes contended for 40 years (1378–1418). France was on the side of the Avignon Popes, while the Empire and England supported the Popes in Rome. Philip the Fair, by arrangement with the Pope, changed the Papal chair to Avignon. During the seventy years of the captivity, when the Church was ruled by French Popes, France underwent the disasters of Crecy and Poitiers, and became almost a province of England.

# CONTENTS

## Part I – The Trial

## Part II – The Rehabilitation

# PART I
## THE TRIAL

*Information as to the Original Documents of the Trial will be found in the Appendix.*

*An Introductory Note on the Maid's Capture at Compiègne and on the Procedure of her Trial is given in the Appendix.*

THE OLD CASTLE OF ROUEN.

## I
## FIRST PROCESS: THE LAPSE
## TRIAL EX OFFICIO
### SIX PUBLIC EXAMINATIONS

*O*n *Wednesday, February 21st, at 8 o'clock in the morning, in the Chapel Royal of the Castle of Rouen. The Bishop and 42 Assessors present.*

We did first of all command to be read the Royal letters conveying surrender and deliverance of the said woman into Our hands; afterwards the letters of the Chapter of Rouen, making concession of territory for Our benefit. This reading ended, M$^{tre.}$ Jean d'Estivet, nominated by Us as Promoter of the Case, did, in Our presence, shew that the aforesaid woman of the name of Jeanne hath been, by the Executor of Our Mandate, cited to appear in this place at this hour and day, here to answer, according to law, to the questions to be put to her.

The said Promoter did then produce Our Mandate, to which is attached the document confirming its execution, and did read them all. Our said Promoter did then require that the said woman should be placed before us, and, in terms of the citation, questioned by Us on divers Articles concerning the Faith, to the which We did agree. But as a preliminary, because the said woman had asked to hear Mass beforehand, We did shew to the Assessors that, by the advice of well-known Doctors and Masters consulted by Us, it hath been decided, considering the crimes of which she is accused, and the impropriety of the dress which she is wearing, that it is right to postpone permission to hear Mass and to assist in Divine Service.

In the meantime, the said woman was brought by the Executor of Our Mandate, and set before Us.

We did then shew that the said Jeanne hath been lately taken[5] in the territory of Beauvais; that many acts contrary to the Orthodox Faith have been committed by her, not only in Our Diocese, but in many others; that the public report, which imputes these misdeeds to her, hath spread in all estates of Christendom; that, in the last place, the most Serene and most Christian our lord the King hath sent and given her up to Us in order that, according to law and right, an action may be brought against her in the matter of the Faith; that, acting upon this common report, upon public rumour, and also on certain information obtained by Us, of which mention hath already been often enough made, by the advice of men versed in sacred and secular Law, We have officially given commandment to cite the said Jeanne to appear before Us, in order through her to obtain truthful answers to the questions to be put to her in matters of the Faith, and in order to act towards her according to law and right; which doth so appear in the letters that the Promoter hath shewn.

---

[5] It is agreed by all authorities that Jeanne was not captured in the Diocese of Beauvais, which ended at the Bridge of Compiègne. Jeanne was taken north of the Bridge, on the right bank of the river, and either in the Diocese of Noyon or Soissons, which of the two has not been determined. The Bishop's assertion is distinctly untrue.

Then, desiring in this particular the blessed succour of Jesus Christ, Who is concerned in this, and wishing only to fulfil the duties of Our office for the exaltation and preservation of the Catholic Faith, We did first charitably warn and require the said Jeanne, seated in Our presence, for the more prompt resolution of the Action and the relief of her own conscience, to speak the whole truth upon all questions which should be addressed to her touching the Faith; and We did exhort her to avoid all subterfuges and shufflings of such a nature as should turn her aside from a sincere and true avowal.

And in the first instance we did require her, in the appointed form, her hand on the Holy Gospels, to swear to speak truth on the questions to be addressed to her.

To which she did reply:

"I know not upon what you wish to question me: perhaps you may ask me of things which I ought not to tell you."

"Swear," We did then say to her, "to speak truth on the things which shall be asked you concerning the Faith, and of which you know."

"Of my father and my mother and of what I did after taking the road to France, willingly will I swear; but of the revelations which have come to me from God, to no one will I speak or reveal them, save only to Charles my King; and to you I will not reveal them, even if it cost me my head; because I have received them in visions and by secret counsel, and am forbidden to reveal them. Before eight days are gone, I shall know if I may reveal them to you."

Again did We several times warn and require her to be willing, on whatsoever should touch on the Faith, to swear to speak truly. And the said Jeanne, on her knees, her two hands resting on the Missal, did swear to speak truth on that which should be asked her and which she knew *in the matter of the Faith*, keeping silence under the condition above stated, that is to say, neither to tell nor to reveal to any one the revelations made to her.

After this oath, Jeanne was interrogated by Us as to her name, and surname, her place of birth, the names of her father and mother, the place of her baptism, her godfathers and godmothers, the Priest who baptized her, etc., etc.

"In my own country they call me Jeannette; since I came into France I have been called Jeanne. Of my surname I know nothing. I was born[6] in the village of Domremy, which is really one with the village of Greux. The principal Church is at Greux. My father is called Jacques d'Arc; my mother, Ysabelle. I was baptized in the village of Domremy.[7] One of my godmothers[8] is called Agnes, another Jeanne, a third Sibylle. One of my godfathers is called Jean Lingué, another Jean Barrey. I had many other godmothers, or so I have heard from my mother. I was, I believe, baptized by Messire Jean Minet; he still lives, so far as I know. I am, I should say, about nineteen years of age. From my mother I learned my Pater, my Ave Maria, and my Credo. I believe I learned all this from my mother."

JEANNE D'ARC'S HOUSE AT DOMREMY.

---

[6] On January 6th, 1412. "*In nocte Epiphiniarum Domini.*" (Letter from Boulainvilliers to the Duke of Milan. Quicherat, vol. v., 116.)

[7] The Font and Holy water stoup in the old Church at Domremy are said to be those in use in the 15th century.

[8] Jeanne appears to have had a great many godparents. In the Enquiry made at Domremy in 1455, eight are mentioned, viz.: Jean Morel, Jean Barrey, Jean de Laxart, and Jean Raiguesson, as godfathers; and Jeannette Thévenin, Jeannette Thiesselin, Beatrix Estellin, and Edith Barrey, as godmothers.

"Say your Pater."

"Hear me in confession, and I will say it willingly."

To this same question, which was many times put to her, she always answered: "No, I will not say my Pater to you, unless you will hear me in confession."

"Willingly," We said to her, "We will give you two well-known men, of the French language, and before them you shall say your Pater."

"I will not say it to them, unless it be in confession."

And then did We forbid Jeanne to go out of the prison which hath been assigned to her in the Castle without Our permission, under pain of the crime of heresy.

"I do not accept such a prohibition," she answered; "if ever I do escape, no one shall reproach me with having broken or violated my faith, not having given my word to any one, whosoever it may be."

And as she complained that she had been fastened with chains and fetters of iron, We said to her:

"You have before, and many times, sought, We are told, to get out of the prison, where you are detained; and it is to keep you more surely that it has been ordered to put you in irons."

"It is true I wished to escape; and so I wish still: is not this lawful for all prisoners?"

We then commissioned as her guard the noble man John Gris,[9] Squire, one of the Body Guard of our Lord the King, and, with him, John Berwoist and William Talbot, whom We enjoined well and faithfully to guard the said Jeanne, and to permit no person to have dealings with her without Our order. Which the aforenamed, with their hands on the Gospels, did solemnly swear.

Finally, having accomplished all the preceding, We appointed the said Jeanne to appear the next day, at 8 o'clock in the morning, before Us in the Ornament Room,

---

[9] John Gris, or Grey, a gentleman in the Household of the Duke of Bedford, afterwards knighted. He was appointed chief guardian to the Maid, with two assistants, all members of the King's Body Guard. They appear to have left her entirely in the hands of the common soldiers five of whom kept constant watch over her.

at the end of the Great Hall of the Castle of Rouen.

*Thursday, February 22nd, in the Ornament Room at the end of the Great Hall of the Castle of Rouen. The Bishop and 48 Assessors present.*

In their presence, We shewed that Jean Lemaître, Deputy of the Chief Inquisitor, had been summoned and required by Us to join himself to the present Action, with Our offer of communicating to him all that hath been done hitherto or shall be done in the future; but that the said Deputy had replied, that, having been commissioned by the Chief Inquisitor for the City and Diocese of Rouen only, and the actual Process being deduced by Us in a territory which hath been ceded to Us by the Metropolitan Chapter, by reason of Our Ordinary Jurisdiction, as Bishop of Beauvais, he had thought it right to avoid all nullity and also for the peace of his own conscience, to refuse to join himself with Us, in the quality of Judge, until he should receive from the Chief Inquisitor a Commission and more extended powers: that, nevertheless, he would have no objection to see the trial continue without interruption.

After having heard Us make this narration, the said Deputy, being present, declared, addressing himself to Us, "That which you have just said is true. It has been, as much as in me lies, and still is, agreeable to me that you should continue the Trial."

Then the said Jeanne was brought before Us.

We warned and required her, on pain of law, to make oath as she had done the day before and to swear simply and absolutely to speak truth on all things in respect of which she should be asked; to which she answered:

"I swore yesterday: that should be enough."

Again We required her to swear: we said to her, not even a prince, required to swear in a matter of faith, can refuse.

"I made oath to you yesterday," she answered, "that should be quite enough for you: you burden me over-much!"

Finally she made oath to speak truth on *that which*

*touches the Faith.*

Then Maître Jean Beaupère, a well-known Professor of Theology, did, by Our order, question the said Jeanne. This he did as follows:

"First of all, I exhort you, as you have so sworn, to tell the truth on that which I am about to ask you."

"You may well ask me some things on which I shall tell you the truth and some on which I shall not tell it you. If you were well informed about me, you would wish to have me out of your hands. I have done nothing except by revelation."

"How old were you when you left your father's house?"

"On the subject of my age I cannot vouch."

"In your youth, did you learn any trade?"

"Yes, I learnt to spin and to sew; in sewing and spinning I fear no woman in Rouen. For dread of the Burgundians, I left my father's house and went to the town of Neufchâteau,[10] in Lorraine, to the house of a woman named La Rousse, where I sojourned about fifteen days. When I was at home with my father, I employed myself with the ordinary cares of the house. I did not go to the fields with the sheep and the other animals. Every year I confessed myself to my own Curé, and, when he was prevented, to another Priest with his permission. Sometimes, also, two or three times, I confessed to the Mendicant Friars; this was at Neufchâteau. At Easter I received the Sacrament of the Eucharist."

"Have you received the Sacrament of the Eucharist at any other Feast but Easter?"

"Pass that by [*Passez outre*]. I was thirteen when I had a Voice from God for my help and guidance. The first time that I heard this Voice, I was very much frightened; it was mid-day, in the summer, in my father's garden. I had not fasted the day before. I heard this Voice to my right, towards the Church; rarely do I hear it without its

---

[10] There is no certain date for this event. By some it is placed between the first and second visits to Vaucouleurs, in 1428; by others, earlier, at the time of the Picard ravages of the neighbourhood in the September of 1426.

being accompanied also by a light. This light comes from the same side as the Voice. Generally it is a great light. Since I came into France I have often heard this Voice."

"But how could you see this light that you speak of, when the light was at the side?"

To this question she answered nothing, but went on to something else. "If I were in a wood, I could easily hear the Voice which came to me. It seemed to me to come from lips I should reverence. I believe it was sent me from God. When I heard it for the third time, I recognized that it was the Voice of an Angel. This Voice has always guarded me well, and I have always understood it; it instructed me to be good and to go often to Church; it told me it was necessary for me to come into France. You ask me under what form this Voice appeared to me? You will hear no more of it from me this time. It said to me two or three times a week: 'You must go into France.' My father knew nothing of my going. The Voice said to me: 'Go into France!' I could stay no longer. It said to me: 'Go, raise the siege which is being made before the City of Orleans. 'Go!' it added, 'to Robert de Baudricourt,[11] Captain of Vaucouleurs: he will furnish you with an escort to accompany you.' And I replied that I was but a poor girl, who knew nothing of riding or fighting. I went to my uncle and said that I wished to stay near him for a time. I remained there eight days. I said to him, 'I must go to Vaucouleurs.'[12] He took me there. When I arrived, I recognized Robert de Baudricourt, although I had never seen him. I knew him, thanks to my Voice, which made me recognize him. I said to Robert, 'I must go into France!' Twice Robert refused to hear me, and repulsed me. The third time, he received me, and furnished me with men;[13] the Voice had told me it would

---

[11] Robert de Baudricourt, Squire, Captain of Vaucouleurs in 1428; afterwards knighted and made Councillor and Chamberlain to the King and Bailly of Chaumont, 1454.

[12] Of the ancient château the "Porte de France" alone survives. From this gate Jeanne rode out with her escort to visit the King at Chinon. The crypt of the chapel remains, where Jeanne constantly prayed.

[13] This is said to have been on account of the impression produced on him by Jeanne's prediction, on February 12th: "To-day the gentle

be thus. The Duke of Lorraine[14] gave orders that I should be taken to him. I went there. I told him that I wished to go into France. The Duke asked me questions about his health; but I said of that I knew nothing. I spoke to him little of my journey. I told him he was to send his son with me, together with some people to conduct me to France, and that I would pray to God for his health. I had gone to him with a safe-conduct: from thence I returned to Vaucouleurs. From Vaucouleurs I departed, dressed as a man, armed with a sword given me by Robert de Baudricourt, but without other arms. I had with me a Knight,[15] a Squire, and four servants, with whom I reached the town of Saint Urbain, where I slept in an Abbey. On the way, I passed through Auxerre, where I heard Mass in the principal Church. Thenceforward I often heard my Voices."

"Who counselled you to take a man's dress?"

To this question she several times refused to answer. In the end, she said: "With that I charge no one." Many times she varied in her answers to this question. Then she said:

"Robert de Baudricourt made those who went with me swear to conduct me well and safely. 'Go,' said Robert de Baudricourt to me, 'Go! and let come what may!' I know well that God loves the Duke of Orleans; I have had more revelations about the Duke of Orleans than about any man alive, except my King. It was necessary for me to change my woman's garments for a man's dress. My counsel thereon said well. I sent a letter to the English before

---

Dauphin hath had great hurt near the town of Orleans, and yet greater will he have if you do not soon send me to him." This "great hurt" proved to be the Battle of Rouvray, in which the French and Scottish troops were defeated by the English under Sir John Fastolf.

[14] Charles I., the reigning Duke de Lorraine in 1428, was in very bad health, and, having no son, the succession was a matter of some anxiety. He died in 1431, and was succeeded by his son-in-law, Réné of Anjou, who had married his only daughter, Isabella. This Réné was a brother of Queen Mary, wife of Charles VII., and father of our own Queen Margaret, married in 1441 to Henry VI.

[15] Jean de Novelomport, called de Metz, Bertrand de Poulengey, Colet de Vienne, the King's Messenger, and three servants.

Orleans,[16] to make them leave, as may be seen in a copy of my letter which has been read to me in this City of Rouen; there are, nevertheless, two or three words in this copy which were not in my letter. Thus, 'Surrender to the Maid,' should be replaced by 'Surrender to the King.' The words, 'body for body' and 'chieftain in war' were not in my letter at all.[17]

"I went without hindrance to the King. Having arrived at the village of Saint Catherine de Fierbois, I sent for the first time to the Castle of Chinon,[18] where the King was. I got there towards mid-day, and lodged first at an inn. After dinner, I went to the King, who was at the Castle. When I entered the room where he was I recognized him among many others by the counsel of my Voice, which revealed him to me. I told him that I wished to go and make war on the English."

"When the Voice shewed you the King, was there any light?"

"Pass on."

"Did you see an Angel over the King?"

"Spare me. Pass on. Before the King set me to work, he had many apparitions and beautiful revelations."

"What revelations and apparitions had the King?"

"I will not tell you; it is not yet time to answer you about them; but send to the King, and he will tell you. The Voice had promised me that, as soon I came to the King, he would receive me. Those of my party knew well that the Voice had been sent me from God; they have seen and known this Voice, I am sure of it. My King and many others have also heard and seen the Voices which came to

---

[16] March 22nd, 1428.

[17] This letter appears later. Jeanne may have forgotten its contents, as both these expressions occur; or the Clerics who acted as her amanuenses may have inserted them without her knowledge.

[18] Jeanne was entertained by command of the King in a small room on the first floor of the Tour de Coudray, within the Castle walls. Her room was approached by a staircase outside the tower. The vaulted roof of the room has fallen in and the fireplace is in ruins, but the room could easily be restored. Jeanne stayed here from March 8th to April 20th, 1429. She was two days at Chinon before she obtained access to the King.

me: there were there Charles de Bourbon[19] and two or three others. There is not a day when I do not hear this Voice; and I have much need of it. But never have I asked of it any recompense but the salvation of my soul. The Voice told me to remain at Saint-Denis, in France; I wished to do so, but, against my will, the Lords made me leave. If I had not been wounded, I should never have left. After having quitted Saint-Denis, I was wounded in the trenches before Paris;[20] but I was cured in five days. It is true that I caused an assault to be made before Paris."

"Was it a Festival that day?"

"I think it was certainly a Festival."

"Is it a good thing to make an assault on a Festival?"

"Pass on."

And as it appeared that enough had been done for to-day, We have postponed the affair to Saturday next, at 8 o'clock in the morning.

*Saturday, 24th February, in the same place. The Bishop and 62 Assessors present.*

In their presence We did require the aforenamed Jeanne to swear to speak the truth simply and absolutely on the questions to be addressed to her, without adding any restriction to her oath. We did three times thus admonish her. She answered:

"Give me leave to speak. By my faith! you may well ask me such things as I will not tell you. Perhaps on many of the things you may ask me I shall not tell you truly, especially on those that touch on my revelations; for you may constrain me to say things that I have sworn not to say; then I should be perjured, which you ought not to wish." [Addressing the Bishop:] "I tell you, take good heed of what you say, you, who are my Judge;[21] you take

---

[19] Charles de Bourbon, Count de Clermont, Governor of the Duchy of the Bourbonnais and the Comté of Auvergne, during the captivity of his father in England.

[20] On September 8th, 1429.

[21] Up to the end of her life, Jeanne spoke of the Bishop as the person responsible for her trial and death. "Bishop, I die through you," was her last speech to him, on May 30th, the day of her martyrdom.

a great responsibility in thus charging me. I should say that it is enough to have sworn twice."

"Will you swear, simply and absolutely?"

"You may surely do without this. I have sworn enough already twice. All the clergy of Rouen and Paris cannot condemn me if it be not law. Of my coming into France I will speak the truth willingly; but I will not say all: the space of eight days would not suffice."

"Take the advice of the Assessors, whether you should swear or not."

"Of my coming I will willingly speak truth, but not of the rest; speak no more of it to me."

"You render yourself liable to suspicion in not being willing to swear to speak the truth absolutely."

"Speak to me no more of it. Pass on."

"We again require you to swear, precisely and absolutely."

"I will say willingly what I know, and yet not all. I am come in God's name; I have nothing to do here; let me be sent back to God, whence I came."

"Again we summon and require you to swear, under pain of going forth charged with that which is imputed to you."

"Pass on."

"A last time we require you to swear, and urgently admonish you to speak the truth on all that concerns your trial; you expose yourself to a great peril by such a refusal."

"I am ready to speak truth on what I know touching the trial."

And in this manner was she sworn.

Then, by Our order, she was questioned by Maître Jean Beaupère, a well-known Doctor, as follows:

"How long is it since you have had food and drink?"[22]

---

[22] This, and a subsequent enquiry, on February 27th, as to Jeanne's habit of fasting, would seem to suggest a desire on the part of the questioner to prove that her visions had a more or less physical cause in a weak bodily state resulting from abstinence. As Jeanne's usual food consisted of a little bread dipped in wine and water, and as she is reported to have had

"Since yesterday afternoon."

"How long is it since you heard your Voices?"

"I heard them yesterday and to-day."

"At what hour yesterday did you hear them?"

"Yesterday I heard them three times,—once in the morning, once at Vespers, and again when the Ave Maria rang in the evening. I have even heard them oftener than that."

"What were you doing yesterday morning when the Voice came to you?"

"I was asleep: the Voice awoke me."

"Was it by touching you on the arm?"

"It awoke me without touching me."

"Was it in your room?"

"Not so far as I know, but in the Castle."

"Did you thank it? and did you go on your knees?"

"I did thank it. I was sitting on the bed; I joined my hands; I implored its help. The Voice said to me: 'Answer boldly.' I asked advice as to how I should answer, begging it to entreat for this the counsel of the Lord. The Voice said to me: 'Answer boldly; God will help thee.' Before I had prayed it to give me counsel, it said to me several words I could not readily understand. After I was awake, it said to me: 'Answer boldly.'" [Addressing herself to Us, the said Bishop:] "You say you are my judge. Take care what you are doing; for in truth I am sent by God, and you place yourself in great danger."

Maître Beaupère, continuing, said:

"Has this Voice sometimes varied in its counsel?"

"I have never found it give two contrary opinions.... This night again I heard it say: 'Answer boldly.'"

"Has your Voice forbidden you to say everything on what you are asked?"

"I will not answer you about that. I have revelations touching the King that I will not tell you."

"Has it forbidden you to tell those revelations?"

"I have not been advised about these things. Give me a

---

when at home (not in war) but one meal a day, it need hardly be supposed that she suffered much from the results of a Lenten Fast.

delay of fifteen days,[23] and I will answer you. If my Voice has forbidden me, what would you say about it? Believe me, it is not men who have forbidden me. To-day I will not answer: I do not know if I ought, or not; it has not been revealed to me. But as firmly as I believe in the Christian Faith and that God hath redeemed us from the pains of Hell, that Voice hath come to me from God and by His Command."

"The Voice that you say appears to you, does it come directly from an Angel, or directly from God; or does it come from one of the Saints?"

"The Voice comes to me from God; and I do not tell you all I know about it: I have far greater fear of doing wrong in saying to you things that would displease it, than I have of answering you. As to this question, I beg you to grant me delay."

"Is it displeasing to God to speak the truth?"

"My Voices have entrusted to me certain things to tell to the King, not to you. This very night they told me many things for the welfare of my King, which I would he might know at once, even if I should drink no wine until Easter, ... the King would be the more joyful at his dinner!"

"Can you not so deal with your Voices that they will convey this news to your King?"

"I know not if the Voice would obey, and if it be God's Will. If it please God, He will know how to reveal it to the King, and I shall be well content."

"Why does not this Voice speak any more to your King, as it did when you were in his presence?"

"I do not know if it be the Will of God. Without the grace of God I should not know how to do anything."

"Has your counsel revealed to you that you will escape from prison?"

"I have nothing to tell you about that."

"This night, did your Voice give you counsel and advice as to what you should answer?"

---

[23] The fifteen days' respite would coincide with the first Examination held in the Prison, May 10th, the first day on which the Allegory of the Sign was given.

"If it did give me advice and counsel thereon, I did not understand."

"The last two occasions on which you have heard this Voice, did a brightness come?"

"The brightness comes at the same time as the Voice."

"Besides the Voice, do you see anything?"

"I will not tell you all; I have not leave; my oath does not touch on that. My Voice is good and to be honoured. I am not bound to answer you about it. I request that the points on which I do not now answer may be given me in writing."

"The Voice from whom you ask counsel, has it a face and eyes?"

"You shall not know yet. There is a saying among children, that 'Sometimes one is hanged for speaking the truth.'"

"Do you know if you are in the grace of God?"

"If I am not, may God place me there; if I am, may God so keep me. I should be the saddest in all the world if I knew that I were not in the grace of God. But if I were in a state of sin, do you think the Voice would come to me? I would that every one could hear the Voice as I hear it. I think I was about thirteen when it came to me for the first time."

"In your youth, did you play in the fields with the other children?"

"I certainly went sometimes, I do not know at what age."

"Do the Domremy people side with the Burgundians or with the opposite party?"

"I knew only one Burgundian[24] at Domremy: I should have been quite willing for them to cut off his head—always had it pleased God."

"The Maxey people, were they Burgundians, or opposed to the Burgundians?"

"They were Burgundians. As soon as I knew that my Voices were for the King of France, I loved the

---

[24] Gérardin of Epinal, to whose child Jeanne was godmother, is probably the person alluded to; he gave witness in 1455 that Jeanne had called him "Burgundian."

Burgundians no more. The Burgundians will have war unless they do what they ought; I know it by my Voice. The English were already in France when my Voices began to come to me. I do not remember being with the children of Domremy when they went to fight against those of Maxey for the French side: but I certainly saw the Domremy children who had fought with those of Maxey coming back many times, wounded and bleeding."

"Had you in your youth any intention of fighting the Burgundians?"

"I had a great will and desire that my King should have his own Kingdom."

"When you had to come into France, did you wish to be a man?"

"I have answered this elsewhere."

"Did you not take the animals to the fields?"

"I have already answered this also. When I was bigger and had come to years of discretion, I did not look after them generally; but I helped to take them to the meadows and to a Castle called the Island,[25] for fear of the soldiers. I do not remember if I led them in my childhood or no."

"What have you to say about a certain tree which is near to your village?"

"Not far from Domremy there is a tree[26] that they call 'The Ladies' Tree'—others call it 'The Fairies' Tree'; near by, there is a spring where people sick of the fever come to drink, as I have heard, and to seek water to restore their health. I have seen them myself come thus; but I do not know if they were healed. I have heard that the sick, once cured, come to this tree[27] to walk about. It

---

[25] A small fortress in an island formed by two arms of the Meuse, nearly opposite the village of Domremy.

[26] According to local tradition, this tree stood to within the last 50 years, and was struck by lightning; another has been planted in its place. The house, in which Jeanne was born, remained in the possession of the De Lys family till the 16th Century, when it passed into the hands of the Count de Salm, Seigneur of Domremy. In the 18th Century it became the property of Jean Gerardin, whose grandson, Nicolas, gave it up in 1818 to the Department of Vosges; so that it is now preserved as National property.

[27] This is probably a survival of the Fontinalia, an old Latin festival. The

is a beautiful tree, a beech, from which comes the 'beau may'—it belongs to the Seigneur Pierre de Bourlement,[28] Knight. I have sometimes been to play with the young girls, to make garlands for Our Lady of Domremy. Often I have heard the old folk—they are not of my lineage—say that the fairies haunt this tree. I have also heard one of my Godmothers, named Jeanne, wife of the Maire Aubery of Domremy, say that she has seen fairies there; whether it be true, I do not know. As for me, I never saw them that I know of. If I saw them anywhere else, I do not know. I have seen the young girls putting garlands on the branches of this tree, and I myself have sometimes put them there with my companions; sometimes we took these garlands away, sometimes we left them. Ever since I knew that it was necessary for me to come into France, I have given myself up as little as possible to these games and distractions. Since I was grown up, I do not remember to have danced there. I may have danced there formerly, with the other children. I have sung there more than danced. There is also a wood called the Oak-wood, which can be seen from my father's door; it is not more than half-a-league away. I do not know, and have never heard if the fairies appear there; but my brother told me that it is said in the neighbourhood: 'Jeannette received her mission at the Fairies' Tree.' It is not the case; and I told him the contrary. When I came before the King, several people asked me if there were not in my country a wood, called the Oak-wood, because there were prophecies[29] which said that from the

---

custom of decorating the wells and springs was kept up in England until the last century, and still exists in a few remote villages. The name 'Well Sunday' survives, though the processions of youths and maidens have long passed away. The 'fontaine aux Groseilliers' is still in existence. It is an oblong tank of water, with the original spring flowing through it. The great beech tree stood close by.

[28] Pierre de Bourlement, Head of the ancient house of Bassigny, and Lord of the Manor of Bourlement. He was the last of his race.

[29] Merlin had foretold the coming of a maiden out of an Oak-wood from Lorraine; and a paper containing a prophecy to this effect had been sent, at the beginning of Jeanne's career, to the English Commander, the Earl of Suffolk. There was also an old prophecy (quoted by Jeanne herself to Catharine Leroyer) that France, which had been "lost by a woman,

neighbourhood of this wood would come a maid who should do marvellous things. I put no faith in that."

"Would you like to have a woman's dress?"

"Give me one, and I will take it and begone; otherwise, no. I am content with what I have, since it pleases God that I wear it."

This done, We stayed the interrogation, and put off the remainder to Tuesday next, on which day We have convoked all the Assessors, at the same place and hour.

*Tuesday, February 27th, in the same place. The Bishop and 54 Assessors present.*

In their presence, We required the said Jeanne to swear to tell the truth on everything touching her Trial.

"Willingly will I swear," she answered, "to tell the truth on everything touching the trial, but *not upon all that I know.*"

We required her again to speak the truth on all which should be asked of her.

"You ought to be satisfied," she answered. "I have sworn enough."

Then, by Our order, Maître Beaupère began to question her. And first he inquired of her, how she had been since the Saturday before?

"You can see for yourself how I am. I am as well as can be."

"Do you fast every day this Lent?"

"Is that in the Case? Well, yes! I have fasted every day during this Lent."

"Have you heard your Voices since Saturday?"

"Yes, truly, many times."

"Did you hear them on Saturday in this hall, where you were being examined?"

---

should be saved by a Maid." The conduct of Isabeau of Bavaria, wife of Charles VI., might certainly be said to have fulfilled the first half of this prophecy; and a tradition in the eastern counties that "deliverance should come from a maid of the Marches of Lorraine" must have directed many hopes to the mission of the Maiden from Domremy, though she herself does not seem to have known of the last prediction until some time later. The Oak-wood covers the hills above Domremy to this day.

"That is not in your Case. Very well, then—yes! I did hear them."

"What did your Voice say to you last Saturday?"

"I did not quite understand it; and up to the moment when I returned to my room, I heard nothing that I may repeat to you."

"What did it say to you in your room, on your return?"

"It said to me, 'Answer them boldly.' I take counsel with my Voice about what you ask me. I will tell willingly whatever I shall have permission from God to reveal; as to the revelations concerning the King of France, I will not tell them without the permission of my Voice."

"Has your Voice forbidden you to tell everything?"

"I did not quite understand it."

"What did your Voice last say to you?"

"I asked counsel about certain things that you had asked me."

"Did it give you counsel?"

"On some points, yes; on others you may ask me for an answer that I shall not give, not having had leave. For, if I answered without leave, I should no longer have my Voices as warrant. When I have permission from Our Saviour, I shall not fear to speak, because I shall have warrant."

"This Voice that speaks to you, is it that of an Angel, or of a Saint, or from God direct?"

"It is the Voice of Saint Catherine and of Saint Margaret.[30] Their faces are adorned with beautiful crowns, very rich and precious. To tell you this I have leave from Our Lord. If you doubt this, send to Poitiers, where I was examined before."

"How do you know if these were the two Saints? How do you distinguish one from the other?"

"I know quite well it is they; and I can easily distinguish one from the other."

"How do you distinguish them?"

---

[30] This is the first identification of the "revelations" with any name; Jeanne had always spoken of her "Voices" or her "Counsel."

"By the greeting they give me. It is seven years now since they have undertaken to guide me. I know them well because they were named to me."

"Are these two Saints dressed in the same stuff?"

"I will tell you no more just now; I have not permission to reveal it. If you do not believe me, go to Poitiers. There are some revelations which come to the King of France, and not to you, who are questioning me."

"Are they of the same age?"

"I have not leave to say."

"Do they speak at the same time, or one after the other?"

"I have not leave to say; nevertheless, I have always had counsel from them both."

"Which of them appeared to you first?"

"I did not distinguish them at first. I knew well enough once, but I have forgotten. If I had leave, I would tell you willingly: it is written in the Register at Poitiers.[31] I have also received comfort from Saint Michael."

"Which of these two appearances came to you first?"

"Saint Michael."

"Is it a long time since you first heard the voice of Saint Michael?"

---

[31] This Examination at Poitiers had taken place in the Chapel attached to the Palace of the Counts of Poitou, which still exists and adjoins the 'Salle des Pas Perdus,' now the Great Hall of the Palais de Justice. It was conducted under the direction of the Archbishop of Rheims during the months of March and April, 1429, and extended over three weeks. At the conclusion, the assembly sent, as the result of their inquiries, a resolution to the King to the effect that he should follow the Maid's guidance, and seek for the sign she promised him in the relief of Orleans, as a proof of the Divine origin of her mission, "for," they added, "to doubt or forsake her without any appearance of evil would be to vex the Holy Spirit, and to make himself unworthy of the help of God: so saith Gamaliel in the Council of the Jews with regard to the Apostles."

Unfortunately, no trace of this Examination has been found: the 'Book of Poitiers' is referred to several times in the Trial; but it was not forthcoming at the time of the Rehabilitation. It was probably lost or destroyed by Jeanne's enemies among her own party. The Archbishop of Rheims would have had it in his charge: and he was consistently opposed to Jeanne throughout. During her stay at Poitiers the Maid lodged in the house of Jean Rabatier.

"I did not say anything to you about the *voice* of Saint Michael; I say I have had great comfort from him."

"What was the first Voice that came to you when you were about thirteen?"

"It was Saint Michael: I saw him before my eyes; he was not alone, but quite surrounded by the Angels of Heaven. I came into France only by the order of God."

"Did you see Saint Michael and these Angels bodily and in reality?"

"I saw them with my bodily eyes as well as I see you; when they went from me, I wept. I should have liked to be taken away with them."

"And what was Saint Michael like?"

"You will have no more answer from me; and I am not yet free to tell you."

"What did Saint Michael say to you this first time?"

"You will have no more answer about it from me to-day. My Voices said to me, 'Reply boldly.' Once I told the King all that had been revealed to me, because it concerned him; but I am no longer free to reveal to you all that Saint Michael said to me." [To Maître Beaupère:] "I wish you could get a copy of this book at Poitiers, if it please God."

"Have your Voices forbidden you to make known your revelations without leave from them?"

"I will answer you no more about it. On all that I have leave, I will answer willingly. I have not quite understood if my Voices have forbidden me to answer."

"What sign do you give that you have this revelation from God, and that it is Saint Catherine and Saint Margaret that talk with you?"

"I have told you that it is they; believe me if you will."

"Are you forbidden to say?"

"I have not quite understood if this is forbidden or not."

"How can you make sure of distinguishing such things as you are free to tell, from those which are forbidden?"

"On some points I have asked leave, and on others I have obtained it. I would rather have been torn asunder by four horses than have come into France without God's leave."

"Was it God who prescribed to you the dress of a man?"

"What concerns this dress is a small thing—less than nothing. I did not take it by the advice of any man in the world. I did not take this dress or do anything but by the command of Our Lord and of the Angels."

"Did it appear to you that this command to take man's dress was lawful?"

"All I have done is by Our Lord's command. If I had been told to take some other, I should have done it; because it would have been His command."

"Did you not take this garment by order of Robert de Baudricourt?"

"No."

"Do you think it was well to take a man's dress?"

"All that I have done by the order of Our Lord I think has been well done; I look for good surety and good help in it."

"In this particular case, this taking of man's dress, do you think you did well?"

"I have done nothing in the world but by the order of God."

"When you saw this Voice coming to you, was there a light?"

"There was plenty of light everywhere, as was seemly." [Addressing herself to Maître Beaupère:] "It does not all come to you!"

"Was there an angel over the head of your King when you saw him for the first time?"

"By Our Lady! if there were, I know nothing of it; I did not see it."

"Was there a light?"

"There were more than three hundred Knights and more than fifty torches, without counting the spiritual light."

"Why was your King able to put faith in your words?"

"He had good signs, and the clergy bore me witness."

"What revelations has your King had?"

"You will not have them from me this year. During

three weeks I was questioned by the clergy at Chinon and at Poitiers. Before he was willing to believe me, the King had a sign of my mission; and the clergy of my party were of opinion that there was nothing but good in my mission."

"Have you been to Saint Catherine de Fierbois?"[32]

"Yes, and I heard there three Masses in one day. Afterwards, I went to the Castle of Chinon, whence I sent letters to the King, to know if I should be allowed to see him; saying, that I had travelled a hundred and fifty leagues to come to his help, and that I knew many things good for him. I think I remember there was in my letter the remark that I should recognize him among all others. I had a sword I had taken at Vaucouleurs. Whilst I was at Tours, or at Chinon, I sent to seek for a sword which was in the Church of Saint Catherine de Fierbois, behind the altar; it was found there at once; the sword was in the

---

[32] According to local tradition, this Church was originally founded by Charles Martel in 732, after his victory over the Saracens, whom he here ceased to pursue, and deposited his sword as an offering. This is by some supposed to have been the sword which later Jeanne sent for; but the legend is not of an early date, and there is no suggestion of the kind in contemporary writings.

According to one authority, the Greffier de la Rochelle, the sword was found in a reliquary, which had not been opened for twenty years or more. The *Chronique de la Pucelle* and the *Journal of the Siege of Orleans* state that it was one of many votive offerings, and was recognized by Jeanne's description of the five crosses on the blade, possibly a Jerusalem Cross. Some of the old Chronicles say that Jeanne told the King she had never been at Fierbois: but this statement is disproved by her own words in this answer. The suggestion that, having been to three Masses in the Church, she might easily have seen the sword, is to some extent answered by the alleged difficulty of the Priests to find, among the many swords there, the one she had specially described.

Of the ultimate fate of this sword there are many versions, and no two agree exactly as to date. It was certainly broken in striking a camp-follower, one of a class the Maid had forbidden to enter the Camp; but whether this was just after the retreat from Paris or earlier, it does not seem possible to decide. Jeanne herself says she "had it up to Saint-Denis" and "Lagny," both of which dates would imply the autumn of 1429: but most witnesses tell the story of its being broken in the July preceding, though several different places are mentioned as the scene of the incident.

ground, and rusty; upon it were five crosses; I knew by my Voice where it was. I had never seen the man who went to seek for it. I wrote to the Priests of the place, that it might please them to let me have this sword, and they sent it to me. It was under the earth, not very deeply buried, behind the altar, so it seemed to me: I do not know exactly if it were before or behind the altar, but I believe I wrote saying that it was at the back. As soon as it was found, the Priests of the Church rubbed it, and the rust fell off at once without effort. It was an armourer of Tours who went to look for it. The Priests of Fierbois made me a present of a scabbard; those of Tours, of another; one was of crimson velvet, the other of cloth-of-gold. I had a third made of leather, very strong. When I was taken prisoner I had not got this sword. I always bore the sword of Fierbois from the time I had it up to my departure from Saint-Denis,[33] after the attack on Paris."

"What blessing did you invoke, or have invoked, on this sword?"

"I neither blessed it, nor had it blessed: I should not have known how to set about it. I cared very much for this sword, because it had been found in the Church of Saint Catherine, whom I love so much."

"Have you been at Coulange-les-Vineuses?"[34]

"I do not know."

"Have you sometimes placed your sword upon an altar; and, in so placing it, was it that your sword might be more fortunate?"

"Not that I know of."

"Have you sometimes prayed that it might be more fortunate?"

"It is good to know that I wished my armour might have good fortune!"

"Had you your sword when you were taken prisoner?"

"No, I had one which had been taken on a Burgundian."

---

[33] On September 13th, 1429.

[34] A small town near Auxerre. In this neighbourhood some of the chronicles place the incident referred to of the breaking of the sword. The question may, therefore, have been intended to elicit the story.

"Where was the sword of Fierbois left?"

"I offered at Saint-Denis a sword and armour;[35] but it was not this sword. I had that at Lagny; from Lagny to Compiègne, I bore the sword of this Burgundian; it was a good sword for fighting—very good for giving stout buffets and hard clouts. To tell what became of the other sword does not concern this Case, and I will not answer about it now. My brothers have all my goods—my horses,[36] my sword, so far as I know, and the rest, which

---

[35] The armour offered at Saint-Denis was the "blanc harnois" she wore during the earlier part of her career. When the church was pillaged by the English troops shortly after, this armour was sent to the King of England; but no further trace of it is known to exist.

[36] Jeanne appears to have been a good horse-woman; she rode "horses so ill-tempered that no one would dare to ride them." The Duke de Lorraine, on her first visit to him, and the Duke d'Alençon, after seeing her skill in riding a course, each gave her a horse; and we read also of a gift of a war-horse from the town of Orleans, and "many horses of value" sent from the Duke of Brittany. She had entered Orleans on a white horse, according to the *Journal du Siège d'Orléans*; but seems to have been in the habit of riding black chargers in war; and mention is also made by Châtelain of a "lyart" or grey. A story, repeated in a letter from Guy de Laval, relates that, on one occasion (June 6th, 1428), when her horse, "a fine black war-horse" was brought to the door, he was so restive that he would not stand still. "Take him to the Cross," she said; and there he stood, "as though he were tied," while she mounted. This was at Selles; and local tradition says that, from her lodging (a Dominican Monastery now the Lion d'Or hotel) the old iron town-cross was visible. It stood until about a century ago some fifteen paces in front of the north door of the Church, and was removed when the cemetery was converted into a market place. The Monastery was the property of the monks of Glatigny.

The writers of the letter referred to above, Guy and André de Laval, were grandsons of Bertrand du Guesclin: the letter was dated Selles, June, 1429. The following are extracts:

"... On Monday (June 6th) I left the King to go to Selles en Berry, four leagues from Saint Aignan. The King had summoned the Maid to come before him from Selles, where she then was, and many said this was much in my favour, so that I might see her. The said Maid treated my brother and me with great kindness: she was armed at all points, save the head, and bore lance in hand. After we had arrived at Selles, I went to her lodging to see her, and she called for wine for me and said she would soon have me drink it in Paris. She seemed to me a thing divine, in all she did and all I saw and heard.

"On Monday evening she left Selles to go to Romorantin.... I saw her mounting her horse armed all in white, save the head, a little axe in her hand.... And then, turning to the door of the Church, which was quite

are worth more than twelve thousand crowns."

"When you were at Orleans, had you a standard, or banner;[37] and of what colour was it?"

"I had a banner of which the field was sprinkled with lilies; the world was painted there, with an angel at each side; it was white, of the white cloth called 'boccassin'; there was written above, I believe, 'Jhesus Maria'; it was fringed with silk."

"The words 'Jhesus Maria' were they written above, below, or on the side?"

"At the side, I believe."

"Which did you care for most, your banner or your sword?"

"Better, forty times better, my banner than my sword!"

"Who made you get this painting done upon your banner?"

"I have told you often enough, that I had nothing done

---

near, she said in a gentle woman's voice, 'You priests and clergy, make processions and prayers to God.' Then she turned again on her way saying, 'Draw on, draw on!' her standard flying, borne by a gracious page, and her little axe in her hand. One of her brothers who arrived eight days since, left also with her, armed all in white."

[37] The banner was painted at Tours, while Jeanne was staying there, before her march to the relief of Orleans. The account for payment, in the "Comptes" of the Treasurer of War, gives: "À Hauvres Poulnoir, paintre, demourant à Tours, pour avoir paint et baillé estoffes pour une grand estandart et ung petit pour la Pucelle ... 25 livres tournois."

The description of this banner varies in different authors. The following account is compiled from them. "A white banner, sprinkled with fleur-de-lys; on the one side, the figure of Our Lord in Glory, holding the world, and giving His benediction to a lily, held by one of two Angels who are kneeling on each side: the words 'Jhesus Maria' at the side; on the other side the figure of Our Lady and a shield with the arms of France supported by two Angels" (*de Cagny*). This banner was blessed at the Church of Saint-Sauveur at Tours (*Chronique de la Pucelle* and *de Cagny*).

The small banner or pennon had a representation of the Annunciation.

There was also a third banner round which the priests assembled daily for service, and on this was depicted the Crucifixion (*Pasquerel*).

Another banner is mentioned by the Greffier de la Rochelle, which Jeanne is said to have adopted as her own private pennon. It was made at Poitiers; and represented on a blue ground a white dove, holding in its beak a scroll, with the words, "De par le Roy du Ciel."

but by the command of God. It was I, myself, who bore this banner, when I attacked the enemy, to save killing any one, for I have never killed any one."

"What force did your King give you when he set you to work?"

"He gave me ten or twelve thousand men. First, I went to Orleans, to the fortress of Saint Loup, and afterwards to that of the Bridge."

"Which fortress was being attacked when you made your men retire?"

"I do not remember. I was quite certain of raising the siege of Orleans; I had revelation of it. I told this to the King before going there."

"Before the assault, did you not tell your followers that you alone would receive the arrows, cross-bolts, and stones, thrown by the machines and cannons?"

"No; a hundred and even more of my people were wounded. I had said to them: 'Be fearless, and you will raise the siege.' Then, in the attack on the Bridge fortress, I was wounded in the neck by an arrow or cross-bolt;[38] but I had great comfort from Saint Catherine, and was cured in less than a fortnight. I did not interrupt for this either my riding or work. I knew quite well that I should be wounded; I had told the King so, but that, notwithstanding, I should go on with my work. This had been revealed to me by the Voices of my two Saints,[39] the blessed Catherine and the blessed Margaret. It was I who first planted a ladder against the fortress of the Bridge, and it was in raising this ladder that I was wounded in the neck by this cross-bolt."

"Why did you not accept the treaty with the Captain of Jargeau?"[40]

"It was the Lords of my party who answered the English that they should not have the fortnight's delay

---

[38] May 7th, 1429.

[39] This prophecy is recorded in a letter written, April 22nd, 1429, a fortnight before the event, by a Flemish diplomatist, De Rotslaer, then at Lyons. Her chaplain, Pasquerel, also states, in his evidence given in 1455, that she had told him of the coming injury on the previous day.

[40] June 11th, 1429.

which they asked, telling them that they were to retire at once, they and their horses. As for me, I told them of Jargeau to retire if they wished, with their doublets,[41] and their lives safe; if not, they would be taken by assault."

"Had you any revelation from your counsel, that is to say from your Voices, to know whether it was right or not to give this fortnight's respite?"

"I do not remember."

At this point, the rest of the enquiry hath been postponed to another day. We have fixed for Thursday the next Meeting, at the same place.

*Thursday, March 1st, in the same place, the Bishop and 58 Assessors present.*

In their presence, We summoned and required Jeanne simply and absolutely to take her oath to speak the truth on that which should be asked her.

"I am ready," she replied, "as I have already declared to you, to speak the truth on all I know touching this Case; but I know many things which do not touch on this Case, and of which there is no need to speak to you. I will speak willingly and in all truth on *all which touches this Case.*"

We again summoned and required her; and she replied:

"What I know in truth *touching the Case*, I will tell willingly."

And in this wise did she swear, her hands on the Holy Gospels. Then she said:

"On what I know touching the Case, I will speak the truth willingly; I will tell you as much as I would to the Pope of Rome, if I were before him."

Then she was examined as follows:

"What do you say of our Lord the Pope? and whom do you believe to be the true Pope?"

"Are there two of them?"

"Did     you     not     receive     a     letter     from     the

---

[41] Gallicè: *"en leur petite cotte," i.e.*, with only the light clothing worn under their armour.

Count d'Armagnac, asking you which of the three Pontiffs[42] he ought to obey?"

"The Count did in fact write to me on this subject. I replied, among other things, that when I should be at rest, in Paris or elsewhere, I would give him an answer. I was just at that moment mounting my horse when I sent this reply."

At this juncture, We ordered to be read the copy of the Count's letter and of Jeanne's reply, which are thus expressed:

"My very dear Lady—I humbly commend myself to you, and pray, for God's sake, that, considering the divisions which are at this present time in the Holy Church Universal on the question of the Popes, for there are now three contending for the Papacy—one residing at Rome, calling himself Martin V., whom all Christian Kings obey; another, living at Paniscole, in the Kingdom of Valence, who calls himself Clement VII.; the third, no one knows where he lives, unless it be the Cardinal Saint Etienne and some few people with him, but he calls himself Pope Benedict XIV. The first, who styles himself Pope Martin, was elected at Constance with the consent of all Christian nations; he who is called Clement was elected at Paniscole, after the death of Pope Benedict XIII., by three of his Cardinals; the third, who dubs himself Benedict XIV., was elected secretly at Paniscole, even by the Cardinal Saint Etienne. You will have the goodness to pray Our Saviour Jesus Christ that by His infinite Mercy He may by you declare to us which of the three named is Pope in truth, and whom it pleases Him that we should obey, now and henceforward, whether he who is called Martin, he who is called Clement, or he who is called Benedict; and in whom we are to believe, if

---

[42] The "three Pontiffs" referred to are Martin V. (Colonna), the real and acknowledged Pope; the schismatic, Clement VIII.; and a mere pretender, Benedict XIV., who was supported only by one Cardinal. The Schism was practically at an end at the time of this letter, as Clement had abdicated a month earlier (July 26th). Clement VIII. is the true title, though called Clement VII. in Count d'Armagnac's letter.

secretly, or by any dissembling, or publicly; for we are all ready to do the will and pleasure of Our Lord Jesus Christ.

"Yours in all things,
"COUNT D'ARMAGNAC."

Jeanne's Reply.
"*Jhesus Maria.*

"Count d'Armagnac, my very good and dear friend, I, Jeanne, the Maid, acquaint you that your message has come before me, which tells me that you have sent at once to know from me which of the three Popes, mentioned in your memorial, you should believe. This thing I cannot tell you truly at present, until I am at rest in Paris or elsewhere; for I am now too much hindered by affairs of war; but when you hear that I am in Paris, send a message to me and I will inform you in truth whom you should believe, and what I shall know by the counsel of my Righteous and Sovereign Lord, the King of all the World, and of what you should do to the extent of my power. I commend you to God. May God have you in His keeping! Written at Compiègne, August 22nd."

Then the Enquiry proceeded thus:
"Is this really the reply that you made?"
"I deem that I might have made this answer in part, but not all."
"Did you say that you might know, by the counsel of the King of Kings, what the Count should hold on this subject?"
"I know nothing about it."
"Had you any doubt about whom the Count should obey?"
"I did not know how to inform him on this question, as to whom he should obey, because the Count himself asked to know whom *God* wished him to obey. But for myself, I hold and believe that we should obey our Lord the Pope who is in Rome. I told the messenger of the Count some things which are not in this copy; and, if the messenger had not gone off immediately, he would have

been thrown into the water—not by me, however. As to the Count's enquiry, desiring to know whom God wished him to obey, I answered that I did not know; but I sent him messages on several things which have not been put in writing. As for me, I believe in our Lord the Pope who is at Rome."

"Why did you write that you would give an answer elsewhere if you believed in the Pope who is at Rome?"

"That answer had reference to other things than the matter of the sovereign Pontiffs."

"Did you say that on the matter of the three sovereign Pontiffs you would have counsel?"

"I never wrote nor gave command to write on the matter of the three sovereign Pontiffs." And this answer she supported by oath.

"Are you in the habit of putting the Names 'Jhesus Maria,' with a cross, at the top of your letters?"

"On some I put it, on others not; sometimes I put a cross as a sign for those of my party to whom I wrote so that they should not do as the letters said."

Here a letter was read from Jeanne to our Lord the King, to the Duke of Bedford, and others, of the following tenour:—

"*Jhesus Maria.*

"King of England; and you, Duke of Bedford, who call yourself Regent of the Kingdom of France; you, William de la Pole, Earl of Suffolk; John, Lord Talbot; and you, Thomas, Lord Scales, who call yourselves Lieutenants to the said Duke of Bedford: give satisfaction to the King of Heaven: give up to the Maid, who is sent hither by God, the King of Heaven, the keys of all the good towns in France which you have taken and broken into. She is come here by the order of God to reclaim the Blood Royal. She is quite ready to make peace, if you are willing to give her satisfaction, by giving and paying back to France what you have taken. And as for you, archers, companions-in-arms, gentlemen and others who are before the town of Orleans, return to your own countries, by God's order; and if this be not done, then hear the message of the Maid, who will shortly come upon you, to your very great hurt. King of England, I am a Chieftain of war and, if this be not done, wheresoever I find your followers in France, I will make them leave, willingly or unwillingly; if they will not obey, I will have them put to death. I am sent here by God, the King of Heaven, body for body, to drive them all out of the whole of France. And if they will obey, I will have mercy on them. And do not think in yourselves that you will get possession of the realm of France from God the King of Heaven, Son of the Blessed Mary; for King Charles will gain it, the true heir: for God, the King of Heaven, so wills it, and it is revealed to him [the King] by the Maid, and he will enter Paris with a good company. If you will not believe the message of God and of the Maid and act aright, in whatsoever place we find you we will enter therein and make so great a disturbance that for a thousand years none in France will be so great. And believe surely that the King of Heaven will send greater power to the Maid, to her and her good men-at-arms, than you can bring to the attack; and, when it comes to blows, we shall see who has the better right from the God of Heaven. You, Duke of Bedford, the Maid prays and enjoins you, that you do not come to grievous hurt. If you will give her satisfactory pledges, you may yet join with her, so that the French may do the fairest deed that has ever yet been done for Christendom. And answer, if you wish to make peace in the City of Orleans; if this be not done, you may be shortly reminded of it, to your very great hurt. *Written this Tuesday in Holy Week*, March 22nd, 1428."

"Do you know this letter?"

"Yes, excepting three words. In place of 'give up to the Maid,' it should be 'give up to the King.' The words 'Chieftain of war' and 'body for body' were not in the letter I sent. None of the Lords ever dictated these letters to me; it was I myself alone who dictated them before sending them. Nevertheless, I always shewed them to some of my party. Before seven years are passed, the English will lose a greater wager than they have already done at Orleans; they will lose everything in France.[43] The English will have in France a greater loss than they have ever had, and that by a great victory which God will send to the French."

"How do you know this?"

"I know it well by revelation, which has been made to me, and that this will happen within seven years; and I am sore vexed that it is deferred so long. I know it by revelation, as clearly as I know that you are before me at this moment."

"When will this happen?"

"I know neither the day nor the hour."

"In what year will it happen?"

"You will not have any more. Nevertheless, I heartily wish it might be before Saint John's Day."

"Did you not say that this would happen before Martinmas, in winter?"

"I said that before Martinmas many things would be seen, and that the English might perhaps be overthrown."[44]

"What did you say to John Gris, your keeper, on the subject of the Feast of Saint Martin?"

"I have told you."

"Through whom did you know that this would happen?"

"Through Saint Catherine and Saint Margaret."

"Was Saint Gabriel with Saint Michael when he came to you?"

"I do not remember."

"Since last Tuesday, have you had any converse with Saint Catherine and Saint Margaret?"

"Yes, but I do not know at what time."

"What day?"

"Yesterday and to-day; there is never a day that I do not hear them."

"Do you always see them in the same dress?"

"I see them always under the same form, and their

---

[43] The English lost Paris in 1436.

[44] Compiègne was relieved early in November; Saint Martin's Day is November 11th.

heads are richly crowned. I do not speak of the rest of their clothing: I know nothing of their dresses."

"How do you know whether the object that appears to you is male or female?"

"I know well enough. I recognize them by their voices, as they revealed themselves to me; I know nothing but by the revelation and order of God."

"What part of their heads do you see?"

"The face."

"These saints who shew themselves to you, have they any hair?"

"It is well to know they have."

"Is there anything between their crowns and their hair?"

"No."

"Is their hair long and hanging down?"

"I know nothing about it. I do not know if they have arms or other members. They speak very well and in very good language; I hear them very well."

"How do they speak if they have no members?"

"I refer me to God. The voice is beautiful, sweet, and low; it speaks in the French tongue."

"Does not Saint Margaret speak English?"

"Why should she speak English, when she is not on the English side?"

"On these crowned heads, were there rings?—in the ears or elsewhere?"

"I know nothing about it."

"Have you any rings yourself?"

[Addressing herself to Us, the Bishop:] "You have one of mine; give it back to me. The Burgundians have another of them. I pray you, if you have my ring, shew it to me."

"Who gave you the ring which the Burgundians [now] have?"

"My father or my mother. I think the Names 'Jhesus Maria' are engraved on it. I do not know who had them written there; there is not, I should say, any stone in the ring; it was given to me at Domremy. It was my brother who gave me the other—the one you have." [Continuing

34

to address herself to Us, the Bishop:] "I charge you to give it to the Church. I never cured any one with any of my rings."

"Did Saint Catherine and Saint Margaret speak to you under the tree of which mention has been made?"

"I know nothing of it."

"Did they speak to you at the spring, which is near the tree?"

"Yes, I have heard them there; but what they said then, I do not know."

"What did they promise you, there or elsewhere?"

"They have never promised me anything, except by God's leave."

"But still, what promises have they made to you?"

"That is not in your Case: not at all. Upon other subjects, they told me that my King would be reestablished in his Kingdom, whether his enemies willed it or no; they told me also that they would lead me to Paradise: I begged it of them, indeed."

"Did you have any other promise from them?"

"There was another, but I will not tell it; that does not touch on the Case. In three months I will tell you the other promise."

"Have your Voices said that before three months you will be delivered from prison?"

"That is not in your Case. Nevertheless I do not know when I shall be delivered. But those who wish to send me out of the world may well go before me."

"Has not your counsel told you that you will be delivered from your actual prison?"

"Speak to me in three months, and I will answer. Moreover, ask of those present, upon oath, if this touches on the Trial."

We, the said Bishop, did then take the opinion of those present: and all considered that this did touch on the Trial.

"I have already told you, you shall not know all. One day I must be delivered. But I wish to have leave to tell you the day: it is for this I ask delay."

"Have your Voices forbidden you to speak the truth?"

"Do you want me to tell you what concerns the King

of France? There are a number of things that do not touch on the Case. I know well that my King will regain the Kingdom of France. I know it as well as I know that you are before me, seated in judgment. I should die if this revelation did not comfort me every day."

"What have you done with your mandrake?"[45]

"I never have had one. But I have heard that there is one near our home, though I have never seen it. I have heard it is a dangerous and evil thing to keep. I do not know for what it is [used]."

"Where is this mandrake of which you have heard?"

"I have heard that it is in the earth, near the tree of which I spoke before; but I do not know the place. Above this mandrake, there was, it is said, a hazel tree."

"What have you heard said was the use of this mandrake?"

"To make money come; but I do not believe it. My Voice never spoke to me of that."

"In what likeness did Saint Michael appear to you?"

"I did not see a crown: I know nothing of his dress."

"Was he naked?"

"Do you think God has not wherewithal to clothe him?"

"Had he hair?"

"Why should it have been cut off? I have not seen Saint Michael since I left the Castle of Crotoy. I do not see him often. I do not know if he has hair."

"Has he a balance?"[46]

"I know nothing about it. It was a great joy to see him;

[45] The mandrake was a part of the accepted paraphernalia of a sorcerer. It was kept wrapped in a silk or linen cloth, and was supposed to preserve its owner from poverty. Brother Richard had recently preached a sermon against them (April, 1429); and many had been burned in consequence.

[46] The balance was a frequent accessory to Saint Michael in the French stained glass windows of the 13th and 14th centuries. A noted example in the Cathedral at Arles represents him weighing the souls of the departed in a balance as big as himself. One of the earliest examples in England is that in a fresco-painting at Preston Manor, Sussex, said to be of the reign of Edward I., in which Saint Michael appears weighing the souls of the faithful, accompanied by Jeanne's saints, Saint Catherine and Saint Margaret.

it seemed to me, when I saw him, that I was not in mortal sin. Saint Catherine and Saint Margaret were pleased from time to time to receive my confession, each in turn. If I am in mortal sin, it is without my knowing it."

"When you confessed, did you think you were in mortal sin?"

"I do not know if I am in mortal sin, and I do not believe I have done its works; and, if it please God, I will never so be; nor, please God, have I ever done or ever will do deeds which charge my soul!"

"What sign did you give your King that you came from God?"

"I have always answered that you will not drag this from my lips. Go and ask it of him."

"Have you sworn not to reveal what shall be asked of you touching the Trial?"

"I have already told you that I will tell you nothing of what concerns my King. Thereon I will not speak."

"Do you not know the sign that you gave to the King?"

"You will not know it from me."

"But this touches on the Trial."

"Of what I have promised to keep secret, I will tell you nothing. I have already said, even here, that I could not tell you without perjury."

"To whom have you promised this?"

"To Saint Catherine and Saint Margaret; and this hath been shewn to the King. I promised them, without their asking it of me, of my own free-will, of myself, because too many people might have questioned me had I not promised it to my Saints."

"When you shewed your sign to the King, were you alone with him?"

"I do not take account of any one else, although there were many people near."

"When you shewed this sign to the King, did you see a crown on his head?"

"I cannot tell you without perjury."

"Had your King a crown at Rheims?"

"I think my King took with joy the crown that he had

at Rheims; but another, much richer, would have been given him later. He acted thus to hurry on his work, at the request of the people of the town of Rheims, to avoid too long a charge upon them of the soldiers. If he had waited, he would have had a crown a thousand times more rich."

"Have you seen this richer crown?"

"I cannot tell you without incurring perjury; and, though I have not seen it, I have heard that it is rich and valuable to a degree."

This done, we put an end to the interrogation and postponed the remainder to Saturday next, 8 o'clock in the morning, in the same place, summoning all the Assessors to be present.

*Saturday, March 3rd, in the same place, the Bishop and 41 Assessors present.*

In their presence, We required the said Jeanne simply and absolutely to swear to speak the truth on what should be asked of her. She replied:

"I am ready to swear as I have already done."

And thus did she swear, her hands on the Holy Gospels.

Afterwards, because she had said, in previous Enquiries, that Saint Michael had wings, but had said nothing of the body and members of Saint Catherine and Saint Margaret, We asked her what she wished to say thereon.

"I have told you what I know; I will answer you nothing more. I saw Saint Michael and these two Saints so well that I know they are Saints of Paradise."

"Did you see anything else of them but the face?"

"I have told you what I know; but to tell you all I know, I would rather that you made me cut my throat. All that I know *touching the Trial* I will tell you willingly."

"Do you think that Saint Michael and Saint Gabriel have human heads?"

"I saw them with my eyes; and I believe it was they as firmly as I believe there is a God."

"Do you think that God made them in the form and fashion that you saw?"

"Yes."

"Do you think that God did from the first create them in this form and fashion?"

"You will have no more at present than what I have answered."

"Do you know by revelation if you will escape?"

"That does not touch on your Case. Do you wish me to speak against myself?"

"Have your Voices told you anything?"

"That is not in your Case. I refer me to the Case. If all concerned you, I would tell you all. By my faith, I know neither the day nor the hour that I shall escape!"

"Have your Voices told you anything in a general way?"

"Yes, truly, they have told me that I shall be delivered, but I know neither the day nor the hour. They said to me: 'Be of good courage and keep a cheerful countenance.'"

"When you first came to the King, did he ask you if you had any revelation about your change of dress?"

"I have answered you about that. I do not remember if I was asked. It is written at Poitiers."

"Do you not remember if the Masters who questioned you in the other Consistory, some during a month, others during three weeks, questioned you about your change of dress?"

"I do not remember. But they asked me where I had assumed this man's dress; and I told them it was at Vaucouleurs."

"Did the aforesaid Masters ask you if it were by order of your Voice that you took this dress?"

"I do not remember."

"Did not your Queen[47] ask you, the first time you went to visit her?"

"I do not remember."

"Did not your King, your Queen, or some of your party, tell you to take off this man's dress?"

"That is not in your Case."

---

[47] Mary of Anjou, wife of Charles VII., daughter of Louis, Duke of Anjou and Yolande of Arragon.

"Were you not so told at the Castle of Beaurevoir?"[48]

[*Here commences the French Version, or Minute, which is collated with the Latin Text.*]

"Yes, truly; and I answered that I would not take it off without leave from God. The Demoiselle de Luxembourg[49] and the Lady de Beaurevoir[50] offered me a woman's dress, or cloth to make one, telling me to wear it. I answered them that I had not leave from Our Lord, and that it was not yet time."

"Did Messire Jean de Pressy[51] and others at Arras never offer you a woman's dress?"

"He and many others have oftentimes offered it to me."

"Do you think that you would have done wrong or committed mortal sin by taking a woman's dress?"

"I did better to obey and serve my Sovereign Lord, who is God. Had I dared to do it, I would sooner have done it at the request of these ladies than of any other ladies in France, excepting my Queen."

"When God revealed it to you that you should change your dress, was it by the voice of Saint Michael, Saint Catherine, or Saint Margaret?"

"You shall not have anything more at present."

"When your King first set you to work, and when you had your banner made, did not the men-at-arms and others have their pennons made in the style of yours?"

"It is well to know that the Lords retained their own

---

[48] Jeanne was taken from Beaurevoir early in August, and removed from there, when the negotiations for selling her were complete, about the middle of November.

[49] Jeanne, Countess de Saint-Pol et Ligny, sister to Count Waleran de Luxembourg and aunt to Jean de Luxembourg.

[50] Jeanne de Bethune, Viscountess de Meaux, wife of Jean de Luxembourg. Both these ladies were at Beaurevoir during Jeanne's captivity, and shewed her great kindness, even interceding for her that she should not be sold to the English.

[51] The Sieur de Pressy, in Artois. Present in the Burgundian camp when Jeanne was taken prisoner, and afterwards at Arras, where she was imprisoned on her way from Beaurevoir to Rouen. The questions seem to suggest that Beaupère had before him some information which has not come down to us.

arms. Some of my companions-in-arms had them made at their pleasure; others not."

"Of what material did they have them made? Of linen or of cloth?"

"It was of white satin; and on some there were fleur-de-lys. In my company I had only two or three lances. But my companions-in-arms now and then had them made like mine. They only did this to know their men from others."

"Did they often renew these pennons?"

"I do not know. When the lances were broken, they had new ones made."

"Have you sometimes said that the pennons which were like yours would be fortunate?"

"I sometimes said to my followers: 'Go in boldly among the English!' and I myself did likewise."

"Did you tell them to carry themselves boldly, and they would be fortunate?"

"I have certainly told them what has happened and what will yet happen."

"Did you put, or did you ever cause to be put, Holy Water on the pennons when they were carried for the first time?"

"I know nothing of it; and if that were done, it was not by my order."

"Did you never see any sprinkled?"

"That is not in your Case. If I ever did see any sprinkled, I am advised not to answer about it."

"Did your companions-in-arms never put on their pennons 'Jhesus Maria'?"

"By my faith! I do not know."

"Have you not yourself carried cloth, or caused it to be carried, in procession round an altar or a church, and afterwards employed this cloth for pennons?"

"No; and I never saw it done."

"When you were before Jargeau, what did you bear at the back of your helmet? Was it not something round?"[52]

---

[52] This may perhaps refer to a popular belief in a halo, as of a Saint, surrounding the Maid's head.

"By my faith! there was nothing."

"Did you ever know Brother Richard?"[53]

"I had not seen him when I came before Troyes."

"What countenance did Brother Richard give you?"

"I suppose after the fashion of the town of Troyes who sent him to me, saying that they feared Jeanne was not a thing that came to them from God. When he approached me, Brother Richard made the sign of the Cross and sprinkled Holy Water; and I said to him: 'Approach boldly, I shall not fly away!'"

"Have you never seen, nor had made, any images or picture of yourself and in your likeness?"

"I saw at Arras a painting[54] in the hands of a Scot: it was like me. I was represented fully armed, presenting a letter to my King, one knee on the ground. I have never seen, nor had made, any other image or painting in my likeness."

"In the house of your host at Orleans, was there not a picture in which was painted three women, with these words: 'Justice, Peace, Union'?"

"I know nothing about it."

"Do you not know that the people of your party had services, masses, and prayers offered for you?"

"I know nothing of it; if they had any service, it was

[53] Brother Richard, a Mendicant Friar; some say, Augustan; some, Cordelier. He was preaching in Paris and the neighbourhood in 1428–9; and said, amongst other things, in a sermon at Sainte Géneviève, April 16th, 1419, that "strange things would happen in 1430." He professed to have been in Jerusalem; and his sermons were so popular that congregations were found to listen to him for 10 or 11 hours, from 5 o'clock in the morning! He was driven out of Paris by the English and went to Troyes, where he joined the Maid.

[54] No absolutely authentic portraits of Jeanne are known. A head of fine work, the portrait of a young girl wearing a casque and of Jeanne's time, is at the Musée Historique at Orleans. Tradition asserts that when Jeanne entered Orleans in triumph with the relieving force a sculptor modelled the head of his statue of St. Maurice from Jeanne herself. This head is a portion of the statue which formerly stood in the church at Orleans dedicated to St. Maurice. The church was demolished in 1850. A photograph from the head is given as the frontispiece to this book, and an admirable copy maybe seen at the Musée du Trocadéro in Paris. It should have been stated on the frontispiece that the original is at Orleans, the copy in Paris.

not by my order; but if they prayed for me, my opinion is they did not do ill."

"Did those of your party firmly believe that you were sent from God?"

"I do not know if they believed it, and in this I refer to their own feeling in this matter. But even though they do not believe, yet am I sent from God."

"Do you not think they have a good belief, if they believe this?"

"If they think that I am sent from God, they will not be deceived."

"In what spirit did the people of your party kiss your hands and your garments?"

"Many came to see me willingly, but they kissed my hands as little as I could help. The poor folk came to me readily, because I never did them any unkindness: on the contrary, I loved to help them."

"What honour did the people of Troyes do you on your entry?"

"None at all. Brother Richard, so far as I remember, entered at the same time as I and our people; I do not recall seeing him at the entry."

"Did he not preach a sermon on your arrival in the town?"

"I did not stop there at all, and did not even sleep there: I know nothing of his sermon."

"Were you many days at Rheims?"

"We were there, I believe, five or six days."

"Did you not act there as Godmother?" ["*lever d'enfant.*"]

"At Troyes I did, to one child. At Rheims, I do not remember it, nor at Château-Thierry. I was Godmother twice at Saint-Denis, in France. Usually, I gave to the boys the name of Charles, in honour of my King; and to the girls, Jeanne. At other times, I gave such names as pleased the mothers."

"Did not the good women of the town touch with their rings that which you wore on your finger?"

"Many women touched my hands and my rings; but I know nothing of their feelings nor their intention."

"Who of your people, before Château-Thierry, caught butterflies in your standard?"

"My people never did such a thing: it is your side who have invented it."

"What did you do at Rheims with the gloves with which your King was consecrated?"

"There were favours of gloves for the knights and nobles at Rheims. There was one who lost his gloves; I did not say he would find them again. My standard has been in the Church of Rheims; and it seems to me it was near the altar.[55] I myself bore it for a space there. I do not know if Brother Richard held it."

---

[55] Latin text adds: "*dum rex suus consecraretur.*" Tradition asserts that at the Coronation Jeanne stood on the left and slightly in front of the altar, coming direct from the sacristy of the cathedral. The coronation throne stood in front of the high altar. The cathedral and its painted glass exist as at the Coronation, with the exception of some comparatively recent stone work surrounding the choir. The Coronation of the Kings of France has taken place at Rheims Cathedral since the twelfth century. The King was not to all intents King of France until he had been anointed by the Holy Oil, brought in great state to the cathedral from the more ancient church of St. Remy.

An inscription on the front of the Hotel Maison Rouge, situated near the west entrance of the cathedral, states that the town entertained Jeanne's father and mother in that house during the Coronation.

RHEIMS CATHEDRAL.

"When you were going through the country, did you often receive the Sacraments of Penance and the Eucharist in the good towns?"

"Yes, from time to time."

"Did you receive the said Sacraments in man's dress?"

"Yes; but I do not remember ever to have received them armed."

"Why did you take the horse of the Bishop of Senlis?"

"It was bought for 200 saluts.[56] If he received these 200 saluts, I do not know. There was a place fixed at which they were to be paid. I wrote to him that he might have his horse back if he wished; as for me, I did not wish it, because it was worth nothing for weight-carrying."

"How old was the child you visited at Lagny?"

"The child was three days old. It was brought before the image of Our Lady. They told me that the young girls of the village were before this image, and that I might wish to go also and pray God and Our Lady to give life to this infant. I went and prayed with them. At last, life returned to the child, who yawned three times, and was

---

[56] About £200.

then baptized; soon after, it died, and was buried in consecrated ground. It was three days, they said, since life had departed from the child; it was as black as my coat; when it yawned, the colour began to return to it. I was with the other young girls, praying and kneeling before Our Lady."

CHURCH OF SAINT REMY.

"Did they not say in the village that it was done through you, and at your prayer?"

"I did not enquire about it."

"Have you ever seen or known Catherine de La Rochelle?"

"Yes, at Jargeau and at Montfaucon in Berry."

"Did not Catherine shew you a lady, robed in white, who, she said, sometimes appeared to her?"

"No."

"What did this Catherine say to you?"

"That a white lady came to her, dressed in cloth-of-gold, who told her to go through the good cities with heralds and trumpets which the King would give to her, and proclaim that any one who had gold, silver, or any concealed treasure should bring it immediately: that those who did not do so, and who had anything hidden, she would know, and would be able to discover the treasure. With these treasures, she told me, she would pay my men-at-arms. I told Catherine that she should return to her husband, look after her home, and bring up her children. And in order to have some certainty as to her mission, I spoke of it, either to Saint Catherine or to Saint Margaret, who told me that the mission of this Catherine was mere folly and nothing else. I wrote to the King as to what he should do about it; and, when I afterwards went to him, I told him that this mission of Catherine was only folly and nothing more. Nevertheless, Brother Richard wished to set her to work; therefore were they both displeased with me,—Brother Richard and she."

"Did you never speak with the said Catherine on the project of going to La Charité-sur-Loire?"

"She did not advise me to go there: it was too cold, and she would not go. She told me she wished to visit the Duke of Burgundy in order to make peace. I told her it seemed to me that peace would be found only at the end of the lance. I asked her if this white lady who appeared to her came to her every night? and I said that, to see her, I would sleep one night with her in the same bed. I went to bed; I watched till midnight; I saw nothing, and then went to sleep. When morning came, I asked her if the White Lady had come. 'Yes, Jeanne,' she answered me, 'while you were asleep she came; and I could not awaken you.' Then I asked her if she would come again the following night. 'Yes,' she told me. For this reason I slept by day that I might be able to watch the night following. I went to bed with Catherine; watched all the night following: but saw nothing, although I asked her often, 'Will she never come?' and she always answered me, 'Yes, in a moment.'"

"What did you do in the trenches of La Charité?"[57]

"I made an assault there; but I neither threw, nor

---

[57] November 9th, 1429.

caused to be thrown, Holy Water by way of aspersion."

"Why did you not enter La Charité, if you had command from God to do so?"

"Who told you I had God's command for it?"

"Did you not have counsel of your Voice?"

"I wished to go into France. The men-at-arms told me it was better to go first to La Charité."

"Were you a long time in the Tower at Beaurevoir?"

"About four months. When I knew that the English were come to take me, I was very angry; nevertheless, my Voices forbade me many times to leap. In the end, for fear of the English, I leaped, and commended myself to God and Our Lady. I was wounded. When I had leaped, the Voice of Saint Catherine said to me I was to be of good cheer,[58] for those at Compiègne would have succour. I prayed always for those at Compiègne, with my Counsel."

"What did you say when you had leaped?"

"Some said I was dead. As soon as the Burgundians saw I was alive, they reproached me with having leapt."

"Did you not say then, that you would rather die than be in the hands of the English?"

"I said I would rather give up my soul to God than be in the hands of the English."

"Were you not then very angry, to the extent of blaspheming the Name of God?"

"Never have I cursed any of the Saints; and it is not my habit to swear."

"On the subject of Soissons[59] and the Captain who surrendered the town, did you not blaspheme God, and say, if you got hold of this Captain you would have him cut in quarters?"

"I have never blasphemed any of the Saints; those who say so have misunderstood."

This done, Jeanne was conducted back to the place which had been assigned as her prison.

### NINE PRIVATE EXAMINATIONS.

---

[58] The Minute adds: "and I should be cured."
[59] Surrendered July 22nd.

*The Bishop decrees that the Enquiries, if any are thought necessary, shall henceforth be made in private.*

Afterwards, We, the Bishop, did say that, in pursuing this Process and without in any way discontinuing it, We would call before Us some Doctors and Masters, experts in law, religious and civil, in order, by them, to gather up and collect what shall seem to them of a nature to be gathered up and collected, in Jeanne's Declarations, as these have already been established by her own answers set down in writing. Their labour ended, if there should remain any points, on the which it would seem Jeanne should submit to more full enquiry, We will make, for this supplementary examination, choice of certain Doctors; and in this manner We shall not fatigue all and each of the Masters, who, at this moment, assist Us in such great numbers. These new enquiries shall also be put into writing, in order that the above-named Doctors and other approved men of science may deliberate and furnish their opinion and advice at the right moment. In the meantime, We invite all the Assessors to study at home the Process, and what they have already gathered from it; to search out the consequences of which the affair is susceptible; and to submit the result of their deliberations either to Us, or to the Doctors who shall be appointed by Us—if they do not prefer rather to reserve themselves for the time and place when they shall have deliberated in full maturity; and to give their opinion on full knowledge of the Process.

In the meantime, We expressly forbid all and each to leave Rouen without Our permission before the full completion of the Process.

*Meeting at the Bishop's House of several Doctors.*

Sunday, March 4th, and the Monday, Tuesday, Wednesday, Thursday, and Friday, 5th, 6th, 7th, 8th, and 9th of the same month, We, the Bishop, assembled in Our dwelling, many grave Doctors-and Masters-in-law, sacred and civil, who were charged by Us to collect all that has been confessed or answered by Jeanne in these Enquiries, and to extract therefrom the points on which she answered in an incomplete manner, and which seem to these

Doctors susceptible of further examination. This double work having been effected by them, We, the said Bishop, by the advice of the said Doctors, decide that there is occasion to proceed to further enquiries. But because Our numerous occupations do not permit Us to attend ourselves,[60] we appoint, to proceed therein, the venerable and discreet person, Jean Delafontaine, Master of Arts and Licentiate in Canon Law, who will interrogate the said Jeanne in Our name. We have for this appointed the 9th March, in presence of the Doctors and Masters, Jean Beaupère, Jacques de Touraine, Nicolas Midi, Pierre Maurice, Thomas de Courcelles, Nicolas Loyseleur, and Guillaume Manchon.

Saturday, March 10th, We, the Bishop, repaired to the part of the Castle of Rouen given to Jeanne as a prison, where, being assisted by Maître Jean Delafontaine, the Commissary appointed by Us, and by the venerable Doctors and Masters in Theology, Nicolas Midi, and Gerard Feuillet (witnesses, Jean Fécard, Advocate; and Maître Jean Massieu, Priest), We summoned Jeanne to make and take oath to speak the truth on what should be asked of her. She replied:

"I promise to speak truth on what touches your Case; but the more you constrain me to swear, the later will I tell you."

Afterwards, the examination of Jeanne by Maître Jean Delafontaine took place as follows:

"On the faith of the oath you have just taken, from whence had you started when you went the last time to Compiègne?"

"From Crespy, in Valois."

"When you were at Compiègne, were you several days before you made your sally or attack?"

"I arrived there secretly early in the morning,[61] and entered the town without the enemy knowing anything of it; and that same day, in the evening, I made the sally in which I was taken."

---

[60] In spite of this assertion, the Bishop was present at *four* out of the nine Examinations.

[61] On May 23rd, 1430.

"When you made your sally, did they ring the bells?"

"If they did ring them it was not by my order or knowledge; I do not think it was so, and I do not remember to have said they rang."

"Did you make this sally by command of your Voice?"

"During the Easter week of last year, being in the trenches of Melun, it was told me by my Voices—that is to say, by Saint Catherine and Saint Margaret—'Thou wilt be taken before Saint John's Day; and so it must be: do not torment thyself about it: be resigned; God will help thee.'"

"Before this occasion at Melun, had not your Voices ever told you that you would be taken?"

"Yes, many times and nearly every day. And I asked of my Voices that, when I should be taken, I might die soon, without long suffering in prison; and they said to me: 'Be resigned to all—thus it must be.' But they did not tell me the time; and if I had known it, I should not have gone. Often I asked to know the hour: they never told me."

"Did your Voices command you to make this sally from Compiègne, and signify that you would be taken if you went?"

"If I had known the hour when I should be taken, I should never have gone of mine own free-will; I should always have obeyed their commands in the end, whatever might happen to me."

"When you made this sally from Compiègne had you any Voice or revelation about making it?"

"That day I did not know at all that I should be taken, and I had no other command to go forth; but they had always told me it was necessary for me to be taken prisoner."

"When you made this sally, did you pass by the Bridge of Compiègne?"

"I passed by the bridge and the boulevard, and went with the company of followers of my side against the followers of my Lord of Luxembourg. I drove them back twice against the camp of the Burgundians, and the third time, to the middle of the highway. The English who were there then cut off the road from me and my people, between us and the boulevard. For this reason, my followers retreated, and, in retreating towards the fields, on the Picardy side, near the boulevard, I was taken. Between Compiègne and the place where I was taken there is nothing but the stream and the boulevard with its ditch."

"Did you not have on the banner you carried a representation of the world, painted with two angels, etc.?"

"Yes; and I had no other."

"What did this signify, to paint God holding the world, and these angels?"

THE BATTLE OF HERRINGS.

From a French Manuscript of the XVth Century.

"Saint Catherine and Saint Margaret told me that I was to take my banner and to carry it boldly, and to have painted on it the King of Heaven. I told my King, much against my will: that is all I can tell of the signification of this painting."

"Have you not a shield and arms?"

"I never had one; but my King has granted arms to my brothers,—that is to say, a shield azure, two fleurs-de-lys of gold, and a sword betwixt. These arms I described in this town to a painter, because he asked what arms I bore. The King gave them to my brothers, [to please[62] them,] without request from me and without revelation."

THE MAID TAKEN PRISONER.

"Had you, when you were taken, a horse, charger, or hackney?"

"I was on horseback; the one which I was riding when I was taken was a demi-charger."

"Who had given you this horse?"

"My King, or his people, from the King's money. I had five chargers from the King's money, without counting my hacks, of which I had more than seven."

"Had you any other riches from your King besides these horses?"

"I asked nothing from my King, except good arms, good horses, and money to pay my household."

"Had you no treasure?"

"The ten or twelve thousand I was worth is not much treasure to carry on war, very little indeed; and such goods are my brothers', in my opinion; what I have is my King's own money."

"What was the sign[63] that came to your King when

---

[62] In the Minute only.

[63] Not in the Minute. Latin text reads: "*quod dedit regi suo dum venit ad eum.*"

you went to him?"

"It was beautiful, honourable, and most credible; the best and richest in the world."

"Then why will you not tell it and shew it, since you wished to have the sign[64] of Catherine de la Rochelle?"

"I might not have asked to know the sign of the said Catherine, had that sign been as well shewn before notable people of the Church and others, Archbishops and Bishops, as mine was before the Archbishop of Rheims and other Bishops whose names I know not. There were there also Charles de Bourbon, the Sire de la Tremouille, the Duke d'Alençon,[65] and many other knights, who saw and heard it as well as I see those who speak to me to-day; and, besides, I knew already, through Saint Catherine and Saint Margaret, that the doings of this Catherine were as nothing."

"Does this sign still last?"

"It is well to know it; it will last a thousand years and more. My sign is with the King's treasure."

"Is it gold, silver, precious stones, or a crown?"

"I will tell you nothing more about it. No man in the world could devise so rich a thing as this sign; but the sign that you need is that God may deliver me from your hands; that is the most sure sign He could send you. When I was about to start to see my King, my Voices told me: 'Go boldly; when thou art before the King, he shall have a sure sign to receive thee and believe in thee.'"

"When the sign came to your King, what reverence did you make to it? Did it come from God?"

"I thanked Our Lord for having delivered me from the trouble that I had with the clergy of my party, who were arguing against me; and I knelt down several times. An Angel from God, and from none other, sent the sign to my King; and for this I have many times thanked Our Lord. The priests of that party ceased to attack me when they

---

[64] The "sign," *i.e.* the appearance of "the White Lady."

[65] Jean, Duke d'Alençon: son of the Duke killed at Agincourt. He was of the blood-royal of France, and had married a daughter of the Duke d'Orléans. Jeanne was on very friendly terms with him, and always called him her "Beau Duc."

had recognized the sign."

"The Clergy of that party then saw the sign?"

"When my King and those who were with him had seen the sign and also the Angel[66] that brought it, I asked my King if he were satisfied. He answered, Yes. Then I left, and went to a little chapel close by. I have since heard that, after I left, more than three hundred persons saw the said sign. For love of me and that I should not be questioned about it, God permitted certain men of my party to see the sign in reality."

"Your King and you, did you do reverence to the Angel who brought the sign?"

"Yes; I made a salutation, knelt down, and took off my cap."

*Monday, March 12th, in the morning; in Jeanne's prison.—Present: The Bishop, assisted by Jean Delafontaine, Commissary; Nicholas Midi and Gerard Feuillet; and as their witnesses: Thomas Fiefvet, Pasquier de Vaux, and Nicolas de Houbent.*

In presence of all the above-named, We required the said Jeanne to swear to speak truth on what should be asked her.

She replied: "*On what touches your Case*, as I have said already, I will willingly speak truth." And thus did she make oath.

Then, by Our order, she was questioned by Maître Jean Delafontaine:

"Did not the Angel who bore the sign to your King speak to him?"

"Yes, he spoke to him; and he told my King it was necessary that I should be set to work, so that the country might be soon relieved."

"Was the Angel who bore the sign to your King the same Angel who had before appeared to you?"

"It is all one; and he has never failed me."

---

[66] The allegory of the Angel sent with a crown, here first given to avoid "perjury," *i.e.*, breaking her promise to preserve the King's secret, is explained by Jeanne herself, on the last day of her life, to mean her own mission from Heaven to lead Charles to his crowning.

"Has not the Angel, then, failed you with regard to the good things of this life, in that you have been taken prisoner?"

"I think, as it has pleased Our Lord, that it is for my well-being that I was taken prisoner."

"Has your Angel never failed you in the good things of grace?"

"How can he fail me, when he comforts me every day? My comfort comes from Saint Catherine and Saint Margaret."

"Do you call them, or do they come without being called?"

"They often come without being called; and other times, if they do not come soon, I pray Our Lord to send them."

"Have you sometimes called them without their coming?"

"I have never had need of them without having them."

"Has Saint Denis appeared to you sometimes?"

"Not that I know."

"When you promised Our Saviour to preserve your virginity, was it to Him that you spoke?"

"It would quite suffice that I give my promise to those who were sent by Him—that is to say, to Saint Catherine and Saint Margaret."

"Who induced you to have cited a man of the town of Toul on the question of marriage?"

"I did not have him cited; it was he, on the contrary, who had me cited; and then I swore before the Judge to speak the truth. And besides, I had promised nothing to this man. From the first time I heard my Voices, I dedicated my virginity for so long as it should please God; and I was then about thirteen years of age. My Voices told me I should win my case in this town of Toul."

"As to your visions, did you speak of them to your Curé or to any other Churchman?"

"No; only to Robert de Baudricourt and to my King. It was not my Voices who compelled me to keep them secret; but I feared to reveal them, in dread that the

Burgundians might put some hindrance in the way of my journey; and, in particular, I was afraid that my father would hinder it."

"Do you think that you did right to go without leave from your father or mother, when you should 'honour your father and mother'?"

"In all things I obeyed them well, except in that of the journey: but afterwards I wrote to them, and they forgave me."

"When you left your father and mother, do you think you sinned?"

"If God commanded, it was right to obey. If God commanded it, had I had a hundred fathers and mothers, and had I been a king's daughter, I should have gone."

"Did you ask your Voices if you should announce your departure to your father and mother?"

"As to my father and mother, my Voices would have been quite willing I should tell them, had it not been for the trouble I should have caused them in speaking of this. As for myself, I would not have told them at any price. My Voices agreed that I might either speak to my father and mother or be silent."

"Did you do reverence to Saint Michael and the Angels when you saw them?"

"Yes; and, after they were gone I kissed the earth where they had been."

"Were they long with you?"

"Very often they came among the faithful [*i.e.*, in church] without being seen; and often I saw them among the faithful."

"Had you had any letters from Saint Michael or from your Voices?"

"I have not permission to tell you. Eight days from this, I will tell you willingly what I know."

"Did not your Voices call you 'Daughter of God, daughter of the Church, great-hearted daughter'?"

"Before the raising of the Siege of Orleans and every day since, when they speak to me, they call me often, 'Jeanne the Maid, Daughter of God.'"

"Since you call yourself a daughter of God, why do

you not willingly say 'Our Father'?"

"I do say it willingly. Last time, when I refused, it was because I meant that my Lord of Beauvais should hear me in confession."

*The same day, Monday, in the afternoon, in the same place.—Present: Jean Delafontaine, Commissary; Nicolas Midi; Gerard Feuillet; Thomas Fiefvet; Pasquier de Vaux; and Nicolas de Houbent.*

The said Jeanne was interrogated as follows by Our order by the said Jean Delafontaine:

"Did not your father have dreams about you before your departure?"

"When I was still with my father and mother, my mother told me many times that my father had spoken of having dreamed that I, Jeannette, his daughter, went away with the men-at-arms. My father and mother took great care to keep me safe, and held me much in subjection. I obeyed them in everything, except in the case at Toul— the action for marriage. I have heard my mother say that my father told my brothers: 'Truly, if I thought this thing would happen that I have dreamed about my daughter, I would wish you to drown her; and, if you would not do it, I would drown her myself!' He nearly lost his senses when I went to Vaucouleurs."

"Did these thoughts and dreams come to your father after you had your visions?"

"Yes, more than two years after I had had my first Voice."

"Was it at the request of Robert de Baudricourt or of yourself that you took man's dress?"

"It was of myself, and at the request of no living man."

"Did your Voices command you to take man's dress?"

"All that I have done of good, I have done by the command of my Voices. As to the dress, I will answer about it another time: at present I am not advised, but to-morrow I will answer."

"In taking man's dress, did you think you were doing wrong?"

"No; even now if I were with those of my own side

and in this man's dress, it seems to me it would be a great good for France to do as I did before I was taken."

"How would you have delivered the Duke d'Orléans?"

"I should have taken enough English prisoners in France to have exchanged him back; if I had not taken enough in France, I should have crossed the sea to seek him in England, by force."

"Did Saint Catherine and Saint Margaret tell you absolutely and without condition that you would take enough English to get the Duke d'Orléans, who is in England, or that otherwise you would cross the sea to seek him?"[67]

"Yes, and I said so to my King: and he allowed me to treat with the English lords who were then prisoners.[68] If I had continued three years without hindrance, I should have delivered him. To do this, it needed less time than three years and more than one. But I do not remember about it."

"What was the sign you gave to the King?"

"I shall take counsel regarding that from Saint Catherine."

*Monday, March 12th, assembled in Our dwelling, summoned by Us, the religious and discreet person, Brother Jean Lemaître, of the Order of Saint Dominic, Deputy of the Inquisitor of the Evil of Heresy in the Kingdom of France, in presence of the Venerable and discreet persons the Lords and Masters, Thomas Fiefvet, Pasquier de Vaux, Nicolas de Houbent, Brother Ysambard de la Pierre.*

We, the Bishop, did shew to the said Deputy, that, at the outset of the Action for Heresy brought by us against the woman, commonly called Jeanne the Maid, We had summoned and required him, the said Deputy, to join with us; and that we had offered to communicate to him the acts, documents and, in one word, all we possess bearing on the matter of the Process. He had then made a

---

[67] In the Minute: "*et l'admener en trois ans*": not in the Latin Text.
[68] The Minute reads: "*la laissant faire de prisonniers.*"

difficulty, not being, he told Us, commissioned except for the City and Diocese of Rouen; and the Action in question being deduced by Us; by right of our jurisdiction of Beauvais, on territory conceded to Us for this purpose. For this cause, in order to give all security to this matter and by an excess of precaution, We have, by the advice of the Masters, decided to write about it to the Chief Inquisitor, requesting him to come himself without delay to Rouen, or specially to appoint a Deputy to whom, for the deduction and completion of the Process, he might wish to give full powers. The said Inquisitor hath received Our letter, and acceding with kindness to Our request, for the honour and exaltation of the Orthodox Faith, he hath specially commissioned and appointed for this Action the said Brother Jean Lemaître, as doth appear in the letters patent furnished and attested with the seal of the Inquisition.

In consequence of this letter, We, the Bishop, summon and require the said Brother Jean Lemaître, here present, in the terms of the said letter, to join with us in this said Action.

To which the said Brother answered: that he would examine the Commission addressed to him, the Process signed by the registrars, and all that it should please Us to communicate to him; and that, all being seen and examined by him, he will give Us an answer and will do for the Holy Inquisition that which is right.

We, the Bishop, added: that the said Deputy had been present at a great part of the Process; that he had, in consequence, been able to hear a great part of Jeanne's answers; that nevertheless We held ourselves satisfied by what he had just said, and would certainly communicate to him the Process and all that had already been done, that he may take fuller cognizance of everything.

*The Deputy Inquisitor joins the Court.*
*Tuesday, March 13th, in the prison. Present: The Bishop and Brother Jean Lemaître, assisted by Jean Delafontaine, Nicolas Midi, and Gerard Feuillet; witnesses, Nicolas de Houbent and Ysambard de la*

*Pierre.*

The said Brother Jean Lemaître declared to Us that seeing the letter addressed to him which we had yesterday communicated, together with the other circumstances of the Process, and all being well considered, he joins himself to Us and is ready to proceed with Us according to law and right.

We, the Bishop, then made known with gentleness to Jeanne this intervention, exhorting and warning her, for the salvation of her soul, to speak the truth on all which should be asked of her.

*The Deputy Inquisitor appoints his Officers.*

And then, the Deputy of the Chief Inquisitor, wishing to proceed regularly in the Process, hath declared his choice of the Officers whose names follow:

1. As Promoter from the Holy Inquisition, Messire Jean d'Estivet, Canon of the Churches of Bayeux and Beauvais.

2. As Registrar of his office, Messire Nicolas Taquel, Priest of the Diocese of Rouen, Notary Public and Registrar of the Archiepiscopal Court of Rouen.

3. As Executor of his Orders and Citations, Messire Jean Massieu, Priest.

4. As keepers of the prison, the noble man, John Gris, Squire of the Body Guard of Our Lord the King, and John Berwoist. These, We, the Bishop, had, with the exception of Messire Nicolas Taquel, but only in that which concerns Our office, already appointed to the same functions, as confirmed for Our part in the letters above quoted, and as confirmed by the said Inquisitor by his letters, of which mention follows. The said officers did then take oath, between the hands of the said Deputy, to faithfully fulfil their functions.

[Here follow the three letters of Nomination of the Promoter, d'Estivet; the Registrar, Taquel; and the Usher, Massieu: dated Tuesday, March 13th: signed Boisguillaume, Manchon: the nomination of Taquel, Registrar, is dated March 14th.]

All which precedes having already taken place, as has been said up to the present time, We, the Bishop, and

Brother Jean Lemaître, Deputy of the Inquisitor, have from this moment proceeded together to all the remainder of the Process, and have questioned or caused questions to be made as it had begun.

*Tuesday, March 13th.—Present: The Bishop, and Brother Jean Lemaître, Jean Delafontaine, Nicolas Midi, Gerard Feuillet; in the presence of Nicolas de Houbent and of Brother Ysambard de la Pierre.*

By Our order, Jeanne was asked as follows:

"What was the sign you gave your King?"

"Will you be satisfied that I should perjure myself?"

"Have you promised and sworn to Saint Catherine that you will not tell this sign?"

"I promised and swore not to tell this sign, and for my own sake, because I was pressed too much to tell it, and then I said to myself: 'I promise not to speak of it to any one in the world.' The sign was that an Angel assured my King, in bringing him the crown, that he should have the whole realm of France, by the means of God's help and my labours; that he was to start me on the work—that is to say, to give me men-at-arms; and that otherwise he would not be so soon crowned and consecrated."

"Have you spoken to Saint Catherine since yesterday?"

"I have heard her since yesterday, and she has several times told me to reply boldly to the Judges on what they shall ask me touching my Case."

"How did the Angel carry the crown? and did he place it himself on your King's head?"

"The crown was given to an Archbishop—that is, to the Archbishop of Rheims—so it seems to me, in the presence of my King. The Archbishop received it, and gave it to the King. I was myself present. The crown was afterwards put among my King's treasures."

"To what place was the crown brought?"

"To the King's Chamber, in the Castle of Chinon."

"What day and what time?"

"The day, I do not know; of the time, it was full day. I have no further recollection of it. Of the month it was

March or April, it seems to me. In this present month of March or next April it will be two years since. It was after Easter."[69]

"Was it the first day that you saw the sign when the King saw it?"

"Yes, he had it the same day."

"Of what material was the said crown?"

"It is well to know it was of fine gold; it was so rich that I do not know how to count its riches or to appreciate its beauty. The crown signified that my King should possess the Kingdom of France."

"Were there stones in it?"

"I have told you what I know about it."

"Did you touch or kiss it?"

"No."

"Did the Angel who brought this crown come from Heaven or earth?"

"He came from above, and I presume that he came by Our Lord's command; he came in by the door of the room. When he came before my King, he did him reverence by bowing before him, and pronouncing the words I have already said; and at the same time the Angel put him in mind of the great patience he had had in presence of so many tribulations. From the door, the Angel walked, and touched the earth, in coming to the King."

"What space was there between the door and the King?"

"My opinion is that there was quite the space of a lance-length [about 10 feet]; and he returned the way he came. When the Angel came, I accompanied him and went with him by the staircase to the King's Chamber. The Angel went in first, then myself, and I said to the King: 'Sire, there is your sign; take it.'"

"Where did the Angel appear to you?"

"I was nearly always at prayer that God might send the sign to the King; and I was at my lodging, at the house of

[69] March 8th, 1428; it was *before* Easter, which in that year fell on March 7th.

a worthy woman,[70] near the Castle of Chinon, when he came; afterwards, we went together to the King. He was accompanied by other Angels whom no one saw. Had it not been for love of me, and to free me of trouble from those that accused me, I think that many who saw the Angel would not have seen him."

"Did all those who were with the King see the Angel?"

"I believe that the Archbishop of Rheims saw him, and so did the Lords d'Alençon, la Trémouille, and Charles de Bourbon. As to the crown, many Clergy and others saw it who did not see the Angel."

"Of what appearance, what height, was this Angel?"

"I have not permission to say; to-morrow I will answer about it."

"All the Angels who accompanied him, had they the same appearance?"

"Some resembled him well enough, others not: at least, so far as I saw. Some had wings, others were crowned. In company with them were Saint Catherine and Saint Margaret, who were with the Angel aforesaid, and the other Angels also, right up to the King's Chamber."

"How did the Angel leave you?"

"He left me in that little Chapel. I was much vexed at his going; I wept; willingly would I have gone with him— that is to say, my soul."

"After the departure of the Angel, did you remain happy [or[71] were you in great fear?"]

"He did not leave me in either fear or terror; but I was grieved at his going."

"Is it for any merit of yours that God sent you this Angel?"

"He came for a great purpose: I was in hopes that the

---

[70] The house in which Jeanne lodged at Chinon is said to have belonged to a certain Regnier de la Barrier, whose widow or daughter is the "worthy woman" referred to. Jeanne was afterwards lodged in the Tower of Coudray, where her room may still be seen. It is approached by a staircase outside the tower. The vaulted roof has fallen in, and the fireplace is damaged, but the walls are intact, and the room could easily be restored. Jeanne stayed in this tower from March 8th to April 20th, 1429.

[71] In the Minute only.

King would believe the sign, and that they would cease to argue with me, and would aid the good people of Orleans. The Angel came for the merits of the King and of the good Duke d'Orléans."[72]

"Why to you rather than to another?"

"It has pleased God so to do by a simple maiden, in order to drive back the enemies of the King."

"Was it told you whence the Angel had taken this crown?"

"It was brought from God; no goldsmith in the world would know how to fashion it so rich and fair."

"Whence did he take it?"

"I refer me to God; and know nothing more of whence it was taken."

"This crown, did it smell well and had it a good odour? did it glitter?"

"I do not remember about it; I will think it over." [Remembering:] "Yes, it smelt good, and will smell good always, if it be well guarded, as it should be. It was in the form of a crown."

"Did the Angel write you a letter?"

"No."

"What sign had your King and the people who were with him and yourself, to believe that it was an Angel?"

"The King believed it by the teaching of the Clergy who were there, and by the sign of the crown."

"But how did the Clergy know it was an Angel?"

"By their knowledge and because they were clerks."

"What have you to say about a married priest and a lost cup that you were to have pointed out?"[73]

"Of all this I know nothing, nor have I ever heard of it."

"When you came before Paris, had you revelations from your Voices to go there?"

"No, I went at the request of the gentlemen who wished to make an attack or assault-at-arms; I intended to go there and break through the trenches."

---

[72] Charles, Duke d'Orléans, then a prisoner in England: one of the five princes of the blood taken at Agincourt.
[73] There is no allusion to either of these in any evidence of the time.

"Had you any revelation to attack La Charité?"

"No, I went there at the request of the men-at-arms, as I said elsewhere."

"Did you have any revelation to go to Pont l'Evêque?"[74]

"After I had had, in the trenches of Melun,[75] revelation that I should be taken, I consulted more often with the Captains of the army; but I did not tell them I had had any revelation that I should be taken."

"Was it well to attack the town of Paris on the day of the Festival of the Nativity of Our Lady?"

"It is well done to observe the Festival of the Blessed Mary, and on my conscience it seems to me that it was, and ever will be, well to observe these festivals, from one end to the other."

"Did you not say before Paris, 'Surrender this town by order of Jesus'?"

"No, but I said, 'Surrender it to the King of France.'"

*Wednesday, March 14th.—Jean Delafontaine, Commissary, assisted by Nicolas Midi and Gerard Feuillet. Witnesses: Nicolas de Houbent and Ysambard de la Pierre.*

Jeanne was interrogated as follows:

"Why did you throw yourself from the top of the Tower at Beaurevoir?"

"I had heard that the people of Compiègne, all, to the age of seven years, were to be put to fire and sword; and I would rather have died than live after such a destruction of good people. That was one of the reasons. The other was that I knew I was sold to the English; and I had rather die than be in the hands of my enemies, the English."

"Did your Saints counsel you about it?"

"Saint Catherine told me almost every day not to leap, that God would help me, and also those at Compiègne. I said to Saint Catherine: 'Since God will help those at Compiègne, I wish to be there.' Saint Catherine said to

---

[74] May, 1430.
[75] Easter week, April 16th–23rd, 1430.

me, 'Be resigned, and do not falter: you will not be delivered before seeing the King of England.' I answered her: 'Truly I do not wish to see him; I would rather die than fall into the hands of the English.'"

"Is it true that you said to Saint Catherine and Saint Margaret: 'Will God leave these good people of Compiègne to die so horribly'?"

"I did not say 'so horribly,' but, 'How can God leave these good people of Compiègne, who have been, and are, so loyal to their lord, to die?' After having fallen, I was two or three days without eating.[76] By the leap I was so injured that I could neither eat nor drink; and all the time I was consoled by Saint Catherine, who told me to confess, and to beg pardon of God; and without fail, those at Compiègne would have help before Saint Martin's Day in the winter. Then I began to recover and to eat, and was soon cured."

"When you made this leap, did you think you would kill yourself?"

"No; but, in leaping, I commended myself to God. I hoped by means of this leap to escape, and to avoid being delivered up to the English."

"When speech returned to you, did you not blaspheme and curse God and His Saints? This is proved by allegation."

"I have no memory of having ever blasphemed and cursed God and His Saints, in that place or elsewhere."

"Will you refer this to the enquiry made or to be made?"

"I refer me to God and not to any other, and to a good confession."

"Do your Voices ask delay to answer you?"

"Sometimes Saint Catherine answers me, but I fail to understand because of the great disturbance in the prison and the noise made by my guards. When I make a request

---

[76] Jeanne says that her leap from the tower was "towards the end," and as the town of Compiègne was in great straits in October, she probably made her attempt at escape towards the end of that month. The army of relief under the Count de Vendôme started on October 25th, and the siege was raised early in November.

to Saint Catherine, both my Saints make request to Our Lord; then, by order of Our Lord, they give answer to me."

"When your Saints come to you, have they a light with them? Did you not see the light on a certain occasion when you heard the Voices in the Castle, without knowing if the Voice were in your room?"

"There is never a day that my Saints do not come to the Castle; and they never come without light. And as to this Voice of which you speak, I do not remember if on that occasion I saw the light or even Saint Catherine. I asked three things of my Voices:—1. My deliverance; 2. That God would come to the help of the French, and protect the towns under their control; 3. The salvation of my soul. [Addressing herself to the Judges:] If it should be that I am taken to Paris, grant, I pray you, that I may have a copy of my questions and answers, so that I may lend them to those at Paris, and that I may be able to say to them: 'Thus was I questioned at Rouen; and here are my answers': in this way, I shall not have to trouble again over so many questions."

"You said that my Lord of Beauvais puts himself in great danger by bringing you to trial; of what danger were you speaking? In what peril or danger do we place ourselves, your Judges and the others?"

"I said to my Lord of Beauvais, 'You say that you are my Judge; I do not know if you are, but take heed not to judge wrongly, because you would put yourself in great danger; and I warn you of it, so that, if Our Lord should punish you for it, I shall have done my duty in telling you.'"

"But what is this peril or danger?"

"Saint Catherine has told me that I shall have help; I do not know if this will be to be delivered from prison, or if, whilst I am being tried, some disturbance may happen, by which I shall be delivered. The help will come to me, I think, in one way or the other. Besides this, my Voices have told me that I shall be delivered by a great victory; and they add: 'Be resigned; have no care for thy martyrdom; thou wilt come in the end to the Kingdom of

Paradise.' They have told me this simply, absolutely, and without fail. What is meant by my martyrdom is the pain and adversity that I suffer in prison; I do not know if I shall have still greater suffering to bear; for that I refer me to God."

"Since your Voices told you that you would come in the end to the Kingdom of Paradise, have you felt assured of being saved and of not being damned in Hell?"

"I believe firmly what my Voices have told me, that I shall be saved; I believe it as firmly as if I were already there."

"After this revelation, do you believe that you cannot commit mortal sin?"[77]

"I do not know, and in all things I wait on Our Lord."

"That is an answer of great weight!"

"Yes, and one which I hold for a great treasure."

*The same day, Wednesday, March 14th, in the afternoon. Present: Jean Delafontaine, Commissary, assisted by Nicolas Midi and Gerard Feuillet. Witnesses: Brother Ysambard de la Pierre and Jean Manchon.*

And in the first place, Jeanne expressed herself thus:

---

[77] The Minute inverts the order of this and the following question and answer.

## GATE TO THE PALACE OF CAUCHON, BISHOP OF BEAUVAIS.

"On the subject of the answer that I made to you this morning on the certainty of my salvation, I mean the answer thus: provided that I keep the promise made to Our Lord, to keep safe the virginity of my body and soul."

"Have you any need to confess, as you believe by the revelations of your Voices that you will be saved?"

"I do not know of having committed mortal sin; but, if I were in mortal sin, I think that Saint Catherine and Saint Margaret would abandon me at once. I do not think one can cleanse one's conscience too much."

"Since you have been in the prison, have you never blasphemed or cursed God?"

"No; sometimes I said: 'bon gré Dieu,' or 'Saint Jean,' or 'Notre Dame': those who have reported otherwise may have misunderstood."

"To take a man at ransom, and to put him to death, while a prisoner, is not that mortal sin?"

"I never did it."

"What did you do to Franquet d'Arras, who was put to death, at Lagny?"

"I consented that he should die if he had merited it, because he had confessed to being a murderer, thief, and traitor; his trial lasted fifteen days; he had for Judge the Bailly of Senlis and the people of the Court at Lagny. I had given orders to exchange this Franquet against a man of Paris, landlord of the Hôtel de l'Ours. When I learnt the death of the latter, and the Bailly told me that I should do great wrong to justice by giving up Franquet, I said to the Bailly, 'As my man is dead, do with the other what you should do, for justice.'"

"Did you give, or cause to be given, money to him who took Franquet?"

"I am not Master of the Mint or Treasurer of France to pay out money so."

"We recall to you:—1. That you attacked Paris on a Feast Day; 2. That you had the horse of my Lord the Bishop of Senlis; 3. That you threw yourself down from the Tower of Beaurevoir; 4. That you wear a man's dress; 5. That you consented to the death of Franquet d'Arras: do you not think you have committed mortal sin in these?"

"For what concerns the attack on Paris, I do not think myself to be in mortal sin; if I have so done, it is for God to know it, and the Priest in confession. As to the horse of my Lord the Bishop of Senlis, I firmly believe I have not sinned against Our Lord: the horse was valued at 200 gold crowns, of which he received assignment; nevertheless, this horse was sent back to the Sire de la Trémouille, to restore it to my Lord of Senlis; it was no good for me to ride; besides, it was not I who took it; and, moreover, I did not wish to keep it, having heard that the Bishop was displeased that it had been taken from him, and, beyond all this, the horse was of no use for warfare. I do not know if the Bishop was paid, nor if his horse was restored to him; I think not. As to my fall from the Tower at Beaurevoir, I did not do it in despair, but thinking to save myself and to go to the help of all those brave folk who were in danger. After my fall, I confessed myself and asked pardon. God has forgiven me, not for any good in me: I did wrong, but I know by revelation from Saint Catherine that, after the confession I made, I was forgiven. It was by the counsel of Saint Catherine that I confessed myself."

"Did you do penance for it?"

"Yes, and my penance came to me in great part from the harm I did myself in falling. You ask me if I believe this wrong which I did in leaping to be mortal sin? I know nothing about it, but refer me to God. As to my dress, since I bear it by command of God and for His service, I do not think I have done wrong at all; so soon as it shall please God to prescribe it, I will take it off."

*The following Thursday, March 15th, in the morning. Present: Jean Delafontaine, Commissary, assisted by Nicolas Midi and Gerard Feuillet. Witnesses: Nicolas de Houbent and Brother Ysambard de la Pierre.*

First of all, Jeanne was charitably exhorted, warned,

and required, if she had done anything which might be against our Faith, that she should refer it to the decision of Holy Mother Church.

"Let my answers," she said, "be seen and examined by the Clergy: then let them tell me if there be anything against the Christian Faith. I shall know surely by my counsel what it is, and will say afterwards what shall be judged and decided. And, moreover, if there be anything wrong against the Christian Faith which Our Lord commanded, I should not wish to maintain it, and should be very sorry to be in opposition."

Then we explained to her about the Church Triumphant and the Church Militant, and the difference between them. Required to submit to the decision of the Church Militant what she had said or done, whether of good or ill:

"I will not answer you anything more about it now," she said.

"Upon the oath that you have taken, tell us, how did you think to escape from the Castle of Beaulieu between two planks of wood?"[78]

"Never was I prisoner in such a place that I would not willingly have escaped. Being in that Castle, I should have shut my keepers in the tower, if it had not been that the porter espied me and encountered me. It did not please God that I should escape this time: it was necessary for me to see the English King,[79] as my Voices had told me, as has been already said."

"Have you had permission from God or your Voices to leave prison when it shall please you?"

"I have asked it many times, but I have not yet had it."

---

[78] There is no fuller account of this attempt. It probably took place during the month of July, and may have been the reason for her removal to the stronger prison of Beaurevoir, early in August.

[79] Henry VI. arrived in Rouen first on July 29th, 1430, when Jeanne was at Beaulieu; he was crowned at Paris in the following November, and returned to Rouen for Christmas, remaining there about six weeks, for the date of his landing at Dover is given as February 11th. It is not improbable that the prisoner may have seen the King, as they were both residing in the same Castle, and her windows looked on the fields, where he would probably take exercise.

Jeanne D'Arc

"Would you go now, if you saw your starting-point?"

"If I saw the door open, I should go: that would be leave from Our Lord. If I saw the door open, and my keepers and the other English beyond power of resistance, truly I should see in it my leave and help sent me by Our Lord. But without this leave, I shall not go, unless I make a forcible attempt to go,[80] and so learn if Our Lord would be pleased: this on the strength of the proverb, 'Help thyself, and God will help thee': I say this in order that, if I do escape, no one may say I did so without God's leave."

"When you asked to hear Mass, did it not seem to you that it would be more proper to be in female dress? Which would you like best, to have a woman's dress to hear Mass, or to remain in a man's dress and not hear it?"

"Give me assurance beforehand that I shall hear Mass if I am in female attire, and I will answer you this."

"Very well, I give you assurance of it: you shall hear Mass if you put on female attire."

"And what say you, if I have sworn and promised to our King my Master, not to put off this dress? Well, I will answer you this: Have made for me a long dress down to the ground, without a train; give it to me to go to Mass, and then on my return I will put on again the dress I have."

"I say it to you once again, do you consent to wear female attire to go and hear Mass?"

"I will take counsel on this, and then I will answer you: but I beseech you, for the honour of God and Our Lady permit me to hear Mass in this good town."

"You consent simply and absolutely to take female attire?"

"Send me a dress like a daughter of your citizens— that is to say, a long 'houppeland.'[81] I will wear it to go and hear Mass. I beseech you as earnestly as I can, permit me to hear it in the dress I wear at this moment and without changing anything!"

---

[80] "*Faceret unam aggressionem;*" *Gallicè*, "*une entreprise.*"
[81] In the Minute: "*mesme le chaperon de femme.*"

"Will you submit your actions and words to the decision of the Church?"

"My words and deeds are all in God's Hands: in all, I wait upon Him. I assure you, I would say or do nothing against the Christian Faith: in case I have done or said anything which might be on my soul and which the clergy could say was contrary to the Christian Faith established by Our Lord, I would not maintain it, and would put it away."

"Are you not willing to submit yourself in this to the order of the Church?"

"I will not answer you anything more about it now. Send me a cleric on Saturday; and, if you do not wish to come yourself, I will answer him on this, with God's help; and it shall be put in writing."

"When your Voices come, do you make obeisance to them as to a Saint?"

"Yes; and if perchance I have not done so, I have afterwards asked of them grace and pardon. I should not know how to do them such great reverence as belongs to them, for I believe firmly they are Saint Catherine and Saint Margaret. I believe the same of Saint Michael."

"For those who are Saints of Paradise, offerings are voluntarily made of candles, etc.: have you never made an offering of lighted candles, or other things, to the Saints who come to you, in the Church or elsewhere, or had Masses said?"

"No, unless it be in the offering of the Mass, in the hands of the Priest, in honour of Saint Catherine, one of the Saints who appeared to me. I have never lighted as many candles as I wish to Saint Catherine and Saint Margaret, who are in Paradise; and I firmly believe it is they who come to me."

"When you place lights before the image of Saint Catherine, do you place them in honour of the one who appears to you?"

"I do it in honour of God, of Our Lady, and of Saint Catherine who is in Heaven, and of her who appears to me."

"Do you place these lights in honour of Saint

Catherine, who has shewn herself to you, who has appeared to you?"

"Yes, I make no difference between the one who has appeared to me, and the one who is in heaven."[82]

"Do you always do, always accomplish, what your Voices command you?"

"With all my power I accomplish the command that Our Lord sends me through my Voices, in so far as I understand them. My Voices command nothing but by the good pleasure of Our Lord."

"In warfare, have you done nothing without counsel of your Voices?"

"I have already answered you thereon: read your book again well, and you will find it. At the request of the men-at-arms, there was an assault made before Paris, and, at the request of the King himself, one also before La Charité. These were neither against nor by the order of my Voices."

"Have you never done anything against their command and will?"

"All that I could and knew how to do, I have done and accomplished to the best of my power. As to the matter of the fall from the keep of Beaurevoir, I did it against their command; but I could not control myself. When my Voices saw my need, and that I neither knew how, nor was able, to control myself, they saved my life and kept me from killing myself. Whatever things I did in my greatest undertakings, they always helped me; and that is a sign they are good spirits."

"Have you no other sign that they are good spirits?"

"Saint Michael assured me of it before the Voices came to me."

"How did you know it was Saint Michael?"

"By the speech and language of the Angels. I believe firmly that they were Angels."

"But how did you know it was the language of Angels?"

---

[82] In the Minute: "*et ne fait point de différence de celle qui est au ciel et celle qui se appert à moi.*"

"I believed it at once, and I had the will to believe it. When Saint Michael came to me, he said to me: 'Saint Catherine and Saint Margaret will come to thee; follow their counsel; they have been chosen to guide thee and counsel thee in all that thou hast to do: believe what they shall tell thee, it is the order of Our Lord.'"

"If the devil were to put himself in the form or likeness of an angel, how would you know if it were a good or an evil angel?"

"I should know quite well if it were Saint Michael or a counterfeit. The first time I was in great doubt if it were Saint Michael; and I was much afraid. I had seen him many times before I knew it was Saint Michael."

"Why did you recognize him sooner that time, when you say you believed it was he, than the first time he appeared to you?"

"The first time I was a young child, and I was much afraid; afterwards, he had taught me so well, and it was so clear to me, that I believed firmly it was he."[83]

"What doctrine did he teach you?"

"Above all things he told me to be a good child, and that God would help me,—to come to the help of the King of France, among other things. The greater part of what he taught me is already in the book in which you are writing: he told me of the great misery there was in the Kingdom of France."

"What was the height and stature of this Angel?"

"On Saturday I will reply, with other things which I should answer, as it shall please God."

"Do you not think it a great sin, and one which offends Saint Catherine and Saint Margaret who appeared to you, to act against their commands?"

"Yes, certainly; and the greatest I have ever committed, in my opinion, has been the leap from the Tower of Beaurevoir; for the which I have besought their mercy, and for all other offences I may have done against

---

[83] "Le vrai office de Monseigneur Saint-Michel est de faire grandes révélations aux hommes en bas, en leur donnant moult sainct conseils." ("*Le Livre des Angeles de Dieu.*"—MS. in the Bibliothèque Nationale, Paris.)

them."

"Will Saint Catherine and Saint Margaret take bodily vengeance for this offence?"

"I do not know, and did not ask them."

"You have asserted that, for speaking the truth, men were sometimes hanged: do you, then, know any crime or fault in yourself for which you should die, if you confessed it?"

"I know of none."

*The following Saturday, March 17th:—Present: Jean Delafontaine, Commissary, assisted by Nicolas Midi, and Gerard Feuillet, in the presence of Ysambard de la Pierre and of Jean Massieu.*

The said Jeanne was required to take the oath already made by her. Afterwards, she was again interrogated:

"In what form, kind, size, and dress did Saint Michael come to you?"

"In the form of a true honest man ['*prud homme*']; of his dress and the rest I will say nothing more. As to the Angels, I saw them with my eyes; you will hear naught else about it. I believe the deeds and words of Saint Michael, who appeared to me, as firmly as I believe that Our Saviour Jesus Christ suffered Death and Passion for us. And that which makes me believe it, is the good counsel, comfort, and good doctrine which he has given me."

"Will you, in respect of all your words and deeds, whether good or bad, submit yourself to the decision of our Holy Mother the Church?"

"The Church! I love it, and would wish to maintain it with all my power, for our Christian Faith; it is not I who should be prevented from going to Church and hearing Mass! As to the good deeds I have done and my coming to the King, I must wait on the King of Heaven, who sent me to Charles, King of France, son of Charles, who was King of France. You will see that the French will soon gain a great victory, that God will send such great doings that nearly all the Kingdom of France will be shaken by them. I say it, so that, when it shall come to pass, it may be remembered that I said it."

"When will this happen?"

"I wait on Our Lord."

"Will you refer yourself to the decision of the Church?"

"I refer myself to God Who sent me, to Our Lady, and to all the Saints in Paradise. And in my opinion it is all one, God and the Church; and one should make no difficulty about it. Why do you make a difficulty?"

"There is a Church Triumphant in which are God and the Saints, the Angels, and the Souls of the Saved. There is another Church, the Church Militant, in which are the Pope, the Vicar of God on earth, the Cardinals, Prelates of the Church, the Clergy and all good Christians and Catholics: this Church, regularly assembled, cannot err, being ruled by the Holy Spirit. Will you refer yourself to this Church which we have thus just defined to you?"

"I came to the King of France from God, from the Blessed Virgin Mary, from all the Saints of Paradise, and the Church Victorious above, and by their command. To this Church I submit all my good deeds, all that I have done or will do. As to saying whether I will submit myself to the Church Militant, I will not now answer anything more."

"What do you say on the subject of the female attire which is offered to you, to go and hear Mass?"

"I will not take it yet, until it shall please Our Lord. And if it should happen that I should be brought to judgment, [and that I have to divest myself in Court,][84] I beseech the lords of the Church to do me the grace to allow me a woman's smock and a hood for my head; I would rather die than revoke what God has made me do; and I believe firmly that God will not allow it to come to pass that I should be brought so low that I may not soon have succour from Him, and by miracle."

"As you say that you bear a man's dress by the command of God, why do you ask for a woman's smock at the point of death?"

---

[84] In the Minute.

"It will be enough for me if it be long."

"Did your Godmother who saw the fairies pass as a wise woman?"

"She was held and considered a good and honest woman, neither divineress nor sorceress."

"You said you would take a woman's dress, that you might be let go: would this please God?"

"If I had leave to go in woman's dress, I should soon put myself back in man's dress and do what God has commanded me: I have already told you so. For nothing in the world will I swear not to arm myself and put on a man's dress; I must obey the orders of Our Lord."

"What age and what dress had Saint Catherine and Saint Margaret?"

"You have had such answers as you will have from me, and none others shall you have: I have told you what I know of it for certain."

"Before to-day, did you believe fairies were evil spirits?"

"I know nothing about it."

"Do you know if Saint Catherine and Saint Margaret hate the English?"

"They love what God loves: they hate what God hates."

"Does God hate the English?"

"Of the love or hate God may have for the English, or of what He will do for their souls, I know nothing; but I know quite well that they will be put out of France, except those who shall die there, and that God will send victory to the French against the English."

"Was God for the English when they were prospering in France?"

"I do not know if God hated the French; but I believe that He wished them to be defeated for their sins, if they were in sin."

"What warrant and what help do you expect to have from Our Lord for wearing this man's dress?"

"For this dress and for other things that I have done, I wish to have no other recompense than the salvation of my soul."

"What arms did you offer at Saint Denis?"

"My whole suit of white armour ['*album harnesium suum*;' *Gallicè*, '*un blanc harnoys*,'] as beseems a soldier, with a sword I had won before Paris."

"Why did you make this offering?"

"In devotion, and as is the custom of soldiers when they have been wounded. Having been wounded before Paris, I offered them at Saint Denis, because that is the war-cry of France."

"Did you do it that these arms might be worshipped?"

"No."

"What was the purpose of these five crosses which were on the sword that you found at Saint Catherine of Fierbois?"

"I know nothing about it."

"Who prompted you to have painted on your standard Angels with arms, feet, legs, and clothing?"

"I have already answered you."

"Did you have them painted as they came to see you?"

"No, I had them painted in the way they are painted in the Churches."

"Did you ever see them in the manner they are painted?"

"I will tell you nothing more."

"Why did you not have painted the brightness that comes to you with the Angels and the Voices?"

"It was not commanded me."

*The same day, March 17th, afternoon. Present: The Bishop and the Deputy Inquisitor, assisted by Jean Beaupère, Jacques de Touraine, Nicolas Midi, Pierre Maurice, Gerard Feuillet, Thomas de Courcelles, Jean Delafontaine; in presence of Brother Ysambard de la Pierre and John Gris.*

We interrogated the said Jeanne, as follows:

"Did the two Angels painted on your standard represent Saint Michael and Saint Gabriel?"

"They were there only for the honour of Our Lord, Who was painted on the standard. I only had these two Angels represented to honour Our Lord, Who was there represented holding the world."

"Were the two Angels represented on your standard those who guard the world? Why were there not more of them, seeing that you had been commanded by God to take this standard?"

"The standard was commanded by Our Lord, by the Voices of Saint Catherine and Saint Margaret, which said to me: 'Take the standard in the name of the King of Heaven'; and because they had said to me 'Take the standard in the name of the King of Heaven,' I had this figure of God and of two Angels done; I did all by their command."

"Did you ask them if, by virtue of this standard, you would gain all the battles wherever you might find yourself, and if you would be victorious?"

"They told me to take it boldly, and that God would help me."

"Which gave most help, you to your standard, or your standard to you?"

"The victory either to my standard or myself, it was all from Our Lord."

"The hope of being victorious, was it founded on your standard or on yourself?"

"It was founded on Our Lord and nought else."

"If any one but you had borne this standard, would he have been as fortunate as you in bearing it?"

"I know nothing about it: I wait on Our Lord."

"If one of the people of your party had sent you his standard to carry, would you have had as much confidence in it as in that which had been sent to you by God? Even the standard of your King, if it had been sent to you, would you have had as much confidence in it as in your own?"

"I bore most willingly that which had been ordained for me by Our Lord; and, meanwhile, in all I waited upon Our Lord."

"For what purpose was the sign you put on your letters and these words: '*Jhesus Maria*'?"

"The clerks who wrote my letters put it; some told me that it was suitable for me to put these two words: '*Jhesus*

*Maria.'"*

"Was it never revealed to you that if you lost your virginity, you would lose your happiness, and that your Voices would come to you no more?"

"That has never been revealed to me."[85]

"If you were married, do you think your Voices would come?"

"I do not know; I wait on Our Lord."

"Do you think, and do you firmly believe, that your King did right in killing, or causing to be killed, my Lord the Duke of Burgundy?"

"It was a great injury to the Kingdom of France; and, whatever there may have been between them, God sent me to the help of the King of France."

"As you have declared to my lord of Beauvais that you will reply to him and his Commissioners as you would before our most holy Lord the Pope, and as there are many questions which you will not answer, would you reply before the Pope more fully than before us?"

"I have answered you all the truth that I know; and if I know anything which comes to my memory that I have left unsaid, I will tell it willingly."

"Does it not seem to you that you are bound to reply more fully to our Lord the Pope, the Vicar of God, on all that might be asked you touching the Faith and the matter of your conscience, than you should to us?"

"Very well; let me be taken before him, and I will answer before him all I ought to answer."

"Of what material was one of your rings, on which was written '*Jhesus Maria*'?"

"I do not exactly know; if it were of gold, it was not fine gold; I do not know if it were of gold or of brass; there were three crosses on it, and no other mark that I know of, except '*Jhesus Maria.*'"

"Why was it that you generally looked at this ring when you were going into battle?"

"For pleasure, and in honour of my father and mother;

---

[85] In the Minute: "*et toute voyes de tout, je m'en attendaye à Notre Seigneur.*"

I had that ring in my hand and on my finger when I touched Saint Catherine as she appeared to me."

"What part of Saint Catherine?"

"You will have no more about it."

"Did you ever kiss or embrace Saint Catherine or Saint Margaret?"

"I have embraced them both."

"Did they smell good?"

"It is well to know, they smelled good."

"In embracing them, did you feel any heat or anything else?"

"I could not have embraced them without feeling and touching them."

"What part did you kiss—face or feet?"

"It is more proper and respectful to kiss their feet."

"Did you not give them crowns?"

"In their honour, I often put crowns on their images in the Churches. As to those who appeared to me, I never gave any to them that I can remember."

"When you placed crowns of flowers on the tree of which you spoke before, did you put them in honour of those who appeared to you?"

"No."

"When these Saints came to you, did you do them no reverence? did you bend the knee before them? did you bow?"

"Yes: and, so far as I could do them reverence, I did; I know it is they who are in the Kingdom of Paradise."

"Do you know nothing of those who came in the air with the fairies?"

"I have never done or known anything about them; but I have heard of them, and that they came on Thursdays; but I do not believe it; I think it is sorcery."

"Did not they wave your standard round the head of your King when he was consecrated at Rheims?"

"No, not that I know of."

"Why was it taken to the Church of Rheims for the consecration more than those of other captains?"

"It had shared the pain, it was only right it should share the honour."

*Meeting at the Bishop's house of the Doctors and Assessors to consider the Case. Sunday of the Passion of our Saviour, 18th day of the month of March. The Bishop and Jean Lemaître, assisted by twelve Assessors, present.*

We, the said Bishop, shewed that Jeanne had lately been questioned during eight days, and that a great number of her replies had been put in writing; to-day we have need of the opinion of the Assessors as to the mode of procedure.

Then We caused to be read a great number of assertions which, by Our order, have been extracted by several Masters from the answers of Jeanne: so that, by means of these assertions, they, the said Assessors, will be able the better to take up the Process as a whole, and thus decide more certainly on what remains to be done.

After this shewing, the said Lords and Masters did deliberate with great solemnity and maturity; and each of them did give us his opinion.

We, the Judges, did then conclude and give order as follows:

Each of the Doctors and Masters shall have the matter to examine and study for his own part in all diligence, and to make research in authentic books for the opinion of the Doctors on each of the said assertions. On Thursday next, We will re-assemble anew to confer upon them. On that day, each one shall submit to Us his opinion.

Besides this, we have given orders that between this and then shall be extracted from the questions and answers of Jeanne certain Articles, which shall be moved against her in the Court before Us, the Judges.

[*The Seventy Articles prepared by the Promoter, which form the Act of Accusation for the Trial in Ordinary, were read to Jeanne by Thomas de Courcelles, on Tuesday, March 27th. These Articles will be found, with Jeanne's replies to them, in the Appendix. The Seventy Articles were afterwards reduced to Twelve by Maître Nicolas Midi. These are given in the Appendix.*]

*Another Meeting in the Bishop's house, in which it is decided to compile Articles from the said Extracts. And the following Thursday, 22nd March, under the presidence of Us, the Bishop, and Maître Jean Lemaître, assisted by 23 Assessors.*

In presence of the above, have been reported sundry assertions gathered and considered in the matter, in a notable and scientific manner, by many Doctors and Masters. In view of these assertions, after having the opinions conferred thereon at length with each of the Assessors, We, the Judges, did conclude and give order that the assertions thus extracted from the register of the declarations of Jeanne shall be drawn up in a very small number of Articles under the form of propositions; that the Articles thus prepared shall be communicated at once to all and each of the Doctors and Masters, who can thus the more easily pronounce their opinion.

On the question of whether Jeanne ought to be again interrogated and examined later on, We will proceed in such sort, with the help of Our Lord, that Our case may be conducted to the praise of God and the exaltation of the Faith, being affected by no blemish.

*The questions are read to Jeanne in prison.*
*On the following Saturday, March 24th, in the prison of Jeanne; Maître Jean Delafontaine, Commissioner for Us, the Bishop, and Brother Jean Lemaître; assisted by J. Beaupère, N. Midi, P. Maurice, G. Feuillet, Thomas de Courcelles, Enguerrand de Champrond.*

In presence of the above-named, We caused to be read to Jeanne the Register which contained the questions made to her and her answers. This reading was made in the presence of the said Jeanne by G. Manchon, Registrar, and in the French language.

But before proceeding to this reading, Our Promoter, Messire d'Estivet, offered to prove, in case Jeanne should not recognize some of her answers, that all the contents of the said Register, questions and answers, had been pronounced as they were there written. And on her side, Jeanne made oath that, during the reading, which was about to be made, she would add or change nothing in her answers that was not the truth.

The Register was then read. In one place during the reading, Jeanne said:

"I have as surname d'Arc or Rommée: in my country the girls take the name of their mother."

Further on, she said:

"Let the questions and answers, all that has to be read, be read without stopping: if I do not contradict at all, I hold it true and acknowledged."

On the subject of the passage relative to her dress, she said in addition:

"Give me a woman's dress to go and rejoin my mother; I will take it that I may get out of prison, because when I am outside I will consider as to what I should do."

The reading of the contents of the said Register being finished, she said:

"I believe certainly to have so spoken as it is written in the Register, and as has been read; I do not contradict on any point."

### Exhortation to Jeanne.

*Palm Sunday, 25th day of March, in the morning, in the prison of Jeanne, in the Castle of Rouen, We, the Bishop, did make an address to Jeanne, in the presence of the venerable Lords and Masters, J. Beaupère, N. Midi, P. Maurice, Thomas de Courcelles.*

We told her, that many times already and notably yesterday, she had requested, because of the solemnity of these days and the time, that she might be permitted to hear Mass to-day, Palm Sunday; in consequence, We were come to ask her if, supposing this favour were accorded to her, she would consent to put off her man's dress, and to take the dress of a woman, as formerly she had been accustomed to wear it in her birth-place, and as worn by all the women of her country?

The said Jeanne answered by again asking of Us permission to hear Mass in the dress she now wears, and in the same dress to receive the Eucharist on Easter Day.

"Reply," We said to her, "to what we ask you; tell us, in the event of your being permitted to hear Mass, if you will consent to abandon the dress you wear."

"I have not consulted thereon," she said, "and cannot yet take a woman's dress."

"Do you wish to have counsel of your Saints to know if you ought to take woman's garments?"

"May I not then," she said, "be permitted to hear Mass in the state in which I am? I desire it ardently! As to changing my dress, I cannot: it is not in my power."

All the Assessors then joined themselves with Us, and each exhorted her, for so great a benefit, and to satisfy the feeling of devotion with which she seemed animated, to consent to take the only garment which was suitable to her sex.

"That," she declared, "is not in my power: if it were, it would soon be done!"

"Speak of it to your Voices," said the Assessors, "to know if you may again take your woman's dress, in order that at Easter you may receive the Viaticum."

"I cannot change my dress: I cannot therefore receive the Viaticum. I beg of you, my Lords, permit me to hear Mass in man's dress; this dress does not weigh upon my soul, and is not contrary to the laws of the Church."

Of all the preceding, Master Jean d'Estivet, Promoter, hath asked that there may be delivered to him a Public Instrument, in the presence of the Lords and Masters, Adam Hillet, William Brolbster, and Pierre Orient, of the Clergy of Rouen, London and Châlons, respectively.

## THE TRIAL IN ORDINARY

*Here begins the Trial in Ordinary, after the Trial Ex-Officio. Monday after Palm Sunday, 26th day of March, in Bishop's House. Present: The Bishop and Brother Jean Lemaître, assisted by 12 Assessors.*

In presence of the above, We caused to be read certain Articles comprising that one which the Promoter intendeth to produce against Jeanne.

After the reading of these Articles, it was decided that, following the preliminary trial until now conducted from our Office, as We, the Bishop, and subsequently We, the Deputy, have decreed and concluded, it will be expedient to proceed henceforward by an action in Ordinary.

It was also decided that the Articles just read have been well put together; that Jeanne should be questioned and heard upon each of them; that these Articles shall be proposed, in the name of the Promoter, by some grave advocate, or by the Promoter himself; that if Jeanne should refuse to answer after a Canonical monition shall have been addressed to her, as a preliminary, the said Articles shall be held as acknowledged.

Following on this decision, We, the Judges, gave order that the Articles of which we treat shall, from to-morrow be proposed by our Promoter; and that Jeanne should be, in like manner, interrogated upon each of them and heard in answer.

### *The Promoter presents his petition.*

*The next day, Tuesday after Palm Sunday, 27th day of March, in the room near the Great Hall of the Castle of Rouen. The Promoter opened the case. Present: The Bishop and Brother Jean Lemaître, assisted by 38 Assessors.*

He then shewed the text of the accusation drawn up by him against Jeanne, in the which are found stated the Articles just spoken of, and of which the tenour shall be written below.

This done, We, the Judges, did request the Lords and Masters here present to deliberate and to give Us their opinion.

This deliberation[86] took place in presence of Jeanne, as follows:

And first, *Maître Nicolas de Venderès* said: that Jeanne should in the first place be compelled to swear what the Promoter hath rightly demanded; that should Jeanne refuse to swear, she be accounted contumacious and excommunicate, and be proceeded against according to law.

*Maître Jean Pinchon*: That the Articles should first be read to her.

*Maître Jean Basset*: That the Articles should be read

---

[86] Given only in the Minute.

to her before she be excommunicated.

*Maître Jean Guerin*: Agrees with preceding.

*Maître Jean Delafontaine*: Of the same opinion as M. Venderès.

*Maître Geoffrey de Crotay*: That she should be given at least three days before being declared excommunicate and convicted; in civil matters there is always a three days' delay for taking the oath.

*Maître Jean Ledoux*: Agrees with preceding.

*Maître Gilles Deschamps*: That the Articles should be read to her, and that a day should be assigned for her to answer.

*Maître Robert Barbier*: Agrees with preceding.

*The Lord Abbot of Fécamp*: She is bound to speak the truth on what touches the Case; that, if she has not already been summoned to that effect, she be so summoned with the due legal interval.

*Maître Jean de Châtillon*: She is bound to speak the truth, her own affairs being in question.

*Maître Erard Ermengard*: Agrees with the Abbot of Fécamp.

*Maître Guillaume Lebouchier*: Agrees with the preceding.

*The Lord Prior of Longueville*: For those things to which she does not know how to answer, it seems to be exacting too much to wish her to reply by "I believe" or "I do not believe."

*Maître Jean Beaupère*: To questions of fact on which she has certain knowledge she should reply at once; to others, on which she has not certain knowledge or which relate to law, delay should be granted if she asks for it.

*Maître Jacques de Touraine*: Agrees with the preceding.

*Maître Nicolas Midi*: The same, with this addition: That the Jurists should be consulted in order to decide if she should be constrained to swear from the present time.

*Maître Maurice Duguesnay*: The same as the Abbot of Fécamp.

*Maître Jean de Nibat*: As to the Articles he would refer to the Jurists; as to the oath, she is bound to swear regarding such things as touch on the Trial or the Faith; if on other subjects she should ask delay, let it be granted to her.

*Maître Jean Lefevre*: Refers to the Jurists.

*Maître Pierre Maurice*: She should answer to what she knows.

*Maître Gerard*: She is bound to reply on oath.

*Maître Jacques Guesdon*: Agrees with preceding.

*Maître Thomas de Courcelles*: She should answer; each Article should be read to her, and she should answer them in order. As to delay, it should be granted to her on such points of the subject as she should request it.

*Maître André Marguerie*: She ought to swear on what touches the Case: as to doubtful points she should be allowed delay.

*Maître Denis Gastinel*: She ought to swear; the Promoter is right to demand her oath; as to what action should be taken in case she should refuse, it would be necessary for him to consult his books.

*Maître Aubert Morel*, and *Maître Jean Duchemin*: She ought to swear.


The opinion of the others is lacking.

Then We, the Judges, considering the request of the Promoter, by the advice of each of the Assessors, gave order, and do give order, that the Articles just produced by the Promoter shall at once be read and shewn in French to the said Jeanne, who, on each of them, shall answer according to knowledge; and if there are any points on which she asks delay, delay of right shall be granted to her.

Then the Promoter did abjure all calumny—that is to say, affirmed upon oath, that he was not led to bring these Articles against the said Jeanne by favour, rancour, hate or fear, but was solely animated by zeal for the Faith.

These preliminaries being completed, We, the Bishop did address to Jeanne a Canonical Admonition. We told her that all the Assessors were ecclesiastical persons of consummate knowledge, experts in law, human and divine, who desired and intended to proceed

against her, as they had already done up to this time, with
kindness and piety, and that, far from seeking vengeance
or punishment, they desired, on the contrary, only her
instruction and return into the way of truth and salvation.
"But because you are neither well enough taught nor
instructed in these arduous matters, by yourself, to
provide what you should do or say, We offer you to
choose for counsel such of the Assessors as you shall be
pleased to point out; if you do not of yourself know how
to make this choice, We offer to do it for you, and to point
out to you some who will counsel you on what you have
to answer or do, on the condition always, that in matters
of pure faith you will answer yourself, and charging you
to swear to speak the truth on those things which are
personal to yourself."

To Our exhortation, Jeanne replied in these terms:
"First, as to that on which you admonish me for my
good and for our Faith, I thank you and all the company
also; as to the counsel which you offer me, also I thank
you; but I have no intention of desisting from the counsel
of Our Lord. As to the oath that you wish me to make, I
am ready to speak the truth on all that touches the Case."

And thus did she swear, her hands on the Holy
Gospels.

After this, by Our order were read the Articles
contained in the document which the Promoter hath just
deposited. Each of these Articles was read to Jeanne in
the French language by Thomas de Courcelles; and she
was called upon to reply in succession to each of these
Articles: which she did. The completion of this formality
hath filled up the end of the Sitting for this day, and all
the Sitting of the next day.

*Jeanne is interrogated in prison on submission to the
Church.*
*And the following Saturday, the last day of the month of
March, Easter Eve, under the presidency of Us, the
aforesaid Judges, in Jeanne's prison, being assisted by
the Lords and Masters, Jean Beaupère, J. de Touraine, N.*

*Midi, P. Maurice, G. Feuillet, G. Haiton, and T. de Courcelles; Guillaume Muton and John Gris, witnesses:*

Jeanne hath been questioned as follows, touching sundry points on which she did, as hath been seen, ask delay for reply:

"Will you refer yourself to the judgment of the Church on earth for all you have said or done, be it good or bad? Especially will you refer to the Church the cases, crimes, and offences which are imputed to you and everything which touches on this Trial?"

"On all that I am asked I will refer to the Church Militant, provided they do not command anything impossible. And I hold as a thing impossible to declare that my actions and my words and all that I have answered on the subject of my visions and revelations I have not done and said by the order of God: this, I will not declare for anything in the world. And that which God hath made me do, hath commanded or shall command, I will not fail to do for any man alive. It would be impossible for me to revoke it. And in case the Church should wish me to do anything contrary to the command which has been given me of God, I will not consent to it, whatever it may be."

"If the Church Militant tells you that your revelations are illusions, or diabolical things, will you defer to the Church?"

"I will defer to God, Whose Commandment I always do. I know well that that which is contained in my Case has come to me by the Commandment of God; what I affirm in the Case is, that I have acted by the order of God: it is impossible for me to say otherwise. In case the Church should prescribe the contrary, I should not refer to any one in the world, but to God alone, Whose Commandment I always follow."

"Do you not then believe you are subject to the Church of God which is on earth, that is to say to our Lord the Pope, to the Cardinals, the Archbishops, Bishops, and other prelates of the Church?"

"Yes, I believe myself to be subject to them; but God must be served first."

"Have you then command from your Voices not to submit yourself to the Church Militant, which is on earth, nor to its decision?"

"I answer nothing from my own head; what I answer is by command of my Voices; they do not order me to disobey the Church, but God must be served first."

"At the Castle of Beaurevoir, at Arras or elsewhere, had you any files?"

"If any were found upon me, I have nothing to say."

This done we did retire, postponing to another day the continuation of this present Trial for Belief.

*Choice is made of assertions on which the deliberation should bear, and these assertions are drawn up in Twelve Articles. The Monday, Tuesday, and Wednesday after Easter, the 2nd, 3rd, and 4th of April, in the year of Our Lord, 1431.*

We, the Judges, have convoked sundry Doctors and Masters with whom we have carefully examined the Seventy Articles which have been recently transcribed, together with the questions and answers of Jeanne, attached to each of these Seventy Articles.

This examination carried out, We did decide that it is expedient to extract from this collection certain assertions and propositions, and to embody these assertions and propositions in Twelve Articles only, which shall thus comprehend, in a summary and succinct manner, the greater part of the sayings of the Accused.

These Twelve Articles having been prepared, We, the Judges, did decree that it is expedient to transmit these Articles to the Doctors, and others, expert in laws Divine and human, in order to have from them, for the benefit of the Faith, advice and counsel on the character of the assertions therein contained. [The Twelve Articles of Accusation will be found in the Appendix.]

*The Twelve Articles are sent to the Committee.*

*The following Thursday, April 5th*, We, the Judges, sent the Articles in question to each of the Doctors and Masters having knowledge thereof, whom we knew were to be found in this town. We accompanied our missive with a letter of requisition for each of them, couched in these terms:

"We, Pierre, by the Divine mercy Bishop of Beauvais, and Brother Jean Lemaître, Vicar of the Inquisition, To you, such an one [here followeth the name, surname, and quality of the Doctor or Master], we pray you, and for the good of the Faith, require you, that before Tuesday next you will give us in writing and under your seal wholesome counsel on the subject of the assertions borne in the Twelve Articles hereto annexed, in order to know if, the said assertions being by you maturely weighed, considered, and compared, all or any of them seem to you contrary to the Orthodox Faith, or, on any point contrary to Holy Writ, to the decisions of the Holy Roman Church, to the decisions of Doctors approved by the Church, or to the Canonical sanction; and if all or any seem to you scandalous, audacious, disturbing to the Commonwealth, injurious, criminal, contrary to good manners, or culpable in any other manner whatsoever; and in effect for you to say what appears to you should be enacted with regard to them in a matter of Faith. Written at Rouen, Thursday after Easter, April 5th, the year of our Lord, 1431."

### EXHORTATIONS AND ADMONITIONS.
*Private Exhortation by the Bishop.*

*Wednesday, 18th day of April*, We, the Judges, having cognizance already by the deliberations and opinions of a great number of Doctors in Theology and in Canon Law, of Licentiates and other Graduates, of the many and considerable errors brought out in the replies and assertions of the said Jeanne, and knowing that she doth expose herself, if she doth not correct herself, to serious dangers:

For this reason, We did decide to exhort her charitably, to admonish her gently, and to cause her to be gently admonished by many men of knowledge and probity, Doctors and others, in order to lead her back into the way of truth and to a sincere profession of our Faith.

To this end, We did to-day repair to the place of her

prison, having with us Guillaume Lebouchier, Jacques de Touraine, Maurice de Quesnay, Nicolas Midi, Guillaume Adelie, Gerard Feuillet, and Guillaume Haiton.

In their presence We, the Bishop, did begin to speak to Jeanne, who declared herself ill.[87] We told her that the Doctors and Masters who accompanied Us were come to see her in a friendly and charitable way, to visit her in her suffering and to bring her consolation and comfort. Then, We recalled to her, that she had been during many days, and at divers times, and in presence of many ecclesiastics full of wisdom, questioned on points, grave and difficult, concerning the Faith; that she had made answers, varied and diverse, which wise and lettered men have examined with the most scrupulous attention; that they have noted many of her words and avowals which, from the point of view of the Faith, have appeared to them perilous; but that she is only a poor illiterate woman, who knoweth not the Scriptures. We come to her and We offer her learned and wise men, watchful and honest, who will give her, as is their duty, the knowledge which she hath not. And at the same time We did exhort the Doctors and Masters here present to give to Jeanne, counsel profitable to the salvation of her body and soul, and this in virtue of the duty which binds them to the doctrine of the true Faith. If Jeanne should know others who appear to her more apt than the Doctors here present, We offer to send them to her to counsel and instruct her on what she should do, maintain, and believe. We added that we are all Clergy, always disposed by vocation, will and inclination, to seek by all means the salvation of body and soul, absolutely, as we should do it for our nearest and for ourselves. We shall be happy to furnish her each day with such men to procure her the instruction that We owe her, and to do towards her all that the Church is accustomed to do in

---

[87] Guillaume Delachambre says that he was sent for by the Cardinal of England and the Earl of Warwick to attend Jeanne, with Desjardins and other Doctors; he was told by Warwick to give all attention to the patient, "as the King would not for anything in the world, that she should die a natural death; she had cost too dear for that; he had bought her dear, and he did not wish her to die except by justice and the fire."

such circumstances, she who shutteth not the fold against the repentant lamb. Finally We told her to take into great consideration this admonition which We address to her for her salvation, and to follow it up efficiently: for, if she should act in opposition to Our words, if she should be obstinate in her own mind in consulting only her inexperienced brain, we must abandon her; and she can see to what peril she doth expose herself in this case. It is this peril which We seek to avoid for her with all the power of Our affection.

To which Jeanne hath answered:

"I thank you for what you say to me for my salvation. It seems to me, seeing how ill I am, that I am in great danger of death: if it be that God may do His pleasure on me, I ask of you that I may have confession, and my Saviour also, and that I may be put in holy ground."

"If you will have the rights [*droits*] and Sacraments of the Church," We said to her, "you must do as good Catholics do, and submit yourself to the Church. If you persevere in your intention of not submitting to the Church, you cannot have the Sacraments you ask administered to you, except the Sacrament of Penance, which We are always ready to give you."

"I have for the moment nothing else to say to you."

"The more you fear for your life, on account of the illness that you have, the more should you amend; you will not have the rights of a Catholic if you do not submit to the Church."

"If my body dies in prison, I trust that you will have it put in holy ground; if you do not have it put there, I place my trust in God!"

"You said in your Trial that if you had said or done anything against the Christian Faith established by Our Lord, you would not maintain it."

"I refer to the answer that I have made to that, and to Our Lord."

"You say you have had many revelations from God by Saint Michael, Saint Catherine and Saint Margaret: if any good person were to come affirming that he had revelations from God touching your mission, would you believe him?"

"There is no Christian in this world who could come to me and say he had had a revelation but that I should know if he were speaking truly or not; I should know it by Saint Catherine and Saint Margaret."

"You imagine then that God can reveal nothing to any one which is unknown to you?"

"I know well that He can; but for me, I should not believe in this case any man or woman if I had not some sign."

"Do you believe that the Holy Scriptures have been revealed by God?"

"You know it well; I know it well!"

"We summon you, We exhort you, We beseech you to take counsel of the Clerks and notable Masters here present, and to believe in the counsel that they will give you for the salvation of your soul. And once more We ask you if you will submit to the Church Militant your sayings and your doings?"

"Whatever may happen to me, I will do and say no other thing than what I have already said in the Trial."

Here the venerable Doctors who were assisting Us did exhort her with the most lively instance and did strive to obtain from her that she would submit herself and her acts to the Church Militant. They cited to her a number of authorities taken from Holy Scripture, and shewed her numerous examples. They enlarged upon these authorities and these examples. One of the Doctors,[88] in his exhortation, brought forward this passage of Matthew, chapter xviii.: "If thy brother sin against thee, go and tell him his fault between thee and him alone"; and this other, "If he will not hear the Church, let him be unto thee as a heathen-man and a publican." He shewed to Jeanne these truths in French, and said to her at the end, that if she would not submit to the Church and obey it, the Church must abandon her as an Infidel [*sarrazine*].

"I am a good Christian," she answered, "I have been baptized; I shall die a good Christian!"

---

[88] Nicolas Midi.

"As you ask that the Church should administer the Eucharist to you, why will you not submit to the Church? It would be administered to you at once."

"Of this submission I will say no more than I have said: I love God, I serve Him; I am a good Christian; I wish to help and maintain the Church with all my power."

"Do you not wish that a good and notable procession might be ordained to restore you to a good estate if you are not therein?"

"I desire that the Church and the Catholics should pray for me."

*Public Admonition by the Judges.*

*Wednesday, the 2nd day of May, the Judges held a sitting in the room of the Castle of Rouen near the Great Hall of the same Castle; assisted by 63 Assessors.*

We, the Bishop, did first address to the above-named the following words:

"After having been thoroughly questioned, this woman hath had to reply to the Articles judicially prepared against her by the Promoter; then We have had a summary made of her avowals and declarations in a succinct and abridged form of assertions in Twelve Articles, which We have addressed to the Doctors and other persons consummate in knowledge of Theology, of Civil Law and of Canon Law, in order to have their advice. By the answers which many amongst them have for some time past been sending, We have been able to recognize that, in their eyes, this woman hath fallen short in many things: but nothing as regards this has as yet been decided by Us; and before We come to a final decision, many honest men, conscientious and wise, have thought it would be well to seek by all means to instruct her on the points in which she seems to be lacking, and to reinstate her in the way and knowledge of the truth. This result We have always desired, and We ardently desire it still. For We ought all to bend ourselves thereto, We who live in the Church, and in the ministration of holy things; We ought to strive to shew to this woman with all gentleness that she is, by her words and by her actions, outside the Faith, the truth, and religion, and to warn her charitably to think of her salvation.

"We were indeed penetrated with this idea when We attempted to convince her, in sending to her, divers times and privately, eminent Doctors, sometimes one, sometimes another. These Doctors have responded to our call with the greatest zeal, and have occupied themselves with her with the greatest gentleness, abstaining in every way from coercion. But the cunning of the Devil has continued to prevail, and their efforts have been able to produce nothing.

"Now that it has become certain to Us that private admonitions are of no effect with her, it appears to Us opportune to assemble you together in a solemn manner, in order that this woman should be admonished before you with gentleness and charity on the necessity of her return [to truth]. Perchance your presence and the exhortations of some among you will better induce her to humility and obedience, and turn her back from continuing obstinate in her own ideas; perchance she will believe the counsels of worthy men, of the wise, versed in the science of the laws, divine and human; she will cease to expose herself to the gravest dangers into which body and soul can fall.

"In order to address to her this solemn admonition, We have chosen an ancient Master in Theology, very learned and singularly well versed in these matters, Maître Jean de Châtillon, Archdeacon of Evreux, who, if it so please him, will shortly accept this charge of demonstrating clearly to this woman sundry points on the which her error is evident, according to what we have already gathered from the opinions which have reached Us, and who will persuade her to leave the criminal path where she now is, to return again to that of truth.

"It is for this purpose that this woman will be brought before you presently; she will, therefore, receive in your presence a solemn admonition. Now, if there be any one among you who thinketh that he hath anything to say or do which may facilitate her return, or instruct her in a manner profitable to the salvation of her body and soul, we beseech him not to hesitate to open himself to Us or to state his views publicly."

Jeanne was then brought, and placed before the assembly.

We, the Bishop, in our name and in the name of the other Judge, did give her counsel to attend to the monitions about to be made to her by the aforesaid Lord Archdeacon, Professor in Sacred Theology, who was about to say many things profitable to the salvation of her body and soul, and that she ought to agree, for if she did not, she would expose herself to great dangers both soul and body.

Then we, the said Judges, did invite the said Lord Archdeacon to proceed with charity to the performance of the said monitions. Obeying our order, the said Lord Archdeacon did begin to instruct the said Jeanne, by shewing her a great number of things contained in a schedule whose tenour will be presently transcribed. He first shewed her that all the faithful in Christ are bound and obliged to believe the Christian Faith, and certain Articles of this Faith; and he did warn and beseech her, by means of a general monition, to correct and amend both herself and her deeds; he reminded her that this was the advice of the venerable Doctors and Masters of consummate experience and skill.

To this general monition, Jeanne replied:

"Read your book" [speaking of the writing which the Lord Archdeacon held in his hand], "read your book, then I will answer. I rely upon God, my Creator, for everything. I love Him with all my heart."

Asked if she had anything more to say to this general monition, she replied:

"I rely on my Judge: He is the King of Heaven and earth."

Afterwards the Lord Archdeacon, proceeding to special monitions, did, in conformity with a writing which he had under his eyes, speak as follows:

[Here follows, in the Original Documents, an Exhortation in Six Articles, addressed to Jeanne in the French language by the Archdeacon, on her submission to the Church, her dress, her Visions and Revelations.]

*Jeanne replies to the Six Articles.*

On the 1st and 2nd Article, she said:

"Thereupon I answer to-day as I have done before."

On the subject of the Church Militant, she said:

"I believe indeed in the Church which is here below; but for my words and deeds, as I have said elsewhere, I rely on and refer me to the only God. I believe that the Church Militant cannot err or fail; but as to my words and deeds, I submit them and refer all to God, Who caused me to do what I have done. I submit me to God, my Creator, Who caused me to do all these things; I refer me to God thereupon and to my own self."

"Do you mean by this to say that you have no judge on earth? Is not our Holy Father, the Pope, your judge?"

"I will say nothing else to you. I have a good Master, that is God; it is to Him I look in everything and to none other."

"If you will not believe in the Church, if you will not believe that Article of the Creed, 'the Church, One, Holy, Catholic,' you will be declared a heretic and, by other judges, punished with the pains of fire."

"I will say no more to you, and, if I saw the fire, I should say all that I am saying to you, and naught else."[89]

"If a General Council—that is to say, our Holy Father the Pope, the Cardinals, Bishops and others—were here, would you not then refer and submit yourself to this Holy Council?"

"You shall drag nothing else from me upon this."

"Will you submit to our Holy Father the Pope?"

"Take me to him, I will reply to him." [She would answer no more.]

On the subject of the 3rd Article, she replied:

"As to my garments, I will indeed take a long dress and a woman's hood to go to Church and to receive there the Sacrament of the Eucharist—as I said elsewhere—provided that, directly after, I may put off that dress and

---

[89] In the margin is written "*Superba responsio.*"

take again what I bear at this moment." And when it was suggested to her that she had taken this dress without necessity, especially while in prison, she said: "When I have done that for which I am sent by God, I will resume woman's dress."

"Do you think you do well to wear a man's dress?"

"I refer me to Our Lord."

"Will you leave off wearing this dress and the believing that you do right in wearing it? Will you resume a woman's dress?"

"I will do nothing different."

On the subject of the 4th Article she replied:

"I have blasphemed neither God nor His Saints."

"When Saint Catherine and Saint Margaret came to you, did you make the sign of the Cross?"

"Sometimes I made it, sometimes not."

On the subject of the 5th Article she answered:

"As to my revelations, I refer me to my Judge—that is to say, to God. My revelations came to me from God direct."

"On the subject of the sign given to your King, will you refer to the Archbishop of Rheims, to the Sire de Boussac,[90] to Charles de Bourbon, to the Seigneur de la Trémouille, and to Etienne, called La Hire, to whom or to some of whom you say that you shewed the crown, these being present when the Angel brought it to the King, who afterwards gave it to the Archbishop? or will you consent to refer to some of your party who may write under their seal about it?"

"Give me a messenger and I will write to them about this Trial." [She would not believe in, or refer otherwise to them.]

On the subject of the 6th Article, she answered:

"I refer to my Judge—that is to say, to Our Lord—and to what I have before answered, which is written in the book."

"If three or four Clergy of your party are sent to

[90] Jean de la Brosse, Marshal of France, called occasionally Marshal de Boussac and de Saint Sevère, being lord of both these territories.

you, coming under a safe conduct, will you refer yourself to them on the subject of your apparitions and of all that is contained in your trial?"

"Let them come; I will answer." [She would not refer nor otherwise submit to them on the subject of the trial.]

"Will you refer or submit yourself to the Church of Poitiers, where you were examined?"

"Do you think you will take me in that way, and draw me to you by it?"

Afterwards, to conclude, she was anew and in full, generally warned by the Lord Archdeacon to submit to the Church under pain of being abandoned by the Church. He said, and repeated to her, that, if the Church abandoned her, she would be in great peril both of body and soul, and would fall into danger of the pains of eternal fire as to her soul and, by sentence of other Judges, into danger of temporal fire for her body.

To which she answered:

"You will not do what you say against me without evil overtaking you, body and soul!"

"Tell us a reason, one only, why you should refuse to refer yourself to the Church."

[But she would make Us no other answer.]

Afterwards, many Doctors and competent people of divers estates and faculties, set themselves to admonish and to counsel her with gentleness. They exhorted her to submit to the Church Universal, to our Holy Father the Pope, and to the Sacred General Council. They explained to her the peril to which she exposed both soul and body in refusing to submit herself and her deeds to the judgment of the Church Militant.

[She answered as before.]

And then We, the Bishop, told Jeanne to think well over it, to take good heed to the monitions, counsels, and exhortations which had just been made to her, and to reflect on them most seriously.

Jeanne expressed herself thus:

"What time will you give me to think over it?"

We told her that she could think over it at once, and answer as she wished. But, as she would reply no more, we retired, and Jeanne was conducted back to prison.

*Wednesday, May 9th, We, the Judges, being in the great Tower of the Castle of Rouen, assisted by the reverend Fathers, Doctors and Masters whose names follow: the Reverend Father Abbot of Corneille de Compiègne, Jean de Chatillon, Guillaume Erard, André Marguerie, Nicolas de Venderès, Guillaume Haiton, Aubert Morel, Nicolas Loyseleur, Jean Massieu: did cause Jeanne to be brought before us.*

We did require and warn her:

To speak the truth to Us on divers and numerous points on which she hath hitherto refused to reply or hath replied untruthfully, the which are established in the highest degree by informations, proofs, and grave presumptions. A great number of these points were read and shewn to her. Then she was told that, if she would not tell the truth, she would immediately be put to the torture, the instruments of which were here, in this same tower, under her eyes. There also were present the executioners, who by Our order had made all the necessary preparations for torturing her, in order to bring her back by this means into the way and knowledge of the truth, and thus to procure for her salvation both of body and soul, which she doth expose to such grave peril by her lying inventions.

To which Jeanne replied in this manner:

"Truly if you were to tear me limb from limb, and separate soul and body, I will tell you nothing more; and, if I were to say anything else, I should always afterwards declare that you made me say it by force. Last Thursday[91] I received comfort from Saint Gabriel; I believe it was Saint Gabriel: I knew by my Voices it was he. I asked counsel of my Voices if I ought to submit to the Church, because the Clergy were pressing me hard to submit, and they said to me: 'If thou willest that God should come to thy help, wait on Him for all thy doings.' I know that Our Lord hath always been the Master of all my doings, and that the Devil hath never had power over

[91] The Day of the Holy Cross, May 3rd.

them. I asked of my Voices if I should be burned, and my Voices answered me: 'Wait on Our Lord, He will help thee.'"

"On the subject of the crown which you say was given to the Archbishop of Rheims, will you defer to him?"

"Make him come here, and I will hear him speak, and then I will answer you. Nevertheless, he dare not say the contrary to what I have said thereon."

Seeing the hardness of her heart, and her manner of replying, We, the Judges, fearing that the punishment of the torture would profit her little, decided that it was expedient to delay it, at least for the present, and until We have had thereupon more complete advice.

*Saturday, May 12th, in the abode of Us, the Bishop,*[92] *We, the Judges, having taken our seats, assisted by the venerable Doctors and Masters whose names follow:— Raoul Roussell, Nicolas de Venderès, André Marguerie, Guillaume Erard, Robert Barbier, Denis Gastinel, Jean Ledoux, Aubert Morel, Thomas de Courcelles, Nicolas Coppequesne, Nicolas Loyseleur, Brother Ysambard de la Pierre.*

We, the Bishop, did make known to the Assessors what had taken place on the previous Wednesday, and ask their counsel on what should be now done; We did in particular consult them on the question of submitting Jeanne to the torture.

[Here follow the deliberations of the fourteen Assessors consulted, only two of whom, Aubert Morel and Thomas de Courcelles, recommended recourse to the torture. Nicolas Loyseleur considered it "a salutary medicine for her soul," but nevertheless agreed that it should not be adopted.]

We, the Judges, after having gathered the opinion of each, taking into consideration the answers made by Jeanne at the Sitting on Wednesday last, taking into consideration also the disposition of her mind, her will so energetically manifested, and all the other circumstances

---

[92] The Minute adds: "in the evening."

of the Case, decide that it is neither profitable nor
expedient to submit her to the torture; and for the rest, We
will proceed later.

[The Twelve Articles of the Indictment, or Accusation,
were sent to the University of Paris, for their
consideration and report, by the hands of Maîtres Jean
Beaupère, Nicolas Midi, Jacques de Touraine, and Gerard
Feuillet, who left Rouen for this purpose on April 19th.
On April 29th, the University was solemnly convoked at
Saint-Bernard to consider the question; on May 14th, the
deliberation of the Faculty of Theology and the Faculty of
Decrees was submitted to all the Faculties, solemnly
assembled for that purpose, and adopted by the University
as its own. Letters from the University of Paris were sent
to the Bishop of Beauvais and to King Henry VI. on the
same day, by the messengers then returning to Rouen.]

*The Bishop communicates the Resolutions of the
University of Paris [approving of the Twelve Articles],
and asks the advice of all the Doctors present. Saturday,
May 19th, in the Chapel of the Archiepiscopal Manor of
Rouen.—Present: the Judges, assisted by 51 Assessors.*

In presence of the above named, We, the Bishop, said:

For a long time, We have been receiving a very
considerable number of Resolutions and opinions, coming
from notable Doctors and Masters, on the subject of the
assertions made and confessed by Jeanne. We might
awhile since have proceeded to the conclusion of the
Process, basing Ourselves on these Resolutions, because
these Resolutions were assuredly quite sufficient. But in
order to testify all honour and all respect towards our
Mother, the University of Paris; to have on the matter a
more full and complete elucidation; to give to consciences
more guarantee and surety: We did decide to send the
assertions in question to Our Mother the University of
Paris, and principally to the Faculties of Theology and of
Decrees; and to beseech the deliberation of the Doctors
and Masters of the said University, principally of the said
two Faculties of Theology and Decrees. The University—
in particular, the said two Faculties—being ardently

enflamed with zeal for the Faith—have maturely and solemnly given their opinion upon each of the assertions, and have sent them to Us in the form of a Public Instrument.

This statement ended, We gave orders that the Resolutions contained in the said Instrument should be read.

Afterwards, upon the reading of the Resolutions of the said two Faculties and the said University, each of the Doctors and Masters present did give and explain his opinion: and this, in addition to the opinion already given for the most part in the deliberations reported above.

The opinion of all is in conformity with the Resolutions of the University and of the two Faculties; and it doth bear not only on the qualifications to be given to the assertions comprised in the Twelve Articles, but also on the manner of proceeding which shall be followed finally.

*Here follow the deliberations of the Doctors and Masters*; [agreeing with the Resolutions of the University, and advising that Jeanne should be again charitably admonished and warned before a final sentence be pronounced.]

For all which, We, the Judges, thanked the reverend Fathers, Lords, and Masters.

We decided that Jeanne should be again warned to return into the way of truth and salvation of soul and body.

Besides, and in accordance with the excellent deliberations which had just taken place, and with the counsels full of sense just enunciated, We decided that We will, after this last monition, pronounce the closing of the Process and give a day for the announcement of the sentence.

## FINAL SESSION AND SENTENCE.
## RECANTATION.

*Wednesday, May 23rd, We, the Judges, assisted by the reverend Fathers and Lords the Bishops of Thérouanne and de Noyon; and the Doctors and Masters Jean de*

*Châtillon, Jean Beaupère, Nicolas Midi, Guillaume Erard, Pierre Maurice, André Marguerie and Nicolas de Venderès, seated ourselves in tribunal in a room in the Castle of Rouen, situated near the place which serves Jeanne as prison.*

We did cause the said Jeanne to be brought before Us, because We judged it profitable to shew her the points on which the Faculties of Theology and Decrees of the University of Paris have declared that she hath erred and fallen short; We have judged it profitable also to make known to her the omissions, crimes and errors which, in the terms of the Resolutions of each of these Faculties, exist on each of these same points; and afterwards, to warn her, or cause her to be warned, to abandon these errors and shortcomings: to correct and submit herself, in fine, to the censure and judgment of Our Holy Mother the Church.

Maître Pierre Maurice, Canon of the Church of Rouen, a celebrated Doctor in Theology, hath been charged by us with this mission, and he hath fulfilled it by addressing to Jeanne the words written by him in French in a schedule thus expressed.

*[Here follows a recapitulation of the Twelve Articles, with the opinion, adverse to Jeanne, given upon them by the Clerics consulted.]*

After these assertions had been thus shewn to her, and the decision of the University of Paris upon each of them had been made known to her, Jeanne was admonished, in the French language, by the said Doctor Pierre Maurice to pay great attention to the character given to her sayings and deeds by this decision of the University of Paris. Above all he did exhort her to reflect well on the gravity of the error contained in her refusal to submit to the Church Militant.

And he concluded by thus speaking to her:

"Jeanne, my very dear friend, it is now time, at the end of your Trial, to reflect well on all that has been said to you. This is the fourth time[93] that the Lord Bishop of Beauvais, the Lord Vicar of the Inquisition, and other

---

[93] April 18th, May 2nd, 19th, and 23rd.

Doctors who have been thereto appointed, have, either in public or in private, in honour and reverence for God, for the Faith, and the Law of Jesus Christ, for the tranquillity of their own consciences and for the alleviation of so great a scandal, admonished you with the greatest zeal— so great is their care for the salvation of your soul and body! Four times have been made known to you the perils which endanger your soul and body, if you do not at last consent to correct yourself and your sayings by submitting to the Church, yourself and your deeds, and by accepting her judgment.

"Up to this time you have obstinately refused. And although many others might long since have declared the Case heard and have given judgment upon you, nevertheless my Lords your Judges, enflamed with zeal for the salvation of your soul and body, desired, in order to have their advice, to send your sayings and deeds to the University, that light of all Science, that extirpator of all error. The resolutions of the University of Paris have come to your Judges. They have then decided, always in the hope of your salvation, to admonish you once again, to again call your attention to your errors, your scandals and all the faults that you have committed in such great number.

"They exhort you, your Judges, they beseech you, they admonish you by the bowels of Our Lord Jesus Christ, Who hath suffered a cruel death for the redemption of man, they beseech you to correct your words, to submit them to the judgment of the Church, as all the faithful are bound and obliged to do. Do not allow yourself to be separated from Our Lord Jesus Christ, Who hath created you to be a sharer in His glory; do not choose the way of eternal damnation with the enemies of God, who daily set their wits to work to find means to trouble mankind, transforming themselves often, to this end, into the likeness of Our Lord, of Angels and of Saints, as is seen but too often in the lives of the Fathers and in the Scriptures.

"Therefore, if such things have appeared to you, do not believe them. The belief which you may have had in such illusions, put it away from you. Believe rather in the words and opinions of the University of Paris and other Doctors, who, knowing the law of God and Holy Scripture, decide that no faith should be placed in such apparitions, nor should faith be placed in any extraordinary apparitions, in any novelty which is not supported by Holy Scripture, by a sign, or by a miracle.

"You have very lightly believed in such things, you who have not turned to God in earnest prayer that He would grant you certainty; you who, to enlighten yourself, have not applied to a prelate or a learned ecclesiastic. This you ought to have done: it was your duty, considering your estate and the simplicity of your knowledge.

"Let us take an example: If your King had given you a treasure to guard, forbidding you to receive any one, whoever it might be, should you not refuse to receive one who presented himself to you, saying he came by order of the King, unless he brought you a letter or some certain sign? For the Church it is the same thing: when Our Lord Jesus Christ, ascending into Heaven, confided the government of His Church to the blessed Apostle Peter and his successors, He forbade us to accept anything from others who might come in His Name, who should have for the support of their mission only their own sayings. You ought not to have put faith in those whom you say came to you; and we also, we ought not to believe in you, since Our Lord hath expressly commanded the contrary.

"Reflect, Jeanne, upon this: if, when you were in your King's realm, a soldier or another, born in his kingdom and placed under his dominion, had suddenly risen and said, 'I will not obey the King, I will not submit either to him or his officers,' would you not have said yourself that this man should be condemned? But what will you say of yourself, you, brought up in the Faith of Christ, if you do not obey the officers of Christ—that is to say, the Prelates of the Church? What judgment will you give on yourself? Cease, therefore, to hold this damnable speech, if you love God, your Creator, your Spouse, and your Salvation: obey the Church, consent to submit to its judgment; know well that, if you do not, if you persevere in your error, your soul will be condemned to eternal punishment; and, for your body, I fear much that it will come to perdition. [*Anima vestra damnabitur supplicio perpetuo crucianda, et de corpore plurimum dubito ne in perditionem veniat.*]

"Let not fear of the world hold you back; do not give way to the fear of losing, by doing as I ask you, the great honours you have received. The honour of God and the salvation of your body and soul must be preferred before all. All is perishable, save only what I tell you to do. If you do it not, you separate yourself from the Church and from the Faith to which you have sworn in Holy Baptism; you detach yourself from the authority of the Church, from the Church which is led, ruled, and governed by the authority of the Spirit of God. Did not God say to the chiefs of the Church: 'He that heareth you heareth Me, he that despiseth you despiseth Me'? If you will not submit to the Church, you separate yourself in deed, and you refuse at the same time to submit yourself to God; you are in error on this article of the Faith, 'the Church, One, Holy, and Catholic.' What this Church and her authority is, hath been sufficiently explained to you in former monitions.

"Thus have my Lords the Bishop of Beauvais and the Vicar of the Inquisition, your Judges, charged me to tell you.

"And now, I admonish, I beseech, I exhort you, in the name of your devotion to the Passion of your Creator, and of the affection you should bear to the salvation of your body and soul, I admonish, I beseech you, amend yourself, return into the way of truth, obey the Church, submit to her judgment and decision.

"In thus acting you will save your soul; you will redeem—so I believe—your body from death. But if you do not, if you persist, know that your soul will be overwhelmed by damnation, and I fear for the destruction of your body.

"May Our Saviour Jesus Christ preserve you from all these evils!"

After being thus admonished and exhorted, Jeanne did reply:

"As to my words and deeds, such as I have declared them in the Trial, I refer to them and will maintain them."

"Do you not, then," We asked her, "think yourself bound to submit your words and deeds to the Church Militant, or to any other but God?"

She replied: "What I have always said in the Trial, and held, I wish still to say and maintain. If I were condemned, if I saw the fire lighted, the faggots prepared, and the executioner ready to kindle the fire, and if I myself were in the fire, I would not say otherwise, and would maintain to the death all I have said."[94]

Then, We, the Judges, asked of the Promoter and of Jeanne herself if they had anything else to say. They replied, No. In consequence, We did proceed to close the Process, following the formula contained in a schedule which We, the Bishop, held in Our hands, and which was thus expressed:

We, the Judges, competent in this Process, declare anew our competence in so far as is necessary;

Considering the declaration just made by the Promoter and the Accused that they have no more to say;

*We declare the Process concluded;*[95] and, this conclusion pronounced, We summon you both to-morrow to hear the law which will be laid down by Us, and the sentence which shall be pronounced by Us, to be afterwards carried out and proceeded with according to law and right.

*On Thursday after Whitsuntide, the 24th day of May in the morning*, We, the Judges, did repair to a solemn Assembly, publicly held in the Cemetery of the Abbey of Saint-Ouen, at Rouen.[96] We did have with us:—*The most*

---

[94] Against this passage is written, on the margin of the original MS. note in the hand of the Registrar Manchon, '*Responsio Johannæ superba.*'

[95] *In ipsâ Causâ concludimus.*

[96] In the Square of Saint-Ouen were two platforms on each side of the south door of the Church: Jeanne and Maître Érard, the preacher, occupied one; the Bishop of Beauvais, together with a great number of Assessors, filled the other. In those days, and up to comparatively recent times, a cemetery occupied this site, which is now a garden. There was ample space for a large crowd to collect on the gently sloping ground facing the south door.

*reverend Father in Christ, Henry, by Divine Permission Priest of the Holy Roman Church, under the title of Saint Eusebius, usually called the Cardinal of England; the reverend Fathers in Christ, the Lords Bishops of Thérouanne, Noyon, and Norwich; the Lords Abbot of Saint Trinité de Fécamp, of Saint Ouen of Rouen, of Jumièges, Bec, Cormeilles, Saint-Michel au Peril-de-la-Mer, Mortemer, and Preaux; the Priors of Longueville-la-Giffard, and Saint Lo of Rouen; and many others.*

Jeanne was placed opposite to Us on a scaffold or platform prepared for this purpose.

First of all, We did charge Maître Guillaume Érard, Doctor in Theology, a preacher of great renown, to pronounce a solemn sermon for the salutary admonition of Jeanne and the great crowd which surrounded us.

This Doctor began by taking for text that Word of God in St. John, Chapter XV., "A branch cannot bear fruit of itself except it abide in the vine." Then he explained solemnly that all Catholics should abide in the true vine of the Holy Mother Church which Christ had planted: he shewed how Jeanne, by many errors and grave crimes, had separated herself from Holy Mother Church, to the great scandal of Christian people. Finally, he admonished and exhorted her and all the people by the most edifying teaching.

In concluding, he spoke to her in these terms:

"Jeanne, behold my Lords your Judges, who, at divers times, have summoned and required you to submit yourself, your words and deeds, to Our Holy Church, shewing you that there doth exist in your words and deeds many things which, as it doth seem to the Clergy, are not good either to say or maintain."

To which Jeanne replied:

"I will answer you. As to my submission to the Church, I have answered the Clergy on this point. I have answered them also on the subject of all the things I have said and done. Let them be sent to Rome to our Holy Father the Pope, to whom after God I refer me as to my words and deeds: I did them by God's order; I charge no one with them, neither my King nor any one else. If there be any fault found in them, the blame is on me, and no one else."

"Will you revoke all your words and deeds which are disapproved by the Clergy?"

"I refer me to God and to our Holy Father the Pope."

SOUTH DOOR OF ST. OUEN AT ROUEN.

Then she was told that this answer would not suffice; that it was not possible to send to seek the Pope from such a distance; that the Ordinaries are Judges, each in their own diocese; that it was necessary she should refer to our Holy Mother the Church; and that she should hold as true all that the Clergy and other people cognizant thereof have said and decided on the subject of her words and deeds.

She was admonished on this to the third monition.

But as this woman would say no more, We, the Bishop, did then begin the reading of Our sentence as follows:

## THE SENTENCE

In the Name of the Lord, Amen.

All the pastors of the Church who have it in their hearts to watch faithfully over their flock, should, when the perfidious Sower of Errors works by his machinations and deceits to infest the Flock of Christ, strive with great care to resist his pernicious efforts with the greatest vigilance and the most lively solicitude, and above all in these perilous times, when so many false prophets are come into the world with their sects of error and perdition, according to the prediction thereof made by the Apostle. Their diverse and strange doctrines might cause the faithful in Christ to stray, if Holy Mother Church, with the aid of wholesome doctrine and canonical sanction, did not study with great zeal to refute their inventions and errors.

Therefore, because that before Us, Pierre by the Divine Mercy Bishop of Beauvais, and before Us, Brother Jean Lemaître, Deputy in this City and Diocese for Maître Jean Graverend, renowned Doctor Inquisitor in France for the Evil of Heresy, specially appointed for this in this Case; because, before Us, competent Judges, thou, Jeanne, commonly called the Maid, hast been indicted and cited in a Case of Faith, on account of thy pernicious errors; after having seen and examined with great attention the whole series of thy Trial[97]....

Our sentence had thus been already read, in great part, when Jeanne did begin to speak and said:

"I will hold[98] all that the Church ordains, all that you, the Judges, wish to say and decree—in all I will refer me to your orders!"

Then many times did she say:

"Inasmuch as the Clergy decide that the apparitions and revelations which I have had are not to be maintained

---

[97] There is no note as to when Jeanne interrupted the Bishop. The Latin gives no hint. It is probable that, during the reading of the sentence, Érard and Loiseleur were trying to induce Jeanne to recant and sign the schedule, and that her abjuration was the result of their endeavours, not of the Bishop's.

[98] The Latin reading is, "Ante finem sententiæ, Johanna, timens ignem, dixit se velle obedire ecclesiæ."

or believed, I will not believe nor maintain them; in all I refer me to you and to our Holy Mother Church!"

## *Abjuration.*

Then, in the presence of all the aforenamed, in presence of an immense number of people and Clergy, she did make and utter her recantation and abjuration, following a formula written in French, which was read to her; a formula which she did pronounce herself, and the schedule of which she did sign with her own hand, and of which the tenour follows:

"All who have erred and been mistaken in the Christian Faith and, by the grace of God, have since returned into the light of truth and the unity of Our Holy Mother Church, should well guard themselves that the Evil One doth not drive them back and cause them to relapse into error and damnation. For this cause, I, Jeanne, commonly called the Maid, a miserable sinner, after that I had recognized the snares of error in the which I was held, and [after] that, by the grace of God, I had returned to our Holy Mother Church, in order that it may be seen that, not feigningly but with a good heart and good will, I have returned thereto; I confess that I have most grievously sinned, in pretending untruthfully to have had revelations and apparitions from God, from the Angels, and Saint Catherine and Saint Margaret; in seducing others; in believing foolishly and lightly; in making superstitious divinations; in blaspheming God and His Saints; in breaking the Divine Law, Holy Scripture, and the lawful Canons; in wearing a dissolute habit, mis-shapen and immodest and against the propriety of nature, and hair clipped 'en ronde' in the style of a man, against all the modesty of the feminine sex; also, in bearing arms in great presumption; in cruelly desiring the effusion of human blood; in saying that all these things I did by the command of God, the Angels, and the aforesaid Saints, and that in these things I did well and was not mistaken; in despising God and His Sacraments; in making seditions; and in being idolatrous, by adoring evil spirits and invoking them. I confess also that I have been schismatic and in many ways have erred from the Faith. The which crimes and errors, from my heart and without lying, I—by the grace of Our Lord, returned into the way of truth, by the holy doctrine and good counsel of you and the Doctors and Masters who have conveyed it to me— abjure as blasphemy and renounce them all, and depart therefrom. And upon all these things aforesaid I submit to the correction, disposal, amendment, and entire decision of our Holy Mother Church and of your good justice. Also I swear and promise to you, to my Lord Saint Peter, Prince of the Apostles, to our Holy Father the Pope of Rome, his Vicar, and his successors, and to you, my Lords, the reverend Father in God my Lord the Bishop of Beauvais, the religious person, Brother Jean Lemaître, Deputy of my Lord the Inquisitor of the Faith, as my Judges, that never, by any exhortation or other manner, will I return to the aforesaid errors, from which it hath pleased Our Lord to deliver and take me; but always I will remain in union with our Holy Mother Church and in the obedience of our Holy Father the Pope of Rome. And this I say, affirm, and swear, by God Almighty and by the Holy Gospels.

"And in sign of this, I have signed this schedule with my signature. (Signed thus): Jehanne +."

After her revocation and her abjuration had been, as has just been said, received by us, the Judges, We, the Bishop, did finally deliver our sentence in these terms:

[The sentence then follows as given above up to the words "thy Trial," and then proceeds:]

... all that therein occurred, principally thine answers, thine avowals, and thine affirmations; after having seen the most renowned decision of the faculties of Theology and Decrees of the University of Paris; after having also seen the decision of the entire University and the numerous Resolutions of so many Prelates, Doctors, and other Masters, who at Rouen or elsewhere have sent in such great numbers their assertions as to thy sayings and deeds; after having had, upon this, advice and mature deliberation of so many Doctors zealous for the Christian Faith; after having weighed and considered all that there is to weigh and consider of what is in the nature of enlightenment; having before our eyes Christ and the honour of the Orthodox Faith, so that our judgment may emanate even from the face of Our Lord: we, the Judges, say and decree: that thou, Jeanne, hast deeply sinned in pretending untruthfully that thy revelations and apparitions are of God; in seducing others; in believing lightly and rashly; in making superstitious divinations; in blaspheming God and the Saints; in prevaricating as to the law, Holy Scripture, and the Canonical sanctions; in despising God in His Sacraments; in fomenting seditions and revolts; in apostatizing; in encouraging the crime of heresy; in erring on numerous points in the Catholic Faith.

But because that, after being many times charitably admonished and long waited for, thou hast at last, with the help of God, returned into the bosom of the Church, thy Holy Mother, with contrite heart, and hast openly revoked thy errors; because, having solemnly and publicly cast these far from thee, thou hast abjured them by the words of thine own mouth, together with the heresy with which thou wast charged: We declare thee set free by these presents, according to the form appointed by Ecclesiastical sanction, from the bonds of excommunications which held thee enchained, charging thee to return to the Church with a true heart and sincere faith, and to observe what hath been already enjoined thee and what shall yet be enjoined thee by us.

But because thou hast sinned rashly against God and Holy Church, We condemn thee, finally, definitely and for salutary penance, saving Our grace and moderation, to perpetual imprisonment, with the bread of sorrow and the water of affliction, in order that thou mayest bewail thy faults, and that thou mayest no more commit [acts] which thou shalt have to bewail hereafter.

*Exhortation made to Jeanne by the Deputy Inquisitor, in Prison. And the same day, Thursday, May 24th, in the afternoon, We, Brother Jean Lemaître, the aforesaid Deputy, assisted by the Lords and Masters N. Midi, N. Loyseleur, Thomas de Courcelles, Brother Ysambard de*

*la Pierre, and several others,*

We did repair to the place in the prison where Jeanne was to be found.

We, and the persons assisting us, did set forth before her how God had on this day had mercy on her, and how the Clergy had shewn themselves merciful in receiving her to the Grace and pardon of Holy Mother Church. In return, it was right that she, Jeanne, should obey with humility the sentence and orders of the Judges and the Ecclesiastics; that she should wholly give up her errors and all her inventions, never to return to them: because, in case she should return to them, the Church could no longer admit her to pardon, and must abandon her altogether. We told her to leave off her man's dress and to take a woman's garments, as the Church had ordered her.

In all our observations Jeanne did reply that she would willingly take woman's garments, and that in all things she would obey the Church.

Woman's garments having been offered to her, she at once dressed herself in them, after having taken off the man's dress she was wearing; and her hair, which up to this time had been cut "en ronde" above her ears, she desired and permitted them to shave and take away.

*Here ends the First Part of the Trial, called "The Lapse."*

BATTLE OUTSIDE ORLEANS.

## II
### SECOND PROCESS: THE RELAPSE
*Monday, May 28th, the day following Trinity Sunday.*

We, the aforesaid Judges, repaired to the place of Jeanne's prison, to learn the state and disposition of her soul. There were found with us the Lords and Masters Nicolas de Venderès, Guillaume Haiton, Thomas de Courcelles, Brother Ysambard de la Pierre; witnesses, Jacques Cannes, Nicolas Bertin, Julien Floquet and John Gris.

And because Jeanne was dressed in the dress of a man—that is to say, a short mantle, a hood, a doublet and other effects used by men—although, by our orders, she had, several days before, consented to give up these garments, we asked her when and for what reason she had resumed this dress.[99]

She answered us:

"I have but now resumed the dress of a man and put off the woman's dress."

"Why did you take it, and who made you take it?"

"I took it of my own free will, and with no constraint: I prefer a man's dress to a woman's dress."

"You promised and swore not to resume a man's dress."

---

[99] Several versions of the reasons which caused Jeanne to resume the forbidden dress were given in the evidence taken at the Rehabilitation, all purporting to have come from her. According to Massieu, her woman's dress was taken away while she was asleep, and the English soldiers refused to give it back to her, offering in its stead the man's dress she had previously worn, 'which they emptied from a sack.' She refused to wear it, reminding them that it was forbidden her; but at last, at mid-day, finding them deaf to her remonstrance, she was obliged to rise and attire herself in the prohibited garments. The Dominican Brothers declared that she had been assaulted by an English milord, as she told them, and that she therefore considered it necessary to return to the protection of her old dress; but considering the type of soldier in whose care she was placed, there seems no need to seek for any further explanation than her own, as given in the text, and as later corroborated by Manchon and De Courcelles. In the Rehabilitation Enquiry, both Jean de Metz and de Poulengey claim to have suggested the male attire. At Poitiers, Jeanne herself stated that she had adopted it as most suitable to her work and the company she must share.

"I never meant to swear that I would not resume it."

"Why have you resumed it?"

"Because it is more lawful and suitable for me to resume it and to wear man's dress, being with men, than to have a woman's dress. I have resumed it because the promise made to me has not been kept; that is to say, that I should go to Mass and should receive my Saviour and that I should be taken out of irons."

"Did you not abjure and promise not to resume this dress?"

"I would rather die than be in irons! but if I am allowed to go to Mass, and am taken out of irons and put into a gracious prison, and [may have a woman for companion[100]] I will be good, and do as the Church wills."

And as We, the Judges, heard from several persons that she had returned to her old illusions on the subject of her pretended revelations, We put to her this question:

"Since last Thursday [the day of her abjuration] have you heard your Voices at all?"

"Yes, I have heard them."

"What did they say to you?"

"They said to me:[101] 'God had sent me word by St. Catherine and St. Margaret of the great pity it is, this treason to which I have consented, to abjure and recant in order to save my life! I have damned myself to save my life!' Before last Thursday, my Voices did indeed tell me what I should do and what I did on that day. When I was on the scaffold on Thursday, my Voices said to me, while the preacher was speaking: 'Answer him boldly, this preacher!' And in truth he is a false preacher; he reproached me with many things I never did. If I said that God had not sent me, I should damn myself, for it is true that God has sent me; my Voices have said to me since Thursday: 'Thou hast done a great evil in declaring that what thou hast done was wrong.' All I said and revoked, I said for fear of the fire."

---

[100] This request is found only in the Minute.

[101] In the margin, the Registrar has written against this answer: "*Responsio mortifera.*"

"Do you believe that your Voices are Saint Catherine and Saint Margaret?"

"Yes, I believe it, and that they come from God."

"Tell us the truth on the subject of this crown which is mentioned in your Trial."

"In everything, I told you the truth about it in my Trial, as well as I know."

"On the scaffold, at the moment of your abjuration, you did admit before us, your Judges, and before many others, in presence of all the people, that you had untruthfully boasted your Voices to be Saint Catherine and Saint Margaret."

"I did not intend so to do or say. I did not intend to deny my apparitions—that is to say, that they were Saint Catherine and Saint Margaret; what I said was from fear of the fire: I revoked nothing that was not against the truth. I would rather do penance once for all—that is die—than endure any longer the suffering of a prison. I have done nothing against God or the Faith, in spite of all they have made me revoke. What was in the schedule of abjuration I did not understand. I did not intend to revoke anything except according to God's good pleasure. If the Judges wish, I will resume a woman's dress; for the rest, I can do no more."

After hearing this, We retired from her, to act and proceed later according to law and reason.

### Final Adjudication.
*The next day, Tuesday, May 29th, in the Chapel of the Archiepiscopal Manor of Rouen, the Judges and 40 Assessors present.*

We, the Bishop, did, in presence of all the above-named, set forth that, after the Sitting held by Us in this same place, on Saturday, May 19th, the Eve of Whitsunday, We had, by the advice of the Assessors, caused Jeanne to be admonished on the following Wednesday, and had made known to her in detail the divers points on which, according to the decision of the University of Paris, she must be considered to have fallen short and erred; We caused her to be exhorted in the most lively manner to abandon her errors, and to return into the way of truth; up to the last moment she refused to agree to these admonitions and these exhortations, and would say nothing more; the Promoter, on his side, asserted that he had nothing more to bring forward against her. We then pronounced the closing of the Case, and summoned the parties on the following day, Thursday, 24th May next, to hear the law pronounced, all whereof is proved by the documents of the Procès Verbal transcribed above.

Afterwards, We did recall what had passed on Thursday, May 24th; how Jeanne, after having on that day received a solemn preachment and numerous admonitions, did end by signing with her own hand her revocation and abjuration; the whole whereof is at greater length recounted in the preceding document. We did add that, in the afternoon of the same day, the Deputy Inquisitor, Our Coadjutor, did go to seek her in her prison, and did charitably admonish her to persist in her good purpose and to guard herself well against any relapse. Obeying the orders of the Church, Jeanne did then put off the dress she was wearing, and take that of a woman; all whereof hath been likewise set forth at greater length as to time and place.

But since that day, driven by the Devil, behold! she hath, in the presence of many persons, declared anew that her Voices and the spirits that appeared to her have returned to her, and have said many things to her; and, casting away her woman's dress she hath again taken male garments. As soon as We, the Judges, did receive information of this lapse, We were eager to return to her and to question her.

And then, in presence of all the above-named, in the said Chapel of the Archiepiscopal Manor of Rouen, We, the Bishop, did order to be read the declarations and affirmations which Jeanne pronounced yesterday before us, and which are reproduced above.

After this reading had been made, We asked advice and counsel thereon from the Assessors. Each one hath given his opinion, as follows:—

*Maître Nicolas de Venderès*: Jeanne should be

considered a heretic: the sentence declaring her to be so, once given by Us, the Judges, she should be abandoned to the secular authority, which should be prayed to act towards her with gentleness. ["*Rogando eam ut cum velit mite agere*," the usual formula for victims sent to the stake.]

*The Reverend Father in Christ, the Lord Gilles, Abbot of the Monastery of the Holy Trinity at Fécamp*: Jeanne is relapsed. Nevertheless, it would be well that the schedule containing her last answers, which hath just been read, should be read anew and set forth to her, reminding her once more of the Word of God; afterwards, We, the Judges, should declare her a heretic and abandon her to the secular authority, praying this authority to deal gently with her.

[The remainder of the Assessors agreed in general with this opinion of the Abbot of Fécamp; some added that she should be again charitably admonished, in regard to the salvation of her soul, and should be told that she had nothing further to expect as to her earthly life.]

After having gathered this advice, We, the Judges, did thank the Assessors, and gave orders that Jeanne should be afterwards proceeded against, as relapsed, according to law and reason.

## Mandate citing Jeanne to appear on Wednesday, May 30th.

"Pierre, by the Divine Mercy Bishop of Beauvais, and Jean Lemaître, Deputy of Maître Jean Graverend, renowned Doctor, appointed by the Holy See Inquisitor of the Evil of Heresy in the Kingdom of France; to all public Priests, to all Curés of this town and of any other place wherever it be in the Diocese of Rouen, to each of them in particular, according as it shall be required: Greeting in Our Saviour. For the causes and reasons to be elsewhere deduced at greater length, a certain woman of the name of Jeanne, commonly called the Maid, having fallen into errors against the Orthodox Faith—errors which she hath publicly abjured before the Church, and to which she hath returned—as is established and proved by her avowals and assertions: We command to all of you and to each in particular, by this requisition, without the one waiting for the other, or excusing himself by another, that you cite the said Jeanne to appear before Us in person to-morrow, at the hour of 8 o'clock in the morning, at Rouen, in the place called the Old Market, in order that she may be declared by us relapsed, excommunicate, and heretic, with the intimation that it shall be done to her as is customary in such cases.

"Given in the Chapel of the Archiepiscopal Manor of Rouen, Tuesday, May 29th, the year of Our Lord, 1431."

*On the following day, Wednesday, 30th of May*, Jeanne, by virtue of the preceding mandate from Us, was cited for the same day, in order to hear the law pronounced, as is proved at greater length by the tenour of the following relation, done for us by the Executor of our mandates:

"To the reverend Father and Lord in Christ, the Lord Pierre, by the Divine Mercy Bishop of Beauvais, and to the venerable and religious person Brother Jean Lemaître, Deputy of Maître Jean Graverend, renowned Doctor, by order of the Holy Apostolic See Inquisitor of the Faith and of the Evil of Heresy in the Kingdom of France: your humble Jean Massieu, Priest, Dean of the Christendom of Rouen[102] sends earnest Greeting, with all protestations of obedience and respect. This is to inform your Reverend Paternities, that I, Massieu, in virtue of your mandate sent to me, to which these presents will be annexed, have cited, speaking to her in person, this woman, commonly called the Maid, to appear before you this day, Wednesday, May 30th, at the hour of eight in the morning, at Rouen, in the place of the Old Market, according to the form and tenour of your said mandate, and to that which I have been ordered to do. All the which, thus done by me, I signify to your Reverend Paternities by these presents, signed by my seal.

"Given in the year of Our Lord 1431, on the aforesaid Wednesday, at 7 o'clock in the morning.

---

[102] An appointment equivalent to a Rural Dean.

"Massieu."

## SENTENCE OF DEATH
*Final Sentence given before the People.*

*Wednesday, May 30th, towards 9 o'clock in the morning,*

We, the Judges, repaired to the place of the Old Market, in Rouen, near the Church of Saint Sauveur.

We were assisted by the reverend Fathers in Christ the Lords Bishops of Thérouanne and Noyon; and by a number of other Lords, Masters, and ecclesiastical personages.

Before Us was brought the said Jeanne, in presence of the people, assembled in this place in an immense multitude.

She was placed upon a scaffold or platform.

For her wholesome admonition and for the edification of the whole multitude, a solemn address was made by the renowned Doctor, Nicolas Midi, who took for his text those words of the Apostle in the first Epistle to the Corinthians, Chapter xii., "If one member suffer, all the members suffer with it."

COURT OF JUSTICE.
From a Miniature by Jean Fouquet.

This address ended, We, the Bishop, did once more admonish Jeanne to look to her salvation, to reflect on her misdeeds, to repent of them, to have a true contrition for them. We exhorted her to believe hereon the opinion of the Clergy, of the notable persons who have taught and instructed her on all that treats of her salvation. We did particularly exhort her to believe the good advice of the two venerable Dominicans[103] who were at that moment beside her, and whom we had sent to her to converse with her up to the last moment and to furnish her in all surety with wholesome admonitions and counsels profitable to her salvation.

Afterwards, We, the Bishop and Vicar aforesaid, having regard to all that has gone before, in which it is shewn that this woman hath never truly abandoned her errors, her obstinate temerity, nor her unheard-of crimes;

---

[103] Brothers Ysambard de la Pierre and Martin Ladvenu.

that she hath even shewn the malice of her diabolical obstinacy in this deceitful semblance of contrition, penitence, and amendment; malice rendered still more damnable by perjury of the Holy Name of God and blasphemy of His ineffable Majesty; considering her on all these grounds obstinate, incorrigible, heretic, relapsed into heresy, and altogether unworthy of the grace and of the Communion which, by our former sentence, We did mercifully accord to her; all of which being seen and considered, after mature deliberation and counsel of a great number of Doctors, We have at last proceeded to the Final Sentence in these terms:

In the Name of the Lord: *Amen.*

At all times when the poisoned virus of heresy attaches itself with persistence to a member of the Church and transforms him into a member of Satan, extreme care should be taken to watch that the horrible contagion of this pernicious leprosy do not gain other parts of the mystic Body of Christ. The decisions of the holy Fathers have willed that hardened heretics should be separated from the midst of the Just, so that to the great peril of others this homicidal viper should not be warmed in the bosom of pious Mother Church. It is for this that We, Pierre, by the Divine Mercy, Bishop of Beauvais, and We, Brother Jean Lemaître, Deputy of the renowned Doctor, Jean Graverend, Inquisitor of the Evil of Heresy, specially delegated by him for this Process, both Judges competent in this Trial, already, by a just judgment, have declared this woman fallen into divers errors and divers crimes of schism, idolatry, invocation of demons and many others. But because the Church closes not her bosom to the child who returns to her, we did think that, with a pure spirit and a faith unfeigned, thou hadst put far from thee thy errors and thy crimes, considering that on a certain day thou didst renounce them and didst publicly swear, vow, and promise never to return to thy errors and heresies, to resist all temptations, and to remain faithfully attached to the unity of the Catholic Church and the communion of the Roman Pontiff, as is proved at greater length in a writing signed by thine own hand. But after this abjuration of thine errors, the Author of Schism and Heresy hath arisen in thine heart, which he hath once more seduced, and it hath become manifest by thy spontaneous confessions and assertions—O, shame!—that, as the dog returns again to his vomit, so hast thou returned to thine errors and crimes; and it hath been proved to us in a most certain manner that thou hast renounced thy guilty inventions and thy errors only in a lying manner, not in a sincere and faithful spirit. For these causes, declaring thee fallen again into thine old errors, and under the sentence of excommunication which thou hast formerly incurred, WE DECREE THAT THOU ART A RELAPSED HERETIC, by our present sentence which, seated in tribunal, we utter and pronounce in this writing; we denounce thee as a rotten member, and that thou mayest not vitiate others, as cast out from the unity of the Church, separate from her Body, abandoned to the secular power as, indeed, by these presents, we do cast thee off, separate and abandon thee;—praying this same secular power, so far as concerns death and the mutilation of the limbs, to moderate its judgment towards thee, and, if true signs of penitence should appear in thee, [to permit] that the Sacrament of Penance be administered to thee.

*Here follows the Sentence of Excommunication,* [the introductory part being word for word the same as the previous sentence, read on May 24th, up to the words "We, the Judges, say and decree"; after which follows:]

... that thou hast been on the subject of thy pretended divine revelations and apparitions lying, seducing, pernicious, presumptuous, lightly believing, rash, superstitious, a divineress and blasphemer towards God and the Saints, a despiser of God Himself in His Sacraments; a prevaricator of the Divine Law, of sacred doctrine and of ecclesiastical sanctions; seditious, cruel, apostate, schismatic, erring on many points of our Faith, and by all these means rashly guilty towards God and Holy Church. And also, because that often, very often, not only by Us on Our part but by Doctors and Masters learned and expert, full of zeal for the salvation of thy soul, thou hast been duly and sufficiently warned to amend, to correct thyself and to submit to the disposal, decision, and correction of Holy Mother Church, which thou hast not willed, and hast always obstinately refused to do, having even expressly and many times refused to submit thyself to our lord the Pope and to the General Council; for these causes, as hardened and obstinate in thy crimes, excesses and errors, WE DECLARE THEE OF RIGHT EXCOMMUNICATE AND HERETIC; and after thine errors have been destroyed in a public preaching, We declare that thou must be abandoned and that We do abandon thee to the secular authority, as a member of Satan, separate from the Church, infected with the leprosy of heresy, in order that thou mayst not corrupt also the other members of Christ; praying this same power, that, as concerns death and the mutilation of the limbs, it may be pleased to moderate its judgment; and if true signs of penitence should appear in thee, that the Sacrament of Penance may be administered to thee.

### *Attestations by the Registrars.*

"I, Boisguillaume, Priest, Registrar above qualified, affirm that I have duly collated the foregoing document with the original Minute of the Process; for which reason I have marked this present copy with my sign manual, the which will be done after me by the two other Registrars, I signing in this place with my own hand.

(*Signed*) "BOISGUILLAUME."

"And I, Guillaume Manchon, Priest, of the Diocese of Rouen, Apostolic and Imperial Notary, I affirm that I assisted in the collation made of the aforesaid Process, with the Registrars signed above and below; I affirm that this collation of the present copy with the original Minute of the Process hath been duly made. For which, in the same way as the two other Registrars, I have subscribed the present copy with my own hand, affixing thereto my sign-manual, to this required.

(*Signed*) "G. MANCHON."

"And I, Nicholas Taquel, Priest of the Diocese of

Rouen, sworn Imperial Public Notary and of the
Archiepiscopal Court of Rouen, called as Registrar to a
part of the foregoing Process, I affirm that I have seen and
heard the present copy collated with the original register
of the said Process; I affirm that this collation hath been
duly made. For which, with the two other Registrars
preceding, I have subscribed with my own hand the
present Process, affixing thereto, here, my sign-manual, to
this required.

(*Signed*) "N. TAQUEL."

[*Here follow the seals of the two Judges, marked in red wax
on the original copies of the Process, prepared to the number of
five.*]

## SUBSEQUENT EXAMINATIONS[104]
## AND
## PROCEEDINGS AFTER THE RELAPSE.

*Information given after the Execution on many things said
by Jeanne, at the end of her life and in articulo mortis.*

Thursday, 7th day of June, 1431, We, the Judges,
did *ex-officio* take information upon certain things which
the late Jeanne had said before persons worthy of credit
when she was still in prison and before being brought to
judgment.

### EXAMINATION OF WITNESSES.

1. *The venerable and circumspect* MAÎTRE NICOLAS
DE VENDERÈS, *licentiate in Canon Law, Archdeacon of
Eu, hath declared upon oath as follows*:

Wednesday, 30th day of May, Eve of the Feast of
Corpus Christi, Jeanne, being still in the prison of the
Castle of Rouen where she was detained, did say that
considering the Voices which came to her had promised
she should be delivered from prison, and that she now
saw the contrary, she realized and knew she had been, and
still was, deceived by them. Jeanne did, besides, say and
confess that she had seen with her own eyes and heard

---

[104] Not included in the Official Text of the Trial.

with her own ears the apparitions and Voices mentioned in the Case.

At this were present, you, the Judges aforesaid, and besides Maître Pierre Maurice, Thomas de Courcelles, Nicolas Loyseleur, Brother Martin Ladvenu, Jean Toutmouillé, Jacques Lecamus, and several others.

BROTHER MARTIN LADVENU, *Priest of the Order of Saint Dominic, did say and depose, upon oath, as follows*:

On the morning of the day on which sentence was delivered and before she was brought to judgment, Jeanne, in presence of Maître Pierre Maurice, Nicolas Loyseleur, and Brother Jean Toutmouillé, who were with me, did say and confess that she knew and recognized that the Voices and apparitions which had come to her, mentioned in the Case, had deceived her, because they had promised she should be delivered and freed from prison; and that she certainly now saw clearly the contrary.

Asked by the Bishop: Who induced Jeanne so to speak?

Replied: Pierre Maurice, Nicolas Loyseleur, and I exhorted her to save her soul, and asked her if it were true that she had these Voices and apparitions? She replied that it was indeed true, and she continued so to tell us up to the end, but without stating decidedly, at least, so far as I understood, under what form the apparitions came to her. All I remember is that she said they came to her in great multitude and in the smallest size [*in magnâ multitudine et quantitate minimâ*]. Besides, I did at this time hear Jeanne say and confess that, inasmuch as the Clergy held and believed that if they were spirits who came to her they proceeded from evil spirits, she also held and believed as did the Clergy, and would no longer put faith in these spirits. And as it appeared to me, Jeanne was then of a sound mind.

Brother Martin Ladvenu did add this: The same day I heard Jeanne say that, although she had stated in her avowals and confessions, and had affirmed above in the course of the Case, that an Angel from God had brought a crown to him whom she called her King, with all other details connected with this fact in the interrogatories, nevertheless, of her free-will and without being constrained thereto, she did this day confess as follows: that in spite of all she had affirmed on the subject of this Angel, no Angel had brought the crown; it was she, Jeanne, who had been the Angel, and who said and promised to him whom she called her King, that, if he would set her to the work, she would have him crowned at Rheims. There was no other crown sent from God, in spite of all she might have affirmed in the course of the Case on the subject of the crown and the sign given to him whom she called her King.

*The venerable and discreet* MAÎTRE PIERRE MAURICE, *Professor in Theology, Canon of Rouen, deposed, upon oath, as follows*:

The day of the sentence, Jeanne being still in the prison, I repaired to her in the morning to exhort her to save her soul. In so exhorting her, I asked her what was the Angel mentioned in the Trial, who, according to her, had brought a crown to him whom she called her King?

She replied that it was herself who was the Angel.

Having questioned her afterwards on the subject of the crown which she had promised to her King, of the multitude of Angels who at that time accompanied her, she replied that it was true that Angels appeared to her under the form of very minute things. Finally, I asked her if this apparition were real? "Yes," she replied, "the spirits did really appear to me—be they good or be they evil spirits—they did appear to me." She also said that she had in particular heard her Voices at the hour of Compline, when the bells rang, and in the morning also, when the bells rang. And when I told her that they were evil spirits—in this, that they had promised her deliverance and had deceived her—"It is true," she replied, "they have deceived me." I also heard her declare that to know whether they were good or evil spirits, she referred to the Clergy. When she thus spoke, Jeanne, so far as it seemed to me, was sound in mind and understanding.

BROTHER JEAN TOUTMOUILLÉ, *Priest, of the Order of Saint Dominic, did say and declare upon oath as follows*:

The day that sentence was given upon Jeanne, Wednesday, Eve of the Feast of Corpus Christi, I accompanied Brother Martin Ladvenu, who, early in the morning, repaired to her to exhort her to save her soul. I first heard Maître Pierre Maurice, who had gone earlier to her, declare she had confessed that all which concerned the crown was fiction: that it was she who was the Angel. The said Master reported all this to us in Latin. Afterwards, Jeanne was questioned on the subject of the Voices and apparitions which had come to her. She replied that she had really heard voices, chiefly when the bells rang Compline or Matins; and she persisted in saying this, although Maître Pierre Maurice told her that, sometimes when the bells rang, one thought one could hear and catch the sounds of human voices. Jeanne did also say and confess that she had had apparitions which came to her in great multitude and in minute quantity— that is to say, under small forms;—she did not perfectly explain the form, or kind, of her apparitions. The same day, after you, the Bishop, had come in with the Lord Deputy Inquisitor into the room where she was detained, you said to Jeanne in French, "Now then, Jeanne, you always told us that your Voices assured you that you would be delivered: you see now how they have deceived you; tell us the truth now." "Truly," Jeanne replied to you, "I see indeed that they have deceived me!" I did not hear her say more, save only that, early in the same day, before you were come to the prison, Jeanne, being asked if her Voices and apparitions proceeded from good or evil spirits, did reply: "I know not—I wait on my Mother, the Church," or "I wait on you, who are of the Church." And, so far as it seemed to me, Jeanne was at this time of sound mind; I heard Jeanne herself then declare that she was of sound mind.

MESSIRE JACQUES LECAMUS, *Priest, Canon of Rheims,*

*did say and declare upon oath as follows*:

Wednesday, Eve of the Feast of Corpus Christi, I went with you, the Bishop, into the room of the Castle of Rouen where Jeanne was detained, and there I heard Jeanne say and confess, publicly and in a voice loud enough to be heard by all those present, that she had had apparitions and had also heard Voices; that these apparitions and Voices had promised her that she should be delivered from prison; but now she saw in truth that they had deceived her, and, for having thus deceived her, she believed they could not be good Voices nor good things. A little while after, she confessed her sins to Brother Martin, of the Order of Saint Dominic. After the Sacrament of Confession and Penitence, when the same Brother was about to administer the Sacrament of the Eucharist to her, and already held in his hands the Consecrated Host, "Do you believe," he asked her, "that this is the Body of Christ?" "Yes," she replied, "and I believe that He alone can deliver me; I ask that It may be administered to me." After the Communion, the same Brother said to her: "Do you still believe in your Voices?" "I believe in God only," she answered, "and will no more put faith in my Voices, for having deceived me on this point."

MAÎTRE THOMAS DE COURCELLES, *Master of Arts, Bachelor of Theology, did say and depose, upon oath, as follows*:

Wednesday, Vigil of the Feast of Corpus Christi, being in the presence of you, the Bishop, in the room of the Castle of Rouen where Jeanne was detained, I heard and understood that you asked Jeanne if it were not true that her Voices had promised to deliver her? She replied that her Voices had truly promised this, and had told her to keep a good countenance; and, "as it seems to me," she added, "I see indeed that I have been deceived." And then you, the Bishop, said to Jeanne, that now she could certainly see her Voices to be only evil spirits and that they did not come from God; for, had they been of such a nature, they would never have said a false thing and thus have lied.

MAÎTRE NICOLAS LOYSELEUR, *Master of Arts, Canon of Rouen and Chartres, said and declared, upon oath, as follows*:

Wednesday, the Vigil of the Feast of Corpus Christi, I repaired in the morning with the venerable Maître Pierre Maurice, to the place where Jeanne, commonly called the Maid, was detained, to exhort and admonish her on the subject of the salvation of her soul. She was besought to speak truth on the subject of that Angel who, she had declared, had brought to him she called her King a crown, very precious, and of the purest gold: she was pledged not to hide the truth, inasmuch as nothing more remained to her but to think of her own salvation. Then I heard her declare that it was she herself who had brought him she called her King the crown in question; that it was she who was the Angel of whom she had spoken; and that there had been no other Angel but herself. Asked if she had really sent a crown to him whom she called her King, she replied that he had no other crown but the promise of his coronation—a promise she had made in giving to her King the assurance that he would be crowned. In the presence of Maître Pierre Maurice, of the two Dominicans, of you, the Bishop, and of several others, I heard her many times declare that "she had really had revelations and apparitions of spirits; that these revelations had deceived her; that she recognized it in this, that they had promised her deliverance, and that she now saw the contrary; that she was willing to refer to the Clergy to know if these spirits were good or evil; that she did not put, and would no more put, faith in them." I exhorted her, to destroy the error that she had sown among the people, to declare publicly that she had herself been deceived, and that through her fault she had deceived the people by putting faith in these revelations and in counselling the people to believe in them; and I told her it was necessary that she should humbly ask pardon. She told me she would do it willingly, but that she did not think she would be able to remember, when the proper moment came—that is to say, when she found herself in the presence of the people; she prayed her Confessor to remind her of this point and of all else which might tend to her salvation. From all this, and from many other indications, I conclude that Jeanne was then of sound mind. She shewed great penitence and great contrition for her crimes. I heard her, in the prison, in presence of a great number of witnesses, and subsequently after sentence, ask, with much contrition of heart, pardon of the English and Burgundians for having caused to be slain, beaten, and damned, a great number of them, as she recognized.

# PART II
## THE REHABILITATION

*In the following Enquiries and Depositions, it has been considered advisable, in order to avoid unnecessary repetitions, to give extracts only from certain of the Depositions. The names of all witnesses are given in full, and no evidence of importance is omitted.*

*In the Original, the whole of the first Enquiry is in French, the second and third are in Latin.*

*An Introductory Note to the Rehabilitation will be found in the Appendix.*

PORTE S<sup>t</sup> HONOR

## THE FIRST ENQUIRY: 1449.

[*The King's Rescript, being a Letter of Commission to Maître Guillaume Bouillé, was granted by Charles VII., for an Enquiry into the case of Jeanne d'Arc.*]

### EXAMINATION OF WITNESSES.

BROTHER JEAN TOUTMOUILLÉ, *of the Order of Saint Dominic, (Examined, 5th day of March), 1449.*[105]

As to the feeling of the Judges and those who

---

[105] 'Old style' is adopted throughout: thus 1449 is given instead of 1449 1450.

conducted the Trial of the said Jeanne, I neither assisted nor was I present at the Trial. I can say nothing, therefore, as to what I saw; but the common report was, that they persecuted her from desire of perverse vengeance, and of this they gave sign and appearance. For, before her death, the English proposed to lay siege to Louviers; soon, however, they changed their purpose, saying they would not besiege the said town until the Maid had been examined. What followed was evident proof of this; for, immediately after she was burnt, they went to besiege Louviers, considering that during her life they could have neither glory nor success in deeds of war.

The day when Jeanne was delivered up to be burned, I was in the prison during the morning with Brother Martin Ladvenu, whom the Bishop of Beauvais had sent to her to announce her approaching death, and to induce in her true contrition and penitence, and also to hear her in confession. This the said Ladvenu did most carefully and charitably; and when he announced to the poor woman the death she must die that day, as the Judge had ordained, and she heard of the hard and cruel death which was approaching, she began, in a sad and pitiful manner, as one distraught, tearing her hair, to cry out: "Alas! am I to be so horribly and cruelly treated? Alas! that my body, whole and entire, which has never been corrupted, should to-day be consumed and burned to ashes! Ah! I would far rather have my head cut off, seven times over, than be thus burned! Alas! had I been in the ecclesiastical prison, to which I submitted myself, and guarded by the Clergy instead of by my enemies, it would not have fallen out so unhappily for me. I appeal to God, the Great Judge, for the great evils and injustice done to me!"

After these complaints, the aforesaid Bishop arrived, to whom she at once said: "Bishop, I die through you." And he began to explain to her, saying: "Ah! Jeanne, have patience; you die because you have not kept to what you promised us, and for having returned to your first evil-doing." And the poor Maid answered him: "Alas, if you had put me in the prisons of the Church Courts, and given me into the hands of competent and suitable ecclesiastical guardians, this would not have happened: for this I summon you before God."

This done, I went out, and heard no more.

BROTHER YSAMBARD DE LA PIERRE, *of the Order of Saint Dominic, of the Convent at Rouen.*

On one occasion, I, with many others, admonished and besought Jeanne to submit to the Church. To which she replied that she would willingly submit to the Holy Father, requesting to be taken before him, and to be no more submitted to the judgment of her enemies. And when, at this time, I counselled her to submit to the Council of Bâle, Jeanne asked what a General Council was. I answered her, that it was an assembly of the whole Church Universal and of Christendom, and that in this Council there were some of her side as well as of the English side. Having heard and understood this, she began to cry: "Oh! if in that place there are any of our side, I am quite willing to give myself up and to submit to the Council of Bâle." And immediately, in great rage and indignation, the Bishop of Beauvais began to call out: "Hold your tongue, in the devil's name!" and told the Notary, he was to be careful to make no note of the submission she had made to the General Council of Bâle. On account of these things and many others, the English and their officers threatened me terribly, so that, had I not kept silence, they would have thrown me into the Seine.

After she had recanted and abjured, and had resumed the dress of a man, I and many others were present when Jeanne excused herself for having dressed again as a man, saying and affirming publicly, that the English had done or caused to be done to her great wrong and violence, when she was wearing a woman's dress; and, in truth, I saw her weeping, her face covered with tears, disfigured and outraged in such sort that I was full of pity and compassion.

When Jeanne was proclaimed an obstinate and relapsed heretic, she replied publicly before all who were present: "If you, my Lords of the Church, had placed me and kept me in your prisons, perchance I should not have been in this way."

After the conclusion and end of this session and trial, the Lord Bishop of Beauvais said to the English who were waiting outside: "Farewell![106] be of good cheer: it is done."

Such difficult, subtle, and crafty questions were asked of and propounded to poor Jeanne, that the great clerics and learned people present would have found it hard to reply; and at [these questions] many of those present murmured.

I was there myself with the Bishop of Avranches,[107] an aged and good ecclesiastic, who, like the others, had been requested and prayed to give his opinion on this Case. For this, the Bishop summoned me before him, and asked me what Saint Thomas said touching submission to the Church. I sent the decision of Saint Thomas in writing to the Bishop: "In doubtful things, touching the Faith, recourse should always be had to the Pope or a General Council." The good Bishop was of this opinion, and seemed to be far from content with the deliberations that had been made on this subject. His deliberation was not put into writing: it was left out, with bad intent.

After Jeanne had confessed and partaken of the Sacrament of the Altar, sentence was given against her, and she was declared heretic and excommunicate.

I saw and clearly perceived, because I was there all the time, helping at the whole deduction and conclusion of the Case, that the secular Judge did not condemn her, either to death or to burning; and although the lay and secular Judge had appeared and was present in the same place where she was last preached to and given over to the secular authority, she was, entirely without judgment or conclusion of the said Judge, delivered into the hands of the executioner, and burnt—it being said to the

---

[106] The word is given in English in the text. Cauchon prided himself on his knowledge of this language.

[107] Jean de Saint Avit, formerly Abbot of Saint-Denis, and, about 1390, Bishop of Avranches. In 1432, he was imprisoned at Rouen, on suspicion of complicity with the French, who wished to get possession of the town.

executioner, simply and without other sentence: "Do thy duty."

Jeanne had, at the end, so great contrition and such beautiful penitence that it was a thing to be admired, saying such pitiful, devout, and Catholic words, that those who saw her in great numbers wept, and that the Cardinal of England and many other English were forced to weep and to feel compassion.

As I was near her at the end, the poor woman besought and humbly begged me to go into the Church near by and bring her the Cross, to hold it upright on high before her eyes until the moment of death, so that the Cross on which God was hanging might be in life continually before her eyes.

Being in the flames, she ceased not to call in a loud voice the Holy Name of Jesus, imploring and invoking without ceasing the aid of the Saints in Paradise; again, what is more, in giving up the ghost and bending her head, she uttered the Name of Jesus as a sign that she was fervent in the Faith of God, just as we read of Saint Ignatius and of many other Martyrs.

Immediately after the execution, the executioner came to me and to my companion, Brother Martin Ladvenu, stricken and moved with a marvellous repentance and terrible contrition, quite desperate and fearing never to obtain pardon and indulgence from God for what he had done to this holy woman. And the executioner said and affirmed that, notwithstanding the oil, the sulphur, and the charcoal which he had applied to the entrails and heart of the said Jeanne, in no way had he been able to burn them up, nor reduce to cinders either the entrails or the heart, at which he was much astonished, as a most evident miracle.

BROTHER MARTIN LADVENU, *of the Order of Saint Dominic, and of the Convent of Saint-Jacques at Rouen.*

Many of those who appeared in the Court did so more from love of the English and the favour they bore them than on account of true zeal for justice and the Catholic Faith. In the extreme prejudice of Messire Pierre Cauchon, Bishop of Beauvais, there were, I assert, two proofs of ill-feeling: the first, when the Bishop, acting as Judge, commanded Jeanne to be kept in the secular prison and in the hands of her mortal enemies; and although he might easily have had her detained and guarded in an ecclesiastical prison, yet he allowed her, from the beginning of the trial to the end, to be tormented and cruelly treated in a secular prison. Moreover, at the first session or meeting, the Bishop aforesaid asked and required the opinion of all present, as to whether it was more suitable to detain her in the secular ward or in the prisons of the Church. It was decided as more correct that she be kept in ecclesiastical prisons rather than in the secular; but this the Bishop said he would not do for fear of displeasing the English. The second proof was that on the day when the Bishop and several others declared her a heretic, relapsed, and returned to her evil deeds, because, in prison, she had resumed a man's dress, the Bishop, coming out of the prison, met the Earl of Warwick and a great many English with him, to whom he said, laughing, in a loud and clear voice: "Farewell! farewell! it is done; be of good cheer," or such-like words.

The Maid revealed to me that, after her abjuration and recantation, she was violently treated in the prison, molested, beaten, and ill-used; and that an English lord had insulted her. She also said, publicly, that on this account she had resumed a man's dress; and, towards the end, she said to the Bishop of Beauvais: "Alas! I die through you, for had you given me over to be kept in the prisons of the Church, I should not have been here!"

When she had been finally preached to in the Old Market-Place and abandoned to the secular authority, although the secular Judges were seated on the platform, in no way was she condemned by any of these Judges; but, without being condemned, she was forced by two sergeants to come down from the platform and was taken by the said sergeants to the place where she was to be burned, and by them delivered into the hands of the executioner.

And in proof of this, a short time after, one called Georges Folenfant was apprehended on account of the

Faith and for the crime of heresy, and was in the same way handed over to the secular justice. In this case, the Judges—to wit, Messire Louis de Luxembourg, Archbishop of Rouen, and Brother Guillaume Duval, Deputy of the Inquisitor of the Faith—sent me to the Bailly of Rouen to warn him that the said Georges should not be treated as was the Maid, who, without final sentence or definite judgment, had been burned in the fire.

The executioner, about four hours after the burning, said that he had never been so afraid in executing any criminal as in the burning of the Maid, and for many reasons: first, for her great fame and renown; secondly, for the cruel manner of fastening her to the stake—for the English had caused a high scaffold to be made of plaster, and, as the said executioner reported, he could not well or easily hasten matters nor reach her, at which he was much vexed and had great compassion for the cruel manner in which she was put to death.

I can testify to her great and admirable contrition, repentance, and continual confession, calling always on the Name of Jesus, and devoutly invoking the Saints in Paradise, as also Brother Ysambard hath already deposed, who was with her to the end, and confirmed her in the way of salvation.

BROTHER GUILLAUME DUVAL, *of the Order of Saint Dominic, and of the Convent of Saint-Jacques at Rouen.*

When the trial of the said Jeanne took place, I was present at one session with Brother Ysambard de la Pierre; and, although we could find no room for ourselves in the consistory, we seated ourselves at the middle of the table, near to Jeanne. When she was questioned or examined, the said Brother Ysambard advised her as to what she should say, nudging her or making some other sign. After the session was over, I and Brother Ysambard, with Maître Jean Delafontaine, were deputed to visit her in prison the same day after dinner and give her counsel; we went together to the Castle of Rouen, to visit and admonish her; and there we found the Earl of Warwick, who attacked the said Brother Ysambard with great anger and indignation, biting insults, and harsh epithets, saying to him: "Why didst thou touch that wicked person this morning, making so many signs? Mort Bleu! villain! if I see thee again taking trouble to deliver her and to advise her for her good, I will have thee thrown into the Seine." At which I and the other companion of the said Ysambard fled for fear to the Convent.

I heard no more, for I was not present at the Trial.

MAÎTRE GUILLAUME MANCHON, *Canon of the Collegiate Church of Notre Dame d'Audely; Curé of the Parish Church of Sainte-Nicolas-le-Peinteur at Rouen, and Notary of the Ecclesiastical Court; Notary of the Trial of Jeanne, from the beginning up to the end, and with him Maître Guillaume Colles, called Bois-Guillaume.*

In my opinion, not only those who had charge of instituting and conducting the Trial—to wit, My Lord of Beauvais and the Masters sent for from Paris for this Case—but also the English, at whose instance the Trial was undertaken, proceeded rather from hatred and anger on account of the quarrel with the King of France, than owing to her support of his party, and for the following reasons:

First, one named Maître Nicolas Loyseleur, a familiar of my Lord of Beauvais, who held altogether to the English side—for, formerly the King being before Chartres, he went to fetch the King of England to raise the Siege—pretended that he belonged to the Maid's country; by this means he found a way to have speech and familiar converse with her, telling her news of her country that would please her. He asked to be her confessor, and of what she told him privately he found means to inform the Notaries: indeed, at the beginning of the Trial, I and Boisguillaume, with witnesses, were put secretly in an adjoining room, where there was a hole through which we could hear, in order that we might report what she said to Loyseleur. As I think, what the Maid said or stated familiarly to Loyseleur he reported to the Notaries; and from this were made memoranda for questions in the

Trial, to find some way of catching her unawares.

When the Trial had begun, Maître Jean Lohier, a grave Norman Clerk, came to this Town of Rouen, and communication was made to him of what the Bishop of Beauvais had written hereon; and the said Lohier asked for two or three days' delay to look into it. To which he received answer that he should give his opinion that afternoon; and this he was obliged to do. And Maître Jean Lohier, when he had seen the Process, said it was of no value, for several reasons: first, because it had not the form of an ordinary Process; then, it was carried on in an enclosed and shut-up place, where those concerned were not in full and perfect liberty to say their full will; then, that this matter dealt with the honour of the King of France, whose side she [the Maid] supported, and that he had not been called, nor any who were for him; then, neither legal document nor articles had been forthcoming, and so there was no guide for this simple girl to answer the Masters and Doctors on great matters, and especially those, as she said, which related to her revelations. For these things, the Process was, in his opinion, of no value. At which my Lord of Beauvais was very indignant against the said Lohier; and although my Lord of Beauvais told him that he might remain to see the carrying out of the Trial, Lohier replied that he would not do so. And immediately my Lord of Beauvais, then lodging in the house where now lives Maître Jean Bidaut, near Saint Nicolas-le-Peinteur, came to the Masters—to wit, Maître Jean Beaupère, Maître Jacques de Touraine, Nicolas Midi, Pierre Maurice, Thomas de Courcelles, and Loyseleur— and said to them: "This Lohier wants to put fine questions into our Process: he would find fault with everything, and says it is of no value. If we were to believe him, everything must be begun again, and all we have done would be worth nothing!" And, after stating the grounds on which Lohier found fault, my Lord of Beauvais added: "It is clear enough on which foot he limps. By Saint John! we will do nothing in the matter, but will go on with our Process as it is begun!" This was on a Saturday afternoon in Lent; and the next morning I spoke with the said Lohier at the Church of Notre Dame at Rouen, and asked him what he thought of the said Trial and of Jeanne? He replied: "You see the way they are proceeding. They will take her, if they can, in her words—as in assertions where she says, '*I know for certain,*' as regards the apparitions; but if she said, '*I think*' instead of the words '*I know for certain*' it is my opinion that no man could condemn her. It seems they act rather from hate than otherwise; and for that reason, I will not stay here, for I have no desire to be in it." And in truth he thenceforward lived always at the Court of Rome, where he died Dean of Appeals.[108]

At the beginning of the Trial, because I was putting in writing for five or six days the answers and excuses of the said Maid, the Judges several times wished to compel me, speaking in Latin, to put them in other terms, by changing the sense of her words or in other ways such as I had not heard. By command of the Bishop of Beauvais, two men were placed at a window near where the Judges sat, with a curtain across the window, so that they could not be seen. These two men wrote and reported what there was in the charge against Jeanne, keeping silence as to her excuses; and, in my opinion, this was Loyseleur. After the sitting was over, in the afternoon, while comparing notes of what had been written, the two others reported differently from me, and had put in none of the excuses; at which my Lord of Beauvais was greatly angry with me. [109] Where *Nota* is written in the Process there was disagreement, and questions had to be made upon it; and it was found that what I had written was true.

In writing the said Process, I was often opposed by my Lord of Beauvais and the Masters, who wanted to compel me to write according to their fancy, and against what I had myself heard. And when there was something which did not please them, they forbade it to be written, saying that it did not serve the Process; but I nevertheless wrote only according to my hearing and knowledge.

Maître Jean Delafontaine, from the beginning of the

---

[108] "*Doyen de la Rote*"—Court of Appeals at Rome.
[109] On the *Minute* of Manchon, which was in the hands of the Judges of the Rehabilitation in 1455.

Trial up to the week after Easter, 1431, took the place of my Lord of Beauvais, to interrogate her, in the absence of the Bishop; and was always present with the Bishop in the conduct of the said Trial. And when the time came that the Maid was summoned to submit herself to the Church by this same Delafontaine, and by Brothers Ysambard de la Pierre and Martin Ladvenu, they advised her that she should believe in, and rely on, our Lord the Pope and those who preside in the Church Militant; and that she should make no question about submitting to our Holy Father the Pope and to the Holy Council; for that there were among them as many of her own side as of the other, many of them notable Clerics, and that if she did not do this, she would put herself in great danger. The day after she had been thus advised, she said that she wished certainly to submit to our Holy Father the Pope and to the Holy Council. When my Lord of Beauvais heard this, he asked who had spoken with the Maid. The Guard replied that it was Maître Delafontaine, his lieutenant, and the two Friars. And at this, in the absence of the said Delafontaine and the Friars, the Bishop was much enraged against Maître Jean Lemaître, the Deputy Inquisitor, and threatened to do him an injury. And when Delafontaine knew that he was threatened for this reason, he departed from Rouen, and did not again return. And as for the Friars, they would have been in peril of death, but for the said Lemaître, who excused them and besought for them, saying that if any harm were done to them, he would never again come to the Trial. And, from that time, the Earl of Warwick forbade any one to visit the Maid, except the Bishop of Beauvais or those sent by him; and the Deputy Inquisitor was not allowed to go without him.

At the end of the sermon at Saint Ouen, after the abjuration of the Maid, because Loyseleur said to her, "Jeanne, you have done a good day's work, if it please God, and have saved your soul," she demanded, "Now, some among you people of the Church, lead me to your prisons, that I may no longer be in the hands of the English." To which my Lord of Beauvais replied, "Lead her back whence she was taken!" For this reason she was taken back to the Castle which she had left. The following Sunday, which was Trinity Sunday, the Masters, Notaries, and others concerned in this Trial were summoned; and we were told that she had resumed her man's dress and had relapsed; and when we came to the Castle, in the absence of my Lord of Beauvais, there came upon us eighty or a hundred English soldiers, or thereabouts, who spoke to us in the courtyard of the Castle, telling us that all of us Clergy were deceitful, traitorous Armagnacs and false counsellors; so that we had great trouble to escape and get out of the Castle, and did nothing for that day. The following day I was summoned; but I replied that I would not go if I had not a surety, on account of the fright I had had the day before; and I would not have gone back if one of the followers of my Lord of Warwick had not been sent as a surety. And thus I returned, and was at the continuation of the Trial, up to the end—except that I was not at a certain examination made by people who had spoken with her privately,[110] as privileged persons; nevertheless, the Bishop of Beauvais wanted to compel me to sign, and this I would not do.

I saw Jeanne led to the scaffold;[111] and there were seven or eight hundred soldiers around her, bearing swords and staves; so that no one was so bold as to speak to her except Brother Martin Ladvenu and Maître Jean Massieu.

Patiently did she hear the sermon right through; afterwards she repeated her thanksgiving, prayers, and

---

[110] This was the Examination called the *Acta Posterius*, which, though included by Cauchon in the Process, is not signed by the Official Registrars, Manchon, Boisguillaume, and Taquel.

[111] Jeanne was burnt in the Market Place at Rouen, where an inscribed stone marks the site. It is stated that the execution took place in front of the Church of St. Sauveur, and facing the principal street which leads to the Market Place, thus accommodating a larger number of spectators than was possible in any other part of the Place.

There is still some dispute as to the actual spot; but as the Cemetery was religious ground and the execution was, nominally at least, a secular one, the ground chosen must have been on land belonging to the municipality of Rouen. Probably this was in the Marché aux Veaux, as we find an order for the burning of a heretic there in 1522, "*lieu accoutumé faire telles exécutions.*"

lamentations most notably and devoutly, in such manner that the Judges, Prelates, and all present were provoked to much weeping, seeing her make these pitiful regrets and sad complaints. Never did I weep more for anything that happened to me; and, for a month afterwards, I could not feel at peace. For which reason, with a part of the money I had for my services I bought a little Missal, so that I might have it and might pray for her. In regard to final repentance, I never saw greater signs of a Christian.

I remember that at the sermon given at Saint Ouen by Maître Guillaume Érard, among other words were said and uttered these: "Ah! noble House of France, which hath always been the protectress of the Faith, hast thou been so abused that thou dost adhere to a heretic and schismatic? It is indeed a great misfortune." To which the Maid made answer, what I do not remember, except that she gave great praise to her King, saying that he was the best and wisest Christian in the world. At which Érard and my Lord of Beauvais ordered Massieu, "Make her keep silence."

MAÎTRE JEAN MASSIEU, *Priest, Curé of one of the Divisions of the Parish Church of Saint-Caudres at Rouen, formerly Dean of the Christendom of Rouen.*

I was at the Trial of the said Jeanne on every occasion when she was present before the Judges and Clerics; and, on account of my office, I was appointed a Clerk to Maître Jean Benedicite,[112] Promoter in this Action. I believe, from what I saw, that the proceedings were taken out of hatred and in order to abase the honour of the King of France whom she served, and to wreak vengeance and bring her to death, not according to reason and for the honour of God and of the Catholic Faith. I say this, because when my Lord of Beauvais, who was Judge in the Case, accompanied by six Clerics—namely, Beaupère, Midi, Maurice, Touraine, Courcelles, and Feuillet, or some other in his place—first questioned her, before she had answered one of them, another of those

---

[112] Cognomen given to the Promoter, d'Estivet.

present would interpose another question, by which she was often hurried and troubled in her answers. And, besides, as I was leading Jeanne many times from her prison to the Court, and passed before the Chapel of the Castle, at Jeanne's request, I suffered her to make her devotions in passing; and I was often reproved by the said Benedicite, the Promoter, who said to me: "Traitor! what makes thee so bold as to permit this Excommunicate to approach without permission? I will have thee put in a tower where thou shalt see neither sun nor moon for a month, if thou dost so again." And when the Promoter saw that I did not obey him, the said Benedicite placed himself many times before the door of the Chapel, between me and Jeanne, to prevent her saying her prayers before the Chapel, and asked expressly of Jeanne: "Is this the Body of Christ?" When I was taking her back to prison, the fourth or fifth day, a priest named Maître Eustace Turquetil, asked me: "What dost thou think of her answers? will she be burned? what will happen?" and I replied: "Up to this time I have seen in her only good and honour; but I do not know what will happen in the end, God knows!" Which answer was reported by the said priest to the King's people; and it was said that I was opposed to the King. On this account, I was summoned, in the afternoon, by the Lord of Beauvais, the Judge, and was spoken to of these things and told to be careful to make no mistake, or I should be made to drink more than was good for me. I think that, unless the Notary Manchon had made excuses for me, I should not have escaped.

When Jeanne was taken to Saint-Ouen to be preached to by Maître Guillaume Érard, at about the middle of the sermon, after she had been admonished by the words of the preacher, he began to cry out, in a loud voice, saying, "Ah! France, thou art much abused, thou hast always been the most Christian country; and Charles, who calls himself thy King and Governor, hath joined himself, as a heretic and schismatic, which he is, to the words and deeds of a worthless woman, defamed and full of dishonour; and not only he, but all the Clergy within his jurisdiction and lordship, by whom she hath been examined and not reproved, as she hath said." Two or three times he repeated these words about the King; and, at last, addressing himself to Jeanne he said, raising his finger: "It is to thee, Jeanne, that I speak, I tell thee that thy King is a heretic and schismatic!" To which she replied: "By my faith! sir, saving your reverence, I dare say and swear, on pain of death, that he is the most noble of all Christians, and the one who most loves the Faith of the Church, and he is not what you say." And then the preacher said to me: "Make her keep silence."

Jeanne never had any Counsel.[113] I remember that Loyseleur was one appointed to counsel her. He was against her, rather deceiving than helping her.

The said Érard, at the end of his sermon, read a schedule containing the Articles which he was inciting Jeanne to abjure and revoke. To which Jeanne replied, that she did not understand what abjuring was, and that she asked advice about it. Then Érard told me to give her counsel about it. After excusing myself for doing this, I told her it meant that, if she opposed any of the said Articles, she would be burned. I advised her to refer to the Church Universal as to whether she should abjure the said Articles or not. And this she did, saying in a loud voice to Érard: "I refer me to the Church Universal, as to whether I shall abjure or not." To this the said Érard replied: "You shall abjure at once, or you shall be burned." And, indeed, before she left the Square, she abjured, and made a cross with a pen which I handed to her.

At the end of the sermon, I advised Jeanne to ask that she might be taken to the prisons of the Church: and it was right she should be taken to the Church prisons, because the Church had condemned her. And this thing was asked of the Bishop of Beauvais by some of those present, whose names I do not know. To which the Bishop replied: "Take her to the Castle whence she came." And so it was done. That day, after dinner, in the presence of the Counsel of the Church, she took off her

---

[113] At the beginning of the Trial, Jeanne had asked for Counsel, and it had been refused.

man's dress and put on a woman's dress, as she was commanded. This was on the Thursday or Friday after Pentecost; and the man's dress was put in a bag in the same room where she was kept prisoner, while she remained guarded in this place, in the hands of five of the English, three of whom stayed all night in the room, and two outside the door of the room. I know of a surety that at night she slept chained by the legs with two pairs of iron chains, and fastened closely to a chain going across the foot of her bed, held to a great piece of wood, five or six feet long, and closed with a key, so that she could not move from her place. When the following Sunday came, being Trinity Sunday, and when it was time to rise, as she reported and said to me, she asked the English guards: "Take off my irons that I may get up." Then one of the English took away from her the woman's garments which she had on her, and they emptied the bag in which was her man's dress, and threw the said dress at her, saying to her: "Get up, and put the woman's dress in the bag." And, in accordance with what he said, she dressed herself in the man's dress they had given her, saying: "Sirs, you know it is forbidden me; without fail, I will not take it again." Nevertheless, they would not give her the other, insomuch that the contention lasted till mid-day, and, finally, she was compelled to take the said dress; afterwards, they would not give up the other, whatever supplications or prayers she might make.

This she told me on the Tuesday following, before dinner, on which day the Promoter had departed in company with the Earl of Warwick, and I was alone with her. Immediately I asked her why she had resumed a man's dress, and she told me what I have just related.

I was not at the Castle on the Sunday, but I met near the Castle those who had been summoned, much overwhelmed and affrighted. They said they had been furiously driven back by the English with axes and swords, and called traitors, and otherwise insulted. On the following Wednesday, the day she was condemned, and before she left the Castle, the Body of Christ was borne to her irreverently, without stole and lights, at which Brother Martin, who had confessed her, was ill-content, and so a stole and lights were sent for, and thus Brother Martin administered It to her. And this done, she was led to the Old Market-Place, and by her side were Brother Martin and myself, accompanied by more than 800 soldiers, with axes and swords. And being in the Old Market-Place, after the sermon, during which she showed great patience and listened most quietly, she evinced many evidences and clear proofs of her contrition, penitence, and fervent faith, if only by her pitiful and devout lamentations and invocations of the Blessed Trinity and the Blessed and Glorious Virgin Mary, and all the Blessed Saints in Paradise—naming specially certain of these Saints: in which devotions, lamentations, and true confession of faith, she besought mercy also, most humbly, from all manner of people of whatever condition or estate they might be, of her own party as well as of the other, begging them to pray for her, forgiving them the harm they had done her, [and thus] she persevered and continued as long a space of time as half-an-hour, and up to the very end.

When she was given over by the Church, I was still with her; and with great devotion she asked to have a Cross: and, hearing this, an Englishman, who was there present, made a little cross of wood with the ends of a stick, which he gave her, and devoutly she received and kissed it, making piteous lamentations and acknowledgments to God, Our Redeemer, Who had suffered on the Cross for our Redemption, of Whose Cross she had the sign and symbol; and she put the said Cross in her bosom, between her person and her clothing. And, besides, she asked me humbly that I would get for her the Church Cross, so that she might see it continually until death. And I got the Clerk of the Parish of Saint-Sauveur to bring it to her; the which, being brought, she embraced closely and long, and kept it till she was fastened to the stake. While she was making these devotions and pious lamentations, I was much hurried by the English and even by some of their Captains, who wished me to leave her in their hands, that she might be put to death the sooner, saying to me, when I was trying to console her on the scaffold: "What, Priest! will you have us dine here?" And immediately, without any form or proof of judgment, they sent her to the fire, saying to the executioner: "Do thine office!" And thus she was led and fastened [to the stake], continuing her praises and devout lamentations to God and His Saints, and with her last word, in dying, she cried, with a loud voice: "Jesus!"

MAÎTRE JEAN BEAUPÈRE, *Master in Theology, Canon of Rouen.*

With regard to the apparitions mentioned in the Trial of the said Jeanne, I held, and still hold, the opinion that they rose more from natural causes and human intent than from anything supernatural; but I would refer principally to the Process.

Before she was taken to Saint-Ouen, to be preached to in the morning, I went alone, by permission, into Jeanne's prison, and warned her that she would soon be led to the scaffold to be preached to, telling her that, if she were a good Christian, she would say on the scaffold that she placed all her deeds and words in the ordering of Our Holy Mother Church, and especially of the Ecclesiastical Judges. And this did she say on the scaffold, being thereto requested by Maître Nicolas Midi. This being noted and considered, she was for a time sent back, after her abjuration; although some of the English accused the Bishop of Beauvais and the Delegates from Paris of favouring Jeanne's errors.

After this abjuration, and after taking her woman's dress which she received in prison, it was reported to the Judges on the Friday or Saturday following that Jeanne had repented of having put off a man's dress and had taken a woman's dress. On this account, my Lord of Beauvais sent me and Maître Nicolas Midi to her, hoping that we should speak to Jeanne and induce and admonish her to persevere in the good intent she had on the scaffold, and that she should be careful not to relapse. But we could not find the keeper of the prison key,[114] and, while we were waiting for the prison guard, several of the English, who were in the courtyard of the Castle, spoke threatening words, as Maître Nicolas Midi told me, to the effect that he who would throw both of us into the water would be well employed. And, hearing these words, we returned; and, on the bridge of the Castle, Midi heard, as he reported to me, like words used by others of the English; at which we were much frightened, and went away without speaking to Jeanne.

As to her innocence, Jeanne was very subtle with the subtlety of a woman, as I consider. I did not understand from any words of hers that she had been violated.

As to her final penitence, I do not know what to say, for, on the Monday after[115] the abjuration, I left Rouen to go to Basle,[116] on the part of the University of Paris. Through this I knew nothing of her condemnation until I heard it spoken of at Lisle in Flanders.

### THE SECOND ENQUIRY[117]: 1452, AND THIRD ENQUIRY: 1455–6.

*[A Rescript was issued by Pope Calixtus III. ordering the Procedure of Revision for the Enquiry of 1455–6.]*

#### EXAMINATION OF WITNESSES.

MANCHON: *Second Examination, 2nd May, 1452. [Additional statements:]*

I have heard that after Jeanne was taken captive by one of the company of the Count de Ligny, she was taken to the Castle of Beaurevoir and detained there three months;

---

[114] There were three keys to the prison, one being in the possession of the Promoter, one of the Inquisitor, and one belonging to the Cardinal.

[115] May 28th.

[116] To the Schismatic Council, then being held at Basle.

[117] Articles for Examination of Witnesses in the Second Enquiry of 1452 were prepared under the direction of Cardinal d'Estouteville and Brother Jean Bréhal, Inquisitor. The witnesses were examined on twelve questions. Articles were also prepared under the direction of Philippe de Rose, Delegate for Cardinal d'Estouteville, the witnesses being examined on twenty-seven questions.

and then, by letters from the King of England to my Lord of Beauvais, she was taken to Rouen and put in prison.

The Bishop of Beauvais held with the English; and, before he took cognizance of the Case, Jeanne was put in irons: after he had informed himself, Jeanne, thus fettered, was given over to the custody of four English, although the Bishop and the Inquisitor had stated and sworn that they would themselves faithfully keep her. Jeanne was treated with cruelty, and, towards the end of the Trial, was shown the torture.

And thus she put on man's clothing and lamented that she did not dare to doff these, fearing that at night the guards might attempt some violence; and once or twice complaint was made to the Bishop of Beauvais, to the Sub-Inquisitor, and to Maître Nicolas Loyseleur that some of these guards had attempted to assault her. The Earl of Warwick, at the statement of the Bishop, the Inquisitor, and Loyseleur, uttered strong threats should they again presume to attempt this; and two other guards were appointed.

SAINT LUCIEN TOWER, BEAUVAIS.
Jeanne is said to have passed a night in this tower on
August 20, 1429.

I, as notary, wrote Jeanne's answers and defence. Two or three writers, who were secretly ensconced near, omitted, in their writing, all that was in her favour.

The Judges desired me to write also in such wise, but I refused.

*Third Examination, 8th May, 1452. [Additional statements:]*

I acted as notary in the Process, by compulsion of the Great Council of the King of England, not daring to contradict their order. The Bishop of Beauvais was not compelled to take up the Process against Jeanne. He did it of free-will. The Inquisitor was summoned and dared not refuse. The Process was carried out by the English at their expense. The Promoter also was not compelled, but came of free-will. The Assessors and Doctors were summoned and dared not refuse.

[With regard to the comparison of the writing of the concealed clerks and the notaries, he adds that] the comparison of notes was made in the house of the Bishop.

Jeanne answered prudently and with simplicity, as might be seen in the Process. She could not have defended herself before such great Doctors had she not been inspired. The examination lasted for two or three hours in the morning, and sometimes as long again in the afternoon of the same day. She was much fatigued by the examination, for the examiners put to her the most subtle questions they possibly could.

The original Process was written by me faithfully, in French, after the first session. Later, I believe it was faithfully translated into Latin. During the Process, and almost up to the close, Jeanne had no Counsel. I do not remember if she asked for one; but, towards the end, she had Maître Pierre Maurice and a Carmelite to direct and instruct her.

On the day of her death, before the sermon and ere she left the Castle, she received the Body of the Lord by the order of the Judges, at her own request.

She was taken to the place of execution by a large

number of soldiers—nearly four score. After the ecclesiastical sentence had been pronounced, and Jeanne given up, she was taken over to the Bailly, there present, who, without any consultation or sentence, made a sign with his hand, saying: "Take her away! Take her away!"

*Fourth Examination, 17th December, 1455. [Additional statements:]*

The sum of a thousand pounds, or crowns, was given by the King of England for the surrender of the Maid; and an annuity of 300 pounds to the soldier of the Duke of Burgundy who had captured her.

I was appointed notary in the Trial, together with a certain Guillaume Boisguillaume.

The copy of the Process shewn to me is the true Copy made. I acknowledge my own and my companion's signatures, and that it is the truth. Two other copies were made. One was given to the Inquisitor, one to the King of England, and one to the Bishop of Beauvais. This Process was made from a certain Minute written in French, by my own hand, which was given up to the Judges, and was afterwards translated from the French into Latin by Monsieur Thomas de Courcelles and myself, in the form in which it now stands, as well and as faithfully as possible, long after the death and execution of Jeanne. As for the Act of Accusation and other parts of the Process, Maître Thomas de Courcelles had very little to do with these, nor did he greatly interfere with them.

With regard to the word *Nota*, written above certain Articles in the Minute, there was, on the first day of the Enquiry, a great tumult in the Chapel of the Castle at Rouen, where, that day, the interrogation was held, so that Jeanne was interrupted at almost every word, whilst she was speaking of her apparitions: Certain secretaries were there—two or three—of the King of England, who registered, as they chose, her words and depositions, omitting all her defence and all which tended to exonerate her. I complained of this, saying it was irregular, and that I would not be responsible, as clerk, in this matter: and, therefore, on the morrow, the place of meeting was changed and convened in a certain hall of the Castle, near the Great Hall, while two English were placed to keep order. When there were difficulties as to Jeanne's answers, and some said she had not replied as I had written, I wrote *Nota* at the top, in order that the questions might be repeated and the difficulties removed. Although it is mentioned in the Process that the Judges stated they had received preliminary evidence, I do not remember to have seen or heard of it; but I know that, if it had been produced, it would have been inserted in the Process.

Jeanne was brought to Rouen and not to Paris, because, as I think, the King of England and the principal people of his Council were there.

At the beginning of the Process, I was sent for to attend a meeting held at a certain house near the Castle, at which were present the Bishop of Beauvais, the Abbé of Fécamp, Maître Nicolas Loyseleur, and many others. The Bishop told me it was necessary that I should serve the King: that they meant to bring a fine case against this said Jeanne, and that I was to recommend another *greffier* to assist me. I therefore nominated Boisguillaume.

I met Lohier in the Church, on the day after the Bishop had asked him to give an opinion on the Process, and enquired what he thought of it. He replied, that the Process was of no value, and could not be maintained, because it was conducted in the Castle and not in a legal court; that it concerned many who were not summoned; that Jeanne had no Counsel: and for many other reasons. He added that, in his opinion, it was their intention to put her to death.

A certain Maître Nicolas de Houppeville was summoned to attend the Trial; and was in great danger, because he refused. Maître Jean Lemaitre, Sub-Inquisitor, delayed as long as possible his attendance at the Trial, and was much vexed at being compelled to attend.

One day, when Jeanne was being questioned, Jean de Châtillon spoke in her favour, saying that she was not compelled to reply to the question put to her, or to that effect. This much displeased the Bishop of Beauvais and his following, and there was a great tumult at his words.

The Bishop ordered him to be quiet, and to let the Judges speak.

On another occasion, when some one was advising and directing Jeanne on the question of submission to the Church, the Bishop said, "Hold your tongue, in the devil's name!" I do not remember the name of him who was thus spoken to.

One day, some one, whose name I do not remember, having spoken of Jeanne in a way which did not please the Earl of Stafford, the latter followed him, sword in hand, to some place of sanctuary; and, if they had not told Stafford that that place was sacred, he would have slain him.

Those who seemed to me most affected [against Jeanne] were Beaupère, Midi, and de Touraine.

One day, I went with the Bishop of Beauvais and the Earl of Warwick to the prison where Jeanne was, and we found her in irons. It was said that at night she was fastened with iron chains; but I did not see her so fastened. There was, in the prison, neither bed nor any kind of couch. There were four or five guards of the lowest kind.

[Manchon supplies a fuller account of the story given in 1450 as to the clerks having overheard Jeanne's confession to Loyseleur:]

After I and Boisguillaume had been appointed notaries, the Earl of Warwick, the Bishop of Beauvais, and Maître Nicolas Loyseleur told us that Jeanne had spoken strange things in regard to her visions, and in order the better to know the truth about them, it was agreed that Maître Nicolas Loyseleur should pretend to be from the Marches of Lorraine—Jeanne's own country— and in the following of the King of France; that he should enter her prison in a layman's habit, and that the guards should retire and leave him alone with her: there was, in a room adjoining the prison, a hole, specially made for the purpose, in order that I and my companion might be there, and hear what was said by Jeanne. Thither we went, unseen by her. Then Loyseleur, pretending to have news, began to question Jeanne of the King's estate and of her revelations. Jeanne replied, believing him to be in fact of her own country and party: and the Bishop and the Earl desired us to put in writing what we had heard. I replied, that this ought not to be, that it was not honest to carry on the Trial by such means, but that, if she spoke thus in open Court, we would willingly register the words. And, ever afterwards, Jeanne had great confidence in this Loyseleur, who often heard her in confession, and would generally have private speech with her before she was taken before the Judges.

The interrogations sometimes lasted three or four hours in the morning; and sometimes difficult and subtle questions arose on the answers, on which she was further examined after dinner for two or three hours. Often they turned from one question to another, changing about, but, notwithstanding this, she answered prudently, and evinced a wonderful memory, saying often, "I have already answered you on this," and adding, "I refer to the clerks."

Long before the [Seventy] Articles were included in the Process, Jeanne had been many times examined, and had given many answers; and from these questions and answers the Articles were drawn up, with the advice of the Assessors. This was done by the Promoter, in order that the material, which was diffuse, might be put in order. Afterwards, she was examined on the whole; and it was concluded by the counsellors—principally those who came from Paris—that it would be well, and according to custom, to reduce these Articles and answers to shorter Articles, bringing together the principal points, in order to have the material in brief, for better and more prompt discussion. On this, there were drawn up the Twelve Articles; but I had no hand in them, nor do I know who composed or extracted them.

[With regard to a Note, dated April 4th, 1431, written in French and contained in the Process, concerning these Twelve Articles, the other two Notaries— Guillaume Colles or Boisguillaume, and Nicolas Taquel—were summoned and questioned, together with deponent. They testified that:]

The Note is in the handwriting of Manchon, but as to

who drew up the Twelve Articles we do not know. It was said to be customary that such Articles should be made and drawn up from the confessions of one accused of Heresy, even as in a matter of Faith was usually done, in Paris, by the Doctors and Masters in Theology. The corrections of these Articles were, we believe, put down as appears in the copy before us; but, whether these corrections were added or not to the copy of the Articles sent to Paris and to those invited to submit an opinion, we do not know. We believe not: for a note, in the handwriting of Maître Guillaume d'Estivet, the Promoter, shews that they were sent by him on the following day without correction.

[Manchon was then asked, if he believed the Articles to be truthfully composed, and if there were not a great difference between them and Jeanne's answers. He replied that, what was in his Process was true. The Articles were not his doing.]

I believe that deliberation was not made on the whole Process, because it was not then in shape. It was brought into its present form only after Jeanne's death. Opinions were given on the Twelve Articles. The Twelve Articles were not read to Jeanne. [Asked again, if he had ever perceived a difference between these Articles and Jeanne's confessions, he said he did not remember. Those to whom they were shown said, that it was the custom to draw up such Articles; but that he had not given his attention to it, and that he should not have dared to argue with such great men.]

During the Trial I was seated at the feet of the Judges with Guillaume Colles and the clerk of Maître Guillaume Beaupère, who was also writing; but there was a great difference in what we had written, and from this arose much contention.

When the Process was complete, opinions were asked for, and from these it was decided that Jeanne should be exhorted; she was left to the counsel of Maître Nicolas Loyseleur, who said to her: "Jeanne, believe me: if you will, you may be saved. Take the dress of your sex, and do all that you are told; otherwise you are in peril of death. If you do what I tell you, you will be saved, and will have much good and not much ill, and you will be given up to the Church." And then she was taken to a scaffold or platform. Two sentences had been prepared, one of abjuration, the other of condemnation: both were in the hands of the Bishop, and, while he was reading the sentence of condemnation, Maître Nicolas Loyseleur continued to press Jeanne to do what he had advised, and to accept the woman's dress. There was a short interval, in which an Englishman addressed the Bishop as a traitor, to which he answered that he lied. At this instant, Jeanne declared herself ready to obey the Church; and then the abjuration was read to her. I do not know if she repeated it, or if, after it was read, she said that she agreed. But she certainly smiled. The executioner was there, with the cart, waiting to take her to the burning.

On Trinity Sunday, I and the other notaries were commanded by the Bishop and Lord Warwick to come to the Castle, because it was said that Jeanne had relapsed and had resumed her man's dress.

When we reached the Court, the English, who were there to the number of about fifty, assaulted us, calling us traitors, and saying that we had mismanaged the Trial. We escaped their hands with great difficulty and fear. I believe they were angry that, at the first preaching and sentence, she had not been burnt.

What she had said in the abjuration she said she had not understood, and that what she had done was from fear of the fire, seeing the executioner ready with his cart.

[Asked, why they had administered the Sacrament to one declared excommunicate and heretic, and if she had been absolved by the forms of the Church, Manchon answered:] There had been much discussion among the Judges and their Counsellors, whether they should offer her the Holy Sacrament, and whether she should be absolved at the place of execution; but I did not see any absolution granted to her. I was so disturbed that for a month I remained terrified.

She never revoked her revelations, but maintained them up to the end.

BROTHER PIERRE MIGIER, *Prior of Longueville, in the diocese of Rouen, S.T.P., First examination, May 2nd, 1452*, [*evidence of no special value.*]

*Second Examination, May 9th, 1452.* [*Additional evidence:*]

At the end of the first sermon at Saint-Ouen, when Jeanne was admonished to recant and she hesitated, one of the English ecclesiastics told the Bishop that he was favouring Jeanne, to which the Bishop replied, "You lie! It is my duty, on account of my profession, to seek the salvation of the soul and body of this Jeanne."

I was accused before the Cardinal of England as a partisan of Jeanne, but I excused myself to the Cardinal, being in fear of my life.

I think the notaries were truthful, and that they wrote with fidelity.

I do not know whether she asked for Counsel, but I think no one would have dared to counsel or defend her, nor would they have been permitted.

She was taken to execution, with great anger, by the English soldiers. When she was given up to the secular authorities by the Church, she began to weep and call upon "Jesus." Then I went away, having so great compassion that I could not witness her death.

*Third Examination, December 16th, 1455.* [*Additional evidence:*]

I heard that, during the Trial, there were certain men hidden behind curtains, who, it was said, were writing down the words and confessions of Jeanne; but I do not know if this is the fact. This I heard from Maître Guillaume Manchon, one of the three Registrars of the Case. I complained of it to the Judges, saying that it did not seem to me to be a good way of acting. But whatever may be the truth of these hidden clerks, I believe truly that the Registrars who signed the Process were trustworthy, and that they faithfully reported what was done in the Trial.

As to the act of recantation, I know it was performed

by her; it was in writing, and was about the length of a *Pater Noster*.

In an old book, in which are the sayings of Merlin the prophet, it is written that a maiden should come from an Oak-wood in the country of Lorraine.

BROTHER YSAMBARD DE LA PIERRE: *Second Examination, May 3rd, 1452.* [*He makes the following additions*:]

The room in which Jeanne was confined was rather dark.

I was at the sermon of Maître Guillaume Érard, who took as his theme, "A branch cannot bear fruit except it abide in the Vine," saying that in France there was no monster such as this Jeanne: she was a witch, heretic, and schismatic; and that the King who favoured her was of like sort for wishing to recover his kingdom by means of such an heretical woman.

The Bishop of Beauvais held with the English. I believe it was he who, at the beginning of the Process, ordered her to be kept in irons, and deputed the English as her keepers, forbidding any to speak with her unless by leave from him, or from the Promoter, Benedicite.

When I was holding the Cross before her, she begged me to descend, as the fire was mounting.

When she spoke of the kingdom and the war, I thought she was moved by the Holy Spirit; but when she spoke of herself she feigned many things: nevertheless, I think she should not have been condemned as a heretic. When the Bishop asked if she would submit to the Church, she enquired, "What is the Church? So far as it is you, I will not submit to your judgment, because you are my deadly enemy." She complained that the Bishop would not allow them to write anything in her excuse, but only what was against her. When she was asked whether she would submit to the judgment of the Pope, she replied that, if they would take her to him, she would be content.

She was adjudged relapsed because she had resumed her man's dress. After she had recanted, she resumed a woman's dress, and begged to be taken to the ecclesiastical prisons; but it was not permitted. I heard from Jeanne, herself, that she had been assaulted by a great lord; and for that reason she had resumed her man's dress, which had been perfidiously left near her. After her resumption of this dress, I heard the Bishop, with some of the English, exulting, and saying publicly to the Earl of Warwick and others: "She is caught this time!"

*Third Examination, May 9th, 1452.*

Some of the Assessors, such as the Bishop of Beauvais, proceeded of their own pleasure; some—to wit, the English Doctors—out of malicious spite; some, Doctors of Paris, from desire of gain; some were induced by fear, as the aforesaid Sub-Inquisitor and others whom I do not remember.

The Process was instituted by the King of England, the Cardinal of Winchester, the Earl of Warwick, and other English, who paid all the expenses. I remember well that Jean, Bishop of Avranches, for having refused to give his advice in the Process, was threatened by the Promoter d'Estivet; and Maître Nicolas de Houppeville, who would not attend the Trial nor give an opinion, was in danger of exile. After the first sermon, at which Jeanne recanted, I, Jean Delafontaine, and Maître Guillaume Vallée, of the Order of Saint Dominic, went to the Castle by order of the Judges to counsel Jeanne that she should persevere in her good purpose. Seeing this, the infuriate English threw themselves upon us, with swords and sticks, and violently drove us out of the Castle; on this occasion, Jean Delafontaine escaped, and left the town and did not return; also I suffered many reproaches from the Earl of Warwick, because I had told Jeanne she should submit to the General Council. [On the day that she said she would submit] Messire Guillaume Manchon, the notary, asked whether he should write down the submission? The Bishop replied, No, it was not necessary. Then Jeanne said to the Bishop: "Ah! you will certainly write what is against me, and will write nothing that is for me." This submission was not registered, and there ensued in the assembly a great murmur.

The examination of Jeanne sometimes lasted three hours in the morning; and sometimes she was examined in the afternoon as well as in the morning; I heard her often complain of over-much questioning.

During the greater part of the Process, when she was asked to submit to the Church, she understood by that term the assembly of Judges and Assessors there present. It was then expounded to her by Maître Pierre Maurice; and, after she knew, she always declared that she wished to submit to the Pope and to be conducted to him.

She was brought in a cart to the cemetery of Saint-Ouen. After the preaching [at the Old Market] there was a long waiting, and then the King's clerks conducted her to the stake, I and Brother Martin Ladvenu accompanying her up to the end.

On this same occasion, the Bishop of Beauvais wept. A certain Englishman, a soldier, who hated her greatly, had sworn to bring a faggot for the stake. When he did so, and heard Jeanne calling on the name of Jesus in her last moments, he was stupefied, and, as it were, in an ecstasy at the spectacle: his companions took him and led him away to a neighbouring tavern. After refreshment, he revived. In the afternoon, the same Englishman confessed, in my presence, to a Brother of the Order of Saint Dominic, that he had gravely erred, and that he repented of what he had done against Jeanne. He held her to be a good woman, for he had seen the spirit departing from her, as it were a white dove, going away from France.

In the afternoon of the same day, the executioner came to the Convent of the Dominicans, saying to them and to Brother Martin Ladvenu, that he feared he was damned because he had burnt a saint.

MAÎTRE PIERRE CUSQUEL, *Citizen of Rouen. First Examination, before Cardinal d'Estouteville, May 3rd, 1452.*

I saw Jeanne brought in by the English.

I did not see her taken to prison, but I saw her two or three times in a chamber in the Castle of Rouen, near the back entrance.

At the time of the Trial, I was in the habit of entering the Castle, thanks to Johnson, master of the masons. Twice I entered her prison and saw her, with her legs shackled and fastened by a long chain to a beam. In my master's house was hung a great cage of iron, in which, it was said, she was to be shut up; but I never saw her in this cage.

I heard that Jeanne was made prisoner in the diocese of Beauvais, and on this account the Bishop undertook the Process against her.

*Second Examination, May 9th, 1452. [He adds to his evidence:]*

The room [where Jeanne was imprisoned] was situated under the stairs, towards the fields.

Maître André Marguérie, or another, said he had enquired as to Jeanne's change of dress, and by some one—I know not whom—was told that he was to hold his tongue, in the devil's name.

I twice entered Jeanne's prison and spoke with her, warning her to speak prudently, and that there was question of her death. The iron cage, which I saw, was intended to detain her in an upright position.

I was not present at the last preaching and condemnation and execution of Jeanne, because my heart could not bear it, for pity of her; but I heard that she received the Body of the Lord before her condemnation.

Maître Jean Tressart, when he returned from the execution, groaning and weeping sadly, lamented to me what he had seen at this place, saying to me: "We are all lost; we have burnt a Saint"; adding, that he believed her soul was in the hands of God because, when she was in the midst of the flames, she constantly called on the name of the Lord Jesus.

*Third Examination, May 11th, 1456. [Additional evidence:]*

I had heard of the visitation ordered by the Duchess of Bedford, but did not know if it were true.

After her death, the English had her ashes collected and thrown into the Seine, because they feared that some might believe she had escaped.

LADVENU: *Second Examination, May 3rd, 1452. [He adds the following to his earlier testimony:]*

I often saw her in the Castle of Rouen, under the custody of the English, ironed and in prison.

I heard Jeanne, by license of the Judges, in confession; I administered to her the Body of Christ; she received it with great devotion and tears which I cannot describe.

The resumption of her man's dress was one of the causes of her condemnation.

*Third Examination, May 9th, 1452. [Additional evidence:]*

I was present at the greater part of the Process, with Brother Jean Lemaître, then Sub-Inquisitor. I saw Maître Nicolas de Houppeville—he who would not assist in the Process—taken to prison. I know well that Jeanne had no director, counsel, nor defender, up to the end of the Process, and that no one would have dared to offer himself as her Counsel, director, or defender, for fear of the English. I have heard that those who went to the Castle to counsel and direct Jeanne, by order of the Judges, were harshly repulsed and threatened.

Directly Jeanne was abandoned by the Church, she was seized by the English soldiers, who were present in large numbers, without any sentence from the secular authority, although the Bailly of Rouen and the Counsels of the Secular Court were present. I know this because I was with her, from the Castle to her last breath.

The executioner, in my presence, gave his testimony that she had been unjustly put to death.

Maître Guillaume Érard, at the sermon which he pronounced at the Cemetery of Saint-Ouen, exclaimed: "Oh, House of France! thou hast never till now nourished a monster in thy bosom; but now thou art disgraced by thy adhesion to this witch, this heretic! this superstitious one!"

*Fourth Examination, December 19th, 1455, and May 13th, 1456. [Additional statements:]*

I have heard it said that the Bishop, and others concerned in the Process, wished to have letters of guarantee from the King of England, and received them; and these are the letters now shewn, signed with the sign manual of Maître Laurence Calot, whose signature I know well. Maître Jean Lemaitre, Sub-Inquisitor, who was concerned in the Trial and who often went with me, was compelled to attend. Brother Ysambard de la Pierre, who was a friend of the Inquisitor, desired on one occasion to direct Jeanne, but was told to hold his tongue, and that, if he did not henceforward abstain from such interference, he would be thrown into the Seine.

On the day of her death I was with her until her last breath. One present said he wished his soul might be where he believed Jeanne's soul was. After the reading of the sentence, she came down from the platform on which the preaching had been, and was led by the executioner, without any sentence from the secular Judges, to the place where the pile was prepared for her burning. The pile was on a scaffold, and the executioner lighted it from below. When Jeanne perceived the fire, she told me to descend and to hold up the Cross of the Lord on high before her that she might see it.

When I was with her, and exhorting her on her salvation, the Bishop of Beauvais and some of the Canons of Rouen came over to see her; and, when Jeanne perceived the Bishop, she told him that he was the cause of her death; that he had promised to place her in the hands of the Church, and had relinquished her to her mortal enemies.

Up to the end of her life she maintained and asserted that her Voices came from God, and that what she had done had been by God's command. She did not believe that her Voices had deceived her: [but that] the revelations which she had received had come from God.

MESSIRE NICOLAS TAQUEL, *Priest, Rector of*

*Basqueville, in the Diocese of Rouen: First Examination, May 8th, 1452.*

About half-way through the Process I was called by the two notaries to assist them. I saw Jeanne in a prison in the Castle of Rouen, in a certain tower near the fields. I never perceived any kind of fear, nor did I know of prohibitions or coercion by the English. I do not remember that she asked to have Counsel, or that they were offered to her; I was not at the opening of the Case. I knew well that Jeanne was in prison. I saw her there, in irons, notwithstanding her weakness. There was an Englishman who had charge of her in the room, without whose leave no one, not even the Judges, might have access to her.

Jeanne was about twenty years of age; though she was as simple as any girl of her age, she could speak well on occasion, sometimes varying her answers, and sometimes not replying to the questions. I certainly heard in the town, that at night, the English, in the absence of the Judges, disturbed her much, saying sometimes that she would die, sometimes that they would kill her; but I do not know if it was true. I was present when some of the Judges put very difficult questions to her, to which she answered that it did not concern her to reply to them. Some of the Doctors present sometimes said to her, "You say well, Jeanne." Sometimes Jeanne, wearied with so many questions, begged for delay till the morrow; and it was granted. Many heard the statement referred to, made by Jeanne, that she would say and do nothing against the Faith. I believe this is written in the Process. I do not remember to have seen any English at the Examinations of Jeanne, with the exception of the guards; nor do I remember any restrictions upon what was done in the Process, although the Judges said it was forbidden to write anything which was not contained in the Process. I do not know that the words of the Seventy Articles were inserted in the Process, nor do I remember that Jeanne, during the whole Trial, said she would not submit to the Ecclesiastical authority, although I occasionally saw her somewhat disturbed; then the Doctors who were present advised her, and sometimes postponed the matter till the morrow.

I saw nothing in Jeanne contrary to a good Catholic. She asked, in my presence, whether she might receive the Sacrament; but I was not permitted to be present at its reception. It was told me that, before she arrived at the place of execution, she made many and devout prayers to God, to the Blessed Mary and the Saints, so that many present were provoked to tears, and, among others, Maître Nicolas Loyseleur, Promoter[118] to the cause, who, leaving her in tears, met certain English in the court of the Castle: these took him to task, calling him traitor, which frightened him so much that, without more ado, he went to the Earl of Warwick to beg his protection; and, had it not been for the said Earl, I think that Loyseleur would have been killed.

After the sentence of the Church had been read, I with many other ecclesiastics retired. I was not present at the execution; but I heard that Jeanne died piously and as a Catholic, calling on the name of the Blessed Virgin Mary.

*Second Examination, May 11th, 1456.* [*Additional evidence*:]

I was one of the notaries, but not at the commencement. I was not there during the time when the Process was carried on in the Great Hall, but only when the sittings were held in the prison. I was first concerned in the Process on the 14th of March, 1430, as appears in my commission, to which I refer; and, from this time to the end of the Process, I was present as notary at the interrogations and answers of Jeanne: I was not permitted to write, but I listened and referred, for the writing, to the other two notaries, Boisguillaume and Manchon, both of whom wrote, especially Manchon.

The said Process was put into its present form a long time after the death of Jeanne, but at what time I do not know. For my labour and trouble I had ten francs, though

---

[118] *Note by Quicherat*: This is an error of the witness. [The Promoter was d'Estivet.]

I had been told I should have twenty; and these ten francs were handed over to me by a certain Benedicite [d'Estivet], but whence the money came I know not.

I heard it said among the notaries that certain Articles were to be made; but as to who drew them up I know not. They were sent to Paris; but whether they were signed or no, I do not remember: I think they were not signed, but, yet, I remember that once something was signed, which was neither Process nor sentence.

[A note of April 4th, 1431, was then shewed to Maître Taquel, containing the Twelve Articles in the form in which they were sent for correction.] He confirmed the handwriting of Manchon, and said he believed he was present on the occasion. He thought no corrections were made.

When the preaching was made at the Place Saint-Ouen, I was not upon the platform with the other notaries. But I was quite close, and could see and hear all that was said and done. I remember well seeing a schedule of abjuration read to Jeanne by Massieu. It was about six lines of large writing; and Jeanne repeated it after Massieu. This letter of abjuration was in French, beginning, "Je, Jeanne," etc. After the abjuration, she was condemned to perpetual imprisonment, and reconducted to the Castle; and after this I was commanded to attend another enquiry; but a tumult arose, and I do not know what happened afterwards. There was another sermon: on that day Jeanne died, and on the morning of the day Jeanne received the Body of Christ. At this last preaching I was present to the end of the sermon; and at its conclusion Jeanne was handed over to the secular authorities. This done, I retired.

MESSIRE PIERRE LEBOUCHIER, *Priest, Curé of the Parish of Bourgeauville: Examined May 8th, 1452.*

An English clerk, Bachelor in Theology, Keeper of the Private Seal of the Cardinal of England, being at the sermon of Saint-Ouen, said these words, in my presence, to the Bishop of Beauvais: "Have done! You favour her overmuch!" Annoyed at these words, the Bishop threw the Process, which he had in his hand, to the ground, saying that he would do nothing more that day, being unwilling to act except according to his conscience.

Jeanne was alone, seated upon a chair; I heard her reply without Counsel. I do not know whether she asked for any or if it were denied her.

She was in prison in the Castle of Rouen. I do not know if she were in irons. No one might speak to her without leave from the English who had charge of her. I did not see her leave the Castle. There were with her certain Englishmen who, I believe, were shut up with her in the same room, to which there were three keys—one kept by the Lord Cardinal or the aforesaid secretary, another by the Inquisitor, and another by Messire Jean Benedicite, the Promoter: for the English feared greatly that she would escape them.

I was not present at the Process; but, after the preaching at Saint-Ouen, Jeanne, with her hands joined together, said in a loud voice that she submitted to the judgment of the Church, and prayed to Saint Michael that he would direct and counsel her.

As soon as the sentence had been read by the Ecclesiastical Judge, [at the Old Market,] she was conducted to the platform of the Bailly by the King's followers, on which platform were the Bailly and other lay officers. She remained there some time with them; and what they did or said I know not, only that she was taken back and given over to the fire after they had departed.

While they were tying her to the stake she implored and specially invoked Saint Michael. She seemed to me a good Christian to the end; the greater number of those present, to the number of ten thousand, wept and lamented, saying that she was of great piety.

I think the English feared Jeanne more than the whole of the rest of the army of the King of France, and that this fear it was which moved them, in my opinion, to bring the Process against her.

MAÎTRE NICOLAS DE HOUPPEVILLE, *Bachelor in Theology, of the diocese of Rouen: First Examination,*

*May 8th, 1452.*

I never thought that zeal of the Faith, nor desire to bring her back to the right way, caused the English to act thus.

Jeanne was brought to the town of Rouen by the English and imprisoned in the Castle; and the Process was, I believe, instituted by them. As to the question of fear and pressure, I do not believe it, so far as it affected the Judges. They acted voluntarily,—principally the Bishop of Beauvais, for I saw him on his return from the negotiations about Jeanne speaking of it with the Regent and the Earl of Warwick: he was exulting and rejoicing in words which I did not understand. He went apart thereupon with the Earl of Warwick; but what was said I know not.

In my judgment, the Judges and Assessors were for the most part uncoerced; for the rest, I believe many were afraid. I heard from Maître Pierre Minier that he had tendered his opinion in writing, but it was not pleasing to the Bishop of Beauvais, who sent him away, telling him that, as a theologian, he was not to meddle any more in the matter, but to leave it to the lawyers.

I was once called at the beginning of the Process. I did not come, being prevented. The second day, when I came, I was not admitted. I was even driven away by the Bishop, because, talking one day with Maître Michel Colles, I had told him that it was dangerous for many reasons to take part in this Process. This was repeated to the Bishop; and for this cause he had me shut up in the King's prison at Rouen, whence I was delivered only by the prayers of the Lord Abbot of Fécamp: and I heard that some, whom the Bishop summoned, advised that I should be exiled to England or elsewhere beyond the bounds of Rouen, had I not been delivered by the Abbot and his friends.

It was reported in the city of Rouen that some one, feigning to be a soldier of the King of France, was secretly introduced to her, persuading her not to submit to the authority of the Church. There were rumours that, on account of this persuasion, Jeanne afterwards wavered in her submission to the Church.

I saw her coming out of the Castle, weeping much, and led to the place of execution by a troop of soldiers, to the number of 120, some with swords and some with clubs. Touched with compassion at this sight I could go no further.

*Re-examined, May 13th, 1456.*

At the beginning of the Process, I was at several consultations, in which I was of opinion that neither the Bishop nor those who wished to take part with him were in the position to act as Judges; I could not see how they could properly proceed, because those opposed to her were acting as Judges, and she had already been examined by the Clergy of Poitiers and the Archbishop of Rheims, the Metropolitan of the Bishop of Beauvais. Owing to this opinion I incurred the wrath of the Bishop, who cited me to appear before him. When I appeared, I told him that I was not his subject, nor was I under his jurisdiction, but in that of Rouen: and so I left him. But when, for this reason, I wished to appear in the Case and presented myself to the authorities of Rouen, I was arrested and taken to the Castle and to the King's prisons. When I asked the cause of my arrest, I was told it was by order of the Bishop of Beauvais. Maître Jean Delafontaine, my friend, wrote to me that I was arrested in consequence of the opinion I had given in this Process; and he warned me, at the same time, of the anger of the Bishop. Thanks to the intervention of the Abbé of Fécamp, I ended by being set at liberty.

[He adds, to his previous statement, that the man who feigned to be a soldier on the side of the King of France was Nicolas Loyseleur.]

MASSIEU: *Second Examination, May 8th, 1452.* [*Additional evidence*:]

On one occasion, Maître Jean de Chatillon, Archdeacon of Evreux and Doctor in Theology, found that Jeanne was being asked questions too difficult for her, and complained of the mode of procedure, saying that they ought not to act in this manner. But the other Assessors told him to let them alone; to which he answered: "I must acquit my own conscience." For this cause he was forbidden, by whom I do not remember, to attend further unless he was summoned.

On Trinity Sunday, in the afternoon, Maître André Marguérie, hearing that Jeanne had resumed her male attire, went to the Castle of Rouen, saying that he must find out why she had done so, and that it was not enough for him merely to see her in this dress. One of the English soldiers, lance in hand, called out to him, "Traitor! Armagnac!" and raised his lance against him, so that Marguérie fled, fearing to be slain, and was in consequence much upset and ill.

At the first sermon, I was on the platform with Jeanne, and read the Schedule of Abjuration to her; at her request and petition I instructed her, shewing her the danger that might arise from abjuration unless the Articles were first seen by the Church, to whom she should refer as to whether she should abjure or not.

Seeing this, Maître Guillaume Érard, the preacher, asked me what I was saying to her, and, when I replied, said: "Read her this schedule, and tell her to sign it." Jeanne answered that she did not know how to sign; she desired that the Articles might be seen and deliberated upon by the Church; [she said] she ought not to abjure this schedule, and requested that she might be placed in the custody of the Church, and no longer be kept by the English. Érard replied that she had had long enough delay, and that, if she did not abjure this schedule, she should be immediately burned; and he forbade me to speak further with her or to give her more counsel.

I remember that incomplete questions were often put to Jeanne, and many and difficult interrogations were made together; then, before she could answer one, another would put a question; so that she was displeased, saying, "Speak one after the other." I marvelled that she could so answer the subtle and captious questions put to her; no man of letters could have replied better.

The examinations lasted generally from eight o'clock to eleven.

I often heard Jeanne say that God would not permit her

to say or do anything against the Catholic Faith. I heard her tell the Judges that, if she had ever said or done anything ill, she was willing to correct and amend according to their decision. I heard Jeanne saying to the Doctors who questioned her: "You ask me of the Church Triumphant and Militant. I do not understand these terms; but I am willing to submit to the Church as a good Christian should."

I know that the whole Process was written in French. I believe it was afterwards translated into Latin. [To his account of her resumption of the man's dress he adds:] On the morrow, after she had been seen in the resumed dress, her woman's dress was restored to her.

At the beginning of the Process, Jeanne asked for Counsel in her replies, she said she was too unlearned to reply; but they answered, that she must speak for herself as best she could, for she should not have Counsel.

[He adds to his account of her last Communion the fact that he was himself present.]

*Further examined, December 17th, 1455, and May 12th, 1456. [Additional evidence:]*

Once, when I was conducting her before the Judges, she asked me, if there were not, on her way thither, any Chapel or Church in which was the Body of Christ. I replied, that there was a certain Chapel in the Castle. She then begged me to lead her by this Chapel, that she might do reverence to God and pray, which I willingly did, permitting her to kneel and pray before the Chapel; this she did with great devotion. The Bishop of Beauvais was much displeased at this, and forbade me in future to permit her to pray there.

Many [in the Trial] had a great hate against her, principally the English, who feared her greatly: for, before she was captured, they did not dare to appear where they believed her to be. I heard it said that the Bishop of Beauvais did everything at the instigation of the King of England and his Council, who were then in Rouen.

Among the Assessors there was complaint that Jeanne was in the hands of the English. Some of them said that she ought to be in the hands of the Church; but the Bishop did not care, and sent her away to the English.

Maître Jean Lefèvre, of the Order of the Hermit Friars of Saint Augustine, now Bishop of Démétriade, seeing Jeanne much fatigued with the questioning as to whether she were in a state of grace, and considering that, though her answers seemed sufficient, she was over-worried by many questioners, remarked that she was being too much troubled. Then the questioners ordered him to be silent: I do not remember who they were.

She was imprisoned in the Castle of Rouen in a room on the second floor, to which one ascended by eight steps. There was a bed in which she slept and a great piece of wood to which she was fastened by iron chains.

There were five English of wretched estate [*houcepailliers*] who kept guard over her; they much desired her death and often derided her, and with this she reproached them.

I learnt from Etienne Castille, locksmith, that he had constructed for her an iron cage in which she was held by the neck, hands and feet, and that she was in this state from the time she was first brought to the town of Rouen until the beginning of the Process. I never saw her in this cage, for, when I fetched her, she was always out of irons.

I know that, by the order of the Duchess of Bedford, a visitation was made by matrons and midwives, among whom were, notably, Anna Bavon and another matron whose name I do not remember. She was found to be virgin, as I have heard from the said Anna. The Duchess of Bedford forbade the guards to offer her any violence.

When Jeanne was questioned, there were with the Bishop six Assessors, who also questioned her in such wise that, when she was occupied in replying to one, another interrupted her answer, so that she often said to them: "Fair sirs, speak one after another."

[To the story of the signing of the abjuration he adds:] Érard, holding the Schedule of Abjuration, said to Jeanne, "Thou shalt abjure and sign this schedule," and passed it to me to read, and I read it in her presence. I remember well that in this schedule it was said that in future she should not bear arms or male attire or short hair, and many other things which I do not remember. I know that this schedule contained about eight lines and no more; and I know of a certainty that it was not that which is mentioned in the Process, for this is quite different from what I read and what was signed by Jeanne. While they were pressing Jeanne to sign her abjuration, there was a great murmur among those present. I heard that the Bishop said to one of them, "You shall pay me for this," and added, that he would not go on unless satisfaction were done him. During this time I was constrained to warn Jeanne of the peril which threatened her if she signed this schedule. I saw clearly that she did not understand it, nor the danger in which she stood. Then Jeanne, pressed to sign, said: "Let the clerics of the Church examine this schedule. It is in their hands I ought to be. If they tell me to sign I will do it willingly." Then Maître Guillaume Érard said: "Do it now, otherwise you will end in the fire to-day." Jeanne replied that she would rather sign than burn; and there arose a great tumult among the people, and many stones were thrown, but by whom I know not. When the schedule was signed, Jeanne asked the Promoter whether she were to be placed in the hands of the Church and where she was to be taken. Then the Promoter replied, that she was to be reconducted to the Castle of Rouen, which in fact was done, and she was put into woman's clothes.

On the morning of Wednesday, the day on which she died, Brother Martin Ladvenu heard her in confession, and afterwards sent me to the Bishop to tell him this fact and that she prayed the Sacrament of the Eucharist might be brought to her. Thereupon, the Bishop convoked some of the Assessors, and at the end of their deliberation he told me to inform Brother Martin that he might take her the Sacrament and whatsoever she desired. Then I returned to the Castle and told this to Brother Martin.

Afterwards, she came out dressed in woman's clothing, and Brother Martin and I led her to the place of execution.

At the end of his sermon, Maître Nicolas Midi said to

her: "Jeanne, go in peace; the Church can no longer defend thee; she leaves thee to the secular arm."

She commended herself to God, to Saint Michael, Saint Catherine, and all the Saints.

I heard it said by Jean Fleury, Clerk to the Bailly, that the executioner related how, when her body was burnt and reduced to powder, her heart remained whole and bleeding. I was told that her ashes and all that remained of her were collected and thrown into the Seine.

MAÎTRE NICOLAS CAVAL, *Priest, Licentiate in Law, Canon of Rouen: First Examination, May 8th, 1452. [Agreed with previous statements.] Further examined, December 19th, 1455, and May 12th, 1456. [Additional evidence:]*

Jeanne had a good memory, for sometimes when she was asked a question she replied, "I have already answered in such a form," and she insisted that it should be ascertained from the notaries on what day she so answered; on which it was found to be as she said, without addition or change: and at this was there much marvel, considering her youth.

MAÎTRE GUILLAUME DU DESERT, *Canon of Rouen: Examined May 8th, 1452.*

I was present at the first preaching at Saint-Ouen, where I saw and heard the recantation made by Jeanne, and that she submitted to the decisions, the judgments, and the commands of the Church. A certain English Doctor who was present, being much displeased that the abjuration was received—because Jeanne was laughing when she pronounced the words—said to the Bishop of Beauvais, the Judge, that he was doing wrong to admit this recantation, since it was a mere farce. The Bishop, irritated, told this person that he lied: for, as Judge in a cause of faith, he must seek rather her salvation than her death.

At this sermon, I heard Jeanne submit to the judgment of the Church.

MAÎTRE ANDRÉ MARGUÉRIE, *Archdeacon: First Examination, May 9th, 1452. Further examined, December 19th, 1455, and May 12th, 1456.*

I heard Jeanne say, that she would believe neither Prelate nor Pope nor any other in [contradiction to] what she had received from God. I think this was one of the reasons why she was proceeded against, so that she should recant.

I was present at the final preaching but not at the execution, for very pity of the deed. Many of those present wept, among others the Cardinal de Luxembourg, then Bishop of Thérouanne.

I know nothing about her devotions; but she said, "Rouen, Rouen, must I die here?"

I can well believe that some of the English acted from hate and fear, but of the more notable ecclesiastics I do not think this. A chaplain of the Cardinal of England, present at the first preaching, said to the Bishop of Beauvais, that he was showing too much favour to Jeanne; but the Bishop said to him, "You lie! For in such a case I would show favour to no one." The Cardinal of England reproved his chaplain and told him to be silent.

MAÎTRE RICHARD GROUCHET, *Priest, Master of Arts, Bachelor of Theology, Canon of the Cathedral Church of La Saussaye in the diocese of Evreux: Examined, May 9th, 1452.*

Maîtres Jean Pigache, Pierre Minier, and I myself, who was with them, gave our opinion only under terror of threats. We stayed to the Trial, but had thoughts of flight. I many times heard from Pierre Maurice that, after the sermon at Saint-Ouen, he had warned Jeanne to hold to her good purpose; and the English, much displeased, threatened to strike him.

I think the notaries wrote with fidelity. I saw and heard that the Bishop of Beauvais bitterly upbraided them when they did not do as he wished: the whole affair, so far as I saw and heard, was carried on tumultuously. So far as I saw, no one was permitted to instruct or counsel Jeanne, nor did I see that she either asked for or was offered

Counsel: but I am not sure of this. I do not know whether any one was in danger of losing his life by defending her, but I know well that when difficult questions were put to Jeanne, whoever wished to direct her was harshly reproved and accused of partiality, sometimes by the Bishop of Beauvais and sometimes by Maître Jean Beaupère, who said to those who wished to advise, that they should leave her to speak and that the business of interrogation was theirs.

Jeanne was in prison, in the Castle of Rouen, where she was guarded and brought backwards and forwards by the English; but as to fetters and chains I know nothing, though I have often heard that she was harshly and straitly bound.

I saw and heard at the Trial that when Jeanne was asked if she would submit to the Bishop of Beauvais and others of the Assessors then named, she replied that she would not, but she would submit to the Pope and the Catholic Church, praying that she might be conducted to the Pope. When she was told that the Process would be sent to the Pope for him to judge, she replied that she did not wish this, because she did not know what might be put in this Process, but that she wished to be taken herself and interrogated by the Pope.

I did not know, nor did I ever hear, that there was ever any secular sentence pronounced against Jeanne. I was not present, but the public voice and rumour said that she had been violently and unjustly done to death.

MESSIRE JEAN LEFEVRE, *Bishop of Démétriade, of the Order of Saint Augustin in the Convent at Rouen, S.T.P.: Examined, May 9th, 1452*.

When Jeanne was asked if she were in the Grace of God, I, who was present, said it was not a suitable question for such a girl. Then the Bishop of Beauvais said to me, "It will be better for you if you keep silent."

Jeanne answered with great prudence the questions put to her, with the exception of the subject of her revelations from God: for the space of three weeks I believed her to be inspired. She was asked very profound questions, as to which she showed herself quite capable; sometimes they interrupted the enquiry, going from one subject to another, that they might make her change her purpose. The Examinations were very long, lasting sometimes two or three hours, so that the Doctors present were much fatigued.

Jeanne had done marvels in war: and, as the English are commonly superstitious, they thought there was a fate with her. Therefore, in my opinion, they, in all their counsels and elsewhere, desired her death.

[When asked how he knew the English were superstitious, he answered that it was commonly so reported, and was a popular proverb.]

I heard from a certain locksmith that he had made an iron cage high enough to allow her to stand upright. [When asked if she were ever put into it:] I believe so; I knew nothing of her keepers.

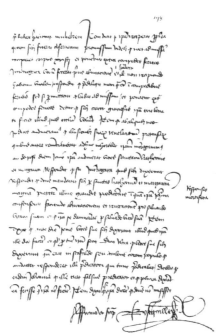

FACSIMILE OF A PAGE OF THE PROCESS OF

## JEANNE D'ARC.

MESSIRE THOMAS MARIE, *Priest, Bachelor in Theology, Prior of Saint Michael, near Rouen, of the Order of Saint Benedict: Examined, May 7th, 1452.*

I have heard, that after the first preaching, when she was taken back to the prison of the Castle, she was the victim of so many oppressions that she said she would rather die than remain with these English.

Where the judgment is not free, neither Process nor sentence is of value; but whether in this Case the Judges and Assessors were free, I know not beyond what I have before stated.

I heard from many that they saw the name Jesus written in the flames of the fire in which she was burnt.

I can well believe that if the English had had such a woman, they would have honoured her much and not have treated her in this manner.

MAÎTRE JEAN DE FAVE, *Master of Arts, Licentiate in Law; living at Rouen; Commissary: Examined, May 9th, 1452.*

After the first preaching, when she was taken back to prison, some of the soldiers insulted her, and their chiefs allowed them to do so. Some of the leaders of the English—as I heard—were angry with the Bishop of Beauvais, the Doctors, and the other Assessors in the Trial, because she had not been convicted and condemned and taken to execution; and I heard it said that some of the English, in their indignation against the Bishop and the Doctors, would have drawn their swords to attack them, if not to slay them, saying that the King was wasting his money on such as they. I also heard that when the Earl of Warwick, after this first sermon, complained to the Bishop and the Doctors, saying that the King was in a bad way, for Jeanne had escaped them, one of them replied: "Take no heed to it, my lord; we shall soon have her again."

The English were discontented with Maître Guillaume Manchon, the notary: they held him in suspicion as favourable to Jeanne, because he had not been willing to come to the Trial, and did not conduct himself to their liking.

MAÎTRE JEAN RICQUIER, *Priest, Curé of Hendicourt* [*testimony of no importance*].

## DEPOSITIONS AT DOMREMY: 1455.

*Twelve questions were prepared for information to be taken in the country of the late Jeanne, commonly called the Maid.*

### EXAMINATION OF WITNESSES.

JEAN MOREL, *of Greux, labourer*.

Jeanne was born at Domremy and was baptised at the Parish Church of Saint Remy, in that place. Her father was named Jacques d'Arc, her mother Isabelle—both labourers living together at Domremy. They were, as I saw and knew, good and faithful Catholics, labourers of good repute and honest life. I lived much with them, I was one of the godfathers of Jeannette. She had three godmothers—the wife of Etienne Thévenin, Beatrix, Widow Estellin, both living at Domremy; and Jeannette, widow of Thiesselin of Viteaux, living at Neufchâteau. From her early youth, Jeannette was brought up with care in the Faith, and in good morals; she was so good that all the village of Domremy loved her. Jeannette knew her Belief and her *Pater* and *Ave* as well as any of her companions. She had modest ways, as beseemed one whose parents were not rich. Up to the time she left her parents she followed the plough and sometimes minded the cattle in the fields. Also she did the usual duties of women, such as spinning, and other things. I know she liked to go often to the Hermitage of the Blessed Marie of Bermont, near Domremy; I often saw her go there. She was there when her parents thought her with the plough or in the fields; and when she heard the Mass-bell, if she were in the fields, she would go back to the village and to the Church, in order to hear Mass. I have been witness of this many times. I have seen her confess at Easter-tide and other solemn Feasts. I saw her confess to Messire

Guillaume Fronte, who was then Curé of the Parish of Saint Remy.

On the subject of the Fairies' tree, I have heard that the Fairies came there long ago to dance; but, since the Gospel of Saint John has been read under the tree, they come no more. At the present day, on the Sunday when in the Holy Church of God the Introit to the Mass 'Laetare Jerusalem' is sung, called with us 'the Sunday of the Wells,' the young maidens and youths of Domremy are accustomed to go there, and also in the spring and summer and on festival days; they dance there and have a feast. On their return, they go dancing and playing to the Well of the Thorn, where they drink and amuse themselves, gathering flowers. Jeanne the Maid went there, like all the other girls at those times, and did as they did; but I never heard say that she went there alone, either to the tree or to the well—which is nearer to the village than the tree—or that she went for any other purpose than to walk about and play like her companions. When Jeanne left her father's house, she went two or three times to Vaucouleurs to speak to the Bailly. I heard it said that the Lord Charles, then Duke of Lorraine, wished to see her, and gave her a black horse.

I have no more to say, except that in the month of July I was at Chalons, at the time when it was said that the King was going to Rheims to be anointed.[119] I found Jeanne at Chalons and she made me a present of a red dress she had been wearing. I know nothing of the enquiry made at Domremy. When Jeanne went to Neufchâteau on account of the soldiers, she was always in the company of her father and mother, who stayed there four days, and then returned to Domremy. I am sure of what I say, because I went with the rest to Neufchâteau

---

[119] Jeanne's father went also to Rheims for the coronation. There still exists in the old accounts of the town an item for his expenses at the inn; and, in the Compte of the Treasurer Raguier there is also an entry of 60 livres tournois, paid Jeanne to give to her father. On the day after the coronation, Jeanne obtained from the King an exemption from taxes for the village of Domremy and Greux: this document, dated July 31st, 1429, still exists in the Archives of France. This exemption from taxes has now lapsed.

and I saw Jeannette there with her parents.

MESSIRE DOMINIQUE JACOB, *Curé of the Parish Church of Montier-sur-Saulx*.

Jeanne was older than I. I knew her and remember her for the three or four years before her departure from home. She was a well-brought-up girl, and well-behaved; and she often attended Church. Sometimes, when the village bell rang for service, I saw her kneel down and pray with great devotion.

BEATRIX, *widow of Estellin, labourer, of Domremy*.

Jeannette was born, at Domremy, of Jacques d'Arc and Isabelle, his wife, labourers, good and true Catholics, honest folk and worthy, according to their ability, but not rich. She was baptised at the Church of Saint Remy. She had as god-fathers, Jean Morel, Jean de Laxart, and the late Jean Raiguesson; and as god-mothers, Jeannette, widow Thiesselin, Jeannette Thévenin, and myself. Jeanne was suitably instructed in the Catholic Faith, like other young girls of her age. Up to her departure, she was properly brought up; she was a chaste maiden, and of modest habits. She frequented with great devotion, churches and holy places; and, after the village of Domremy was burned, she went on Feast Days to attend Mass at Greux. She confessed willingly at festivals, principally at the Feast of the most Holy Easter, the Resurrection of our Lord Jesus Christ. I do not think there was any one better than she in our two villages. She employed herself at home with many duties in the house, spinning hemp or wool, following the plough, or going to harvest, according to the season. When it was her father's turn, she sometimes kept the cattle and the flocks of the village for him. When Jeannette went to Neufchâteau, all the village had fled. I saw her there, always with her father and mother. Up to her going into France, Jeannette had never obeyed any one or worked for any one but her father.

JEANNETTE, *wife of Thévenin, cartwright* [*gave*

*evidence similar to the preceding, as did*] JEAN MOEN, *of Domremy, cartwright, living at Coussey, near Neufchâteau*, [*and*] JACQUIER *of Saint Amance, near Nancy.*

MESSIRE ETIENNE OF SIONNE, *Curé of the Parish Church of Roncessey-sous-Neufchâteau.*

Many times I heard Messire Guillaume Fronte, in his lifetime Curé of Domremy, say that Jeanne the Maid was a simple and good girl, pious, well-brought-up, and God-fearing, and without her like in the whole village. Often did she confess her sins; and, if she had had money, she would have given it to him, he told me, to say Masses. Every day, when he celebrated Mass, she was there. I heard it said by a great number of persons that Jeannette, when she went to Neufchâteau, lived with a worthy woman named La Rousse; and that she always remained in the company of her father and the other inhabitants of Domremy, who had fled there.

JEANNETTE, *widow of Thiesselin of Viteaux, formerly clerk at Neufchâteau.*

I often saw her confess to Messire Guillaume Fronte, the Curé of the parish. She never swore, and, to affirm strongly, contented herself with saying, "Without fail!" She was no dancer; and, sometimes, when the others were singing and dancing, she went to prayer. Jeannette was fond of work, spinning, looking after the house, and, when necessary, taking her turn at minding her father's cattle. There is a tree by us called the Ladies' Tree, because, in ancient days, the Sieur Pierre Granier, Seigneur de Bourlement, and a lady called Fée met under this tree and conversed together: I have heard it read in a romance. The Seigneurs of Domremy and their ladies—at least, the Lady Beatrix, wife of Pierre de Bourlement, and the said Pierre—accompanied by their daughters, came sometimes to walk round this tree. In the same way, every year the young girls and youths of Domremy came to walk there, on the Laetare Sunday—called 'the Sunday of the Wells': they ate and danced there, and went to drink at the Well of the Thorn. But I do not remember if Jeanne were ever under this tree. I never heard anything evil said about her on account of this tree.

LOUIS DE MARTIGNY, *Squire, living at Martigny-les-Gerbonveaux, near Neufchâteau.*

I heard that Jeanne, when she wanted to go into France, went first to the Bailly of Chaumont, and afterwards to the Lord Duke de Lorraine, who gave her a horse and some money. Bertrand de Poulengey, Jean de Metz, Jean Dieu-le-Ward, and Colet de Vienne afterwards conducted her to the King.

THÉVENIN LE ROYER, *Cartwright, a native of Chermisey, near Neufchâteau, residing at Domremy, husband of one of Jeanne's God-mothers* [*evidence similar to the preceding*].

BERTRAND LACLOPPE, *thatcher, of Domremy.*

One day, a man[120] of Burey-le-Petit came to seek Jeanne at Domremy, and took her to speak with the Bailly of Vaucouleurs: I heard say that it was this Bailly who sent her to the King. The soldiers having come to Domremy, all the people of the village went to take refuge at Neufchâteau. Jeannette and her parents did as the others did: she stayed there about four days, always in their company.

PERRIN LE DRAPIER, *of Domremy, Churchwarden of the Parish Church and Bell-ringer.*

From her earliest years till her departure, Jeannette the Maid was a good girl, chaste, simple, modest, never blaspheming God nor the Saints, fearing God. She loved to go to Church and confessed often. I can attest what I say, for I was then attached to the Church of Saint Remy, and often I saw Jeanne come there to Mass and other Offices. When I forgot to ring for Service, Jeanne scolded me, saying I had done wrong; and she promised to give me some of the wool of her flock if I would ring more diligently. Often she went with her sister and others to the

---

[120] Durand Laxart, her uncle.

Church and Hermitage of Bermont. She was very charitable, and very industrious, employed herself in spinning and divers other works in her father's house; sometimes she went to the plough, or took care of the flock when it was her turn. When Jeanne left her father's house, she went with her uncle Durand Laxart to Vaucouleurs, to seek Robert de Baudricourt, who was then captain there.

GERARD GUILLEMETTE, *labourer, of Greux.*

When Jeanne left her father's house, I saw her pass before my father's house, with her uncle Durand Laxart. "Adieu," she said to my father, "I am going to Vaucouleurs." I heard afterwards that she had gone to France. I was at Neufchâteau with Jeanne and her parents. I saw her always with them, excepting that, for three or four days, she did, under their eyes, help the hostess at whose house they were lodging,—an honest woman named La Rousse. I know well that they only remained at Neufchâteau four or five days. When the soldiers had gone, Jeanne returned to Domremy with her parents.

HAUVIETTE, *wife of Gerard of Syonne, near Neufchâteau.*

She was a good girl, simple and gentle; she went willingly and often to Church, and Holy places. Often she was bashful when others reproached her with going too devotedly to Church. There was a tree in the neighbourhood that, from ancient days, had been called the Ladies' Tree. It was said formerly that ladies, called Fairies, came under this tree; but I never heard any one say they had been seen there. The young people of the village were accustomed to go to this tree, taking food with them, and to the Well of the Thorn.[121]

[*Ad fontem Rannorum*, or, "*ad Rannos*"] on the Sunday of 'Laetare Jerusalem,'[122] called the Sunday of the

---

[121] This is also called the "Fontaine aux Groseilliers"; the Latin name is probably intended for Rhamnus, the Buckthorn.
[122] Mid-Lent Sunday, the 4th Sunday in Lent; so-called, because the introit for the day begins, "*Laetare Jerusalem*," &c.

Wells. I often went there with Jeanne, who was my friend, and with other young girls on the said Sunday of the Wells. We ate there, ran about, and played. Also, we took nuts to this tree and well. I did not know of Jeanne's departure: I wept much; I loved her dearly for her goodness and because she was my friend. Jeanne was always with her father and mother at Neufchâteau. I also was at Neufchâteau, and saw her there all the time.

JEAN WATERIN, *labourer, of Greux*.

I saw Jeannette very often. In our childhood, we often followed together her father's plough, and we went together with the other children of the village to the meadows or pastures. Often, when we were all at play, Jeannette would retire alone to "talk with God." I and the others laughed at her for this. She was simple and good, frequenting the Church and Holy places. Often, when she was in the fields and heard the bells ring, she would drop on her knees.

GERARDIN, *labourer, of Epinal*.

Of her departure for Vaucouleurs I know nothing. But, at the time when she was thinking of leaving the village, she said to me, one day: "Gossip, if you were not a Burgundian, I would tell you something." I thought it was on the subject of some marriage which she might have in her head. After her departure, I saw her at Chalons,—I and four other inhabitants of this place. She told us she feared nothing but treason.

SIMONIN MUSNIER, *labourer, of Domremy*.

I was brought up with Jeannette, close to her house. I know that she was good, simple and pious, and that she feared God and the Saints. She loved Church and Holy places; she was very charitable, and liked to take care of the sick. I know this of a surety, for, in my childhood, I fell ill, and it was she who nursed me. When the Church bells rang, I have seen her kneel down and make the sign of the Cross.

ISABELLETTE, *wife of Gerardin, labourer, of Epinal.*

From my childhood I knew the parents of Jeannette; as to Jeannette, herself, I knew her in my youth and as long as she remained with her parents. She was very hospitable to the poor, and would even sleep on the hearth in order that the poor might lie in her bed. She was not fond of playing, at which we, her companions, complained. She liked work; and would spin, labour with her father, look after the house, and sometimes mind the sheep. She was never seen idling in the roads; she was more often in Church at prayer.

I often saw her at confession, for she was my gossip, and god-mother to my son Nicolas. I was often with her, and saw her go to confession to Messire Guillaume, who was then our Curé. When all was well at the château, the Seigneurs and their ladies often came to walk beneath the Ladies' Tree, on the Sunday of Laetare, which we call 'the Sunday of the Wells'; and on certain other days, in fine weather, they brought with them the village boys and girls. The Seigneur Pierre de Bourlement and his lady, who was from France, took me there on the said Sunday of the Wells many times in my childhood, with other children. It was the custom to go every year, on this Sunday, to play and walk round this tree. Jeannette went with us, we each brought provisions, and, the meal ended, went to refresh ourselves at the Well. The same thing takes place now, with our children.

MENGETTE, *wife of Jean Joyart, labourer.*

My father's house joined the house of Jacques d'Arc: so I knew her well. We often spun together, and together worked at the ordinary house-duties, whether by day or night. She was a good Christian, of good manners and well brought up. She loved the Church, and went there often, and gave alms from the goods of her father. She was a good girl, simple and pious—so much so that I and her companions told her she was too pious.

MESSIRE JEAN COLIN, *Curé of the Parish Church at Domremy and Canon of the Collegiate Church of Saint-*

*Nicolas de Brixey, near Vaucouleurs.*

While Jeanne was at Vaucouleurs, she confessed to me two or three times. It seemed to me, to my knowledge, that she was an excellent girl, with all the signs of a perfect Christian and of a true Catholic; she was fond of going to Church. I saw her at Vaucouleurs, when she wanted to go into France, and saw her mount on horseback; with her were Bertrand de Poulengey, Jean de Metz, Colet de Vienne, horse-soldiers and servants of Robert de Baudricourt.

COLIN, *son of Jean Colin, labourer.*

I heard Durand Laxart say, that she told him he must conduct her to Vaucouleurs, that she wished to go into France, and that she would tell her father she was going to the house of the said Durand to nurse his wife. And this, Durand told me, was done; and then, with the consent of her father, she went to Vaucouleurs to seek Robert de Baudricourt.

JEAN DE NOVELEMPORT, *Knight, called Jean de Metz.*

When Jeannette was at Vaucouleurs, I saw her dressed in a red dress, poor and worn; she lived at the house of one named Henri Leroyer. "What are you doing here, my friend?" I said to her. "Must the King be driven from the kingdom; and are we to be English?" "I am come here," she answered me, "to this royal town,[123] to speak to Robert de Baudricourt, to the end that he may conduct me or have me conducted to the King: but Robert cares neither for me nor for my words. Nevertheless, before the middle of Lent, I

---

[123] "*Ad cameram regis.*"

CHÂTEAU DE VAUCOULEURS,
Porte de France.

must be with the King—even if I have to wear down my feet to the knees! No one in the world—neither kings, nor dukes, nor the daughter of the King of Scotland,[124] nor any others—can recover the kingdom of France; there is no succour to be expected save from me; but, nevertheless, I would rather spin with my poor mother— for this is not my proper estate: it is, however, necessary that I should go, and do this, because my Lord wills that I should do it." And when I asked her who this Lord was, she told me it was God. Then I pledged my faith to her, touching her hand, and promised that, with God's guidance, I would conduct her to the King. I asked her when she wished to start. "Sooner at once than to-morrow, and sooner to-morrow than later," she said. I asked her if she could make this journey, dressed as she was. She replied that she would willingly take a man's dress. Then I gave her the dress and equipment of one of my men. Afterwards, the inhabitants of Vaucouleurs had a man's dress made for her, with all the necessary requisites; I also procured for her a horse at the price of

---

[124] Margaret, daughter of James I. of Scotland, who was betrothed to Louis, afterwards Louis XI.

about sixteen francs. Thus dressed and mounted, and furnished with a safe-conduct from the Sieur Charles, Duke de Lorraine, she went to visit the said Lord Duke. I accompanied her as far as Toul. On the return to Vaucouleurs, the first Sunday in Lent,[125] which is called 'Dimanche des Bures'—and it will be, if I mistake not, twenty-seven years from that day to the coming Lent[126]— I and Bertrand de Poulengey, with two of my men, Colet de Vienne, the King's Messenger, and the Archer Richard, conducted the Maid to the King, who was then at Chinon. The journey was made at the expense of Bertrand de Poulengey and myself. We travelled for the most part at night, for fear of the Burgundians and the English, who were masters of the roads. We journeyed eleven days, always riding towards the said town of Chinon. On the way, I asked her many times if she would really do all she said. "Have no fear," she answered us, "what I am commanded to do, I will do; my brothers in Paradise have told me how to act: it is four or five years since my brothers in Paradise and my Lord—that is, God—told me that I must go and fight in order to regain the kingdom of France." On the way, Bertrand and I slept every night by her—Jeanne being at my side, fully dressed. She inspired me with such respect that for nothing in the world would I have dared to molest her; also, never did I feel towards her—I say it on oath—any carnal desire. On the way she always wished to hear Mass. She said to us: "If we can, we shall do well to hear Mass." But, for fear of being recognized, we were only able to hear it twice. I had absolute faith in her. Her words and her ardent faith in God inflamed me. I believe she was sent from God; she never swore, she loved to attend Mass, she confessed often, and was zealous in giving alms. Many times was I obliged to hand out to her the money she gave for the love of God. While we were with her, we found her always good, simple, pious, an excellent Christian, well-behaved, and God-fearing. When we arrived at Chinon,[127] we

---

[125] February 13th, 1428.
[126] 1455.
[127] March 6th, 1428.

presented ourselves to the King's Court and Council. I know she had there to submit to long enquiries.

MICHAEL LEBUIN, *labourer, of Domremy*.

I knew Jeannette from my earliest youth. Of Jeanne's departure for Vaucouleurs I knew nothing. But, one day—the Eve of Saint John the Baptist[128]—she said to me: "Between Coussy and Vaucouleurs there is a young girl, who, before the year is gone, will have the King of France consecrated." And, in truth, the following year the King was crowned at Rheims.[129] When Jeanne was a prisoner I saw Nicolas Bailly, Notary of Andelot, coming to Domremy, one day, with several other persons. At the request of Jean de Torcenay, Bailly of Chaumont for the pretended King of France and England, he proceeded to make enquiries into the conduct and life of Jeanne. But he could not induce the inhabitants of Vaucouleurs to depose. I believe that they questioned Jean Begot, at whose house they were staying. Their enquiry revealed nothing against Jeanne.

GEOFFROY DE FAY.

I saw Jeanne the Maid when she came to Maxey-sur-Vays.[130] When Jeanne came to Maxey, she came sometimes to my house. I always thought her a good girl, simple and pious. Many times I heard her speak; she said that she wished to go into France.

DURAND LAXART, *of Burey-le-Petit*.

Jeanne was of the family of Jeanne, my wife. I knew Jacques d'Arc and Isabelle, his wife, the parents of Jeanne the Maid: they were good and faithful Catholics, and of good repute. She was a girl of good disposition, devout, patient, loving the Church, going often to confession, and giving to the poor all that she could. I can attest this, having been witness thereof, both at Domremy and at my

[128] June 23rd, 1428.
[129] July 17th, 1429.
[130] Near Vaucouleurs.

own house at Burey, where she passed six weeks.[131] I went to fetch her from her father's and brought her to my house; she told me she wished to go into France, to the Dauphin, to have him crowned. "Was it not foretold formerly," she said to me, "that France should be desolated[132] by a woman, and should be restored by a maid?" She told me she wished to go, herself, and seek Robert de Baudricourt, in order that he might have her conducted to the place where the Dauphin was. But many times Robert told me to take her back to her father and to box her ears. When she saw that Robert would not do as she asked, she took some of my garments and said she would start. She departed, and I took her to Vaucouleurs [*i.e.* Saint-Nicolas[133]].—Thence she returned, and went with a safe-conduct to the Sieur Charles de Lorraine. The Duke saw her, spoke to her, and gave her four francs,[134] which Jeanne showed to me. She came back to Vaucouleurs; and the inhabitants bought for her a man's garments and a complete warlike equipment. Alain de Vaucouleurs and I bought her a horse for the price of twelve francs, which we paid, and which was repaid to us later by the Sieur Robert de Baudricourt. This done, Jean de Metz, Bertrand de Poulengey, Colet de Vienne, together with Richard the Archer and two men of the suite of Jean de Metz and Bertrand, conducted Jeanne to the place where the Dauphin was.

All this, as I now say it, I told to the King. I know no more, except that I saw her at Rheims at the King's crowning.

CATHERINE, *wife of Leroyer.*

Jeanne, when she had left her parents, was brought to our house at Vaucouleurs by Durand Laxart, her uncle;

---

[131] This covers the period of several visits, made between May 1428, and February 1429.

[132] The mother of Charles VII., who denied the legitimacy of her own son, being Burgundian at heart, and ratified the iniquitous Treaty of Troyes, so disastrous for France.

[133] In the text Vaucouleurs is an obvious misprint for Saint-Nicolas.

[134] He also gave her a horse; *cf.* previous depositions.

she wished to go to the place where the Dauphin was. I had occasion to know her well; she was an excellent girl, simple, gentle, respectful, well-conducted, loving to go to Church.

She lived with us at Vaucouleurs, at different times about three weeks. She spoke to the Sieur Robert de Baudricourt, that he might have her conducted to the Dauphin, but Sieur Robert would not listen to her. One day, I saw Robert de Baudricourt—then captain of Vaucouleurs—and Messire Jean Fournier, our Curé, come in to our house to visit her. After they were gone, she told me that the Priest had his stole, and that, in presence of the said captain, he adjured her, saying: "If you are an evil spirit, avaunt! If you are a good spirit, approach!" Then Jeanne drew near the Priest and threw herself at his knees: she said he was wrong to act so, for he had heard her in confession. When she saw that Robert refused to conduct her to the King, she said to me that, nevertheless, she would go and seek the Dauphin. "Do you not know," she said, "the prophecy which says that France, lost by a woman, shall be saved by a maiden from the Marches of Lorraine?" I did indeed remember the prophecy, and remained stupefied. Jacques Alain and Durand Laxart took her to Saint-Nicolas,[135] then came back with her to Vaucouleurs.

HENRI LEROYER, *cartwright, formerly of Vaucouleurs.*

Jeanne, when she came to Vaucouleurs, lodged in our house. She said to us, "It is necessary that I should go to the noble Dauphin; my Lord the King of Heaven wills that I should go; I go in the name of the King of Heaven; even if I have to drag myself thither on my knees, I shall go!" When she arrived at our house, she was wearing a woman's dress, of a red colour. At Vaucouleurs she received the gift of a man's dress and a complete

---

[135] Saint-Nicolas-du-Port—then a celebrated centre of pilgrimage—near Nancy. As both Poulengey and Laxart connect this pilgrimage with her visit to the Duke de Lorraine, whose residence was at Nancy, it is clear that Saint-Nicolas-du-Port is meant, and not the Chapel of St. Nicolas near Vaucouleurs.

equipment; then, mounted on a horse, she was conducted to the place where the Dauphin was, by Jean de Metz, Bertrand de Poulengey, and two of their servants—Colet de Vienne, and Richard the Archer. I saw them depart, all six, and Jeanne with them. When she spoke of leaving, she was asked how she thought she could effect such a journey and escape the enemy. "I fear them not," she answered, "I have a sure road: if the enemy are on my road, I have God with me, Who knows how to prepare the way to the Lord Dauphin. I was born to do this."

ALBERT D'OURCHES, *Seigneur of Ourches, near Commerey*.

I saw Jeanne at Vaucouleurs when she arrived to be taken to the King. Many times I heard her then say that she wished to go to the King, and that some one would conduct her to him, for it would be to the great benefit of the Dauphin.

This maiden always seemed to me very well behaved. I should have been well pleased to have had a daughter as good as she.

NICOLAS BAILLY, *Tabellion (Notary) and Deputy Royal at Andelot*.

As Tabellion I was appointed by the Sieur Jean de Torcenay, Knight, then Bailly of Chaumont, by the authority of the pretended King of France and England, and, with me, the late Gerard Petit—then Provost of the said Andelot[136]—to proceed to an enquiry on the subject of Jeanne, at that time detained in prison at Rouen. Many times, in her youth, I saw Jeanne before she left her father's house: she was a good girl, of pure life and good manners, a good Catholic who loved the Church and went often on pilgrimage to the Church of Bermont, and confessed nearly every month—as I learned from a number of the inhabitants of Domremy, whom I had to question on the subject at the time of the enquiry that I

[136] The village of Domremy, although in the territory of Lorraine, belonged to France, not to Lorraine; for administrative purposes it was a dependance of Champagne.

made with the Provost of Andelot. When I and the late Gerard made this enquiry, we examined twelve or fifteen witnesses. Afterwards, we certified the information before Simon de Thermes, Squire, Lieutenant of the Captain of Montclair.

GUILLOT JACQUIER, *of Andelot, King's Sergeant*; [*evidence similar to the preceding.*]

BERTRAND DE POULENGEY, *Squire*.

After her departure from her father's roof, I often saw Jeanne at Vaucouleurs and during the war. I remember often to have heard this Ladies' Tree spoken of. I have even sat beneath it, but that was a dozen years before I saw Jeanne. Jeanne came to Vaucouleurs, I think, about Ascension Day.[137] I saw her speaking to the Captain, Robert de Baudricourt. She told him that "she came to him in the name of her Lord; that the Dauphin must be compelled to persevere and to give battle to his enemies, that the Lord would give him succour before the middle of Lent; that the kingdom belonged not to him, the Dauphin, but to her Lord; that her Lord would have the Dauphin King and hold the kingdom in trust; that she would make him King, in spite of his enemies, and would conduct him to his coronation." "But who is this Lord of whom you speak?" asked Robert of her. "The King of Heaven," she replied. That time she went back to her father's house, accompanied by one of her uncles, named Durand Laxart. Later, towards the commencement of Lent, she came back to Vaucouleurs to seek companions, so as to go to the Dauphin. Then Jean de Metz and I offered to conduct her to the King—at that time Dauphin. After a pilgrimage to Saint-Nicolas, she went to seek the Lord Duke de Lorraine, who had sent her a safe-conduct and asked to see her. She then returned to Vaucouleurs and lodged in the house of Henry Leroyer. Then Jean de Metz and I, aided by many others of Vaucouleurs, so wrought that she put off her woman's dress, which was of

---

[137] May 13th, 1428.

a red colour;[138] we procured for her a tunic and man's dress—spurs, leggings, sword, and such-like—and a horse. Then we started with her to seek the Dauphin, together with Julian, my servant, Jean de Honecourt, servant of Jean de Metz, Colet de Vienne, and Richard the Archer. On starting, the first day, fearing to be taken by the Burgundians and the English, we travelled all night. Jeanne said to me and to Jean de Metz, while we were journeying, that it would be well for us to hear Mass; but while we were in the enemy's country, we could not, for fear of being recognized. At night, Jeanne slept beside John de Metz and myself, fully dressed and armed. I was young then; nevertheless I never felt towards her any desire: I should never have dared to molest her, because of the great goodness which I saw in her. We were eleven days on the road, during which we had many anxieties. But Jeanne told us always that we had nothing to fear, and that, once arrived at Chinon, the noble Dauphin would show us good countenance. She entirely abstained from swearing. I felt myself inspired by her words, for I saw she was indeed a messenger of God; never did I see in her any evil, but always she was as good as if she had been a saint. We took our road thus, and, without many obstacles, gained Chinon, where the King—then Dauphin—was staying. There the said maid was presented to the nobles in the King's suite, to whom I refer for the actions of the said Jeanne.

MESSIRE HENRI ARNOLIN, *of Gontrecourt-le-Château, near Commercy, Priest*; [*testimony of no importance*].

MESSIRE JEAN LEFUMEUX, *of Vaucouleurs, Canon of the Chapel of Saint Mary at Vaucouleurs, and Curé of the Parish Church of Ugny.*

I know that Jeanne came to Vaucouleurs, and said that she wished to go to the Dauphin. I was then young, and attached to the Chapel of the Blessed Mary at Vaucouleurs. I often saw Jeanne in this Chapel; she behaved with great piety, attended Mass in the morning,

---

[138] See Deposition of Jean Morel.

and remained a long time in prayer. I have also seen her[139] in the crypt of the Chapel on her knees before the Blessed Mary, her face sometimes bent to the ground, sometimes raised to heaven. She was a good and holy maiden.

JEAN JACQUARD, *labourer, of Greux; son of Jean, called* GUILLEMETTE; [*evidence similar to the preceding*].

## DEPOSITIONS AT ORLEANS: 1455.

JEAN,[140] *Bastard of Orleans, Count de Dunois*.

I think that Jeanne was sent by God, and that her behaviour in war was a fact divine rather than human. Many reasons make me think so.

I was at Orleans, then besieged by the English, when the report spread that a young girl, commonly called the Maid, had just passed through Gien, going to the noble Dauphin, with the avowed intention of raising the siege of Orleans and conducting the Dauphin to Rheims for his anointing. I was then entrusted with the care of the town of Orleans and was Lieutenant-General of the King in affairs of war. In order to be better informed on the subject of this young girl, I sent to the King the Sieur de Villars, Seneschal of Beaucaire, and Janet de Tilly,[141] who was afterwards Bailly of Vermandois.

They returned from the King, and reported to me publicly, in presence of all the people of Orleans [assembled] to know the truth, that they had seen the Maid arrive at Chinon. They said that the King at first had no wish to listen to her: she even remained two days, waiting, until she was permitted to present herself before him, although she persisted in saying that she was come to raise the siege of Orleans, and to conduct the Dauphin

---

[139] This Chapel in the crypt may still be seen at Vaucouleurs.

[140] Jean, a natural son of Louis, Duke d'Orléans, was brought up with the family of Orleans, and acknowledged by Valentine, the widowed Duchess, after the murder of his father in 1407. At 25 years of age, in company with de Gaucourt, he defeated the English under Warwick at Montargis in 1427, and afterwards defended Orleans till its relief in 1429. He was created Count de Dunois, in 1439.

[141] Then Captain of Blois.

to Rheims, in order that he might be consecrated; she at once asked for men, arms and horses.

Three weeks or a month elapsed, during which the King had her examined by Clergy, Prelates, and Doctors in Theology, as to her words and deeds, in order to know if he might receive her with safety. Then the King assembled an army to conduct to Orleans a convoy of supplies.

COUNT DE DUNOIS,
Bastard of Orleans.

Hearing the opinion of the Clergy and Prelates that there was no evil in this Maid, the King sent her with the Lord Archbishop of Rheims,[142] then Chancellor of France, and the Sieur de Gaucourt, then Grand Steward, to Blois, where those were who had the charge of escorting the convoy—that is, the Sieurs de Rais[143] and de Boussac,

---

[142] Regnault de Chartres.
[143] Gilles de Laval, Seigneur de Rais, notorious for the horrible excesses which brought him to the scaffold in 1440.

Marshals of France; de Coulent, Admiral of France; La Hire; and Ambroise de Loré, who was afterwards Governor of Paris. All, at the head of the army transporting the convoy, came, with Jeanne, in good order, by way of the Sologne, to the Loire, facing the Church of Saint Loup. But the English were there in great number: and the army escorting the convoy did not appear to me, nor to the other captains, in sufficient force to resist them and to ensure the entrance of the convoy on that side. It was necessary to load the convoy on boats, which were procured with difficulty. But to reach Orleans it was necessary to sail against the stream, and the wind was altogether contrary.

Then Jeanne said to me: "Are you the Bastard of Orleans?" "Yes," I answered; "and I am very glad of your coming!" "Is it you who said I was to come on this side [of the river], and that I should not go direct to the side where Talbot and the English are?" "Yes, and those more wise than I are of the same opinion, for our greater success and safety." "In God's Name," she then said, "the counsel of My Lord is safer and wiser than yours. You thought to deceive me, and it is yourselves who are deceived, for I bring you better succour than has ever come to any general or town whatsoever—the succour of the King of Heaven. This succour does not come from me, but from God Himself, Who, at the prayers of Saint Louis and Saint Charlemagne, has had compassion on the town of Orleans, and will not suffer the enemy to hold at the same time the Duke[144] and his town!"

At that moment, the wind, being contrary, and thereby preventing the boats going up the river and reaching Orleans, turned all at once and became favourable. They stretched the sails; and I ordered the boats to the town, which I entered with Brother Nicolas de Geresme, then Grand Prior in France of the Order of Rhodes. We passed before the Church of Saint Loup in spite of the English. From that time I put good hope in her, even more than before. I had begged her to cross the river and to enter the

---

[144] The Duke was then a prisoner in England.

town, where many were longing for her. She had made a difficulty about it, not wishing, she said, to abandon her army or her followers who were duly confessed, penitent, and of good will; and on their account she refused to come. Thereupon, I went in search of the captains who had charge of the convoy and the army, and besought them, for the welfare of the King, to allow Jeanne to enter Orleans at once, and that they should go up the river—they and the army—to Blois, where they should cross the Loire so as to return to Orleans, for there was no nearer place of crossing. They consented; and Jeanne then came with me. She had in her hand a banner, white in colour, on which was an image of Our Lord holding in His Hand a lily. La Hire crossed the Loire at the same time as she, and entered the city with her and ourselves. All this was much more the work of God than of man: the sudden change of wind immediately Jeanne had announced it; the bringing in of the convoy of supplies in spite of the English, who were in much greater force than all the King's army; and the statement of Jeanne that she had seen Saint Louis and Saint Charles the Great praying God for the safety of the King and of the City.

Another circumstance made me think these deeds were the work of God. I wished to go towards the army which had turned back on Blois and which was marching to the relief of Orleans; Jeanne would not wait for them nor consent that I should go to meet them: she wished to summon the English to raise the siege at once on pain of being themselves attacked. She did, in fact, summon them by a letter which she wrote to them in French, in which she told them, in very simple terms, that they were to retire from the siege and return to England, or else she would bring against them a great attack, which would force them to retreat. Her letter was sent to Lord Talbot. From that hour, the English—who, up to that time, could, I affirm, with two hundred of their men, have put to rout 800 or 1,000 of ours—were unable, with all their power, to resist 400 or 500 French; they had to be driven into their forts, where they took refuge, and from whence they dared not come forth.

There is another fact which made me believe she was from God. The 27th of May,[145] very early in the morning, we began the attack on the Boulevard[146] of the bridge. Jeanne was there wounded by an arrow which penetrated half-a-foot between the neck and the shoulder; but she continued none the less to fight, taking no remedy for her wound. The attack lasted throughout, from the morning until 8 o'clock in the evening, without hope of success for us: for which reason I was anxious that the army should retire into the town. The Maid then came to me, praying me to wait yet a little longer. Thereupon she mounted her horse, retired to a vineyard, all alone by herself, remained in prayer about half an hour, then, returning and seizing her banner by both hands, she placed herself on the edge of the trench. At sight of her the English trembled, and were seized with sudden fear; our people, on the contrary, took courage and began to mount and assail the Boulevard, not meeting any resistance. Thus was the Boulevard taken and the English therein put to flight: all were killed, among them Classidas[147] and the other principal English captains of the Bastille, who, thinking to gain the Bridge Tower, fell into the river, where they were drowned. This Classidas was he who had spoken of the Maid with the greatest contempt and insult.

The Bastille taken, we re-entered the town of Orleans—the Maid and all the army—where we were received with enthusiasm. Jeanne was taken to her house, to receive the care which her wound required. When the surgeon had dressed it, she began to eat, contenting herself with four or five slices of bread dipped in wine and water, without, on that day, having eaten or

---

[145] 7th of May.

[146] Antiquarians state that the Café le Bœuf at Orleans covers the ancient "Boulevard" captured by Jeanne d'Arc. This redoubt adjoined the "Tourelles" and was close to the bridge of Orleans. Many steps below ground, and entered from the Café le Bœuf, is a room of carefully constructed masonry, being the interior of a tower, with embrasures for cannon, and iron rings to which cannons were attached.

[147] *i.e.*, William Glasdale, Bailly of Alençon. He was Captain of the Fort of the Tourelles, called here the Bridge Tower.

drunk anything else.

The next day, early in the morning, the English came out of their camp and placed themselves in order of battle. At this sight, Jeanne got up and put on a light coat of mail; she forbade the English to be attacked or in any way molested but [gave orders] that they should be allowed to depart, which they did, without any pursuit. From that moment the town was delivered.

After the deliverance of Orleans, the Maid, with myself and the other captains, went to seek the King at the Castle of Loches, praying him to attack immediately the towns and the camps on the Loire, Mehun, Beaugency, Jargeau, in order to make his consecration at Rheims more free and sure. This she besought the King often, in the most urgent manner, to hasten, without longer delay. The King used the greatest haste possible, and sent, for this purpose, the Duke d'Alençon, myself and other captains, as well as Jeanne, to reduce these towns and camps. All were reduced in a few days—thanks alone, as I believe, to the intervention of the Maid.

After the deliverance of Orleans, the English assembled together a numerous army, to defend the aforesaid towns, which they occupied. When we had invested the camp and bridge of Beaugency, the English army arrived at the camp of Meung-sur-Loire, which was still under their control. But this army could not come to the help of the English besieged in the camp of Beaugency. At the news of the taking of this camp, all the English divisions joined together into one complete army; and we thought they would offer us battle: we made our dispositions accordingly. In presence of the Constable, myself, and the other captains, the Duke d'Alençon asked Jeanne what was to be done. She answered thus, in a loud voice: "Have all of you good spurs?" "What do you mean?" asked those present of her; "are we, then, to turn our backs?" "Nay," she replied, "it is the English who will not defend themselves, and will be beaten; and you must have good spurs to pursue them." And it fell out thus, as she had predicted: the English took to flight, and of killed and prisoners there were more than 4,000.

At Loches, after the raising of the siege of Orleans, I remember that, one day, the King, being in his private room with the Sieur Christopher d'Harcourt, the Bishop of Castres,[148] his Confessor, and the Sieur de Trèves, who was formerly Chancellor of France,[149] Jeanne and I went to seek him. Before entering, she knocked at the door; as soon as she had entered, she knelt before the King, and, embracing his knees, said these words: "Noble Dauphin! hold no longer these many and long councils, but come quickly to Rheims to take the crown for which you are worthy!" "Is it your Counsel who told you this?" said Christopher d'Harcourt. "Yes," she answered, "and my Counsel urges me to this most of all." "Will you not say, here, in presence of the King," added the Bishop, "what manner of Counsel it is which thus speaks to you?" "I think I understand," she said, colouring, "what you want to know; and I will tell you willingly." Then said the King: "Jeanne, will it please you to say, in presence of the persons who are listening to us, what has been asked you?" "Yes, Sire," she answered. And then she said this, or something approaching it: "When I am vexed that faith is not readily placed in what I wish to say in God's Name, I retire alone, and pray to God. I complain to Him that those whom I address do not believe me more readily; and, my prayer ended, I hear a Voice which says to me: 'Daughter of God! go on! go on! go on! I will be thy Help: go on!' And when I hear this Voice, I have great joy. I would I could always hear it thus." And, in repeating to us this language of her Voice, she was—strange to say!—in a marvellous rapture, raising her eyes to Heaven.

After the victories of which I have just spoken, the nobles of the Blood Royal and the captains wished the King to go into Normandy, and not to Rheims. But the Maid was always of opinion that it was necessary to go to

---

[148] Gerard Machet, according to the *Chronique de la Pucelle*; he was not Bishop until after the death of Jeanne.

[149] Robert le Maçon, Chancellor, in 1418, was harassed by the opposition of the Burgundian faction and the favourites of the Dauphin. He retired in 1421, and acted henceforward as a simple Councillor.

Rheims, that the King should be consecrated, giving as a reason that, if once the King were consecrated and crowned, the power of his adversaries would decline, and that in the end they would be past the power of doing any injury, either to him or to his kingdom. And all consented to her opinion. The place where the King first halted, with his army, was under the town of Troyes; he there took counsel with the nobles of the Blood, and the other captains, to decide whether they should remain before this town, in order to lay siege to it, or whether it would not better avail to pass on and march straight to Rheims, leaving Troyes alone. The Council were divided in opinion, and no one knew which course to pursue, when Jeanne suddenly arrived, and appeared in the Council. "Noble Dauphin," she said, "order your people to come and besiege the town of Troyes, and lose no more time in such long councils. In God's Name, before three days are gone, I will bring you into this town by favour or force, and greatly will the false Burgundy be astounded." Then Jeanne, putting herself at the head of the army, had the tents placed right against the trenches of the town, and executed many marvellous manœuvres which had not been thought of by two or three accomplished generals working together. And so well did she work during the night, that, the next day, the Bishop[150] and citizens came all trembling and quaking to place their submission in the King's hands. Afterwards, it was known that, at the moment when she had told the King's Council not to pass by the town, the inhabitants had suddenly lost heart, and had occupied themselves only in seeking refuge in the Churches. The town of Troyes once reduced, the King went to Rheims, where he found complete submission, and where he was consecrated and crowned.

Jeanne was accustomed to repair daily to Church at the time of Vespers, or towards evening; she had the bells rung for half-an-hour, and collected together all the Mendicant Friars who were following the army. Then she

---

[150] Jean Leguise, ennobled by Charles VII. for his share in the surrender of the town.

began to pray, and had an anthem in honour of the Blessed Mary, Mother of God, sung by the Mendicant Friars.

When the King came to La Ferté and to Crespy-en-Valois, the people ran about him, crying "Noel!" The Maid was then riding between the Archbishop of Rheims and myself: "This is a good people," she said to us; "I have seen none elsewhere who rejoiced as much at the coming of so noble a King. How happy should I be if, when my days are done, I might be buried here!" "Jeanne," then said the Archbishop to her, "in what place do you hope to die?" "Where it shall please God," she answered; "for I am not certain of either the time or the place, any more than you are yourself. Would it might please God, my Creator, that I might retire now, abandon arms and return to serve my father and mother and to take care of their sheep with my sister and my brothers, who would be so happy to see me again!"

RHEIMS CATHEDRAL.

There was never any one more sober. I often heard it said by the Sieur Jean d'Aulon, Knight, now Seneschal of

Beaucaire, who had been appointed by the King to watch over her, as being the wisest and most worthy in the army, that he did not think there had ever been a more chaste woman. Neither I nor others, when we were with her, had ever an evil thought: there was in her something divine.

Fifteen days after the Earl of Suffolk[151] had been made prisoner at the taking of Jargeau, a writing was sent to him containing four lines, in which it was said that a Maid should come from the Oak-wood who would ride on the backs of the archers and against them.[152]

Although Jeanne sometimes spoke in jest of the affairs of war, and although, to encourage the soldiers, she may have foretold events which were not realized, nevertheless, when she spoke seriously of the war, and of her deeds and her mission, she only affirmed earnestly that she was sent to raise the siege of Orleans, and to succour the oppressed people of that town and the neighbouring places, and to conduct the King to Rheims that he might be consecrated.

SIEUR DE GAUCOURT.[153]

I was at the Castle of the town of Chinon when Jeanne arrived there, and I saw her when she presented herself before the King's Majesty with great lowliness and simplicity; a poor little shepherdess! I heard her say these words: "Most noble Lord Dauphin, I am come and am sent to you from God to give succour to the kingdom and

---

[151] William de la Pole, Earl of Suffolk, Grand Steward of the King of England.

[152] The prophecy of Merlin, as it appears in MS. 7301 of the Bibliothèque Nationale, runs: "*Descendit virgo dorsum sagittari et flores virgineos obscultabit.*"

[153] Raoul, *not* Jean, de Gaucourt, Grand Steward, born 1370. Fought, in 1394, under the banner of Jean de Nevers, afterwards Duke of Burgundy, for Sigismund, King of Hungary, against Bajazet; and was knighted on the field of Nicopolis, from which only himself, his leader, and twenty-two other French nobles escaped. He defended Harfleur against Henry V., in 1415, and was a prisoner for ten years, being one of those specially named by Henry in his dying commands to Bedford as prisoners "to be kept." In 1425, he was ransomed for the sum of 20,000 gold crowns; in 1427, he aided Dunois at the victory of Montargis, and afterwards in the defence of Orleans.

to you."

After having seen and heard her, the King, so as to be better instructed about her, put her under the protection of Guillaume Bellier, his Major-Domo, my Lieutenant at Chinon, afterwards Bailly of Troyes,[154] whose wife was most devout and of the best reputation. Then he had her visited by the Clergy, by Doctors, and by Prelates, to know if he could lawfully put faith in her. Her deeds and words were examined during three weeks, not only at Chinon, but at Poitiers. The Examinations finished, the Clergy decided that there was nothing evil in her deeds nor in her words. After numerous interrogations, they ended by asking her what sign she could furnish, that her words might be believed? "The sign I have to shew," she replied, "is to raise the siege of Orleans!" Afterwards, she took leave of the King, and came to Blois, where she armed herself for the first time, to conduct a convoy of supplies to Orleans and to succour the inhabitants.

[On the subject of the sudden change of wind and of the way in which the convoy of supplies was brought into Orleans, the witness deposed as the Sieur de Dunois. He added only this: Jeanne had expressly predicted that, before long, the weather and the wind would change; and it happened as she had foretold. She had, in like manner, stated that the convoy would enter freely into the town.

The declaration of the witness agrees equally with that of the Sieur de Dunois as to the taking of the Bastille, the raising of the siege, and the expulsion of the English.

On all the other points the Sieur de Gaucourt is also in perfect agreement, in matter and form, with the said Sieur de Dunois, as to all that concerns the setting free of Orleans, the taking of the camps and the towns on the borders of the Loire.

He agrees equally on all points with what concerns the journey of the King for the ceremony of his consecration at Rheims.

---

[154] Quicherat thinks there is an error of copy here; that Bellier could not have been Bailly of Troyes when that town was in the hands of the English, nor could he at any time have combined so high an office with the lieutenancy of Chinon.

Jeanne, he adds, was abstemious in food and drink; nothing came from her lips but excellent words, which could serve only for edification and good example. No one could be more chaste, ... she had always at night a woman in her room. She confessed herself frequently, being often in prayer, hearing Mass every day, and constantly receiving the Sacrament of the Eucharist; she would not suffer any to use in her presence shameful or blasphemous words, and by her speech and actions she shewed how much she held such things in horror.]

MAÎTRE FRANÇOIS GARIVEL, *Councillor-General to the King.*

I remember that, at the time of the coming of Jeanne the Maid, the King sent her to Poitiers, where she lodged with Maître Jean Rabateau, then King's Advocate in Parliament. In this town of Poitiers were deputed [to examine Jeanne], by the King's Order, certain venerable Doctors and Masters,—to wit, Pierre de Versailles, then Abbot of Talmont, afterwards Bishop of Meaux; Jean Lambert; Guillaume Aimery, of the Order of Saint Dominic; Pierre Séguin, of the Carmelite Order, Doctors in Theology; Mathieu Message, and Guillaume Le Marie, Bachelors in Theology, with many others of the King's Councillors, licentiates in Canon and Civil Laws. Many times and often, during the space of three weeks, they examined Jeanne, studying and considering her deeds and words; and finally, taking into consideration her condition and her answers, they said that she was a simple girl, who, when interrogated, persisted in her answer, that she was sent from the God of Heaven in favour of the noble Dauphin, to replace him in his kingdom, to raise the siege of Orleans, and to conduct the King to Rheims for his consecration; and that first she must write to the English and command them to retire, for such was the Will of God.

When I asked Jeanne why she called the King *Dauphin*, and not *King*, she replied that she should not call him King till he had been crowned and anointed at Rheims, to which city she meant to conduct him.

Afterwards, the Clergy told Jeanne she ought to shew them a sign by which it might be believed that she was sent from God; but she replied: "The sign given to me from God is to raise the siege of Orleans; I have no fear that it will be done, if the King will give me soldiers, as few as he may like."

She was a simple shepherd-maiden, who confessed often; she was entirely devoted to God, and frequently received the Sacrament of the Eucharist.

At last, after long examinations made at great length by clerics of various faculties, all decided and concluded that the King might lawfully receive her, and might send a body of soldiers to the siege of Orleans, for that there was nothing found in her which was not Catholic and reasonable.

GUILLAUME DE RICARVILLE,[155] *Seigneur de Ricarville, Steward to the King.*

I was in Orleans—then besieged by the English—with the Count de Dunois and many other captains, when news came that there had passed through the town of Gien a shepherdess, called the Maid, conducted by two or three gentlemen of Lorraine, from which country she came; that this Maid said she was come to raise the siege of Orleans, and that afterwards she would lead the King to his anointing; for thus had she been commanded by God.

Notwithstanding this, she was not readily received by the King, who desired that she should first be examined, and that he should know something of her life and estate, and if it were lawful for him to receive her. Therefore, the Maid, by the King's order, was examined by many Prelates, Doctors, and Clergy, who found evidence in her of good life, honest estate, and praiseworthy repute; nor was there aught in her which should cause her to be repelled.

---

[155] Master of the Horse, Counsellor and Steward to the Court. He was made prisoner in 1437, but ransomed from the English for 500 crowns. In 1459, he was sent by Charles VII. to Bordeaux, in order to settle a dispute between the municipal authority and some English ships. He was living in 1472, and in receipt of a pension from Louis XI.

She lived honourably, most soberly as to food and drink, was chaste and devout, hearing Mass daily, and confessing often, communicating with fervent devotion every week. She reproved the soldiers when they blasphemed or took God's Name in vain; also when they did any evil or violence. I never observed in her aught deserving reproof, and from her manner of life and actions I believe she was inspired by God.

MAÎTRE REGINALD THIERRY, *Dean of the Church of Meung-sur-Yèvre; Surgeon to the King.*

I saw Jeanne with the King at Chinon, and heard what she said; to wit, that she was sent from God to the noble Dauphin, to raise the Siege of Orleans, and to conduct the King to his anointing and coronation.

When the town of Saint-Pierre-le-Moustier was taken,[156] by assault, Jeanne being there, the soldiers wanted to pillage the Church and to seize the sacred vessels and other treasure there hidden; but Jeanne prohibited and forbade them with great energy, so that nothing was taken away.

JEAN LUILLIER, *Burgher of Orleans.*

Many of the inhabitants of Orleans desired the coming of the Maid, for they had heard the current rumour that she had told the King how she was sent from God to raise the siege then held against the town; the inhabitants were then in such straits, on account of the English, that they knew not where to turn, except to God.

I was in the town when Jeanne reached it. She was received with as much rejoicing and acclamation from old and young, of both sexes, as if she had been an Angel of God; because we hoped through her to be delivered from our enemies, which indeed was done later.

When Jeanne was come into the City, she exhorted us all to hope in God; saying that, if we had good hope and trust in God, we should escape from our enemies. She said, moreover, she would summon the English to leave

---

[156] In December, 1429.

the town, and drive them away before she permitted any attack to be made; and this she did, summoning the English by letter, in which she told them to retire from the siege and return to England, or else she would make them retreat by force. From that time the English were terrified, nor had they power to resist as before; so that a few of our people might often fight with a great number of the English, and in such manner that they no longer dared to come out of their forts.

On the 27th May,[157] 1429, I remember well that an assault was made on the enemy in the Fort of the Bridge, in which Jeanne was wounded by an arrow; the attack lasted from morning till evening, and in such manner that our men wished to retreat into the town. Then Jeanne appeared, her standard in her hand, and placed it on the edge of the trench; and immediately the English began to quake, and were seized with fear. The army of the King took courage, and once more began to assail the Boulevard; and thus was the Boulevard taken, and the English therein were all put to flight or slain. Classidas and the principal English captains, thinking to retreat into the Tower of the Bridge, fell into the river, and were drowned; and the fort being taken, all the King's army retired into the city.

On the next day, very early in the morning, the English came out of their tents and ranged themselves in order of battle, as it seemed. Hearing this, the Maid rose from her bed and armed herself; but she would not allow any one to attack the English, nor to ask anything of them, but that they should be permitted to depart: and so, indeed, they did, no one pursuing them; and from that hour the town was free from the enemy.

I believed, like all in the town, that, had the Maid not come in God's Name to our help, we should soon have been, both town and people, in the hands of the enemy: we did not believe it possible for the army then in the town to resist the power of the enemy who were in such force against us.

---

[157] 7th May.

JEAN HILAIRE and GILLES DE SAINT MESNIN, [*Evidence of no importance*].

JACQUES L'ESBAHY.

I remember that two heralds were sent on the part of the Maid to Saint-Laurent, one named Ambeville, and the other Guienne, to Talbot, the Earl of Suffolk, and Lord Scales, telling the English in God's name to return to England, or evil would come to them. The English detained one of these heralds, named Guienne, and sent back the other—Ambeville—to the Maid, who told her that the English were keeping back his companion Guienne to burn him. Then Jeanne answered Ambeville and assured him in God's Name that no harm should happen to Guienne, and told him to return boldly to the English, that no evil should happen to him, but that he should bring back his comrade safe and sound. And so it was.

When Jeanne first entered Orleans, she went, before all else, to the Great Church, to do reverence to God, her Creator.

GUILLAUME LE CHARRON, *Burgher of Orleans* [*testified to the same effect*].

COSMA DE COMMY, *Burgher of Orleans*.

I heard Maître Jean Maçon, a famous Doctor in Civil and Canon Law, say that he had many times examined Jeanne as to her deeds and words, and he had no doubt she was sent from God; that it was a wondrous thing to hear her speak and answer; and that he had found nothing in her life but what was holy and good.

MARTIN DE MAUBOUDET, JEAN VOLANT, GUILLAUME POSTIAU, DENIS ROGER, JACQUES DE THOU,[158] JEAN

---

[158] Seigneur de Bignon, whose father was distinguished at the siege of Orleans. He was great-grandfather of Christopher de Thou, first President of the Parliament of Paris.

CARRELIER, AMIAN DE SAINT-MESMIN,[159] *all burghers of Orleans, gave witness to the same effect.*

JEAN DE CHAMPEAUX.

On a certain Sunday I saw those of Orleans preparing for a great conflict against the English, who were drawn up in order of battle. Seeing this, Jeanne went out to the soldiers; and then she was asked, if it were well to fight against the English on that day, being Sunday; to which she answered that she must hear Mass; and then she sent to fetch a table, and had the ornaments of the Church brought, and two Masses were celebrated, which she and the whole army heard with great devotion. Mass being ended, Jeanne asked if the English had their faces turned toward us; she was told no, that their faces were turned towards Meung. Hearing this, she said: "In God's Name, they are going; let them depart; and let us give thanks to God and pursue them no further, because it is Sunday."

*This story is confirmed by* PIERRE JONGAULT, PIERRE HUE, JEAN AUBERT, GUILLAUME ROUILLART, GENTIAN CABU, PIERRE VAILLANT, *and* JEAN COULON, *all burghers of Orleans.*

All agreed that they never perceived anything by which they could conjecture that Jeanne attributed to herself the glory of her wonderful deeds; but she ascribed all to God, and, so far as she could, resisted when the people sought to honour her or give her the glory; she preferred to be alone rather than in others' society, except when she was engaged in warfare.

JEAN BEAUHARNAYS.[160]

I often saw Jeanne while in Orleans; there was nothing in her which could merit reproof; she was humble, simple, chaste, and devoted to God and the

---

[159] Head of one of the principal families of Orleans. Amian de Saint-Mesmin was ennobled in 1460, on account of his services. He died at the ripe age of 118 years.

[160] Brother-in-law to Louis de Contes, Jeanne's page, and owner of the lordships of la Chaussée and Miramion. From his younger brother, Guillaume, descended the Beauharnais who was husband to Josephine and father of Eugène.

Church. I was always much comforted in talking with her.

MAÎTRE ROBERT DE FARCIAUX, *Priest, Licentiate in Law, Canon and Sub-Dean of the Church of Saint-Aignan at Orleans; testified to the same effect.*

MAÎTRE PIERRE COMPAING, *Priest, Licentiate in Law, Canon of Saint-Aignan.*

I have seen Jeanne, at the Elevation of the Host, weeping many tears. I remember well that she induced the soldiers to confess their sins; and I indeed saw that, by her instigation and advice, La Hire and many of his company came to confession.

The SIEURS PIERRE DE LA CENSURE, *Priest, Canon and Warden of Saint-Aignan*; RAOUL GODART, *Priest, Licentiate in Decrees, Prior of Saint Samson, and Canon of Saint-Aignan at Orleans*; HERVÉ BONART, *Prior of Saint-Magloire, of the Order of Saint-Augustine*; The SIEUR ANDRÉ BORDES, *Canon of Saint-Aignan; and* JEANNE, *wife of* GILLES DE SAINT-MESMIN. *All agreed with the preceding as to Jeanne's life and morals.*

JEANNE, *wife of* GUY BOYLEAUD; GUILLEMETTE, *wife of* JEAN DE COULONS; JEANNE, *widow of* JEAN DE MOUCHY, *gave similar testimony.*

CHARLOTTE,[161] *wife of* GUILLAUME HAVET.

At night I slept alone with Jeanne; I never saw anything evil in her, either in word or deed, but always simplicity, humility and chastity. She was in the habit of confessing frequently and hearing Mass daily. She often told my mother, in whose house she lodged, that she must put trust in God, and that God would help the town of Orleans, and drive away the enemy.

She was accustomed, before going to an assault, to take account of her conscience, and to receive the Sacrament after hearing Mass.

REGINALDE, *widow of* JEAN HURÉ.

---

[161] Daughter of Jacques Bourchier, Treasurer of Orleans, at whose house Jeanne lodged.

I remember well to have seen and heard, one day, a great lord, walking along the street, begin to swear and blaspheme God; which, when Jeanne saw and heard, she was much perturbed, and went up to the lord who was swearing, and, taking him by the neck, said, "Ah! master, do you deny Our Lord and Master? In God's Name, you shall unsay your words before I leave you." And then, as I saw, the said lord repented and amended his ways, at the exhortation of the said Maid.

PETRONILLE, *wife of* JEAN BEAUHARNAIS; *and* MASSEA, *wife of* HENRI FAGONE; *testified to the same effect.*

## DEPOSITIONS IN PARIS: 1455–6.

[*No questions for the Examinations at Paris and Rouen appear in the Rehabilitation Reports, but, as M. Jules Fabre was the first to point out, the numbers appended to the answers correspond with the first thirty-three of the hundred and one Articles of the Act of Accusation.*]

### EXAMINATION OF WITNESSES.

MAÎTRE JEAN TIPHAINE, *Priest, Master in Arts and Medicine, Canon of the Sainte Chapelle, Paris.*

On the first four Articles, I declare that I knew nothing of Jeanne until she was brought to the town of Rouen for her trial. I was summoned to take part. At first I would not go; but I was commanded a second time, and was present and heard the enquiry and her answers: she made many beautiful answers. When I was present at this Trial, the Judges and the Assessors were in the small hall behind the Great Hall of the Castle; and she answered with much prudence and wisdom and with great bravery.

On the occasion when I was present, Maître Beaupère was the principal questioner; and Jacques de Touraine, of the Order of Friars Minor, also questioned her. I well remember that this Maître Jacques once asked her, if she was ever in a place in which the English were overcome; to which she answered: "In God's name, surely. How mildly you put it! Why, have many not fled from France and gone back to their own country?"[162] And there was a great lord of England, whose name I do not remember, who said, hearing this: "Truly this is a brave woman! Would she were English!" And this he said to me and to Maître Guillaume Desjardins. No Doctor, however great and subtle he might be, had he been questioned by so many Doctors and before so great an assembly as was this Jeanne, but would have been perplexed and upset. With regard to the illness of Jeanne during the Trial, I was summoned by the Lords Judges to visit her, and was brought to her by one named d'Estivet; in presence of this d'Estivet, Maître Delachambre, and several others, I felt her pulse in order to know the cause of the malady, and asked what ailed her and from what she suffered. She replied that some carp had been sent her by the Bishop of Beauvais, and that she doubted this was the cause of her illness. Upon this, d'Estivet, who was present, found fault with her, saying she had spoken ill, and called her "paillarde," saying: "Thou paillarde! thou hast been eating sprats and other unwholesomeness." She answered that she had not; and then they—Jeanne and d'Estivet— exchanged many abusive words. Afterwards, I wished to know further as to the malady of Jeanne, and learnt that she had had severe vomiting. Except as to her malady, I gave no opinion.[163]

MAÎTRE GUILLAUME DELACHAMBRE, *Master in Arts and Medicine.*

I gave no opinion during the Trial, but allowed myself to affix my signature, under compulsion from the Bishop of Beauvais. I made excuses to him that in these matters it did not belong to my profession to give an opinion: however, finally, the Bishop forced me to subscribe as others had done, saying that otherwise some ill would befall me for having come to Rouen. I say, too, that threats were also used against Maître Jean Lohier and

---

[162] See decrees of Henry VI. against fugitives, "*terrificatos incautionibus puellae.*"
[163] Nevertheless, his name appears as having agreed with the Abbot of Fécamp in his opinion of the Condemnation.

Maître Nicolas de Houppeville, who, not wishing to take part in the Trial, were threatened with the penalty of drowning.

Sometimes it was the Abbot of Fécamp who interrogated Jeanne. Once, I saw the Abbot of Fécamp interrogating Jeanne, and Maître Jean Beaupère interrupted with many and divers questions. Jeanne would not reply to them both at once, saying that they did her much harm by thus vexing her, and that she would reply presently. As to her illness, one day the Cardinal of England and the Earl of Warwick having sent for me, I found myself associated with Guillaume Desjardins and other doctors. The Earl of Warwick told us that Jeanne had been ill and that we had been sent for to give her all our attention, for the King would not, for anything, that she should die a natural death: he had bought her too dear for that, and he intended that she should die at the hands of justice, and should be burnt. For this, I and Guillaume Desjardins and others visited her. Desjardins and I felt her pulse on the right side, and found fever, from which we recommended she should be bled. "Away with your bleeding!" said Warwick, "she is artful, and might kill herself." Nevertheless, we did bleed her, and she recovered. One day, after she had recovered, there arrived a certain Maître Guillaume d'Estivet, who used evil words against Jeanne, calling her ... and a *paillarde*. This abuse upset her to such a point that the fever returned, and she had a relapse. And this being brought to the notice of the Earl, he forbade d'Estivet to abuse Jeanne from that day forth.

I was present at a sermon of Maître Guillaume Érard. I do not remember the sermon, but I remember well the Abjuration made by Jeanne. She was long in doing this. Maître Guillaume Érard decided her by saying that, if she did what he advised her, she would be delivered from prison. She abjured on this condition and no other, and immediately read a small schedule containing six or seven lines on a piece of paper folded in two. I was so near her that, in all truth, I could see the lines and their form.

For the rest, I can only say that I was present at the last

discourse made in the Old Market-Place of Rouen by Maître Nicolas Midi. As soon as the sermon was over, Jeanne was burnt, the stake being already prepared. Her pious lamentations and ejaculations made many weep; only some English were laughing. I heard her say these or like words: "Alas! Rouen, I fear me that thou wilt have to suffer for my death." Shortly after she began to cry "Jesus" and to invoke St. Michael; and then she perished in the flame.

*The Reverend Father in God, the Lord* JEAN DE MAILLY, *Bishop of Noyon.*

I knew nothing of Jeanne before she came to Rouen; and I saw her only two or three times. I do not remember either being present at the Trial or giving my opinion.

I remember that, the day before the discourse at St. Ouen, I was present at an Exhortation addressed to Jeanne; but what was said or done I do not remember. I was present also on the day after, when a sermon was given at St. Ouen by Maître Guillaume Érard. There were two galleries or scaffolds: on one were the Bishop of Beauvais, myself and others; and on the other the preacher, Maître Guillaume Érard, and Jeanne. The words of the preacher I do not remember; but I remember well that, either then or on the preceding day, Jeanne said that, if there had been aught evil in her words or deeds, whatever of either good or ill had been in her speech or action came from herself alone, and not from her King. After the sermon, I perceived that Jeanne was ordered to do or say something. I believe it was to abjure; they said to her: "Jeanne, do what you are advised. Would you cause your own death?" These words verily moved her to make her Abjuration. After this Abjuration, many said that it was a mere trick, and that she had acted only in derision.

I remember to have heard—from whom I cannot recall—that the man's dress was returned to her by the window.

For the rest, I was present at the last sermon on the day she was burnt. There were three galleries or scaffolds: one where sat the Judges, one where many Bishops sat, myself among them, and one where wood was prepared for the burning of Jeanne. At the end of the sermon the sentence was pronounced which delivered Jeanne to secular justice. After this sentence was pronounced, Jeanne began to make many pious exclamations and lamentations; and among other things she said that nothing she had done, either good or ill had been suggested by the King. Thereupon I left, not wishing to see the burning of Jeanne. I saw many of the bystanders weeping.

As to certain letters of guarantee which the King of England gave to the Bishop of Beauvais and others concerned in this Trial, in which I, the Bishop of Noyon, am mentioned as having been present, I can well believe that it was so, though I do not remember much about it.

MAÎTRE THOMAS DE COURCELLES, *S.T.P., Canon of Paris.*

I believe that the Bishop of Beauvais undertook the Trial brought against Jeanne in the matter of the Faith because he was a Counsellor of the King of England, and also Bishop of Beauvais, in which territory Jeanne had been taken captive.

I have heard it said that money was given to the Inquisitor by a certain Surreau, receiver-general, for his participation in the said Trial; but I never heard that the Bishop received anything.

At the time when Jeanne was brought to Rouen, I, being in Paris, was summoned by the Bishop of Beauvais aforesaid to proceed to Rouen for the Trial. I went in the company of Maîtres Nicolas Midi, Jacques de Touraine, Jean de Rouel,[164] and others whom I do not remember, to the town of Rouen, at the expense of those who took us, among whom was Maître Jean de Reynel.[165]

About that time Maître Jean Lohier came to the town of Rouen, and order was given to put him in possession of

[164] Not mentioned elsewhere.
[165] Secretary to the King of England.

the details of the Action. And when the said Lohier had
seen the evidence, he told me that evidently they ought
not to proceed against Jeanne in a matter of Faith without
previous information as to the charges of guilt, and that
the law required such information.

I remember well that in the first deliberation, I never
held Jeanne to be a heretic, except in that she obstinately
maintained she ought not to submit to the Church; and
finally—as my conscience can bear me witness, before
God—it seems to me that my words were: "Jeanne is now
what she was. If she was heretic then, she is so now." Yet
I never positively gave an opinion that she was a heretic. I
may add that in the first deliberations there was much
discussion and difficulty among those consulted as to
whether Jeanne should be reputed a heretic. I never gave
an opinion as to her being put to the torture.[166]

Many of the Assessors were of opinion and advised
that Jeanne should be put in the hands of the Church, into
an ecclesiastical prison; but I do not remember that this
subject formed a part of our discussions.

Certain Articles, to the number of twelve, were made
and extracted from the confessions and answers of the
said Jeanne. They were drawn up, I verily believe, by the
late Maître Nicolas Midi. It was on these Twelve Articles,
thus extracted, that all deliberations and opinions were
made and given. I do not know if there was ever any
question of correcting them, or if they were corrected.

I often heard from Maître Nicolas Loiseleur that he
many times visited Jeanne in an assumed dress; but what
he said I know not: and I always counselled him that he
should reveal himself to Jeanne, and let her know that he
was a priest. I believe he heard Jeanne in confession.

After the first preaching came word that Jeanne had
resumed a man's attire; and immediately the Bishop went
to the prison, accompanied by myself, and questioned her
as to her reasons for resuming this dress. She replied that
she had resumed it because it seemed to her more suitable

---

[166] It is, however, stated that, on being consulted, he did advise the
extreme measure of putting Jeanne to the torture.

to wear man's clothing, being with men, than a woman's dress.

I was present at the last preaching made in the Old Market-Place, on the day of her death. I did not see her burnt, for, after the sermon and the reading of the sentence, I went away.

### MAÎTRE JEAN MONNET, *S.T.P., Canon of Paris*.

Three or four times I went to the Trial and wrote out the questions put to Jeanne and her answers, not as notary but as clerk and servant to Maître Jean Beaupère. Among other things, I remember hearing Jeanne say to me and to the other notaries, that we were not writing properly; and often did she correct us. Often, in these questions and answers, when questioned on something which I could see she ought not to answer, she said that she would refer to the conscience of the questioner as to whether she ought to answer or not.

I was present at the preaching at Saint-Ouen, seated on the platform at the feet of Maître Jean Beaupère, my master. When the preaching was finished, and while the sentence was being read, Jeanne said that if she were advised by the clerics and if their consciences approved, she would willingly do as they recommended. Hearing this, the Bishop of Beauvais asked the Cardinal of England what he ought to do in face of this submission of Jeanne. To which the Cardinal answered the Bishop, that he should receive Jeanne to penitence. And therefore he laid on one side the sentence which he had begun to read, and admitted Jeanne to penitence. I saw the Schedule of Abjuration, which was then read; it was a short schedule, hardly six or seven lines in length. I remember well that Jeanne referred to the consciences of the Judges as to whether she ought to abjure or not. It was said that the executioner was already on the spot, expecting that she would be handed over to the secular power. I left Rouen on the Monday or Sunday before the death of Jeanne.

LOUIS DE CONTES.[167]

The year that Jeanne came to Chinon I was fourteen or fifteen years old. I was page to the Sieur de Gaucourt, Captain of the Castle. Jeanne arrived at Chinon in the company of two gentlemen, who conducted her to the King. I saw her many times going and coming to the King; there was given her for residence the Tower of Coudray, at Chinon. I resided and lived with her all the time that she stayed there, passing all the time with her, except at night, when she always had women with her. I remember well that while she was living at Coudray persons of great estate came many days to visit her there. I do not know what they did or said, because when I saw them coming I retired; nor do I know who they were. Very often while she lived in this town I saw her on her knees praying; but I did not understand what she was saying; sometimes also I saw her weep.

Shortly afterwards she was taken to Poitiers; then to Tours, where she resided with a woman called Lapau. In this place the Duke d'Alençon made her a present of a horse, which I saw at the house of the woman Lapau. At Tours I became her page; with me also was one named Raymond. From that time I remained with her, and was always with her as her page, at Blois, as well as at Orleans, and until she reached the walls of Paris.

While she was at Tours the King gave her a complete suit of armour and an entire military household. From Tours she went to Blois with the army, who had great faith in her. Jeanne remained some time with the army at Blois; how long I do not remember. Then it was decided that she should go to Orleans by the Sologne. She started fully armed, accompanied by her men-at-arms, to whom she said without ceasing that they were to put all their confidence in Our Lord and to confess their sins. On the way I saw her during this journey receive the Sacrament of the Eucharist.

---

[167] Louis de Contes was brother-in-law of Beauharnais, the Bourgeois of Orleans. He was a son of Jean de Contes, Captain of Châteaudun, and Chamberlain to the Duke d'Orléans.

CHINON.

Having arrived near Orleans on the side of the Sologne, Jeanne with many others and myself were conducted to the opposite side of the Loire, on which side is the city of Orleans; and from thence we entered the said town. In her journey from Blois to Orleans, Jeanne had been all bruised, because on the night of the start from Blois she had slept fully armed. At Orleans she lived at the house of the Treasurer[168] of the Town, facing the Bannier Gate; and in this house she received the Sacrament. The day after her arrival she went to seek the Sieur Bastard of Orleans, with whom she had an interview. On her return I saw she was quite vexed that, as she told me, the captains had decided not to attack the English on that day. She went nevertheless to a Boulevard which the French were occupying, opposite to one garrisoned by the English, and there she spoke with them, telling them to retire in God's Name, or otherwise she would drive them away. One of them, called the Bastard of Granville, assailed her with many insults: "Do you wish us," he said, "to surrender to a woman?" At the same time, he called the Frenchmen who were with her "maquereaux mescreans." Then Jeanne returned to her lodging, and went up into her chamber: I thought she was going to sleep: shortly afterwards, there she was, coming down from her chamber; "Ah! bloodthirsty boy," she said

---

[168] Jacques Bouchier.

to me, "you did not tell me that the blood of France was being shed!"[169] And she ordered me to go and look for her horse. At the same time she was being armed by the lady of the house and her daughter. When I returned with her horse I found her already armed: she told me to go and seek her banner, which had been left in her chamber: I passed it to her through the window. Immediately she rode hastily towards the Burgundy gate, whither the lady with whom she lodged told me to follow her, which I did. The attack took place against the Fort of Saint Loup; and in this attack the Boulevard was taken. On the way Jeanne met several of the French wounded, at which she was much disturbed. The English were preparing to resist when Jeanne advanced against them in all haste. As soon as the French saw her they began to shout aloud; and thus was the Fort of Saint Loup taken. I heard it said that the English ecclesiastics had taken their ornaments, and had thus come before her; that Jeanne had received them without allowing any harm to be done them, and had had them conducted to her lodging; but that the other English had been killed by the people of Orleans.

In the evening Jeanne returned to supper in her lodging. She had always most sober habits: many times I saw her eat nothing during a whole day but a morsel of bread. I was astonished that she ate so little. When she was in her lodging she ate only twice a day.

The next day, towards 3 o'clock, the soldiers of the King crossed the Loire to attack the Fort of Saint-Jean-le-Blanc, which they took, as also the Fort of the Augustins.[170] Jeanne crossed the river with them, and I accompanied her: then she re-entered Orleans, and went back to sleep at her lodging with some women, as she was in the habit of doing: for every night, as far as possible, she had a woman to sleep by her, and when she could not find one in war, or in camp, she slept fully dressed.

The following day, in spite of many Lords pretending that it was exposing the King's followers to too great a

---

[169] ["*Ha! sanglant garçon, vous ne me dyriez pas que le sanc de France feust repandu!*"]

[170] *Cælestinorum*, in the text.

danger, she had the Burgundy gate opened, and a small gate near the great tower: she then crossed the water with some of her followers to attack the Fort of the Bridge, which the English still held. The King's troops remained there from morning to night, and Jeanne was wounded: it was necessary to take off her armour to dress the wound; but hardly was it dressed when she armed herself afresh and went to rejoin her followers at the attack and the assault, which had gone on from morning without ceasing. And when the Boulevard was taken Jeanne still continued the assault with her men, exhorting them to have a good heart and not to retire, because the fort would very soon be theirs. "When," she told them, "you see the wind drive the banner towards the fort, it will be yours!" But the evening was drawing on, and her followers, seeing they made no way, despaired of success; yet Jeanne persisted always, assuring them they would take the fort that day. Then they prepared to attempt a last assault; and when the English saw this they made no resistance, but were seized with panic, and nearly all were drowned; nor did they during this attack even defend themselves. Those who survived retreated the next day to Beaugency and Meung. The King's army followed them, Jeanne accompanying it. The English offered to surrender Beaugency by agreement, or to fight; but on the day of combat they retired again; and the army began afresh to pursue them. On this day La Hire commanded the vanguard, at which Jeanne was much vexed, for she liked much to have the command of the vanguard. La Hire threw himself on the English, and the King's army was victorious: nearly all the English were slain.

Jeanne, who was very humane, had great compassion at such butchery. Seeing a Frenchman, who was charged with the convoy of certain English prisoners, strike one of them on the head in such manner that he was left for dead on the ground, she got down from her horse, had him confessed, supporting his head herself, and comforting him to the best of her power.

Afterwards she went with the army to Jargeau, which was taken by assault, with many English, among whom were Suffolk and de la Pole[171]. After the deliverance of Orleans, and all these victories, Jeanne went with the army to Tours, where the King was. There it was decided that the King should go to Rheims for his consecration. The King left with the army, accompanied by Jeanne, and marched first to Troyes, which submitted; then to Chalons, which did the same; and last to Rheims, where our King was crowned and anointed in my presence—for I was, as I have already said, page to Jeanne, and never left her. I remained with her until she arrived before Paris.

She was a good and modest woman, living as a Catholic, very pious, and, when she could, never failing to be present at the Mass. To hear blasphemies upon the Name of Our Lord vexed her. Many times when the Duke d'Alençon swore[172] or blasphemed before her, I heard her reprove him. As a rule, no one in the army dared swear or blaspheme before her, for fear of being reprimanded.

She would have no women in her army. One day, near Château-Thierry, seeing the mistress of one of her followers riding on horseback, she pursued her with her sword, without striking her at all; but with gentleness and charity she told her she must no longer be found amongst the soldiers, otherwise she would suffer for it.

I know nothing more, not having seen her after Paris.

GOBERT THIBAUT, *Squire to the King of France.*

I was at Chinon when Jeanne came to seek the King, who was then residing in that city. Before this, I knew nothing of her; but henceforward I had more acquaintance with her, for, when I went with the King to the town of Poitiers, Jeanne was also taken thither and lodged in the house of Jean Rabateau. I know that Jeanne was questioned and examined in the town of Poitiers by the late Maître Pierre de Versailles, S.T.P.,—then Abbot of

---

[171] John de la Pole, Captain of Avranches, brother of the Earl of Suffolk.
[172] Jeanne's hatred of swearing is noticed by many of her followers, and in her hearing they endeavoured to abstain from it. La Hire, whose language was apparently the most violent, was permitted by her to employ the mild expletive 'Par mon martin,' 'By my baton,' an expression she herself is constantly reported to have used.

Talmont and, at the time of his death, Bishop of Meaux,—and by Maître Jean Erault, S.T.P. I went with them by the command of the late Lord Bishop of Castres. As I have said, she was living in the house of Rabateau, in which house de Versailles and Erault talked with her in my presence. When we arrived at her house, Jeanne came to meet us, and striking me on the shoulder said to me that she would gladly have many men of such good-will as I. Then Maître Pierre de Versailles told Jeanne that he had been sent to her from the King. She replied: "I well believe that you have been sent to question me," adding, "I know neither A nor B."

Then she was asked by them for what she had come. She replied; "I am come from the King of Heaven to raise the siege of Orleans and to conduct the King to Rheims for his crowning and anointing." And then she asked if they had paper and ink, saying to Maître Jean Erault: "Write what I say to you. You, Suffolk, Classidas, and La Poule, I summon you by order of the King of Heaven to go back to England." Versailles and Erault did nothing more on this occasion, so far as I remember. Jeanne remained in the town of Poitiers as long as the King did.

Jeanne said that her Counsel had told her she should have gone more quickly to the King. I saw those who had brought her—Jean de Metz, Jean Coulon, and Bertrand Pollichon,[173] with whom I was very friendly and familiar. I was present one day when they told the late Bishop of Castres—then Confessor to the King—that they had travelled through Burgundy and places occupied by the enemy, yet had they always travelled without hindrance, at which they much marvelled.

I heard the aforesaid Confessor say that he had discovered in a writing that there should come a maiden who would aid the Kingdom of France.

I do not know whether Jeanne was examined otherwise than as aforesaid. I heard the said Lord Confessor and other Doctors say that they believed Jeanne to be sent from God, and that they believed it was she of

---

[173] A nickname of Poulengey.

whom the prophecies spoke; because, seeing her actions, her simplicity, and conduct, they thought the King might be delivered through her; for they had neither found nor perceived aught but good in her, nor could they see anything contrary to the Catholic faith.

On the day that the Lord Talbot, who had been taken at Patay, was brought to the town of Beaugency, I arrived at that town; and from thence Jeanne went with the men-at-arms to Jargeau, which was taken by assault, and the English were put to flight.

Jeanne assembled an army between Troyes and Auxerre, and found large numbers there, for every one followed her. The King and his people came without hindrance to Rheims. Nowhere was the King turned back, for the gates of all cities and towns opened themselves to him.

SIMON BAUCROIX, *Squire.*

It was Jeanne's intention that the army should go towards the Fort or Bastille of Saint-Jean-le-Blanc: but this was not done; and they went to a place between Orleans and Jargeau, whither the inhabitants of Orleans sent boats to receive the provisions and to take them into the town; and the said provisions were put into the boats and brought into the town. And because the army was not able to cross the Loire, it was decided to return and cross the river at Blois: for there was no bridge nearer within the King's jurisdiction. At this Jeanne was very indignant, fearing they would not be willing to fall back, and so would leave the work unfinished. Neither could she go with them to Blois; but she crossed the river with about 200 lances in boats to the other bank, and entered Orleans by land. The Marshal de Boussac went that night to seek the King's army which had gone to Blois; and I remember that shortly before the arrival of the said Marshal at Orleans, Jeanne said to Sieur Jean d'Aulon that the Marshal would arrive, and that she knew well he would come to no harm.

When Jeanne was in her lodging, she, being led by the Spirit, cried out: "In God's Name! our people are hard pressed." Then she sent for a horse; and, arming herself, she went to the Fort of Saint Loup, where there was an assault being made by the King's people on the English: and no sooner had Jeanne joined in the attack, than the fort was taken.

The next day the French in company with Jeanne went to attack the Fort of Saint-Jean-le-Blanc, and drew near to the island; and when the English saw that the King's army had crossed the water, they quitted the Fort of Saint-Jean-le-Blanc, and retreated to another fort near the Augustins. And there I saw the King's army in great peril. "Let us advance boldly in God's Name," said Jeanne: and they advanced on the English, who, now in much danger, held their three forts.[174] At once, without much difficulty, this fort of the Augustins was taken; and the captains then advised Jeanne to re-enter Orleans; but this she would not do, saying, "Shall we leave our men?" The next day they attacked the fort at the end of the bridge, which was very strong and almost impregnable, so that the King's army had much to do; and the attack lasted the whole day, up to nightfall. I saw the Seneschal of Beaucaire break up the bridge with a bombard. When evening came and they despaired of gaining the fort, orders were given that Jeanne's standard should be brought to the fort; and this being done another attack was made on the fort, and thereupon without much difficulty the King's army entered with the standard; and the English fled, in such manner that when they reached the end of the bridge it broke down beneath them, and many were drowned.

The next day the King's army sallied out to give battle to the English; but they, on seeing the French, fled. When Jeanne saw them in flight and the French following after, she said to the French: "Let the English go, and slay them not; let them go; it is enough for me that they have retreated." On that day, they escaped from the city of Orleans and turned back on Blois, which they reached the same day.

---

[174] These three forts were on the left bank of the Loire; the fort of the Tourelles, of the Augustins, and of Saint-Privé were further west.

Jeanne stayed there two or three days; and from thence she went to Tours, and to Loches, where the King's army was preparing to go to Jargeau; and from thence they went to attack that town.

In war time, she would not permit any of those in her company to steal anything; nor would she ever eat of food which she knew to be stolen. Once, a Scot told her that he had eaten of a stolen calf: she was very angry, and wanted to strike the Scot for so doing.

She would never permit women of ill-fame to follow the army; none of them dared to come into her presence; but, if any of them appeared, she made them depart unless the soldiers were willing to marry them.

ORLEANS CATHEDRAL.

She was good not only to the French, but also to the enemy. All this I know of a surety, for I was for a long time with her, and many times assisted in arming her.

Jeanne lamented much, and was displeased when

certain good women came to her, wishing to salute her: it seemed to her like adoration, at which she was angered.

MAÎTRE JEAN BARBIN, *Doctor of Laws, King's Advocate.*

I was sent to Poitiers, where I saw Jeanne for the first time. When she arrived at the town she was lodged in the house of Maître Jean Rabateau; and while there I have heard the wife of Rabateau say that every day after dinner she was for a long time on her knees, and also at night; and that she often went into a little oratory in the house and there prayed for a long time. Many clergy came to visit her,—to wit, Maître Pierre de Versailles, S.T.P., sometime Bishop of Meaux, and Maître Guillaume Aimery, S.T.P. There were also other graduates in theology, whose names I do not remember, who questioned her in like manner at their will.

I heard from these said Doctors that they had examined her and put many questions, to which she replied with much prudence, as if she had been a trained divine; that they marvelled at her answers, and believed that, taking into account her life and conversation, there must have been in her something divine.

In the course of these deliberations Maître Jean Erault stated that he had heard it said by Marie d'Avignon,[175] who had formerly come to the King, that she had told him that the kingdom of France had much to suffer and many calamities to bear: saying moreover that she had had many visions touching the desolation of the kingdom of France, and amongst others that she had seen much armour which had been presented to her; and that she was alarmed, greatly fearing that she should be forced to take it; but it had been said to her that she need fear nothing, that this armour was not for her, but that a maiden who should come afterwards should bear these arms and deliver the kingdom of France from the enemy. And he believed firmly that Jeanne was the maiden of

---

[175] A woman called "la gasque d'Avignon," whose predictions made much stir at the beginning of the fifteenth century.

whom Marie d'Avignon thus spoke.

All the soldiers held her as sacred. So well did she bear herself in warfare, in words and in deeds, as a follower of God, that no evil could be said of her. I heard Maître Pierre de Versailles say that he was once in the town of Loches in company with Jeanne, when the people, throwing themselves before the feet of her horse, kissed her hands and feet; and he said to Jeanne that she did wrong to allow what was not due to her, and that she ought to protect herself from it lest men should become idolatrous; to which she answered: "In truth, I know not how to protect myself, if God does not protect me."

DAME MARGUERITE LA TOUROULDE, *widow of the late Réné de Bouligny, Councillor to the King.*

I was at Bourges when Jeanne arrived at Chinon, where the Queen was. In those days there was in the kingdom—especially in that part still obedient to the King—such great calamity and penury as was sad to see; so that the followers of the King were almost in despair: and this I know, because my husband was then Receiver-General, and at that time neither of the King's money nor of his own had he four crowns.

The town of Orleans was in the hands of the King, and there was no way of help. And in this calamity came Jeanne, and I firmly believe that she came from God and was sent for the relief of the King and his faithful subjects, who then were without hope save in God.

I did not see Jeanne until the time when the King came from Rheims, where he was consecrated. He came to Bourges, where was the Queen, and I with her. When the King approached, the Queen went to meet him as far as the town of Selles-en-Berry, and I accompanied her. While the Queen was on the way, Jeanne encountered and saluted her, and was then taken on to Bourges, and by command of my Lord d'Albret lodged in my house, although my husband had said that she was to be lodged with a certain Jean Duchesne.

She remained with me for the space of three weeks—sleeping, drinking, and eating [in the house]. Nearly every night I slept with her, nor did I ever perceive aught of evil in her, but she comported herself as a worthy and Catholic woman, often confessing herself, willingly hearing Mass, and many times asking me to accompany her to matins, which at her request I often did. We often talked together, and I would say to her: "If you do not fear to go to the attack, it is because you know that you will not be killed": to which she would reply that she had no greater security than other soldiers. Sometimes Jeanne would tell me how she had been examined by the Clergy, and that she had made them the answer: "There are books of Our Lord's besides what you have."

I heard from those that brought her to the King that at first they thought she was mad, and intended to put her away in some ditch, but while on the way they felt moved to do everything according to her good pleasure. They were as impatient to present her to the King, as she was to meet him, nor could they resist her wishes.

They testified as others did to the purity of her conduct and influence.

Jeanne told me that the Duke de Lorraine who was ill, wished to see her, that she talked with him, and told him that he was not living well, and that he would never be cured unless he amended; also she exhorted him to take back his good wife.[176]

Jeanne had great horror of dice.

I remember that many women came to my house while Jeanne was living there, and brought *pater nosters* and other religious objects that she might touch them; but Jeanne laughed, saying: "Touch them yourselves. Your touch will do them as much good as mine."

Jeanne was very liberal in almsgiving, and willingly succoured the poor and indigent, saying that she had been sent for their consolation.

... I have no doubt that she was virgin. According to my knowledge she was quite innocent, unless it be in warfare. She rode on horseback and handled the lance like

---

[176] The devoted Margaret of Bavaria, who was separated from him on account of his evil life.

the best of the knights, and the soldiers marvelled.

JEAN MARÇEL, *Burgess of Paris*.

Maître Jean Sauvage, of the Order of Saint Dominic, who often talked with me of Jeanne, has told me that he was engaged in the Process against her; but it was difficult to make him speak of it. He did once say, that he had never seen a woman of such years give so much trouble to her examiners, and he marvelled much at her answers and at her memory. Once the notary reporting what he had written, she declared that she had not said what they had made her say, and referred it to those present, who all recognized that Jeanne was right, and the answer was corrected.

I was present at the sermon at Saint-Ouen; and there for the first time I saw Jeanne. I remember that Maître Guillaume Érard preached in presence of the said Jeanne, who was in a man's dress. But what was said or done in the sermon I know not. I was at some distance from the Preacher. I heard it said that Maître Laurence Calot said to Maître Pierre Cauchon, that he was too slow in pronouncing judgment, and that he was not judging rightly; to which Maître Pierre Cauchon replied that he lied.

I was also at the second preaching, on the day that Jeanne was burnt, and saw her in the flames calling out in a loud voice many times "Jesus!" I believe firmly that she died a Catholic and ended her days well in good Christian estate; and this I know from what I had from the monks who were with her in her last hours. I saw many—the greater part of those present—weeping and bewailing for pity, and saying that Jeanne had been unjustly condemned.

THE DUKE D'ALENÇON.[177]

When Jeanne arrived at Chinon, I was at Saint Florent. One day, when I was hunting quails, a messenger came to inform me that there had come to the King a young girl,

---

[177] Jean, Duke d'Alençon, son of the Duke killed at Agincourt. He was of the Blood Royal, descended from Philip II.

who said she was sent from God to conquer the English and to raise the siege then undertaken by them against Orleans. It was for this reason that I went on the following day to Chinon, where I found Jeanne talking with the King. Having approached them, she asked me who I was. "It is the Duke d'Alençon," replied the King. "You are welcome," she then said to me, "the more that come together of the blood of France the better it will be." The next day she went to the King's Mass; and when she perceived him she made a profound salutation. After Mass the King took her into his private room, where he kept me with him, as well as the Sieur de la Tremouille, after having sent away all the others. Jeanne then made several requests to the King—amongst others that he would make a gift of his kingdom to the King of Heaven, because the King of Heaven, after this gift, would do for him as He had done for his predecessor, and reinstate him in all his rights. Many other things were said, up to the hour of dinner, which I do not remember. After dinner the King went for a walk; Jeanne coursed before him, lance in hand. Seeing her manage her lance so well I gave her a horse.

Following on this the King caused her to be examined by the Clergy. Choice was made of the Bishop of Chartres, the King's Confessor; the Bishop of Senlis[178], Mende and Poitiers; Maître Pierre de Versailles, since Bishop of Meaux; Maître Jourdin Morin, and many others whose names I do not recall. They questioned her in my presence and asked why she had come, and who had caused her to come to the King? She replied that she had come from the King of Heaven, that she had voices and a Counsel which told her what she was to do; but I do not remember if she made known what those voices told her.

One day when dining with me she told me that the clergy had examined her well, but that she knew and could do more than she had told them. The King, when he had heard the report of his commissioners, wished that

[178] The Bishop referred to is Simon Bonnet, Bishop of Senlis at that time, not the partisan of the English who occupied the seat in 1429.

she should still go to Poitiers, in order to submit to another examination. I did not assist at this examination; I only knew it to be afterwards reported to the Council, that the examiners at Poitiers held the opinion that there was nothing in her contrary to the Faith, and that the King, considering his extreme necessity, might make use of her assistance.

On receiving this news the King sent me to the Queen of Sicily[179] to prepare a convoy of supplies for the army, which was then being directed against Orleans. I found with the Queen the Sieur Ambroise de Loré,[180] and the Sieur Louis—his other name I do not remember—who prepared the convoy: but money was lacking, and in order to obtain it I returned to the King, to whom I made known that the supplies were prepared, and that it only remained to procure the necessary money to pay for them and for the army. The King then sent people who delivered the necessary sums; so that in the end soldiers and supplies were ready, and there was nothing more to be done but to gain Orleans, and try to raise the siege.

With this army Jeanne was sent. The King had caused armour to be made for her.[181]

The King's army started with Jeanne. What happened on the way, and afterwards in Orleans, I know only by hearsay—for I was not present, not having then gone to Orleans—but I went there shortly after, and saw the works which had been raised by the English before the town. I was able to study the strength of these works; and I think that, to have made themselves masters of these—

---

[179] Yolande, daughter of John I. of Aragon; wife of Louis XI., Duke of Anjou, and titular King of Sicily. She was the mother of Mary, wife of Charles VII., and grandmother of Margaret, afterwards wife of Henry VI.

A receipt is recorded, in *Quicherat* (III. 93), for the carriage of corn, on her behalf, from Orleans to Blois.

[180] A captain of some repute, exchanged for Talbot after the Battle of Patay.

[181] In the Accounts (formerly kept in the Chambre des Comtes at Paris), of Maître Hemon Raguier, Treasurer of War, there is an item relating to this suit of armour: "To the Master Armourer, for a complete harness for the said Pucelle, 100 livres tournois."

above all, the Fort of the Tourelles at the end of the Bridge, and the Fort of the Augustins—the French needed a real miracle. If I had been in either one or the other, with only a few men, I should have ventured to defy the power of a whole army for six or seven days: and they would not have been able, I think, to have mastered it. For the rest, I heard from the captains and soldiers who took part in the siege, that what had happened was miraculous; and that it was beyond man's power.

I did not see Jeanne from the time she left the King until after the raising of the siege of Orleans. After this siege, we succeeded in assembling as many as 600 lances, with which we decided to march on Jargeau, then occupied by the English. That night we slept in a wood. On the following morning we were joined by another division, under the guidance of the Sieur Bastard of Orleans, the Sieur Florent d'Illiers,[182] and many other captains. When we were all joined together, we found ourselves to number about 1,200 lances. There was then contention among the captains: some were of opinion that the attack should be made; and others opposed it, seeing the great strength of the English and their large numbers. Jeanne, seeing us thus divided, said: "No, do not fear their numbers; do not hesitate to make the attack; God will conduct your enterprise; if I were not sure that it is God Who guides us, I would rather take care of the sheep than expose myself to such great perils!" On these words we marched to Jargeau, counting on gaining the suburbs that day and passing the night there. But on the news of our approach, the English came to meet us and at first drove us back. Seeing this Jeanne seized her standard and began the attack, telling the soldiers to have good courage. We succeeded so well that we were able that night to camp in the suburbs. I think truly it was God Who was leading us; for, in the night that followed, we kept no guard; so that, had the English made a sally, we must have been in great danger. The next morning we prepared

---

[182] A street in Orleans is still called after d'Illiers, then Captain of Châteaudun.

artillery and had the machines and bombards placed in position. Then we consulted for some time as to what should be done against the English in Jargeau in order to take the town. While we were deliberating, we were told that La Hire was in conference with the English Lord Suffolk. I and the other captains were much provoked at this, and sent for La Hire, who came at once. The attack being resolved upon, the Heralds-at-Arms began to sound, "To the Assault!" "Forward, gentle Duke, to the assault!" cried Jeanne to me. And when I told her it was premature to attack so quickly: "Have no fear," she said to me, "it is the right time when it pleases God; we must work when it is His Will: act, and God will act!" "Ah! gentle Duke," she said to me, later, "art thou afraid? dost thou not know that I promised thy wife[183] to bring thee back, safe and sound?"

And indeed when I left my wife to come with Jeanne to the head-quarters of the army, my wife had told me that she feared much for me, that I had but just left prison[184] and much had been spent on my ransom, and she would gladly have asked that I might remain with her. To this Jeanne had replied: "Lady, have no fear; I will give him back to you whole, or even in better case than he is now."

During the assault on Jargeau Jeanne said to me: "Go back from this place, or that engine"—pointing out an engine of war in the city—"will kill you." I retired, and shortly after that very engine did indeed kill the Sieur de Lude in that very place from which she told me to go away. On this account I had great fear, and wondered much at Jeanne's words and how true they came. Afterwards, Jeanne made the attack; in which I followed her. As our men were invading the place, the Earl of Suffolk made proclamation that he wished to speak with me, but we did not listen, and the attack continued. Jeanne was on a ladder, her standard in her hand, when her

---

[183] Jeanne, daughter of the Duke d'Orléans.

[184] The Duke d'Alençon, at the age of eighteen, had been taken prisoner at the battle of Verneuil, in 1424, and kept for five years in the Castle of Crotoy, where Jeanne herself was afterwards imprisoned.

standard was struck and she herself was hit on the head by
a stone which was partly spent, and which struck her
calotte.[185] She was thrown to the ground; but, raising
herself, she cried: "Friends! friends! come on! come on!
Our Lord hath doomed the English! They are ours! keep a
good heart." At that moment the town was carried; and
the English retired to the bridges, where the French
pursued them and killed more than 1,100 men.

The town taken,[186] Jeanne and the army went to
Orleans; then from Orleans to Meung-sur-Loire, where
were the English under the command of 'the child of
Warwick' and Scales. Beneath the walls of Meung, I
passed the night in a Church with a few soldiers, and was
in great peril. The day after the taking of Meung, we went
to Beaugency; and in the neighbourhood of this town we
rallied to us a part of the army with which we attacked the
English who were in Beaugency. In consequence of our
attack the English abandoned the town and retired into a
camp which we had watched during the night for fear they
should beat a retreat. We were there when the news
reached us that the Constable was coming to join us:
Jeanne, the other Captains, and I myself were much
troubled by this news, and wished to retire, because we
had orders from the King not to receive the said Constable
into our company. I told Jeanne that if the Constable came
I should retire. The next day, before his arrival, we
learned that the English were marching upon us in great
number, under the command of Talbot.[187] Our men
immediately called "To arms!" and, seeing that I wished
to retire because of the arrival of the Constable, Jeanne
told me that we must help one another. The English
surrendered their camp by agreement, and retreated by a
safe-conduct which I gave them: for I was then Lieutenant
to the King, and thus in command of the army. We

---

[185] Head-covering without visor, "*chapeline casque léger en forme de calotte sans masque.*"
[186] Jargeau was taken on June 11th, 1429.
[187] John Talbot, afterwards Earl of Shrewsbury. He was exchanged for Ambroise de Loré and killed while attempting the relief of Châtillon, then besieged by Dunois.

thought they had retired, when a man of La Hire's company told us they were marching upon us, and that in a moment we should have them before us, to the number of a thousand men-at-arms. Jéanne asked what this messenger had stated; and when she knew what was going on she said to the Lord Constable,[188] "Ah! fair Constable, you have not come by my will, but now you are here you are welcome." Many were in fear and said it would be well to await the arrival of the cavalry. "In God's Name!" exclaimed Jeanne, "we must fight them at once: even if they were hanging from the clouds we should have them, because God has sent us to chastise them." She assured us she was certain of obtaining the victory, saying in French: "The gentle King shall have to-day the greatest victory he has ever had. My Counsel has told me they are all ours." Without great difficulty the English were beaten and slain, and Talbot made prisoner. There was a great slaughter. Then the army went to Patay, where Talbot was brought before me and the Constable in the presence of Jeanne. I said to Talbot that in the morning I had never expected what had happened. "It is the fortune of war,"[189] he replied. Afterwards we returned to the King, and it was decided to direct our way towards Rheims for his coronation and consecration.

Many times in my presence Jeanne told the King she would last but one year and no more; and that he should consider how best to employ this year. She had, she said, four duties to accomplish: to beat the English; to have the King crowned and consecrated at Rheims; to deliver the

---

[188] Arthur, Count de Richemont, Constable of France, brother of the Duke of Britanny. He was one of the Princes of the Blood taken at Agincourt, but was released on parole; and Henry V. dying soon after, he claimed his freedom, saying he had given his word to the King alone. He married a sister of the Duke of Burgundy and widow of the late Dauphin. Although friendly to the French cause, he was distrusted by Charles, and, at this time, was in disgrace. He was uncle to the Duke d'Alençon, his sister Mary having married the preceding Duke. He succeeded to the Duchy of Britanny in 1453, but died childless.

[189] It was after this battle of Patay that Sir John Fastolf, one of the English captains, was deprived of the Garter, for his conduct in retreating before the French army.

Duke d'Orléans from the hands of the English;[190] and to raise the siege of Orleans.

Jeanne was a chaste maiden; she hated the women who follow in the train of armies. I saw her one day at Saint Denis on the return from the coronation, pursuing one of them sword in hand: her sword was broken on this occasion. She was very vexed if she heard any of the soldiers swear. She reproved me much and strongly when I sometimes swore; and when I saw her I refrained from swearing.

So far as I could judge, I always held her for an excellent Catholic, and a modest woman: she communicated often, and, at sight of the Body of Christ, shed many tears. In all she did, except in affairs of war, she was a very simple young girl; but for warlike things—bearing the lance, assembling an army, ordering military operations, directing artillery—she was most skilful. Every one wondered that she could act with as much wisdom and foresight as a captain who had fought for twenty or thirty years. It was above all in making use of artillery that she was so wonderful.

---

[190] Louis, Duke d'Orléans, taken prisoner at Agincourt, in 1415, was imprisoned in England until the year 1440, when he was ransomed at the price of 54,000 nobles (about £36,000), the negotiations being carried out on the English side by Cauchon, Bishop of Beauvais.

THE COUNT DE RICHEMONT,
Constable of France.

BROTHER JEAN PASQUEREL.[191]

The first time I heard of Jeanne, and that she had come to find the King, I was at Anche,[192] in which town was her mother[193] and some of those who had accompanied her thither. One day, they invited me to go with them and see her, and told me they would not leave me till I had seen

---

[191] Of the Order of Hermit Friars of Saint Augustin, living at their Convent in Tours in 1429, and at Bayeux in 1456.

[192] There is some doubt as to the identity of this town. The text gives "Aniciensis," which would refer to Puy-en-Valais; but this, Quicherat says, is unlikely, owing to the distance, and proposes to substitute "Anceinsi," *i.e.*, Anche. Fabre, following Simon de Lune, is in favour of the former reading, as the town was one noted for pilgrimages; and, in the Lent of 1429, there was an unusual number of pilgrims, in honour of the special feast of La Vierge Noire de Puy, which, in that year, fell on Good Friday. This fact might account for the presence of Jeanne's mother at Puy, and of the men-at-arms, who had escorted the Maid to Chinon.

[193] Quicherat prefers to read, "brother."

her. I came then with them to Chinon; then to Tours, in which town I was at that time Reader in a Convent; and there we found her lodging in the house of a citizen named Jean Dupuy,[194] a burgher of Tours. My companions addressed Jeanne in these terms: "Jeanne, we bring you this good father; when you know him you will love him much." "I am very glad to see you," she said to me; "I have already heard of you; I should like to-morrow to confess myself to you."

The next day, indeed, I heard her in confession, and recited Mass before her. From that day onward, I always followed her and was always with her as her Chaplain, until Compiègne, where she was taken prisoner.

On her arrival at Chinon, I heard that she had been visited on two occasions by women. The Lady de Gaucourt and the Lady de Trèves, it is said, were those who visited her.

Afterwards, she was taken to Poitiers, to be examined there by the Clergy of that University as to what should be done with regard to her. Maître Jourdin Morin, Maître Pierre de Versailles, since deceased as Bishop of Meaux, and many others, after having questioned her, came to the conclusion that, in view of the necessity which weighed upon the Kingdom, the King might make use of her aid, and that they had found nothing in her contrary to the Catholic Faith. She then returned to Chinon, and thought she would be allowed to speak with the King; but it was not yet to be. At last, by the advice of the Council, she was permitted an interview with the King. The day on which this interview was to take place, just as she entered the Castle, a man, mounted on horseback, said, "Is that the Maid?" He insulted her, and swore with horrid blasphemy. "Oh! in God's Name," she said to him, "dost thou blaspheme God, thou who art so near thy death!" And, an hour after, this man fell into the water and was drowned. I report this fact as I gathered it from Jeanne and from many others, who said they had been witnesses

---

[194] Probably the husband of the woman named Lapau, mentioned by Louis de Contes.

of it.

CHARLES VII.
(Gallery of the Louvre.)

It was the Sieur Count de Vendôme who brought her
into the King's apartment. When he perceived her, the
King asked her her name. "Gentle Dauphin," she replied,
"I am called Jeanne the Maid; and the King of Heaven
sends you word by me that you will be consecrated and
crowned at Rheims, and that you will be the lieutenant of
the King of Heaven, who is King of France." After the
King had asked her a number of questions, she said to
him, "On the part of My Lord, I tell thee thou art true heir
of France and son of the King[195]; and He sends me to lead
thee to Rheims to the end thou mayst receive thy
crowning and thy consecration, if thou wilt." At the close
of this interview, the King said that Jeanne had confided
to him secrets which were not known and could not be
known except by God, which gave him great confidence
in her. All this I heard from Jeanne, but without having
been witness of it.

---

[195] Doubt had been thrown on the fact here stated, since Charles VII.'s
mother, Queen Isabeau, had denied her son's legitimacy.

She told me she was not pleased at so many examinations; that they prevented her carrying out the work for which she was sent, and that it was quite time for her to act. She told me she had asked from the Messengers of her Lord—that is to say, God—who appeared to her, what she ought to do; and they had told her to take the banner of her Lord. It was for this she had her banner made, on which was painted the image of Our Saviour seated in judgment on the clouds of Heaven, with an Angel holding in his hand a fleur-de-lys which Christ was blessing. I was at Tours with her when this banner was painted.[196]

A short time after Jeanne departed with the army to the succour of the town of Orleans, which was then besieged; I went with her, and did not leave her until the day when she was taken at Compiègne. I acted as her Chaplain, confessed her, and sang Mass for her. She was, indeed, very pious towards God and the Blessed Mary, confessing nearly every day and communicating frequently. When she was in a neighbourhood where there was a Convent of Mendicant Friars, she told me to remind her of the day when the children of the poor received the Eucharist, so that she might receive it with them; and this she did often: when she confessed herself she wept.

When Jeanne left Tours to go to Orleans, she prayed me not to forsake her, and to remain always with her as her Confessor; this I promised to do. We were at Blois about two or three days, waiting for the supplies with which the boats were to be loaded. At Blois she told me to have a banner made, round which the Priests might assemble, and to have painted thereon the Image of Our Saviour crucified. I had it done, as she required of me. As soon as this banner was made, Jeanne, twice a day, morning and evening, charged me to assemble the Priests around this banner: they then sang anthems and hymns to the Blessed Mary. Jeanne was with them, permitting only

[196] The account for this banner appears in the 13th Compte of Maître Hemon Raguier, Treasurer of War: 25 liv. tour. were paid to "Hauves Poulnois, painter, living at Tours, for painting and procuring materials for a great standard, and a small one for the Maid."

the soldiers who had that day confessed themselves to join her; she told her people to make confession, if they wished to come to this assemblage. There were Priests always ready to confess those in the army who wished to apply to them.

*Reproduced from an engraving of the XVIIth Century.*

On leaving Blois to march to Orleans, Jeanne made all the Priests assemble round this banner; and in this wise they marched at the head of the army. They departed, thus assembled, from the side of the Sologne, singing the "*Veni Creator Spiritus*" and many other anthems. On that and the two following days, we slept in the fields. On the third day, we arrived at Orleans, where the English held their siege right up to the bank of the Loire: we approached so close to them that French and English could almost touch one another. The French had with them a convoy of supplies; but the water was so shallow that the boats could not move up-stream, nor could they land where the English were. Suddenly the waters rose, and the boats were then able to land on the shore where the [French] army was. Jeanne entered the boats, with some of her followers, and thus came to Orleans. As for myself I returned to Blois, by Jeanne's command, with the Priests and the banner. Then, some days after, accompanied by the whole army, I came to Orleans by way of the Beauce—always with this same banner surrounded by Priests—meeting no obstacle. When Jeanne knew of our approach, she came to meet us; and together we entered Orleans without difficulty, bringing in the provisions in sight of the English. This was a marvellous thing; for the English were in great number

and strength, all prepared for fight. They had opposite
them our army, very inferior to theirs: they saw us; they
heard our Priests singing; I was in the midst of the Priests
bearing the banner. The English remained immovable,
never attempting to attack either the Priests or the army
which followed them.

As soon as we entered Orleans, the French sallied
from the town at Jeanne's urgent entreaties, and went to
attack the English, who were shut up in the Fort of Saint
Loup. After dinner the other Priests went with me to seek
Jeanne at her residence. When we arrived, we heard her
calling out: "Where are those who should arm me? The
blood of our people is falling to the ground!" And, so
soon as she was armed, she sallied from the town and
made for the Fort of Saint Loup, where the attack was
taking place. On the road she met many wounded
soldiers; the sight of them distressed her much. She went
to the assault, and did so well, that by force and violence
the fort was at last taken, and all the English who were
there were taken prisoners. I remember that this took
place on the Eve of the Ascension of Our Saviour.

When the Fort of Saint Loup was taken, the
English died there in great numbers. Jeanne was much
afflicted when she heard that they had died without
confession, and pitied them much. On the spot she made
her confession. She ordered me to invite the whole army
to do likewise, and to give thanks to God for the victory
just gained. Otherwise, she said, she would help them no
more, but would abandon them. On this day, the Eve of
the Ascension, she predicted that within five days the
siege would be raised, and that not a single Englishman
would be left within the walls of Orleans.[197] And so it
was: for on this Wednesday, as I have already said, the
Fort of Saint Loup was taken, which formerly had been a
convent.[198] More than one hundred men of distinction
were found there, all well armed, not one escaping. In the
evening, when Jeanne returned to her lodging, she told me

---

[197] The siege was raised on the 8th of May.
[198] Established on the site of a convent in the previous December.

that on the following day, the Ascension of Our Saviour, she would not fight, nor even put on her armour; and that she wished, out of respect for the Festival, to confess and to receive the Sacrament of the Eucharist. And this was done.

On Ascension Day, she ordered that no one should go out of the town to the attack on the same day without first making confession, and forbade women of bad reputation to follow her, lest, on account of sin, God should cause us to lose the battle. All these orders were carried out. It was on Ascension Day that she wrote to the English, entrenched in their forts, a letter thus couched:

"You, men of England, who have no right in this kingdom of France, the King of Heaven orders and commands you by me, Jeanne the Maid, that you quit your strong places, and return to your own country; if you do not I will cause you such an overthrow as shall be remembered for all time. I write to you for the third[199] and last time, and shall write to you no more.

Signed thus—

"*Jhésus Maria*, JEHANNE LA PUCELLE."

And lower:

"I would have sent you this letter in a more suitable manner, but you keep back my heralds: you have kept my herald Guyenne; I pray you to send him back, and I will send you some of your people who have been taken at the Fort of Saint Loup,—for all were not killed there."

As soon as this letter was written, Jeanne took an arrow, on the point of which she fastened this letter with a thread, and ordered an archer to shoot this arrow towards the English, crying out, "Read! here is news!" The English received the arrow with this letter, which they read. After having read it they began to cry out with all their power: "It is news sent to us from the ... of the Armagnacs!" At these words Jeanne began to cry, shedding many tears, and prayed the God of Heaven to

---

[199] The first letter was sent on March 22nd, 1429: of the second nothing is known.

*Jeanne D'Arc*

come to her aid. Soon she appeared to be consoled, having had, as she said, news from her Lord. In the evening after supper, she ordered me to rise earlier than I had done on Ascension Day, because she wished to confess very early in the morning: and this she did.

The next day, Friday, I rose very early; confessed her, and sang Mass before her and all her followers: she then started with them at once for the attack, which lasted from morning to evening. On this day the Fort of the Augustins was taken, after a great assault. Jeanne, who was accustomed to fast every Friday, could not do so on that day because she was too troubled, and she took supper. After this supper there came to her a noble and valiant captain, whose name I do not remember. He told her that all the captains were assembled in Council; that they had taken into consideration the small number of their forces in comparison with the large forces of the English, and the abundant grace which God had granted them in the success already obtained: "The town is full of supplies; we could keep it well while we await fresh succour, which the King could send us; it does not seem," he ended by saying, "expedient to the Council that the army should go forth to-morrow." "You have been to your Counsel," Jeanne answered him, "and I have been to mine; and believe me the Counsel of God will be accomplished and will succeed; yours on the contrary will perish." And addressing herself to me who was near her: "Rise to-morrow morning even earlier than you did to-day; do your best; keep always near me; for to-morrow I shall have yet more to do, and much greater things; to-morrow blood shall flow from my body, above the breast."

THE BRIDGE OF ORLEANS ON THE LAST DAY OF
THE ENGLISH SIEGE, SUNDAY, MAY 8, 1429.

THE BRIDGE SHORTLY BEFORE ITS DEMOLITION
IN 1760.

*Reproduced by kind permission of M. Herluison, Vice-President of the Archæological Society Of Orleans.*

On the Saturday, therefore, very early in the morning I rose and celebrated Mass; then Jeanne went to the attack of the Bridge Fort, in which was the Englishman, Clasdas.[200] The attack lasted from morning to sunset without interruption. At this assault, after dinner, Jeanne, as she had predicted, was struck by an arrow above the breast. When she felt herself wounded, she was afraid, and wept; but she was soon comforted, as she said. Some of the soldiers seeing her severely wounded wished to "charm" her; but she would not, saying: "I would rather die than do a thing which I know to be a sin; I know well that I must die one day, but I know not when, nor in what manner, nor on what day; if my wound may be healed without sin, I shall be glad enough to be cured." Oil of olive and lard were applied to the wound. After the dressing, she confessed herself to me, weeping and lamenting. Then she returned in all haste to the attack, crying: "Clasdas! Clasdas! yield thee, yield thee to the King of Heaven! Thou hast called me ... I have a great pity for thy soul, and for thy people." At this moment Clasdas, fully armed from head to foot, fell into the Loire, where he was drowned. Jeanne, moved to pity at this sight, began to weep for the soul of Clasdas, and for all the others who, in great number, were drowned, at the same time as he. On this day, all the English who were on the other side of the bridge were taken and killed. The next day—which was a Sunday—before sunrise all the English who were still in the plains around Orleans grouped themselves together, and came to the foot of the trenches of the town. From thence they departed for Meung-sur-Loire, where they remained for several days. On this Sunday[201] there was in Orleans a solemn

---

[200] *i.e.*, Glasdale.

[201] 8th May. The commemoration of the relief of Orleans was made a national festival by Louis XI. and confirmed by Richelieu. This day is still kept in the town with great rejoicings and religious processions: it has been celebrated, excepting during the Revolution, ever since the relief of the city.

procession and a sermon. It was then decided to go and seek the King; and Jeanne went thither. The English entrenched themselves in Jargeau, which was soon taken by assault. Finally, they were entirely defeated at Patay.

I often heard her say of her work that it was her mission; and when people said to her: "Never have such things been seen as these deeds of yours. In no book can one read of such things," she answered: "My Lord has a book in which no Clerk has ever read, how perfect soever he may be in clerkship!"

In war and in camp, when there was not enough provision, she would never eat stolen food. I firmly believe she was sent from God on account of her good works, and her many virtues; even on the poor English soldiers she had so much compassion that, when she saw them dying or wounded, she had them confessed. So much did she fear God, that for nothing in the world would she displease Him. When she was wounded in the shoulder by an arrow—which went through from one side to the other—some spoke of "charming" her, promising in this manner to cure her on the spot. She replied that it would be a sin, and that she would rather die than offend God by such enchantments.

I marvel much that such great Clerks as those who caused her death at Rouen should have dared such a crime as to put to death so poor and simple a Christian, cruelly and without cause—sufficient at least for [the penalty of] death: they might have kept her in prison or elsewhere; but she had so displeased them that they were her mortal enemies; and thus, it seems, they assumed the responsibility of an unjust court. Her actions and her deeds are all perfectly known to our Lord the King and to the Duke d'Alençon, who knew certain secrets which they might declare if they would.

As for me I know no more than what I have said, unless it be that many times Jeanne expressed to me a desire that, if she were to die, the King would build a Chapel, where the souls of those who had died in defence of the kingdom might be prayed for.

MAÎTRE JEAN DE LENOZOLLES, *Priest, of the Order of St. Pierre Celestin.*

At the time when Jeanne was at Rouen, I was in the service of Maître Guillaume Érard, with whom I came from Burgundy. After we had arrived, I heard talk of this Trial; but of what was done therein I know nothing, for I left Rouen and went to Caen, and stayed there until the feast of Pentecost; at this feast I returned to Rouen to meet my master, who told me that he had a heavy task— to preach a sermon for this Jeanne, which much displeased him. He said he would he were in Flanders: this business disturbed him much.

I saw Jeanne at the second sermon; and in the morning before the sermon I saw the Body of Christ carried to the said Jeanne with much solemnity, and the singing of Litanies and intercession "*Orate pro eâ*," and with a great multitude of candles; but who decided or ordered this, I know not. I was not present at the reception, but I afterwards heard it said that she received It with great devotion and abundance of tears.

SIMON CHARLES, *President of the Council.*

The year in which Jeanne came to seek the King was the very year in which the King sent me as ambassador to Venice. I returned about the month of March, at which time I heard from Jean de Metz, who had conducted her, that she had visited the King. When Jeanne came to Chinon, there was discussion in the Council as to whether the King should hear her or not. And first she was questioned as to why and to what end she had come; and she began by replying that she would answer nothing except to the King. She was compelled, by order of the King, to state the cause of her mission.

She said she had two commands from the King of Heaven: the one to raise the siege of Orleans, the other to conduct the King to Rheims for his coronation and anointing.

Hearing this, some of the King's Council said that the King ought not to put faith in this Jeanne; others said that, as she declared she was sent from God and commanded to speak to the King, the King ought at least to hear her. The King desired that she should first be examined by the Clergy and Ecclesiastics, and this was done; after many difficulties it was arranged that the King should hear her. I have heard the Seigneur de Gaucourt relate that, when she was at Orleans, the King's people had decided it was not well to make the attack. This happened on the day when the Fort of the Augustins was taken and he, de Gaucourt, had been commissioned to guard the gates of the town that none should go out. Jeanne, discontented with the orders of the generals, was of opinion that the King's soldiers with the people of the town should go out and attack the fort; and many of the soldiers and people of the city agreed with her. Jeanne told de Gaucourt that he was a bad man, saying to him: "Whether you will or no, the soldiers shall come; and they will succeed this time as they have succeeded before." And, against the will of the said Lord de Gaucourt, the soldiers left the city and marched to the assault of the bastille of the Augustins, which was taken by force. My Lord de Gaucourt added that he had come that day into great peril.

The King made a treaty with the people of Troyes, and entered the town of Troyes in great array, Jeanne carrying her banner by his side. Shortly after, the King left Troyes and went with his army to Chalons, and thence to Rheims. When the King feared to find resistance at Rheims, Jeanne said to him: "Have no fear! for the burghers of the city will come out to meet you;" and she said that, before he got near the city of Rheims, the burgesses would meet him. The King feared their resistance because he had no artillery or engines for carrying on a siege, in case they should prove rebellious. Jeanne told him that he must go forward boldly and fear nothing, for if he would go forward like a man he would soon obtain all his kingdom.

THIBAULD D'ARMAGNAC, *Knight, Seigneur de Termes, bailiff of Chartres*.

I knew nothing of Jeanne until she came to Orleans to raise the siege made by the English, in the defence of which town I was in the company of my lord of Dunois.

I afterwards saw her at the assault of the Forts of Saint Loup, the Augustins, Saint-Jean-le-Blanc, and at the Bridge. In all these assaults she was so valorous and comported herself in such manner as would not have been possible to any man, however well versed in war; and all the captains marvelled at her valour and activity and at her endurance.

I believe that she was good and worthy, and that the things she did were divine rather than human. She often reproved the vices of the soldiers; and I heard from a certain Maître Robert Baignart, S.T.P., of the Order of Saint Dominic, who often heard her in confession, that Jeanne was a godly woman, that all she did came from God, that she had a good soul and tender conscience.

After the raising of the siege of Orleans, I with many others of the army went with Jeanne to Beaugency, where the English were. The day that the English lost the battle of Patay, I and the late La Hire, knowing that the English were assembled and prepared for battle, told Jeanne that the English were coming and were all ready to fight. She replied, speaking to the captains: "Attack them boldly, and they will fly; nor will they long withstand us." At these words, the captains prepared to attack: and the English were overthrown and fled. Jeanne had predicted to the French that few or none of them should be slain or suffer loss: which also befell, for of all our men there perished but one gentleman of my company.

Apart from affairs of war, she was simple and innocent; but in the conduct and disposition of troops and in actual warfare, in the ordering of battle and in animating the soldiers, she behaved as the most skilled captain in the world who all his life had been trained in the art of war.

RAIMOND, SIEUR DE MACY, *Knight*.

I knew nothing of Jeanne until I saw her in prison, in the Castle of Beaurevoir, where she was detained for and in the name of the Count de Ligny; then I saw her often and many times talked with her: she would allow no familiarity, but repelled such with all her power; she was indeed of modest bearing, both in words and deeds.

She was taken to the Castle of Rouen, where she was placed in a prison facing the fields. Whilst she was there, in this prison, came the Count de Ligny, on whom I was in attendance. The Count de Ligny desired to see Jeanne, and came to visit her, in company of the Earls of Warwick and Stafford, the present Chancellor of England, then Bishop of Thérouanne, the brother[202] of the Count de Ligny, and myself. He said to her: "Jeanne, I have come to ransom you, if you will promise never again to bear arms against us." She answered: "In God's Name, you mock me, for I know well that you have neither the will nor the power;" this she repeated often, because the Count persisted in his statement. "I know well," she ended by saying, "that the English will do me to death, thinking after my death to gain the kingdom of France; but if they were a hundred thousand more 'godons'[203] than they are at present, they would not have the kingdom." Indignant at these words, the Earl of Stafford half drew his dagger to kill her, but the Earl of Warwick withheld him. After this, while I was still at Rouen, Jeanne was taken to the Place St. Ouen, where a sermon was preached to her by Maître Nicolas Midi,[204] who, amongst other things, said, in my hearing: "Jeanne, we have great compassion for thee; it behoves thee to revoke what thou hast said, or we must give thee up to the secular judges." She answered, that she had done no evil, that she believed in the Twelve Articles of the Faith and in the Ten Commandments of the Decalogue; adding, that she referred herself to the Court of Rome, and that she wished to believe all things in which Holy Church believed. Notwithstanding this, they pressed her much to recant, to which she answered: "You take much pains to seduce me;" and, to escape danger, she said at last that she was content to do all they required. Then a Secretary of the King of England there present, named Laurence Calot,

---

[202] Louis de Luxembourg.
[203] "Godon," or "goddam," a common term for the English in the Middle Ages and to the present day.
[204] An error; the first sermon was by Érard.

drew from his pocket a little written schedule, which he handed to Jeanne to sign. She replied that she could neither read nor write. Notwithstanding this Laurence Calot, the Secretary, handed Jeanne the schedule and a pen to sign it; and by way of derision Jeanne made some sort of round mark. Then Laurence Calot took her hand with the pen and caused her to make some sort of signature,—what, I cannot remember.

I believe her to be in Paradise.

COLETTE, *wife of* PIERRE MILET.

I first knew of Jeanne when she came to Orleans; she was lodged in the house of one Jacques Bouchier, where I went to visit her. Jeanne continually spoke of God, saying, "My Lord hath sent me to succour the good town of Orleans." I often saw her attend Mass with great devotion, as a good Christian and Catholic. During the time she was at Orleans, for the raising of the siege, Jeanne was sleeping in the house of her host, Jacques le Bouchier; on the Vigil of the Ascension, she suddenly awoke, and, calling her page, Mugot,[205] said to him: "In God's Name! This is ill done. Why was I not sooner awakened? Our people have much to do." Then she asked for her armour, and armed herself, her page bringing round her horse; then, all armed, she mounted, lance in rest, and began to ride along the main street so rapidly that the stones struck fire. She made straight for Saint Loup; and gave order, by sound of trumpet, that nothing should be taken from the Church.

On the morning of the day that the Fort of the Bridge was taken, Jeanne was still in the house of her host when a fish was brought to her: on seeing it she said to her host, "Take care of it till the evening, because I will bring you back a 'godon' and I shall return by the bridge."

Jeanne was very frugal in eating and drinking. There was nothing but modesty in her conduct, in her actions, and in all her manner of life. I believe firmly that her deeds and actions were rather the works of God than of

---

[205] Louis de Contes, called "Imerguet" and "Mugot" by his companions.

man.

PIERRE MILET, *Clerk to the Electors of Paris.*

Soon after she came to Orleans, she sent to the English, who were besieging the town, and summoned them in a kind of simple schedule written in her mother-tongue, which I read myself, notifying that it was the will of God that they should depart:

["Messire vous mande que vous en aliez en vostre pays, car c'est son plaisir, ou sinon je vous feray ung tel hahay...."[206]]

MAÎTRE AIGNAN VIOLE, *Licentiate in Law, Advocate of the Court of Parliament.*

On the Sunday after the taking of the Forts of the Bridge and of Saint Loup, the English were drawn up in order of battle before the town of Orleans, at which the greater part of [our] soldiers wished to give combat, and sallied from the town. Jeanne, who was wounded, was with the soldiers, dressed in her light surcoat. She put the men in array, but forbade them to attack the English, because, she said, if it pleased God and it were His will that they wished to retire, they should be allowed to go. And at that the men-at-arms returned into Orleans.

It was said that Jeanne was as expert as possible in the art of ordering an army in battle, and that even a captain bred and instructed in war could not have shown more skill; at this the captains marvelled exceedingly.

She frequently confessed, often received the Holy Sacrament, and, in all her deeds and conversation, bore herself most worthily, and in everything save in warfare she was marvellously simple.

## DEPOSITIONS AT ROUEN: 1455–6.

GUILLAUME COLLES, *or* BOISGUILLAUME, *Priest, Notary Public.*

---

[206] The phrase is left thus unfinished in all the MSS. It is quoted in the Latin texts in the original French, as above.

I knew nothing of Jeanne till she was brought to Rouen for her trial, at which I was one of the notaries. In the copy of the Process shown to me, I recognize my own signature at the end. It is the true Process made against Jeanne, and is one of five similar copies made. In the said Process were associated with me Maître Guillaume Manchon and Maître Pierre Taquel. In the morning we registered the notes and answers, and in the afternoon we collected them together. For nothing in the world would we have failed in anything that should have been done.

I remember well that Jeanne answered more prudently when questioned a second time upon a point whereon she had been already questioned; she failed not to say that she had elsewhere replied, and she told the notaries to read what she had already said.

Maître Nicolas Loyseleur, feigning to be a cobbler—a captive on the part of the King of France, and from Lorraine—obtained entrance to Jeanne's prison, to whom he said that she should not believe the Churchmen, "because," he added, "if you believe them, you will be destroyed." I believe the Bishop of Beauvais knew this well, otherwise Loyseleur would not have done as he did. Many of the Assessors in the Process murmured against him. It is said that Loyseleur died suddenly at Bâle; and I have heard that, when he saw Jeanne condemned to death, he was seized with compunction and climbed into the cart, earnestly desiring her pardon; at which many of the English were indignant; and that, had it not been for the Earl of Warwick, Loyseleur would have been killed; the said Earl enjoined him to leave Rouen as soon as he possibly could, if he wished to save his life.

In the same way, Maître Guillaume d'Estivet got into the prison, feigning to be a prisoner—as Loyseleur had done. This d'Estivet was Promoter, and in this matter was much affected towards the English, whom he desired to please. He was a bad man, and often during the Process spoke ill of the notaries and of those who, as he saw, wished to act justly; and he often cruelly insulted Jeanne, calling her foul names. I think that, in the end of his days, he was punished by God; for he died miserably. He was found dead in a drain outside the gates of Rouen.

Jeanne was often disconcerted by questions which were subtle and not pertinent. I remember that, on one occasion, she was asked if she were in a state of grace. She replied, that it was a serious matter to answer such a question, and at last said: "If I am, may God so keep me. If I am not, may God so place me. I would rather die than not be in the love of God." At this reply the questioners were much confounded, and broke up the sitting; nor was she further interrogated on that occasion.

On the Sunday following the first sentence, I was summoned to the Castle with the other notaries to see Jeanne dressed in man's dress; we went to the Castle, entered the prison, and there saw her. Questioned as to why she had resumed it, she made excuses, as appears in the Process. I think, perhaps, that she was induced to act thus, for I saw many of those concerned in the Process applauding and rejoicing that she had resumed her old dress; yet some lamented, among whom I saw Pierre Maurice grieving much.

On the following Wednesday, Jeanne was taken to the Old Market of Rouen, where a sermon was preached by Maître Nicolas Midi upon the Sentence of Relapse pronounced by the Bishop of Beauvais. After this sentence was read, she was taken by the civil authorities, and, without further trial or sentence, was led to the executioner, to be burnt. And I know, of a truth, that the Judges and their adherents were henceforward notorious to the population: after Jeanne was burnt, they were pointed at by the people and hated; and I have heard it maintained that all who were guilty of her death came to a shameful end. Maître Nicolas Midi died of leprosy a few days later; and the Bishop died suddenly while he was being shaved.

JEAN LEMAIRE, *Priest, Curé of the Church of St. Vincent at Rouen*; [evidence of no special value.]

MAUGIER LEPARMENTIER, *Clerk, Apparitor of the Archiepiscopal Court of Rouen.*

I knew nothing of Jeanne until she came to Rouen. I

was summoned to the Castle of Rouen, with my assistants, to submit Jeanne to torture. On this occasion, she was questioned on various subjects and answered with such prudence that all present marvelled. Then I and my associates retired without doing anything.

She was a prisoner in the Castle, in a great tower. I saw her when I was summoned to the torture, as aforesaid. I was present at the first preaching at St. Ouen, and also at the last at the Old Market, on the day when Jeanne was burnt. Wood was prepared for the burning before the preaching was finished or the sentence pronounced; and as soon as the sentence was read by the Bishop, without any interval, she was taken to the fire. I did not notice that any sentence by the civil authorities was read. When she was in the fire she cried, more than six times, "Jesus!" And with the last breath she cried with a loud voice, so that all present might hear, "Jesus!" Nearly all wept for pity. I have heard it said that, after the burning, her ashes were collected and thrown into the Seine.

*Pierre Cauchon,*
*Bishop of Beauvais. Died Bishop of Lisieux 1442.*
*Tomb formerly in the Cathedral of Lisieux.*

LAURENCE GUESDON, *Burgher of Rouen, and Advocate in the Civil Courts.*

I knew nothing of Jeanne till she was brought to Rouen; but I was so anxious to see her that I went to the Castle, and there saw her for the first time. I did not see her again until the time of the preaching at Saint Ouen.

I was at the final sermon in the Old Market Place, at Rouen; I went as Bailly, for whom I was then acting as deputy. The sentence by which Jeanne was handed over to the civil authorities was read; and, as soon as it was pronounced,—at once, without any interval of handing her over to the Bailly, without more ado, and before either the Bailly or myself, whose office it was, had given sentence,—the executioner seized her and took her to the place where the stake was already prepared: and she was burned. And this I hold was not a right proceeding: for soon after, a malefactor named George Folenfont was in like manner handed over, by sentence, from the ecclesiastical to the civil authorities; and, after the sentence, the said George was conducted to the Cohue,[207] and there condemned by the secular justice, instead of being immediately conducted to execution.

I think Jeanne died as a Catholic, for, in dying, she cried on the name of the Lord Jesus. She was very devout, and nearly all present were moved to tears. After she was dead, the ashes that remained were collected by the executioner and thrown into the Seine.

JEAN RICQUIER, *Priest, Chaplain in the Cathedral of Rouen, and Curé of the Church at Hendicourt.*

I first saw Jeanne at the sermon at Saint Ouen, and again at the Old Market. I was then about twenty.

At the time when Jeanne was brought to Rouen, I was in the choir of the Cathedral, and sometimes heard of the Trial from the Clergy of the Cathedral.

I was present at the sermon in the Old Market, on the day Jeanne died. I know she was handed over by the ecclesiastical authorities. I saw the English followers and soldiers seize her, and lead her immediately to the place of execution; nor did I see any sentence read by the secular authorities.

On that morning, before the sermon, Maître Pierre Maurice came to visit her; to whom she said, "Maître Pierre, where shall I be this evening?" Maître Pierre replied, "Have you not a good hope in God?" She answered that she had; and that, God willing, she would be in Paradise. This I heard from the aforesaid Maître Pierre. When Jeanne saw that they were setting fire to the pile, she began to say, with a loud voice, "Jesus!" and constantly, to the end, she cried, "Jesus!"

And after she was dead, because the English feared that people would say she had escaped, they ordered the executioner to part the flames a little, in order that those

---

[207] The Court of the Bailiff.

present might see she was dead. I was near to Maître Jean Alépée, at that time Canon of Rouen, and heard him say these words, weeping greatly: "God grant that my soul may be in the place where I believe this woman's to be!"

JEAN MOREAU, *Visitor in the city of Rouen.*

I live at Rouen; but I came from Viville, in Bassigny,—not far from Domremy, where Jeanne was born.

At the time when Jeanne was at Rouen, and during the Trial against her, a man of note from Lorraine came to the town. We soon made acquaintance, being of the same country. He told me that he came from the Marches of Lorraine, and that he had been called to Rouen, having been commissioned to get information in the native country of the said Jeanne, and to hear what was said about her. This he had done, and had brought it to the Bishop of Beauvais, expecting to have satisfaction for his labour and expense. But the Bishop blamed him for a traitor and a bad man, and said he had not done in this as he had been told. My compatriot complained that he could not get any wage from the Bishop, who found his information of no use: he told me that in this information he had learnt nothing of Jeanne which he would not willingly know of his own sister, although he had made enquiries in five or six parishes near Domremy as well as in the village itself. I remember it was said that she had committed the crime of *lèse majesté*,[208] and had led the people away.

HUSSON LE MAÎTRE, *of Viville, in Bassigny, Coal Merchant.*

I knew nothing of Jeanne until she came to Rheims, for the King's coronation, in which town I was then living. Thither came also her father and her brother Pierre, both of whom were friendly with me and my wife, as we were compatriots; and they called my wife "neighbour."

I was in my own neighbourhood when Jeanne went

---

[208] "*Crimen læsæ majestatis.*"

to Vaucouleurs, to Robert de Baudricourt, that she might get an escort to go to the King. I then said it was by the grace of God, and that Jeanne was led by the Spirit of God. Jeanne requested the said Robert to give her an escort to conduct her to my lord the Dauphin.

I heard, at the time when she was taken from Vaucouleurs to the King, that some of the soldiers who conducted her feigned to be on the other side, and, when those who were with her pretended to fly, she said to them: "Fly not, in God's Name! they will do us no harm." When she came to the King, she recognized him, though she had never seen him before; and afterwards she took the King without hindrance to Rheims, where I saw her; and from Rheims the King went to Corbignac, and afterwards to Château Thierry, which was surrendered to the King. And there arrived news that the English were come to fight against the King; but Jeanne told the King's people not to fear, for the English would not come.

PIERRE DARON, *Locum Tenens, Deputy to the Bailiff of Rouen.*

I knew nothing of Jeanne until she was brought to Rouen, where, at that time, I was Procurator of the town. Having much curiosity to see the said Jeanne, I enquired the best means to accomplish this: and a certain Pierre Manuel, Advocate of the King of England, who was also anxious to see her, came, and together we went to see her.

We found her in the Castle, in a certain turret, in shackles, with a great piece of wood chained to her feet, and having many English guards. And Manuel said to her, in my presence, jokingly, that she would never have come there if she had not been brought: and he asked her if she knew, before she was captured, that she would be taken; to which she replied that she had feared it. When he asked her, afterwards, why, if she feared to be taken prisoner, she did not guard herself on the day that she was captured, she replied that she did not know either the day or hour when she was to be taken.

I saw her once again during the Trial, when she was being brought from the prison to the great hall of the

Castle.

I heard from several, during the Trial, that Jeanne was quite wonderful in her answers, and that she had a remarkable memory; for, on one occasion, when questioned as to a point on which she had answered eight days before, she replied: "I was asked about this eight days ago, and thus replied." Boisguillaume, the other notary, said she had not answered; and, when some of those present declared that what Jeanne said was true, the answers of that day were read: and it was found that Jeanne had spoken right. At this she rejoiced, saying to Boisguillaume that, if he made mistakes again, she would pull his ears!

I was present at the sermon at the Old Market on the day that Jeanne died. Among other things, I heard her say: "Ah! Rouen, Rouen, wilt thou be my last dwelling?" She inspired in all the greatest pity, and many were moved to tears; many, too, were much displeased that Jeanne had been executed in the town of Rouen. At the close of her life, she continually cried "Jesus!" Her ashes and remains were afterwards collected and thrown into the Seine.

BROTHER SÉGUIN DE SÉGUIN, *Dominican, Professor of Theology, Dean of the Faculty of Theology of Poitiers.*

I saw Jeanne for the first time at Poitiers. The King's Council was assembled in the house of the Lady La Macée, the Archbishop of Rheims, then Chancellor of France, being of their number. I was summoned, as also were Jean Lombart, Professor of Theology of the University of Paris; Maître Guillaume le Maire, Canon of Poitiers and Bachelor in Theology; Maître Guillaume Aymerie, Professor of Theology, of the Order of Saint Dominic; Brother Pierre Turrelure; Maître Jacques Maledon; and many others whose names I do not remember. The Members of the Council told us that we were summoned, in the King's name, to question Jeanne and to give our opinion upon her. We were sent to question her at the house of Maître Jean Rabateau, where she was lodging. We repaired thither and interrogated her.

Among other questions, Maître Jean Lombart asked

her why she had come; that the King wished to know what had induced her to come to him. She answered, in a grand manner, that "there had come to her, while she was minding the cattle, a Voice, which told her that God had great compassion for the people of France, and that she must go into France." On hearing this, she began to weep; the Voice then told her to go to Vaucouleurs, where she would find a Captain who would conduct her safely into France and to the King, and that she must not be afraid. She had done what the Voice had ordered, and had come to the King without meeting any obstacle.

Thereupon, Guillaume Aymerie put to her this question: "You assert that a Voice told you, God willed to deliver the people of France from the calamity in which they now are; but, if God wills to deliver them, it is not necessary to have soldiers." "In God's Name!" Jeanne replied, "the soldiers will fight, and God will give the victory." With which answer Maître Guillaume was pleased.

I, in my turn, asked Jeanne what dialect the Voice spoke? "A better one than yours," she replied. I speak the Limousin dialect. "Do you believe in God?" I asked her. "In truth, more than yourself!" she answered. "But God wills that you should not be believed unless there appear some sign to prove that you ought to be believed; and we shall not advise the King to trust in you, and to risk an army on your simple statement." "In God's Name!" she replied, "I am not come to Poitiers to shew signs: but send me to Orleans, where I shall shew you the signs by which I am sent:" and she added: "Send me men in such numbers as may seem good, and I will go to Orleans."

And then she foretold to us—to me and to all the others who were with me—these four things which should happen, and which did afterwards come to pass: first, that the English would be destroyed, the siege of Orleans raised, and the town delivered from the English; secondly, that the King would be crowned at Rheims; thirdly, that Paris would be restored to his dominion; and fourthly, that the Duke d'Orléans should be brought back from England. And I who speak, I have in truth seen these four things accomplished.

JEANNE D'ARC.
From a Miniature of the XVth Century.

We reported all this to the Council of the King; and we were of opinion that, considering the extreme necessity and the great peril of the town, the King might make use of her help and send her to Orleans.

Besides this, we enquired into her life and morals; and found that she was a good Christian, living as a Catholic, never idle. In order that her manner of living might be better known, women were placed with her who were commissioned to report to the Council her actions and ways.

As for me, I believed she was sent from God, because, at the time when she appeared, the King and all the French people with him had lost hope: no one thought of aught but to save himself.

I remember that Jeanne was asked why she always marched with a banner in her hand? "Because," she answered, "I do not wish to use my sword, nor to kill any one."

When she heard any one taking in vain the Name of God, she was very angry; she held such blasphemies in horror: and Jeanne told La Hire, who used many oaths and swore by God, that he must swear no more, and that, when he wanted to swear by God, he should swear *by his staff*. And afterwards, indeed, when he was with her, La Hire never swore but by his staff.

TESTIMONY OF D'AULON:[209] 1456.

And first, Deponent saith that, twenty years ago or thereabouts, the King being in the town of Poitiers, he [d'Aulon] was told that the said Maid, who was from the country of Lorraine, had been brought to the said Lord by two gentlemen, the same being of the company of Messire Robert de Baudricourt, Knight—the one named Bertrand; the other Jean de Metz—and presented [to the King]; to see whom (the said Maid) the Deponent visited the said town of Poitiers;

That, after the presentation, the Maid spoke privately to our Lord the King, and told him several secret things— what, he [the Deponent] knew not: saving that, shortly after, the King sent to fetch some of the people of his Council, among whom was the Deponent. He [the King] then informed them that the Maid had told him she was sent from God to help him to recover his kingdom, which at that time was for the most part occupied by his ancient enemies, the English;

That, after these words had been declared to the people of his Council by the King, it was agreed to interrogate the Maid—who, at that time, was of the age of sixteen years or thereabouts—upon sundry points touching the Faith;

That, to do this, the King sent for certain Masters in Theology, Jurists, and other expert people, who should well and diligently examine her on these points;

---

[209] The examination of d'Aulon, who served Jeanne d'Arc as Steward, and who, at the time of being examined, was Seneschal of Beaucaire, is the only evidence preserved in the original French.

THE BATTLE OF PATAY.

LA HIRE AND XANTRAILLES.

That he was present at the said Council when the Masters made their report on what they had found in the Maid; at which it was publicly said by one of them, that they did not see, know, or recognize in the Maid anything, excepting only whatever should be in a good Christian and true Catholic: and for such they held her, and it was their opinion that she was very worthy;

Also that, the report being made to the said King by the Masters, the Maid was then handed over to the Queen of Sicily, the mother of our Sovereign Lady the Queen, and to certain ladies with her, by whom the Maid was seen, visited, and privately looked at and examined; and after examination made by these matrons, the lady stated to the King that she and the other ladies found most surely that this was indeed a true Maid ...;

That he was present when the lady made her report;

That, these things being heard, and considering the great goodness in the Maid, and that God had sent her to him, as she had said, it was by the King concluded in his Council that henceforward he would make use of her help in his wars, inasmuch as for this she had been sent;

That, it was then decided she should be sent to the city of Orleans, at that time besieged by the enemy;

That, for this end people were given for her own service, and others to conduct her;

That, the guard and conduct of the same was appointed by our Lord the King;

Also that, for the safety of her body the King caused to be made armour fit for the Maid's body, and, this done, appointed a certain number of men-at-arms for the same [Maid] and for those of her company, to lead and conduct them safely to the City of Orleans;

That, immediately afterwards, he [the Deponent] took the road with them, following in this direction;

That, as soon as it came to the knowledge of my Lord Dunois—then called the Bastard of Orleans, who was in the city of Orleans in order to keep and guard it from the enemy—that the Maid was coming that way, he assembled together a certain number of men of war to meet her, such as La Hire and others. And to do this, and more safely to lead and conduct her to the city, this Lord and his followers placed themselves in a boat, and went to meet her by the river Loire, about a quarter of a league distant, and there found her;

That, the Maid and the Deponent immediately entered the boat, while the remainder of her soldiers turned back toward Blois. And, with the Lord Dunois and his followers, they entered the city sure and safe; in which [city] the Lord Dunois lodged her well and comfortably in the house of one of the principal burghers of the city, who had married one of the principal women thereof;

That, after the said Lord Dunois, La Hire, and certain other captains of the party of our Lord the King, had conferred with the Maid as to what was expedient to do for the guardianship, keeping, and defence of the city, and also by what means the enemy could be best harassed, it was between them agreed and concluded to be necessary that a certain number of men-at-arms of their party, then near Blois, should be sent for and brought. To put this into execution, and to fetch them to the city, were appointed the Lord Dunois and the Deponent, and certain other captains, with their followers, who sent to the country of Blois to bring the same;

That, as soon as they were ready to depart and bring those who were in the country of Blois, and that this came to the notice of the Maid, immediately she mounted her horse, and, together with La Hire and a certain number of her followers, she went out into the fields to keep the enemy from doing them injury. And, in order to do this, the Maid placed herself with her followers between the army of the enemy and the city of Orleans; and so wrought, that,—thanks to God!—notwithstanding the great power and number of the soldiers in the army of the enemy, the Lord Dunois and the Deponent, with all their followers, passed through, and safely went their way: and in the same way returned the Maid and her followers to the city;

That, as soon as she knew of the coming of the aforesaid, and that they brought with them those whom they had gone to fetch for the reinforcement of the city, immediately the Maid mounted her horse and, with a party of her followers, went to meet them, to support and succour them, if there were need of it;

That, in the sight and knowledge of the enemies, the Maid, Dunois, Maréchal La Hire, and the Deponent, with their followers, entered the city without any opposition whatsoever;

Moreover, that, the same day, after dinner, came the said Lord Dunois to the lodging of the Maid, where she and the Deponent had dined together. And, in speaking to her, Dunois told her that he knew, of a truth, from people of worth, that one named Fastolf, captain of the enemy, would shortly join the enemy at the siege, not only to give them help and reinforce them, but also to victual them, and that he was then at Vinville. At which words the Maid much rejoiced—so it seemed to the Deponent—and said to my Lord Dunois these or such-like words: "Bastard, Bastard, in the Name of God I command thee that, so soon as thou knowest of the coming of the said Fastolf, thou dost let me know; for, if he pass without my knowing, I promise thee I will have thy head." To which replied the Lord Dunois, that of this he had no fear, for he would certainly let her know;

That, after these words, the Deponent being tired and overdone, placed himself on a couch in the chamber of the Maid, to rest himself a little, and also the Maid placed herself with her hostess on another bed in the same way, to sleep and rest; but, as the Deponent was beginning to take his rest, suddenly the Maid, though asleep, arose from her bed and, making a great noise, awoke him. And then the Deponent asked of her what she wanted; to which she answered: "En Nom Dè! my Counsel hath told me that I should attack the English; but I know not if I should attack their bastilles or go against Fastolf, who would victual them"; on which the Deponent immediately rose, and, as soon as he could, armed the Maid;

That, as soon as he had armed her, they heard a great noise and cry made by those of the city, saying that the enemy were doing much harm to the French. Then the Deponent armed himself, and, while he was so doing, without his knowledge, the Maid left the room, and went forth into the street. Here she found a page, on horseback, who at once dismounted from the horse; and immediately she mounted thereon, and, as straight and as speedily as she could, she took her way direct to the Burgundy Gate, where was the greatest noise;

That, the Deponent immediately followed the Maid; but, go as quickly as he might, she was already at the gate;

That, as they were coming to the gate, they saw being

carried away one of the people of the city, who was terribly wounded; and then the Maid asked of those carrying him who this man was. They replied that he was a Frenchman. Then she said she had never seen French blood without feeling her hair stand on end;

That, at the same time, the Maid, the Deponent, and many other men of war of their company, went out from the city to help the French, and to harass the enemy to the best of their power; but, as soon as they were outside the city, the Deponent was told that never had there been seen so many men-at-arms of their side as were now there;

That, after this passage, they took their road towards a very strong fort of the enemy, called the Fort of Saint Loup, which was at once attacked by the French, and, with very little loss to them, was taken by assault; and all the enemy within were killed or taken: and the fort remained in the hands of the French;

That, this being done, the Maid and those of her company returned into the city of Orleans, where they refreshed themselves and rested that day;

That, next day, the Maid and her people, considering the great victory obtained by them the day before over their enemies, sallied from the town in good order, to attack another fort in front of the city, called the Fort of Saint-Jean-le-Blanc: for which purpose, seeing that they could not get there by land—because their enemies had made another very strong fort, at the foot of the bridge of the city, so that it was impossible for them to cross [the bridge]—it was decided among them to pass over to a certain island in the river Loire, and there to assemble their entire army: and, in order to take the Fort of Saint-Jean-le-Blanc and to cross to the other arm of the river Loire, two boats were brought, of which a bridge was made, for the attack of the fort;

That, this done, they went to the fort, which they found quite deserted; for the English who were therein, so soon as they perceived the coming of the French, went away, retreating to another stronger and greater fort, called the Fort of the Augustins;

That, seeing the French were not powerful enough to

take the fort, it was decided they should return without doing anything further;

That, in order to return and cross more safely, the most notable and valiant of the party of the French were ordered to remain behind, in order to keep the enemy from troubling them on their return; and for this were appointed Messires de Gaucourt, de Villars, then Seneschal of Beaucaire, and the Deponent;

That, while the French were returning from the Fort of Saint-Jean-le-Blanc to the island, the Maid and La Hire both crossed over, each with a horse, in a boat from the other side of the island; and on these horses they mounted as soon as they had crossed, each with lance in hand. As soon as they saw that the enemy was making a sally from the fort to rush upon their people, immediately the Maid and La Hire, who were always in the front to protect them, couched their lances and were the first to attack the enemy; others then followed and began to attack the English, in such wise that they forcibly constrained them to retreat and enter the Fort of the Augustins;

And, while this was going on, the Deponent, being in guard of a passage with others appointed and ordered thereto—among whom was a very valiant man-at-arms of the country of Spain, named Alphonse de Partada—saw passing before them another man-at-arms of their company, a tall man, big and well armed, to whom, because he was about to pass on, the Deponent remarked that he ought to remain there for a time, with the others, and make resistance to the enemy, should need arise; and he immediately replied that he would do nothing [of the kind]. Then Alphonse said he also would remain with the others, and that there were many as valiant men as he who would remain willingly; who answered Alphonse, that it would not be he. Upon which there were between them certain proud words, so much that they decided to go, both of them, the one and the other, against the enemy; and then it would be seen which was the more valiant, and which of the two would best do his duty. And, taking one another by the hand, at the greatest pace they could, they went towards the fort of the enemy, and so to the foot of the palisade;

That, as they reached the palisade of the fort, the Deponent saw within the palisade a tall, strong and powerful Englishman, armed at all points, who so resisted them that they could not enter. Then the Deponent shewed the Englishman to a man named Maître Jean the Cannoneer, telling him to shoot at the Englishman; for he was doing much harm and injury to those who wished to approach the fort. This Maître Jean did; for, as soon as he saw him, he aimed a shot at him, so that he fell dead to the ground; then the two men-at-arms won the passage, by which all the others of their company crossed, and entered the fort, which most fiercely and with great persistence they assailed on all sides, so that within a short time they won it and took it by assault. There were killed or taken the greater part of the enemy; and those who were able to save themselves retreated into the Fort of Tourelles, at the foot of the bridge. Thus, the Maid and those who were with her obtained victory over the enemy that day. And the great battle was won; and the Lords and their people with the Maid remained before the same [fort] all that night;

Moreover, that, the next day, in the morning, the Maid sent to fetch all the lords and captains before the captured fort, to consult as to what more should be done; by the advice of whom it was concluded and resolved to attack this day a great Boulevard, which the English had made, before the Fort of Tourelles, and that it was expedient to gain it before doing anything else. To do and put this into execution, the Maid, the captain, and their people, on this day, very early in the morning, went from one place to the other, before the Boulevard, and on this they made the assault from all sides, making every effort to take it, in such manner that they were before the Boulevard from morning till sunset without being able to take it or gain it. And the lords and captains who were with her, seeing that they could not well gain it this day, considering the hour, which was late, and that all were very tired and worn out, it was agreed amongst them to sound the retreat for the army; which was done; and, at sound of the trumpet-call, each one retreated for that day. In making this retreat, because the Deponent, who was carrying the standard of the Maid, and holding it upright before the Boulevard, became fatigued and worn-out, he gave the standard to one named La Basque, who was of the following of De Villars; and because the Deponent knew La Basque to be a valiant man, and feared that, by reason of the retreat, evil would ensue, and that the fort and Boulevard would remain in the hands of the enemy, he had an idea that, if the standard were pushed to the front,—from the great affection which he knew the soldiers had for it—they might for this reason gain the Boulevard. Then the Deponent asked La Basque, if he were to enter and go to the foot of the Boulevard, would he follow him; who said and promised that he would; then the Deponent entered the trench, and went up to the foot of the sides of the Boulevard, covering himself with his shield for fear of the stones, and left his companion on the other side, believing he would follow him step by step. But when the Maid saw her standard in the hand of La Basque, and because she believed she had lost it, as he who bore it had gone into the trench, the Maid came and took the standard by the end in such wise that he could not hold it, crying, "Ha! my standard! my standard!" and shook the standard in such wise that the Deponent thought that, in so doing, the others might imagine she was making some sign to them; then the Deponent cried: "La Basque, is this what thou didst promise me?" Then La Basque so pulled at the standard that he dragged it from the hand of the Maid; and, this being done, he went to the Deponent and brought the standard. On this account all the army of the Maid assembled together and rallied again, and, with great fierceness, assailed the Boulevard, so that, shortly after, the Boulevard and the fort were taken by them, and abandoned by the enemy, the French [on their return] entering the city of Orleans by the bridge;

And the Deponent saith that, on this very day, he had heard it spoken by the Maid: "In God's Name, we shall enter the town this night by the bridge." This done, the Maid and her followers returned into the town of Orleans, in which the Deponent had her [wound] dressed, for she had been wounded by an arrow in the assault;

Also that, next day, all the English still remaining before the town on the other side of the Fort of Tourelles, raised the siege and retreated, being discomfited and in confusion. Thus, by the help of God and the Maid, was the city delivered from the hands of the enemy;

Moreover, that, some time after the return from the consecration of the King, he [the King] was advised by his Council—then at Meung-sur-Yèvre—that it was most necessary to recover the town of La Charité, which was held by the enemy; but that first must be taken the town of Saint Pierre le Moustier, which likewise was held by the enemy;

That, to do this and to collect men, the Maid went to the town of Bourges, in which she assembled her forces; and from thence, with a certain number of men-at-arms, of whom Lord d'Elbret was the head, she went to besiege the town of Saint Pierre le Moustier;

That, after the Maid and her followers had made siege against the town for some time, an assault was ordered to be made against the town; and so it was done, and those who were there did their best to take it; but, on account of the great number of people in the town, the great strength thereof and also the great resistance made by those within, the French were compelled and forced to retreat, for the reasons aforesaid; and at that time, the Deponent was wounded by a shot in the heel, so that without crutches he could neither keep up nor walk: he noticed that the Maid was left accompanied by very few of her own people and others; and the Deponent, fearing that trouble would follow therefrom, mounted a horse, and went immediately to her aid, asking her what she was doing there alone and why she did not retreat like the others. She, after taking her helmet ["*salade*"] from her head, replied that she was not alone, and that she had yet in her company fifty thousand of her people, and that she would not leave until she had taken the town;

And the Deponent saith that, at that time—whatever she might say—she had not with her more than four or five men, and this he knows most certainly, and many others also, who in like manner saw her; for which cause he told her again that she must leave that place, and retire as the others did. And then she told him to have faggots and hurdles brought to make a bridge over the trenches of the town, in order that they might approach it the better. And as she said these words to him, she cried in a loud voice: "Every one to the faggots and hurdles, to make the bridge!" which was immediately after done and prepared, at which the Deponent did much marvel, for immediately the town was taken by assault, without very great resistance;

That, all the deeds of the Maid seemed to him to be more divine and miraculous than otherwise, and that it was not possible for so young a Maid to do such things without the Will and Guidance of Our Lord;

Also that, for the space of a whole year, by command of our Lord the King, he remained in the company of the Maid, during which time he neither saw nor knew of anything in her which should not be in a good Christian; and he has always seen and known her to be of very good life and modest conversation in all and every one of her acts;

Also that, he knew the Maid to be most devout; that she shewed herself very reverent in hearing the Divine Service of our Lord, which she would constantly hear, that is to say, High Mass, on solemn days, wherever she was, with the Hours following; and on other days Low Mass; and that she was accustomed to hear Mass daily if it were possible;

That, many times he saw and knew that she confessed herself and received Our Lord, and did all that belongs to a good Christian to do, and that, never when he was conversing with her, did he hear her swear, blaspheme, or perjure the Name of Our Lord, nor the Saints, for whatever cause or occasion it might be;

And that, in his opinion, she was a good Christian, and must have been inspired; for she loved everything that a good Christian ought to love, and especially she loved a good honest man ["*bon prudhomme*"] whom she knew to be of chaste life; ... Also that, when the Maid had anything to do for the conduct of war, she told the Deponent that her Counsel had advised her what she ought to do;

That, he asked her who was the Counsel, and that she replied there were three Counsellors, of whom one always remained with her; another went away, but came often, to visit her; and the third was he with whom the two others consulted. And it happened that, one time, among others, the Deponent prayed and besought her that she would shew him the Counsel; to whom she replied that he was not worthy, nor of sufficient virtue to see them: and upon this the Deponent desisted from speaking or asking her further about them;

And the Deponent firmly believes as aforesaid, that, considering the deeds, actions and great leadership of the Maid, she was full of all the virtue which might or should be in a good Christian;

And thus he hath deposed, as is above written, without love, favour, hate, or suborning, but for the truth, and as he knew it to be in the Maid.

## SENTENCE OF REHABILITATION.

In the name of the Holy and Undivided Trinity, Father, Son, and Holy Ghost, Amen!

The Providence of the Eternal Majesty, the Saviour Christ, Lord God and Man, hath instituted, for the rule of His Church Militant, the Blessed Peter, and his Apostolic Successors; He hath made them His principal representatives, and charged them, by the light of truth, which He hath manifested to them, to teach men how to walk in the paths of justice, protecting the good, relieving the oppressed in the whole universe, and, by a reasonable judgment, bringing back into the right road those who have turned therefrom:

Invested with this Apostolic authority for the matter in question, we Jean of Rheims, Guillaume of Paris, and Richard of Coutances, by the Grace of God Archbishop and Bishops, and Jean Bréhal, of the Order of Saint Dominic, Professor of Sacred Theology, one of the two

Inquisitors of the Heretical Evil for the Realm of France, all four Judges specially delegated by our most Holy Lord the Pope actually reigning:

Having seen the solemn Process brought before us, by virtue of the Apostolic Mandate addressed to us, and by us respectfully accepted:

In the Case concerning the honest woman, Widow Isabelle d'Arc, mother, Pierre and Jean d'Arc, brothers german, natural and legal, of the deceased Jeanne d'Arc, of good memory, commonly called the Maid:

The said Case brought in their name,

Against the Sub-Inquisitor of the Heretical Evil for the Diocese of Beauvais, the Promoter of the Officiality of the said Diocese of Beauvais, and also the Reverend Father in Christ and Lord Guillaume de Hellande, Bishop of Beauvais, and against all others and each in particular who might be thought to be therein interested, all together respectively Defendants, as well conjointly as separately:

Having seen, in the first place, the peremptory citation and the execution of this citation made against the said Defendants, at the request not only of the said Plaintiffs but of the Promoter of our Office appointed by us, sworn and created, to the end that the said Defendants might see the carrying out of the said Rescript, hear the conclusions against them, and answer themselves; and to proceed, in one word, according to right:

Having seen the request of the said Plaintiffs, their deeds, reasons, and conclusion set down in writing under the form of Articles, putting forward a declaration of nullity, of iniquity, and of cozenage against a certain Process in a pretended Trial for the Faith, formerly done and executed in this city against the above-named woman, now deceased, by the late Lord Pierre Cauchon, then Bishop of Beauvais, Jean Lemaître, then Vice-Inquisitor of the said Diocese of Beauvais, and Jean d'Estivet, Promoter, or having at least acted in this capacity; the said request putting forward and inferring further the breaking down and annulling of the Process in question and of all which followed it, to the justification of the said Deceased, and to all the other ends therein enumerated:

Having seen, read, re-read and examined the original books, instruments, means, acts, notes and protocols of the said Process, shewn and sent to us, in virtue of the compulsory letters, by the Registrars and others whose signatures and writings have been, as a preliminary, acknowledged in our presence:

After having studied at length all these documents, not only with the said Registrars and other officials appointed in the said Process, but also with those of the Counsellors who were called to the same Process, those, at least, whom we have been able to bring before us:

And after having ourselves collated and compared the final text, with the Minute itself of the said Process:

Having considered also the Preparatory Enquiries,— first, those which were conducted by the Most Reverend Father in Christ the Lord Guillaume, Cardinal Priest under the title of Saint-Martin-les-Monts,[210] then Legate of the Holy Apostolic See in the Kingdom of France, assisted by the Inquisitor, after the examination which had been made by the said Cardinal-Legate of the books and instruments then presented:

Having afterwards considered the Preparatory Enquiry conducted at the beginning of the actual Process by us or our Commissaries:

Having considered also divers treatises[211] which had come from the Prelates, Doctors, and men of learning, the most celebrated and the most authorized, who, after having studied at length the books and instruments of the said Process, have separated from these books and instruments the doubtful points which they would have to elucidate in their said treatises composed afterwards and brought to light, whether by the order of the most Reverend Father aforesaid or of us:

Having considered the Articles and Interrogations to be submitted to the witnesses, presented to us in the name of the Plaintiffs and of our Promoter, and after many citations admitted in proof by us:

---

[210] Guillaume d'Estouteville: Enquiry of 1452.
[211] See Appendix: Note on Documents of Rehabilitation Enquiry.

Having considered the depositions and attestations of the witnesses heard on the subject of the said Articles and Interrogations on the life of the said Deceased in the place of her birth;—on her departure; on her examination before several Prelates, Doctors, and others having knowledge thereof, in presence notably of the Most Reverend Father Reginald, then Archbishop of Rheims and Metropolitan of the said Bishop of Beauvais: an examination made at Poitiers and elsewhere, on several occasions; on the marvellous deliverance of the city of Orleans; on the journey to the city of Rheims and the coronation of the King; and the divers circumstances of the Trial, the qualifications, the judges, and the manner of proceeding:

Having considered also letters, instruments, and measures, besides the letters, depositions and attestations just mentioned, sent to us and produced in the course of law:

Having afterwards heard our Promoter, who, considering these productions and these sayings, declares himself fully joined with the Plaintiffs:

Having heard the other requests and reserves made by our Promoter, in his own name as well as in that of the Plaintiffs, the said requests and reserves admitted by us and received at the same time as certain reasons of law briefly formulated, of a nature also to impress our minds:

After the Case had been concluded, in the Name of Christ, and this day had been assigned by us to give sentence:

After having, with great matureness, weighed, examined, all and each one of the aforesaid things, as well as certain Articles beginning with these words "A certain Woman, &c.,"[212] which the Judges in the first Process did pretend to have extracted from the confessions of the said Deceased, and which have been submitted by us to a great number of staid persons for their opinion; Articles which our Promoter, as well as the Plaintiffs aforesaid, attacked as iniquitous, false, prepared without reference to the confessions of Jeanne, and in a lying manner:

---

[212] *Viz.*, the Twelve Articles.

That our present Judgment may come as from the Face of God Himself, Who weigheth the spirits, Who alone infallibly knoweth His revelations, and doth hold them always at their true value, Who bloweth where He listeth, and doth often choose the weak to confound the strong, never forsaking those who trust in Him, but being their Support in their sorrows and their tribulations:

After having had ripe deliberation, as much on the subject of the Preparatory Enquiries as on the decision itself, with persons at the same time expert, authorized, and prudent:

Having considered their solemn decisions, formulated in the treatises written out in a compendious manner, and in numerous consultations:

Having considered their opinion, written or verbal, furnished and given, not only on the form but also on the basis of the Process, and according to which the actions of the said Deceased, being worthy of admiration rather than of condemnation, the judgment given against her should, in form as well as in basis, be reprehended and detested:

And because on the question of revelations it is most difficult to furnish a certain judgment, the Blessed Paul having, on the subject of his own revelations, said that he knew not if they came to him in body or in spirit, and having on this point referred himself to God:

In the first place, we say, and, because Justice requires it, we declare, that the Articles beginning with the words "A woman," which are found inserted in the pretended Process and Instrument of the pretended sentences, lodged against the said Deceased, ought to have been, have been, and are, extracted from the said pretended Process and the said pretended confessions of the said Deceased, with corruption, cozenage, calumny, fraud and malice:

We declare, that on certain points the truth of her confessions has been passed over in silence; that on other points her confessions have been falsely translated—a double unfaithfulness, by which, had it been prevented, the mind of the Doctors consulted and the Judges might have been led to a different opinion:

We declare, that in these Articles there have been added without right many aggravating circumstances, which are not in the aforesaid Confessions, and many circumstances both relevant and justifying have been passed over in silence:

We declare, that even the form of certain words has been altered, in such manner as to change the substance:

For the which, these same Articles, as falsely, calumniously, and deceitfully extracted, and as contrary even to the Confessions of the Accused, we break, annihilate, and annul; and, after they shall have been detached from the Process we ordain, by this present judgment, that they be torn up:

In the second place, after having examined with great care the other parts of the same said Process—particularly the two sentences which the Process contained, designated by the Judges as "Lapse" and "Relapse"—and after having also for a long time weighed the qualifications of the Judges and of all those under whom and in whose keeping the said Jeanne was detained:

We say, pronounce, decree, and declare, the said Processes and Sentences full of cozenage, iniquity, inconsequences, and manifest errors, in fact as well as in law; We say that they have been, are, and shall be—as well as the aforesaid Abjuration, their execution, and all that followed—null, non-existent, without value or effect.

Nevertheless, in so far as is necessary, and as reason doth command us, we break them, annihilate them, annul them, and declare them void of effect; and we declare that the said Jeanne and her relatives, Plaintiffs in the actual Process, have not, on account of the said Trial, contracted nor incurred any mark or stigma of infamy; we declare them quit and purged of all the consequences of these same Processes; we declare them, in so far as is necessary, entirely purged thereof by this present:

We ordain that the execution and solemn publication of our present Sentence shall take place immediately in this city, in two different places, to wit,

To-day in the Square of Saint Ouen, after a General Procession and a public Sermon:

To-morrow, at the Old Market-Place, in the same place where the said Jeanne was suffocated by a cruel and horrible fire, also with a General Preaching and with the placing of a handsome cross for the perpetual memory of the Deceased and for her salvation and that of other deceased persons:

We declare that we reserve to ourselves [the power] later on to execute, publish, and for the honour of her memory to signify with acclaim, our said sentence in the cities and other well-known places of the kingdom wherever we shall find it well [so to do], under the reserves, finally, of all other formalities which may yet remain to be done.

This present Sentence hath been brought out, read and promulgated by the Lords Judges, in presence of the Reverend Father in Christ the Lord Bishop of Démétriade, of Hector de Coquerel, Nicolas du Boys, Alain Olivier, Jean du Bec, Jean de Gouys, Guillaume Roussel, Laurent Surreau, Canons; of Martin Ladvenu, Jean Roussel, and Thomas de Fanouillères.

Maître Simon Chapitault, Promoter; Jean d'Arc and Prevosteau for the other Plaintiffs.

Done at Rouen in the Archiepiscopal Palace, in the year of our Lord 1456, the 7th day of the month of June.

THE HÔTEL DE VILLE: COMPIÈGNE.

# APPENDIX
## NOTE ON ORIGINAL DOCUMENTS OF THE PROCESS OF CONDEMNATION

1. *The Minute.*

The original French notes of the Trial, taken down at the time by the Registrars, formed the material on which the Authentic Document was subsequently based. A part of this original MS. is still in existence in the National Library at Paris, and is known as the 'MS. D'Urfé.' It begins with March 3rd, the day of the last Public Examination, and is apparently in the handwriting of Manchon, the Registrar, who had the whole in his own possession at the time of the Trial of Rehabilitation. The Fragment was discovered among the MSS. of the D'Urfé Library in the reign of Louis XVI. by Laverdy.

2. *The Authentic Document.*

This was the original Latin translation of the Minute, made by Thomas de Courcelles, signed by the Registrars, and attested by the seals of the two Judges. No trace of this first document can be found; but the Bishop of Beauvais caused five complete and legally attested copies to be made, three of these being in the writing of Manchon, the Registrar, of which there are still in existence, (1) Copy made for the King of England, now in the Library of the Corps Législatif in Paris; (2) Copy for the Bishop of Beauvais, formerly in the Colbert Library; and (3) Copy for the Inquisitor, formerly in the Dupuy Library—the last two being now in the National Library at Paris. The two other copies are lost, one having been sent to the Pope, whilst the other was the property of Manchon himself.

Besides these Original Documents, there are also seven copies of the Process, of different dates: five in the National Library, one in the Vatican, and one at Geneva.

### NOTE ON THE DOCUMENTS CONNECTED WITH THE TRIAL OF REHABILITATION

In the Preface to the Authentic Document of the Rehabilitation, the Notaries, Denis Lecomte and François Ferrebouc, state that they have prepared under their seals three copies of the Process of Rehabilitation, one containing also the entire Process of the Trial of Condemnation: this Copy is unfortunately lost. The two still in existence, both in the National Library of Paris, contain only the text of the Trial of 1455–6. In one of these Manuscripts are inserted the Eight Memorials presented to the Holy See in favour of Jeanne.

The Second Manuscript contains only the Memorial of Gerson. Other Documents connected with the Enquiries may be found in *Quicherat*, Vol. II., and in Lanery d'Arc's *Mémoires et Consultations en faveur de Jeanne d'Arc*, the most important being the *Opinions* of sundry learned Doctors given in 1452, and the *Recollectio* of Jean Bréhal in 1456.

## INTRODUCTORY NOTE TO THE TRIAL

In order to understand more fully the course of events in the last year of Jeanne's life, it may be well to give in some detail the story of her capture at Compiègne on May 23rd, 1430, and of the negotiations and legal preliminaries which preceded the opening of the Case in the following February. Strangely enough, there is in the Trial of Rehabilitation absolutely no witness to this period. It may therefore be more satisfactory to quote at some length from the contemporary Chronicles, which, as regards the Capture itself, are fortunately very explicit.

In the early dawn of Tuesday, May 23rd, Jeanne started from Crespy with about 400 followers to reinforce the garrison of Compiègne, then besieged by the combined forces of England and Burgundy. Of the events of that day there is no better account than that given in the Chronicle of Percival de Cagny,[213] which reads as follows:—

'The 23rd day of the month of May, the Maid, being in the said place of Crespy, learned that the Duke of Burgundy,[214] with a great number of men-at-arms and

---

[213] *Chronicles of the Dukes of Alençon.*
[214] Philip the Good, son of Jean Sans-Peur, the Duke murdered at the Bridge of Montereau in 1418 by the Armagnac faction; he was consequently an ally of England. Anne, his sister, married John, Duke of

others, and the Earl of Arundel, had come to besiege the said town of Compiègne. About midnight she departed from the said place of Crespy, in the company of 300 or 400 fighting men. And although her followers said to her, that she had too few people with her to pass through the army of the Burgundians and of the English, she exclaimed: "By my staff! [*Par mon martin!*] we are enough; I am going to see my good friends of Compiègne."

'She arrived at the said place about sunrise, and, without loss or disturbance either to herself or to her followers, she entered the said town. On the same day the Burgundians and English had come to make an assault in the field before the said town. There were done many feats of arms on the one side and on the other. The Burgundians and English, knowing that the Maid was in the town, thought that those within would sally forth in great strength, and for this the Burgundians placed a strong ambush of their followers under cover of a lofty mountain near by, named the Mount of Clairoy. And, about nine in the morning, the Maid heard that the assault was hot and fierce in the field before the said town. She armed herself and her followers, mounted on horseback, and went to join the *mêlée*. And no sooner was she come than the enemy turned back and were put to flight. The Maid charged hard upon the flank of the Burgundians. Those in ambush gave warning to their followers, who turned back in great disorder, and then, breaking up their ambuscade, they spurred on to place themselves between the town-bridge and the Maid and her company. And the one part of them turned right on the Maid in such force that those of her company could not withstand them, and said to the Maid, "Strive hard to regain the town, or you and we are lost."

---

Bedford. Efforts were constantly made by both sides to secure the sympathies of so powerful an ally; but after the death of his sister in 1432, the Duke's attachment to the English cause waned; and in 1435, a week after the death of Bedford, he made peace with Charles VII., and signed the Treaty of Arras, which practically restored France to the King. He died in 1467, and was succeeded by his son Charles the Bold.

'When the Maid heard them speak thus, she cried to them, angrily, "Silence! It only depends on you to discomfit them. Think only of striking them down." But whatsoever she might say, these people would not believe it, and forcibly compelled her to withdraw to the bridge. And when the Burgundians and English saw that she was returning to the town, they, by supreme effort, reached the end of the bridge. And great feats of arms were done there. The captain of the place, seeing vast multitudes of Burgundians and English about to cross the bridge, for the fear that he had of the loss of the place, commanded the bridge of the town to be raised and the gates closed. And there remained the Maid hemmed in without, and few of her followers with her. When her enemies saw this, all made effort to seize her. She resisted stoutly against them, but in the end was taken by five or six acting together, some laying hands on her, others on her horse, and each saying, "Surrender to me and give parole." She answered and said, "I have sworn and given my parole to Another than you, and to Him will I give my oath." And, saying these words, she was taken to the lodging of Messire Jehan de Luxembourg.

'Messire Jehan de Luxembourg[215] had her kept in his lodging for three or four days; and, after that, he remained at the siege of the said town and had the Maid sent to a castle named Beaulieu, in Vermandois. And there was she kept prisoner during the space of four months or thereabouts. After this, the said de Luxembourg, by means of the Bishop of Thérouanne,[216] his brother, and

---

[215] Jean de Luxembourg, Sire de Luxembourg and de Choques, nephew of the Constable Waleran de Luxembourg. A captain of Free-Lances in the service of the Duke of Burgundy, afterwards Count de Ligny and Guise, and a knight of the Toison d'Or. He remained true to the English, even after his chief had made terms with Charles, and died in 1441, still obstinately refusing to recognize the Treaty of Arras.

[216] Louis de Luxembourg, Bishop of Thérouanne, 1414, and Chancellor of France for Henry VI., 1425, surnamed "Le Renard"; afterwards Archbishop of Rouen, Bishop of Hély, and Cardinal. A warm adherent of the English cause, and a consistent supporter of Bedford and Warwick. It was he who received information of the capture of Jeanne on May 25th, and himself went with the news to the Parliament. When

Chancellor of France for the English King, delivered her to the Duke of Bedford, Lieutenant in France for the King of England, his nephew, for the price of fifteen or sixteen thousand *saluts* [the *salut* being worth about £1] paid to the said de Luxembourg. Thus was the Maid put into the hands of the English and taken to the Castle of Rouen, at which the said Duke then held his residence. She being in prison in the said Castle of Beaulieu, he who had been her steward[217] before her capture, and who served her in prison, said to her, "That poor town of Compiègne, which you have so much loved up to this time, will fall again into the hands and the power of the enemies of France!"

'And she answered him, "It will not be, for all the places which the King of Heaven hath subdued and put into the hands and jurisdiction of the gentle King Charles by my means, will not be retaken by his enemies, so long as he will take pains to keep them."'

The following additional details in regard to the Capture of the Maid are taken from George Chatellain's *Histoire de Philippe Le Bon*:—'The Maid, passing the nature of woman, did bear great weight, and took much pains to preserve her company from loss, remaining in the rear as becomes the chief and as the most valiant of the troop, when fortune did so permit, for the ending of her glory and for the last time that ever she should bear arms. An archer, a hard man and very churlish, having great spite that a woman of whom he had heard so much talk should drive back so many valiant men as she had done, caught her from one side by her surcoat of cloth-of-gold, and dragged her from her horse to the ground: she could find neither rescue nor help from her followers that she might be remounted, notwithstanding the pains they took. But a man-at-arms,

---

the tide turned, and Charles VII. was able to establish himself in his kingdom, the Bishop retired to England, and there died, 1443.

[217] Jean D'Aulon. Formerly a squire in the service of the King, appointed Chief of Jeanne's Household by Charles VII., in 1428. He remained with her from that time till her capture at Compiègne; was taken prisoner with her, and carried to Beaulieu, but was ransomed during the autumn. He was afterwards knighted, and made Seneschal of Beaucaire.

named the Bastard de Wandonne,[218] who arrived just as she fell, pressed her so closely that she gave him her parole, for that he said he was a man of noble birth. The which man-at-arms, more joyful than if he had gotten a king into his hands, took her hastily to Marigny, and there kept her under guard till the end of the affair. And there were taken also with her, Pouthon the Burgundian, a gentleman-at-arms of the French party; the brother of the Maid; her steward; and certain others, in small numbers, who were taken to Marigny and held in safe keeping.'

On the same day, the Duke of Burgundy wrote the following letter to the people of Saint Quentin:—

'By order of the Duke of Burgundy, Count of Flanders, Artois, Burgundy, and Namur.

'Very dear and well-beloved, knowing that you desire to have news of us, we signify to you that this day, the 23rd May, towards six o'clock in the afternoon, the adversaries of our Lord the King [Henry VI.] and of us, who were assembled together in great power, and entrenched in the town of Compiègne, before which we and the men of our army were quartered, have made a sally from the said town in force on the quarters of our advanced guard nearest to them, in the which sally was she whom they call the Maid, with many of their principal captains. In the encounter with whom, our fair cousin, Messire Jehan de Luxembourg, who was there present, and others of our people, and some of the people of our Lord the King whom he had sent before us to pass over to Paris, made great and bitter resistance. And presently we arrived in person and found that the said adversaries were already driven back, and by the pleasure of our blessed Creator, it had so happened and such grace had been granted to us, that the said Maid had been taken; and with her many captains, knights, squires and others were taken, drowned, and killed, of whom to this hour we yet know

---

[218] Lionel Bastard de Wandonne; now *Wandomme*, a castle in Artois; a captain in the service of Jean de Luxembourg, to whom the Maid finally surrendered at Compiègne. For his share of the reward he received 300 pounds *rente*. He was afterwards Count de Nesle and Beaulieu, in Vermandois.

not the names, only that none of our followers nor the followers of my Lord the King are either killed or taken, and that only twenty are wounded, thanks to God. The which capture, as we certainly hold, will be great news everywhere; and by it will be recognized the error and foolish belief of all those who have shewn themselves well-disposed and favourable to the doings of the said woman. And this thing we write for our news, hoping that in it you will have joy, comfort, and consolation, and will render thanks and praise to our Creator, Who seeth and knoweth all things, and Who by His blessed pleasure will conduct the rest of our enterprizes to the good of our said Lord the King and his kingdom, and to the relief and comfort of his good and loyal subjects.

'Very dear and well-beloved, the Holy Spirit have you in His Holy Keeping.

'Written at Codun, near Compiègne, the 23rd day of May. Subscribed: To our very dear and good friends the Clergy, citizens and inhabitants of Saint Quentin, in Vermandois.'

In the Notes of Clement de Fauquembergue, Registrar of the Parliament of Paris, occurs the following passage:—'Thursday, the 25th day of May, 1430, Messire Louis de Luxembourg, Bishop of Thérouanne, Chancellor of France, received letters from Messire Jean de Luxembourg, Knight, his brother, making mention, among other things, that on Tuesday last, in a sally made by the captains and men-at-arms of Messire Charles de Valois, then in the town of Compiègne, against the people of the Duke of Burgundy, encamped and come against the said town with the intention of besieging it, the people of the said De Valois were in such manner compelled to retreat that many of them had no time to enter again into the said town. And many of them threw themselves into the river adjacent to the walls, to the peril of their lives; others remained prisoners of the said Messire Jean de Luxembourg, and the followers of the said Duke of Burgundy, who, among others, seized and held prisoner this woman whom the followers of the said Messire

Charles called the Maid.'[219]

The news of the Maid's capture was received in Paris with much rejoicing,[220] and *Te Deums* were ordered to be sung in the Churches. The University and the Inquisition at once took up the matter, and wrote on the following day, May 26th, to the Duke of Burgundy, requesting him to claim the prisoner as a heretic against the Church. Six weeks later, on July 14th, letters were sent from the University both to the Duke and to Jean de Luxembourg to the same effect. On the same day, Cauchon, Bishop of Beauvais, acting for the Regent Bedford, arrived at the Burgundian camp to negotiate for the purchase of the Maid. He claimed her as a prisoner of the Church, but nevertheless offered the usual ransom of a king, 10,000 livres tournois [about £16,000 of our present value].

The arrangements presented, however, matters of long deliberation. The Duke and Jean de Luxembourg, whether from scruples of conscience or in hope of still higher ransom from the party of the King of France, were in no hurry to part with their prisoner. She had been removed to the Castle of Beaulieu at the end of May; and here she remained until August, with her faithful follower d'Aulon still in attendance on her. No records remain of her sojourn; but she herself gives evidence at the Trial of her attempt to escape, which was all but successful. Early in August, she was sent to Beaurevoir, where for a time she had the society of the wife and the aunt of Jean de Luxembourg. Of the latter, the Countess de Ligny, she spoke at the Trial in terms of great affection. Whilst at Beaurevoir, she heard of the negotiations for her delivery to the English. In despair for herself, and overwhelmed with grief for the sorrows of her beloved friends of Compiègne, who were then in great straits, she threw

---

[219] The much-vexed question of the date of the Capture seems to be decided by these two last contemporary documents. The same date, May 23rd, is also given in the Chronicle of William of Worcester.

[220] The news, received in the letter from Jean de Luxembourg, was communicated by his brother, the Bishop of Thérouanne, to the Parliament.

herself[221] from the top of the Keep, a height of sixty feet, hoping, as she afterwards said, at least to escape from her enemies. She was taken up, stunned, but not severely injured by her fall, and was kept in closer ward until, in the middle of November, the arrangements for her purchase were completed. From Beaurevoir she was removed to Arras; thence to Crotoy, where she was handed over to the tender mercies of the English, who kept her, in comparatively easy confinement, until it should be decided where the Trial was to take place—the University claiming her for Paris, the Regent preferring to keep her more strictly within his own power. In December, a decision was arrived at. Rouen was fixed upon as the most suitable place, both as a stronghold of the English and as the residence of the Regent and the Court. To Rouen, accordingly, the Maid was brought, and there lodged in a tower of the Castle, under the guard of English soldiers.

The room in which she was confined was situated in a tower of the Castle of Rouen, now no longer in existence; it was on the first floor, up eight steps;[222] not far from the back entrance,[223] and facing the fields.[224] There were three keys to the prison: one retained by the Cardinal of England or his Secretary, one kept by the Inquisitor, and one by the Promoter.[225] The Maid was under the close surveillance of five common soldiers (*houcepailliers*), three of whom remained in the room day and night, while two guarded the door.[226] She was heavily ironed, and chained to a beam which crossed the end of her bed.[227] It is reported also that a cage, in which she could stand upright had been made for her; but, although this is mentioned by several persons, no one can remember to have seen it in use. The Castle being under the control of

---

[221] Or let herself down, as some state, by a rope that was too short to reach the ground.

[222] Massieu.

[223] Cusquel.

[224] Taquel.

[225] Lebouchier.

[226] Massieu.

[227] *Ibid.*

the Governor, the Earl of Warwick, the captive was officially in his hands; and for this reason the guardians appointed later to see to her safe custody were members of his household or of the Royal Bodyguard: John Gris or Grey, Talbot, and Berwoist, whose commission is made out by the authority of the Bishop on March 13th.

Many of the Assessors considered that Jeanne should have been placed in the prisons of the Church, and not left in the hands of the English. Lefevre remarks that no one dared say this; and De Courcelles states that it was never brought up as a matter for consultation, although Ladvenu refers to a discussion at the first Session, during which, in response to a generally expressed opinion that Jeanne should be placed under Ecclesiastical ward, the Bishop announced that this could not be done "for fear of the English." At this first Session, February 21st, neither Ladvenu nor De Courcelles was present.

The Trial opened, according to the Official Report, on January the 9th. It was based on the Procedure of the trials of the Holy Office; and, although the Inquisitor himself was not *officially* present until a month later, the Inquisitorial form was punctiliously observed. This form was as follows:—

1. *Process ex officio.*

Enquiry as to facts of accusation.

Examination of the Accused on the results of this enquiry.

The Promoter then draws up the case, if any be undertaken.

2. *Process in ordinary.*

Trial and examination of the Accused, sometimes by torture.

Sentence.

This Procedure was carefully observed in the case of Jeanne. The process *ex officio*, beginning in January, with the suppressed Domremy Enquiry, comprised the Six Public and Nine Private Examinations, and ended with the drawing up of the Seventy Articles, the Act of Accusation, on March 26th. The Process in Ordinary began on March 27th, with the reading of the Seventy

Articles and Jeanne's examination upon them. She was brought into the Torture Chamber on May the 9th; but the decision of the greater number of the Assessors being against the use of extreme measures, nothing was done. The Sentence was read on May 24th, condemning her to perpetual imprisonment.

Of the legality of the Trial there were grave doubts, expressed both at the beginning and also later on, when some opportunity had been given by the Public Examinations for those not absolutely prejudiced against the Accused, to form an opinion as regards the impartiality of the Judges. On the first day, Houppeville, whose testimony was given in full at the Rehabilitation, was present in Court; but, having dared to express his opinion that the action to be undertaken was fraught with some danger, he was afterwards refused admission, and was sent for by the Bishop to be reprimanded. As he was not in the Diocese of Beauvais he refused submission; but his appeal to his own Chapter at Rouen was disregarded, and he was thrown into prison, from which he was only released some days later through the intervention of the Abbot of Jumièges.

Lohier, a celebrated legal authority, who was present in Rouen during the earlier part of the Examination, expressed his opinions to the Bishop at some length, stating that the whole Trial was absolutely worthless: (1) on account of its form, (2) that the Assessors were not at liberty to hold their own views, the Trial being in the Castle and therefore not in open Court, (3) that no opportunity was given to the party of the French King to speak for themselves, (4) that Jeanne herself was allowed no Counsel,[228] nor had proper documents been prepared to support the Accusation. The Bishop, furious at this interference, summoned a meeting at his house to discuss the matter, and announced his decision to take no notice

---

[228] According to the rules of Inquisitorial Trials it was not necessary to grant an advocate to the accused. In the "Directorium Inquisitorum" the Decretal on the treatment of Heretics empowers the Bishop and the Judge of the Inquisition, acting conjointly, to dispense with other assistance, and to act alone.

of the opinions thus expressed, but to continue as before. On the following day, Lohier left Rouen, remarking to the Registrar of the Trial: "It seems to me they act more from hate than aught else: and for this reason I will not stay here, for I do not wish to be in it."

Massieu, the Usher of the Court, afterwards stated that Jeanne had asked for Counsel, and had been refused; but there is no reference to any such request in the message he gives from her at the time of her citation.[229]

The Bishop's violent resentment at any interference is noted by more than one witness; and, indeed, the whole conduct of the Trial may be not inaptly described in the words of one of the Assessors, Maître Grouchet: "all was violence in this affair."

The Trial itself was held in the Castle of Rouen, where Henry VI. had just been spending Christmas in state.

At the First Session, in the Castle Chapel, the noise and disturbance were so great that it was decided that future Sessions should be held in a smaller room, and from this time the Court met in the Ornament Room, opening from the Great Hall. Two Englishmen kept the door.[230]

The Meetings of May 19th and May 29th, preliminary to the closing of the First and Second Processes, respectively were held outside the Castle in the Chapel of the Archiepiscopal Manor, possibly with a view to giving an air of greater publicity to the proceedings. The room in which the instruments of torture were exhibited to Jeanne is on the ground-floor of the only part of the old Castle now standing, called the Great Tower. The smaller tower, in which Jeanne's prison was situated, was still in ruins until the beginning of the present century, and went by the name of the Tower of La Pucelle; but it has now entirely disappeared.

The three Registrars, Manchon, Boisguillaume, and Taquel (the last only after March 14th), were seated at the feet of the Judges. The clerks of Beaupère and Erard, Jean

---

[229] See "Execution of the Mandate," Feb. 20th.
[230] Manchon.

de Monnet and Jean de Lenozelles, were sometimes with them; two English clerks, under the direction of Loyseleur, were hidden behind a curtain.[231]

Jeanne was seated on a chair, and questioned, generally from 8 to 11 a.m., by the Bishop and the six University Delegates. Sometimes they all spoke together, insomuch that Jeanne protested: "Beaux Seigneurs, faites l'un après l'autre."[232]

In the evidence given at the Rehabilitation, we learn that on more than one occasion Jeanne received advice from friendly Assessors, notably from Brother Duval and Brother Ysambard de la Pierre; but their well-meant interference seems only to have further incensed her Judges against her, and occasionally produced a violent altercation.

On the other hand, Jeanne was cruelly misled by Nicolas Loyseleur, one of the Canons of Rouen, who disguised himself as a fellow-countryman of the Marches of Lorraine, and, by false messages from her friends, wormed himself into the confidence of the Maid, even inducing her to allow him to act as her Confessor: nor did he scruple to report any admission she might make to the Bishop and the Inquisitor. The Registrars, Manchon and Boisguillaume, were even required by Cauchon to place themselves in a room adjoining the prison, provided with a so-called "Judas" ear, in order that they might take notes of the conversation between the prisoner and Loyseleur: but this, to their everlasting honour, they refused to do.

The Registrars appear to have had their difficulties from the very beginning. The notes taken by them at the morning sittings were read over in the presence of some of the Assessors at the Bishop's lodgings in the afternoon, and compared with those made by the concealed English clerks. Differences of opinion arose very often; but the officials refused to allow their own notes to be overridden, and, whenever any disputed point was referred to the Accused, their version was always found to

---

[231] *Ibid.*
[232] Massieu.

be correct. These notes were finally drawn up by
Manchon in a complete form, and upon them is based the
whole account of the Trial as it appears in the Latin
translation, the subsequent work of Thomas de
Courcelles.

## ACT OF ACCUSATION PREPARED BY THE PROMOTER
### The Seventy Articles

[The Seventy Articles, prepared by the Promoter,
d'Estivet, which form the Accusation of the Trial in
Ordinary, were read to Jeanne by Thomas de Courcelles,
on Tuesday, March 27th. In her replies, here given,
Jeanne refers constantly to previous answers. The dates of
Examinations, in which these are said to occur, follow in
notes.]

ARTICLE I. And first, according to Divine Law, as
according to Canon and Civil Law, it is to you, the
Bishop, as Judge Ordinary, and to you, the Deputy, as
Inquisitor of the Faith, that it appertaineth to drive away,
destroy, and cut out from the roots in your Diocese and in
all the kingdom of France, heresies, witchcrafts,
superstitions, and other crimes of that nature; it is to you
that it appertaineth to punish, to correct and to amend
heretics and all those who publish, say, profess, or in any
other manner act against our Catholic Faith: to wit,
sorcerers, diviners, invokers of demons, those who think
ill of the Faith, all criminals of this kind, their abettors
and accomplices, apprehended in your Diocese or in your
jurisdiction, not only for the misdeeds they may have
committed there, but even for the part of their misdeeds
that they may have committed elsewhere, saving, in this
respect, the power and duty of the other Judges competent
to pursue them in their respective dioceses, limits, and
jurisdictions. And your power as to this exists against all
lay persons, whatever be their estate, sex, quality, and
pre-eminence: in regard to all you are competent Judges.

"What have you to say to this Article?"

"I believe surely that our Lord the Pope of Rome, the
Bishops, and other Clergy, are established to guard the

Christian Faith and punish those who are found wanting therein: but as for me, for my doings I submit myself only to the Heavenly Church—that is to say, to God, to the Virgin Mary, and to the Saints in Paradise. I firmly believe I have not wavered in the Christian Faith, nor would I waver."

ARTICLE II. The Accused, not only this year, but from her infancy, and not only in your Diocese, Bishop, and your jurisdiction, Deputy, but also in many other places of this kingdom, hath done, composed, contrived and ordained a number of sacrileges and superstitions: she made herself a diviner; she caused herself to be adored and venerated; she hath invoked demons, and evil spirits; consulted them, associated with them, hath made and had with them compacts, treaties, and conventions, hath made use of them, hath furnished to others, acting in the same manner, aid, succour, and favour, and hath, in much, led them on to act like herself; she hath said, affirmed, and maintained that to act thus, to use witchcraft, divinations, superstitions, was not a sin, was not a forbidden thing, but, on the contrary, a thing lawful, to be praised, worthy of approval; also she hath led into these errors and evil doings a very great number of persons of divers estates, of both sexes, and hath imprinted on their hearts the most fatal errors. Jeanne hath been taken and arrested within the limits of your diocese of Beauvais, in the very act (*flagrante delicto*) of perpetrating all these misdoings.

"What have you to say to this Article?"

"I deny ever having used witchcraft, superstitious works, or divinations. As to allowing myself to be adored, if any kissed my hands and my garments, it was not my doing or by my wish; I sought to protect myself from it, and to prevent it as much as in me lay. And as for the rest of the Article, I deny it."

ARTICLE III. The Accused hath fallen into many diverse and detestable errors which reek of heresy. She hath said, vociferated, uttered, published and inculcated within the hearts of the simple, false and lying propositions allied to heresy, even themselves heretical, contrary to our Catholic Faith and its principles, to Gospel rules, and to the Statutes established or approved by General Councils; propositions, contrary not only to the Divine Law but also to Canon and Civil Law; propositions scandalous, sacrilegious, contrary to good manners, offensive to pious ears: she hath furnished help, counsel and favour to the people who dogmatized, affirmed, or promulgated such propositions.

"What have you to say to this Article?"

"I deny it, and on the contrary affirm that I have always upheld the Church so far as it lay in my power."

ARTICLE IV. But it is time to instruct you more fully and more directly, my Lords and Judges, on the offences, excesses, crimes, and misdemeanours, committed by the Accused in the diocese of Beauvais and elsewhere, in many and divers places.

It is true that the Accused was born in the village of Grus [Greux], of Jacques d'Arc and Isabelle, his wife; that she lived until seventeen years old or thereabouts in the village of Domremy, on the Meuse, in the diocese of Toul, in the Bailly of Chaumont, in Bassigny, in the provosty of Montclère and Andelot. In her childhood, she was not instructed in the beliefs and principles of our Faith; but by certain old women she was initiated in the science of witchcraft, divination, superstitious doings, and magical arts. Many inhabitants of these villages have been known for all time as using these kinds of witchcraft: Jeanne hath herself said that she learned from several, notably from her godmother, many things touching her visions and the apparitions of fairies; through others also, she hath been penetrated by the detestable and pernicious errors of these evil spirits—so much so, that, in these interrogations before you, she hath confessed that even now she doth not know if these fairies were evil spirits or not.

"What have you to say to this Article?"

"For the first part it is true, in so far as concerns my father, my mother, and the place of my birth. As to the fairies, I do not know what they are. On what touches my teaching, I learnt to believe, and have been brought up well and duly to do what a good child ought to do. For what concerns my godmother, I refer to what I have said on another occasion. You ask me to say the Creed? Ask my confessor, to whom I said it."

ARTICLE V. Near the village of Domremy there is a great tree, big and ancient; it is called "the Charmed Tree of the Fairy of Bourlement": near by is a spring; round this tree and this spring live, it is said, evil spirits called fairies, with whom those who use witchcraft are accustomed to come and dance at night.

"What have you to say to this Article?"

"For the tree and the spring, I refer to my previous answers. The rest, I deny."[233]

ARTICLE VI. Accustomed to frequent this tree and this spring, above all by night, sometimes also by day, but at the times when the Church celebrates the Divine Office, Jeanne, in order to find herself more alone, danced roundelays around this tree and this spring; from time to time she hung from its branches garlands of herbs and flowers woven by her own hands, accompanying her dances with songs mingled with invocations, sorceries, and other witchcrafts: the garlands thus left overnight on the following morning were not to be found.

"What have you to say to this Article?"

"I refer for a part to my previous answers; the rest I deny."[234]

ARTICLE VII. Jeanne was in the habit of carrying about with her a mandrake, hoping thereby to secure fortune and riches in this world, she, in fact, believed that the mandrake has the virtue of procuring fortune.

"What have you to say about the mandrake?"

"I deny it entirely."[235]

ARTICLE VIII. Towards her twentieth year, Jeanne, of her own wish, and without permission of her father and mother, went to Neufchâteau, in Lorraine, and was in service for some time at the house of a woman, an inn-

---

[233] Cf. 3rd Public Examination, February 24th; 5th Public Examination, March 1st; 8th Private Examination, 17th; and 9th Private Examination, March 17th.
[234] Cf. 3rd Public Examination, February 24th.
[235] Cf. 5th Public Examination, March 1st.

keeper named La Rousse, where lived women of evil life, and where soldiers were accustomed to lodge in great numbers. During her stay in this inn, Jeanne sometimes stayed with these evil women, sometimes took the sheep into the fields, or led the horses to watering in the meadows and pastures: it was there that she learnt to ride on horseback and to use arms.

"What have you to say to this Article?"

"I refer to what I said elsewhere. I deny the rest."[236]

ARTICLE IX. Whilst she was in service with these women Jeanne indicted a young man before the Officials at Toul for breach of promise; many times she repaired to Toul for this end, and spent thus nearly all that she had. This young man refused to marry her, because he knew she had been connected with evil women. He died during the trial. Jeanne then, unable to remain longer, quitted the service of this woman.

"What have you to say to this Article?"

"On the subject of this trial for marriage I have answered elsewhere and refer to my answer. I deny the rest."[237]

ARTICLE X. After having quitted the service of La Rousse, Jeanne pretended, and still doth pretend, to have had continually during five years, visions and apparitions of Saint Michael Saint Catherine, and Saint Margaret. They revealed to her, she says, by order of God, that she should raise the siege of Orleans and crown Charles, whom she calls her King; and that afterwards she would drive out his enemies from the realm of France. In spite of her father and mother, she left home, of her own motion, of her sole inspiration, and went to Robert de Baudricourt, captain of Vaucouleurs, to whom she communicated, in virtue of the order of Saint Michael, Saint Catherine, and Saint Margaret, the visions and revelations that God had made to her, asking of the said Robert to find her the means to accomplish what had been revealed to her. Twice repulsed by Robert, she returned twice to her

---

[236] Cf. 2nd Public Examination, February 22nd, and 3rd Public Examination, February 24th.
[237] Cf. 2nd Private Examination, March 12th.

parents. Returning a third time to the attempt, on a pretended order sent to her by revelation, she was then admitted and received by the said Robert.

"What have you to say to this Article?"

"I refer to what I said before."[238]

ARTICLE XI. Having become familiar with the said Robert, Jeanne boasted that, after having done and accomplished all that had been commanded her of God, she would have three sons, of whom the first should be Pope, the second Emperor, and the third King. Robert de Baudricourt, hearing this, said to her, "Would I could be father to one myself, if they are to be such great people! my own value would thereby be the greater!" "Nay, nay, gentle Robert," replied Jeanne, "it is not time; the Holy Spirit will accomplish it."[239] This is the tale which the said Robert hath in many places often affirmed, told and published, and this in presence of prelates, lords, and high personages.

"What have you to say to this Article?"

"I refer to what I have already said.[240] I never boasted that I should have three children."[241]

ARTICLE XII. In order the more openly and better to attain her end, Jeanne asked of Robert de Baudricourt to have made for her a man's dress and armour appropriate. This captain, with great repugnance, ended by acquiescing in her request. These garments and armour made and furnished, Jeanne, rejecting and abandoning women's clothing, her hair cut a-round like a young coxcomb, took shirt, breeches, doublet, with hose joined together and fastened to the said doublet by twenty points, long leggings laced on the outside, a short mantle [surcoat] to the knees, or thereabouts, close-cut cap, tight-fitting boots or buskins, long spurs, sword, dagger,

---

[238] Cf. 2nd Public Examination, February 22nd; 3rd Public Examination, February 24th; 4th Public Examination, February 27th; 5th Public Examination, March 1st; 2nd Private Examination, March 12th; 3rd Private Examination, March 12th.

[239] This answer is given in French in the text.

[240] No previous answer is recorded.

[241] Cf. 2nd Private Examination, March 12th.

breastplate, lance and other arms in fashion of a man of war, affirming that in this she was executing the order of God, as had been prescribed to her by revelation.

"What have you to say on this Article?"

"I refer to what I said before."

"Did you then take this costume, these arms, and all this warlike apparel by the order of God?"

"On this also I refer to what I said before."[242]

ARTICLE XIII. Jeanne attributes to God, His Angels and His Saints, orders which are against the modesty of the sex, and which are prohibited by the Divine Law, things abominable to God and man, interdicted on pain of anathema by ecclesiastical censure, such as dressing herself in the garments of a man, short, tight, dissolute, those underneath as well as above. It is in virtue of these pretended orders that she hath attired herself in sumptuous and stately raiment, cloth-of-gold and furs; and not only did she wear short tunics, but she dressed herself in tabards, and garments open at both sides; and it is notorious that she was taken prisoner in a loose cloak of cloth-of-gold. She was always seen with a cap on her head, her hair cut short and a-round in the style of a man. In one word, putting aside the modesty of her sex, she acted not only against all feminine decency, but even against the reserve which beseems men of good morals, wearing ornaments and garments which only profligate men are accustomed to use, and going so far as to carry arms of offence. To attribute all this to the order of God, to the order which had been transmitted to her by the Angels and even by Virgin Saints, is to blaspheme God and His Saints, to destroy the Divine Law and violate the Canonical Rules; it is to libel the sex and its virtue, to overturn all decency, to justify all examples of dissolute living, and to drive others thereto.

"What have you to say to this Article?"

"I have not blasphemed God nor His Saints."[243]

---

[242] Cf. 2nd Public Examination, February 22nd; 4th Public Examination, February 27th; 3rd Private Examination, March 12th; and 8th Private Examination, March 17th.

[243] The two following questions and answers appear in the Minute

ARTICLE XIV. Jeanne affirms that she has done right in attiring herself in garments worn only by dissolute men; she doth profess that she will continue to retain them until she shall have received, by revelation, the express order of God: by this, she outrages God, the Angels, and the Saints.

"What have you to say to this Article?"

"I do no wrong in serving God; to-morrow I will answer you."

[One of the Assessors]: "Did you have revelation or order to wear a man's dress?"

"I have already answered that elsewhere. I refer to my previous sayings. To-morrow I will answer. I know well who made me take a man's dress; but I do not know how I can reveal it."[244]

ARTICLE XV. Jeanne, having many times asked that she might be permitted to hear Mass, hath been invited to quit the dress she now wears and to take again her woman's dress; she hath been allowed to hope that she will be admitted to hear Mass and to receive Communion, if she will renounce entirely the dress of a man and take that of a woman, as beseems her sex; she hath refused. In other words, she hath chosen rather not to approach the Sacraments nor to assist in Divine Service, than to put aside her habit, pretending that this would displease God.

---

only:—

"But, Jeanne, the Holy Canons and Holy Writ declare that women who take men's dress or men who take women's dress, do a thing abominable to God. How then can you say that you took this dress at God's command?"

"You have been answered. If you wish that I should answer you further, grant me delay, and I will answer you."

"Will you not take the dress of a woman to receive your Saviour on Easter Day?"

"Neither for that nor for anything else will I yet put off my dress. I make no difference between man's dress and woman's dress for receiving my Saviour. I ought not to be refused for this question of dress." Cf. 4th Public Examination, February 27th, and 6th Public Examination, March 3rd.

[244] Cf. 3rd Public Examination, February 24th; 3rd Private Examination, March 12th; 8th Private Examination, March 17th. These questions and answers come after Article XIII. in the minute.

In this appears her obstinacy, her hardness of heart, her lack of charity, her disobedience to the Church, and her contempt of Divine Sacraments.

"What have you to say to this Article?"

"I would rather die than revoke what I have done by the order of Our Lord."

"Will you, to hear Mass, abandon the dress of a man?"

"I will not abandon it yet; the time is not come. If you refuse to let me hear Mass, it is in the power of Our Lord to let me hear it, when it shall please Him, without you. I recollect being admonished to take again a woman's dress. As to the irreverence and such like things, I deny them."[245]

ARTICLE XVI. Previous to, and since her capture, at the Castle of Beaurevoir and at Arras, Jeanne hath been many times advised with gentleness, by noble persons of both sexes, to give up her man's dress and resume suitable attire. She hath absolutely refused, and to this day also she refuses with persistence; she disdains also to give herself up to feminine work, conducting herself in all things rather as a man than as a woman.

"What have you to say on this Article?"

"At Arras and Beaurevoir I was invited to take a woman's dress; then I refused, and I refuse still. As to the women's work of which you speak, there are plenty of other women to do it."[246]

ARTICLE XVII. When Jeanne found herself in the presence of Charles, thus attired and armed, she promised him these three things among others: that she would raise the siege of Orleans; that she would have him consecrated at Rheims; that she would avenge him on his enemies, who, all of them, English or Burgundians, should be, thanks to her, killed or driven out of the kingdom. Many times and in many places did she repeat publicly the same

---

[245] Cf. 7th Private Examination, March 15th; 8th Private Examination, March 17th.

After Article XV., the following sentence is inserted in the Extracts, but is not in the Procès. "She added that the Demoiselle de Luxembourg prayed the Seigneur de Luxembourg not to give her up to the English."

[246] Cf. 6th Public Examination, March 3rd.

boasts; and, to give them greater weight, then and often afterwards, she did use divinations, and by these means unveiled the morals, the entire life, the most secret acts, of persons who came before her, whom she had never before seen or known; she boasted of knowing all by revelation.

"What have you to say on this Article?"

"In the name of God I brought the news to my King that Our Lord would restore the kingdom to him, cause him to be crowned at Rheims, and drive out all his enemies; I was a messenger from God, when I told the King boldly to set me to work and I would raise the siege of Orleans. I mean, in so saying, the whole kingdom; and if my Lord of Burgundy and the other subjects of the King do not return to their obedience, the King will know how to make them by force. As to the end of the Article, of knowing Robert de Baudricourt and my King, I hold to what I said before."[247]

ARTICLE XVIII. So long as Jeanne remained with Charles, she did dissuade him with all her power, him and those with him, from consenting to any treaty of peace, any arrangement with his adversaries; inciting them always to murder and effusion of blood; affirming that they could only have peace by sword and lance; and that God willed it so, because otherwise the enemies of the King would not give up that which they held in his kingdom; to fight against them thus, is, she told them, one of the greatest benefits that can happen to all Christendom.

"What have you to say on this Article?"

"As to my Lord of Burgundy, I requested him by my ambassadors and my letters that he would make peace between my King and himself; but as to the English, the peace they need is that they may go away to their own country, to England. I have answered on the remainder of the Article; and I refer to this answer."[248]

ARTICLE XIX. It was by consulting demons and using divinations, that Jeanne sent to look for a sword hidden in

---

[247] Cf. 2nd Public Examination, February 22nd; 4th Private Examination, March 13th.
[248] Cf. 4th Public Examination, February 27th.

the Church of Saint Catherine de Fierbois: (perchance she had already maliciously, fraudulently, and deceitfully hidden or caused to be hidden this sword in the same church, to seduce the princes, nobles, clergy, and people, to induce them to believe more easily that she knew by revelation in what place this sword was). By this stratagem and others of a like nature she succeeded in inspiring an absolute faith in all her words.

"What have you to say to this Article?"

"I refer to what I said before; I deny all the rest."[249]

ARTICLE XX. She hath put faith in her ring, in her banner, in certain pieces of linen, and pennons which she carried or caused to be carried by her people, and also in the sword found by revelation, according to her, at Saint Catherine de Fierbois, saying that these things were very fortunate. She made thereon many execrations and conjurations, in many and divers places, publicly asserting that by them she would do great things and would obtain victory over her enemies; that to those of her people who carried pennons of this kind no ill could happen. She said all this at Compiègne on the eve of the day when, having sallied to attack my lord the Duke of Burgundy, she was taken prisoner and many of her followers were wounded, killed, or taken. She said as much at Saint Denis, when she incited her army to attack Paris.

"What have you to say on this Article?"

"I refer to what I have already said. In all I have done there was never any sorcery or evil arts. As for the good luck of my banner, I refer it to the fortune sent through it by Our Lord (*de bonâ fortunâ sui estandart se refert ad fortunium quod Dominus Noster in es transmissit*)."[250]

ARTICLE XXI. Jeanne, by temerity or presumption, hath caused to be written certain letters at the head of which she placed the names 'Jhésus Maria,' with a cross in the middle. These letters she caused to be addressed in

---

[249] Cf. 4th Public Examination, February 27th; 8th Private Examination, March 17th.
[250] Cf. 5th Public Examination, March 1st; 6th Public Examination, March 3rd; 9th Private Examination, March 17th.

her name to our Lord the King, to my Lord of Bedford, Regent of France, to the lords and captains who were then at the siege of Orleans, containing a number of things wicked, pernicious, contrary to the Catholic Faith, the tenour of which is found in the Article which follows:

"What have you to say to this Article?"

"I did not send the letters of which you speak in pride or in presumption, but by command of Our Lord. I remember and acknowledge the contents of these letters, with the exception of three words. If the English had believed my letters, they would only have been wise; and before seven years are gone they will perceive it well enough!"[251]

ARTICLE XXII. Tenour of the letter:[252]

"What have you to say to this letter?"

"I remember having it written except three words, which I did not dictate. If the English had believed my words they would have acted wisely. Before seven years are gone, they will feel the truth of what I wrote to them, and for that, I refer to the answer which I made elsewhere."

ARTICLE XXIII. The tenour of the letter contained in the preceding Article proves well that Jeanne hath been the sport of evil spirits, and that she often consulted them to know what she ought to do; or, at least, that, to seduce the people, she imagined these inventions by lying or wickedness.

"What have you to say to this Article?"

"I deny ever having done anything under the inspiration of evil spirits."[253]

ARTICLE XXIV. Jeanne hath gravely misused the names "Jhésus Maria" and the sign of the cross placed beside them; it was understood between her and her people that, when they saw on her letters these words and this sign, they were to do the contrary of what she wrote: and, in fact, they did do the contrary.

---

[251] Cf. 2nd Public Examination, February 22nd; 6th Public Examination, March 3rd.

[252] *Vide* 5th Public Examination, March 1st: pages 36–38.

[253] Cf. 4th Public Examination, February 27th.

"What have you to say to this Article?"

"I refer to what I said before."[254]

ARTICLE XXV. Usurping the office of Angels, Jeanne hath said and affirmed that she hath been sent by God; and she hath said this even for cases which tend openly to violence and effusion of human blood: a proposition the most foreign to all holiness, horrible and abominable to all pious souls.

"What have you to say to this Article?"

"First, I begged them to make peace; and it was only in case they would not make peace that I was ready to fight."[255]

ARTICLE XXVI. Jeanne, being at Compiègne in August of 1429, did receive from the Count d'Armagnac a letter of which the tenour forms the article which follows.

"What have you to say to this Article?"

"I refer to what I said before."[256]

ARTICLE XXVII. Tenour of the said letter.[257]

ARTICLE XXVIII. To this letter Jeanne did send in answer the letter signed with her name, found in the Articles which follow.

ARTICLES XXIX. AND XXX. Letter of Jeanne to the Count d'Armagnac.[258]

"What have you to say on these Articles, XXVII., XXVIII., XXIX., XXX., which have been read to you with great care, from the first word to the last?"

"I refer to what I answered on Article XXVI."[259]

*Continuation of the Reading of the Articles in Open Court.*

[The next day, Wednesday, March 28th, in the same room, near the great Hall of the Castle of Rouen, before the Bishop and Brother Jean Lemaître, assisted by 35

---

[254] Cf. 9th Private Examination, March 17th.
[255] Cf. 3rd Public Examination, February 24th; 9th Private Examination, March 17th.
[256] Cf. 5th Public Examination, March 1st.
[257] *Vide* 5th Public Examination, March 1st: pages 34–35.
[258] *Vide ante*, page 35.
[259] Cf. 5th Public Examination, March 1st.

Assessors.]

Before them hath been resumed the reading, begun the preceding day, of the Articles in the document produced by the Promoter. Their contents in French, being shewn to Jeanne, Article by Article, she hath been questioned on each of these Articles and hath continued to reply, as here followeth, after having anew sworn to speak truth on everything touching the Trial.[260]

ARTICLE XXXI. From the time of her childhood and since, Jeanne hath boasted, and every day still doth boast, of having had, and of still having, numerous revelations and visions on the subject which, although she hath been on this charitably admonished and legally required to swear, she hath not made, nor wished to make, nor is now willing to make, any oath. She will not even make known the revelations made to her, by words nor by signs. This she hath postponed, contested, refused, and doth now also postpone, contest, and refuse. Many times hath she said and affirmed in a formal manner, in Court and outside, that she will not make known these revelations and visions to you, her Judges, even if her head should be cut off, or her body dismembered. "They shall not drag it from my mouth," she hath said, "neither the sign that God revealed to me, nor the means whereby I knew that this sign came to me from God."

"What have you to say on this Article?"

"As to revealing the sign and the other things, of which you speak, I may well have said I will not reveal them. I add, to what I before acknowledged that I should have said I would not reveal it without leave from Our

---

[260] The following incident occurs in the Minute only:

The Bishop, referring to the promise given on the previous day by Jeanne that she would answer on the subject of her dress, asks that, before proceeding with the reading, this answer may be given. To which Jeanne replies:

"The dress and the arms that I wear, I wear by the permission of God: I will not leave them off without the permission of God, even if it cost me my head: but, if it should so please Our Lord, I will leave them off: I will not take a woman's dress if I have not permission from Our Saviour."

Lord."[261]

ARTICLE XXXII. By this refusal to make known these pretended revelations, you may and should presume strongly that the revelations and visions of Jeanne, if she had them always, came to her from lying and evil spirits rather than from good. And all the world may take it for certain, considering her cruelty, her pride, her dress, her actions, her lies, the contradictions here given in various Articles, that all these together constitute in this respect the most powerful of presumptions, both of law and right.

"What have you to say on this Article?"

"I did it by revelation, from Saint Catherine and Saint Margaret; and I will maintain it even unto death. If I put on my letters the names 'Jhésus Maria,' it was because I was advised to do so by certain persons of my party; sometimes I used these names, sometimes not. As to that passage in my answer of which you remind me, 'All that I did, I did by the counsel of Our Lord,' it should be completed thus: 'All that I did *well*.'"

"Did you do well or ill to advance on La Charité?"

"If it were ill done, it will be confessed."

"Did you do well to advance on Paris?"

"The gentlemen of France wished to advance on Paris. In doing this, it seems to me they did their duty in going against their enemies."

ARTICLE XXXIII. Jeanne hath presumptuously and audaciously boasted, and doth still boast, of knowing the future and of having foreseen the past, of knowing things that are in the present, but hidden or unknown; all which, an attribute of the Deity, she claims for herself, a simple and ignorant creature.

"What have you to say on this Article?"

"It is in Our Lord's power to give revelations to whom He pleases; that which I said of the sword of Fierbois and

---

[261] Cf. 2nd Public Examination, February 22nd; 3rd Public Examination, February 24th; 4th Public Examination, February 27th; 5th Public Examination, March 1st; 7th Private Examination, March 15th; 8th Private Examination, March 17th.

of things to come, I knew by revelation."[262]

ARTICLE XXXIV. Obstinate in her temerity and presumption, Jeanne hath said, proclaimed, and published, that she recognized and discerned the voices of Archangels, Angels, and Saints; she hath affirmed and doth still affirm that she knoweth how to distinguish their Voices from human voices.

"What have you to say on this Article?"

"I hold by what I have already said: of my pretended temerity, and, of that which has been concluded against me, I refer to Our Lord, my Judge."[263]

ARTICLE XXXV. Jeanne hath boasted and affirmed that she did know how to discern those whom God loveth and those whom He hateth.

"What have you to say on this Article?"

"I hold by what I have already said elsewhere of the King and the Duke d'Orléans; of the others I know not; I know well that God, for their well-being,[264] (*pro ediis corporum suorum*), loves my King and the Duke d'Orléans better than me. I know it by revelation."[265]

ARTICLE XXXVI. Jeanne hath said, affirmed, and boasted, she doth say, affirm, and every day boast, that she hath known, and could know exactly—and that not only herself, but also others through her means recognized and surely knew—the Voice which came to her, although from its nature a voice must be invisible to every human being.

"What have you to say to this Article?"

"I hold by what I have said elsewhere."[266]

ARTICLE XXXVII. Jeanne doth confess to having frequently done the contrary to what hath been

---

[262] Cf. 3rd Public Examination, February 24th; 4th Public Examination, February 27th; 5th Public Examination, March 1st; 6th Public Examination, March 3rd; 1st Private Examination, March 10th; 3rd Private Examination, March 12th; 5th Private Examination, March 14th.
[263] Cf. 4th Public Examination, February 27th; 5th Public Examination, March 1st; 7th Private Examination, March 15th.
[264] Minute reads: "pour l'aise de son corps."
[265] Cf. 2nd Public Examination, February 22nd; 3rd Public Examination, Feb. 24th; 8th Private Examination, March 17th.
[266] Cf. 2nd Public Examination, February 22nd.

commanded her by the revelations she doth boast to have had from God; for example, when she retired from St. Denis, after the assault on Paris, and when she leaped from the top of the tower of Beaurevoir. By this, it is manifest, either that she hath had no revelations from God, or that, if she hath had them, she hath despised them. And she it is, who, after this, doth dare to affirm that she is in all things guided and governed by commands from on high and by revelation! Besides, she hath said that, when she had had the order not to leap from the top of the tower, she was compelled to act contrary to this order, without being able to resist the constraint put upon her will; in the which she appears to think wrongly on the matters of Free-will and to fall into the error of those who believe that man is led by Fate or by some other irresistible power.

"What have you to say to this Article?"

"I hold by what I have said elsewhere. I state in addition that when I left St. Denis I had permission from my Voices."

"In acting against your Voices, do you think you committed mortal sin?"

"I have answered elsewhere to that; I refer to that answer. On the concluding part of this Article, I refer me to God."[267]

ARTICLE XXXVIII. Jeanne, from the time of her childhood, hath said, done, and committed a great number of crimes, sins and evil deeds—shameful, cruel, scandalous, dishonouring, unworthy of her sex; now she doth say and affirm that all that she hath done hath been with the approbation and by the will of God; that she hath done nothing and now doeth nothing which proceedeth not from God, by means of the revelations transmitted to her by the Holy Angels and the Holy Virgins, Catherine and Margaret.

"What have you to say on this Article?"

---

[267] Cf. 2nd Public Examination, February 22nd; 1st Private Examination, March 10th; 7th Private Examination, March 15th.

"I refer to what I have said elsewhere."[268]

ARTICLE XXXIX. Although the Just sin seven times a day, Jeanne hath said and published that she hath never committed, or, at least, that she doth believe never to have committed, mortal sin. Nevertheless, as many Articles of the present accusation prove, she hath indeed practised, and on a vast scale, acts customary to nations who are at war, and others yet more grave.

"What have you to say on this Article?"

"I have answered it; I refer to what I have said elsewhere."[269]

ARTICLE XL. Forgetful of her salvation, impelled by the devil, she is not and hath not been ashamed several times and in many and divers places to receive the Body of Christ, having upon her a man's dress of unseemly form, a dress which the laws of God and man do forbid her to wear.

"What have you to say on this Article?"

"I have answered elsewhere. I rely upon what I have said before. I rely upon Our Lord."[270]

ARTICLE XLI. Jeanne, as one desperate, for hate and contempt of the English, and foreseeing the destruction of Compiègne, which she believed to be imminent, did attempt to kill herself by throwing herself down from the top of a tower; at the instigation of the devil, she took it into her head to commit this action; she applied herself to commit it; she did commit it in so far as she was able; on the other hand, in so throwing herself down, she was so well impelled and guided by a diabolic instinct that she had in view rather the safety of her body than that of her soul and of many others. Often indeed, hath she boasted that she would kill herself rather than that she should be delivered to the English.

"What have you to say on this Article?"

---

[268] Cf. 3rd Public Examination, February 24th; 7th Private Examination, March 15th.

[269] Cf. 3rd Public Examination, February 24th; 5th Public Examination, March 1st; 6th Private Examination, March 14th.

[270] Cf. 6th Public Examination, March 3rd.

"I rely upon what I have said before."[271]

ARTICLE XLII. Jeanne hath said and published that Saint Catherine and Saint Margaret and Saint Michael have bodies—that is to say, head, eyes, face, hair, etc.; that she hath touched them with her hands; that she hath kissed them and embraced them.

"What have you to say on this Article?"

"I have already answered it, and I rely upon what I have said."[272]

ARTICLE XLIII. Jeanne hath said and published that the Saints, the Angels, and the Archangels speak the French language and not the English language, because the Saints, the Angels, and the Archangels are not on the side of the English, but of the French; she hath outraged the Saints in glory, in implying to them a mortal hatred against a Catholic realm and a nation devoted, according to the will of the Church, to the veneration of all the Saints.

This Article having been set forth to Jeanne word for word, she only answered thus:

"I rely on Our Lord, and upon what I have replied before."[273]

ARTICLE XLIV. Jeanne hath boasted and doth yet boast, she hath published and doth publish, that Saint Catherine and Saint Margaret have promised to lead her to Paradise, and have assured her that she will obtain heavenly joy if she preserve her virginity; she affirms she is certain of this.

"What have you to say on this Article?"

"I rely on Our Lord and on what I answered elsewhere."[274]

ARTICLE XLV. Although the judgments of God are impenetrable to us, nevertheless Jeanne hath said, uttered, declared, and promulgated that she hath known and can

---

[271] Cf. 6th Public Examination, March 3rd; 5th Private Examination, March 28th.

[272] Cf. 9th Private Examination, March 17th.

[273] Cf. 5th Public Examination, March 1st.

[274] Cf. 5th Private Examination, March 14th; 6th Private Examination, March 14th; 5th Public Examination, March 1st.

know those who are Saints, Archangels, Angels, or the elect of God; she knoweth how to discern them.

"What have you to say on this Article?"

"I refer to what I have already said."[275]

ARTICLE XLVI. She hath said that, before leaping from the tower of Beaurevoir, she did most lovingly entreat Saint Catherine and Saint Margaret for the people of Compiègne, saying to these Saints in a reproachful manner, "And how can God allow these people of Compiègne, who are so loyal, to die thus miserably?" In the which did appear her impatience and her irreverence towards God and the Saints.

"What have you to say on this Article?"

"I refer to what I have already said."[276]

ARTICLE XLVII. Provoked with her wound, Jeanne, after the leap from the tower of Beaurevoir, seeing she had not attained her end, began to blaspheme God and the Saints, abjuring them with horrible taunts, insulting them terribly, to the great confusion of all those present. In the same way, when she was in the Castle of Rouen, many times, and on different days, did she blaspheme and deny God, the Blessed Virgin, and the Saints, in impatience and resentment at being brought for judgment before an ecclesiastical tribunal and forced to appear there.

"What have you to say on this Article?"

"I hold by Our Lord and by what I have already said."[277]

ARTICLE XLVIII. Jeanne hath said that she did and doth still believe that the spirits which appear to her are Angels and Archangels and the Saints of God, as firmly as she believes in the Christian Faith, and in the Articles of that Faith, although she can report no sign which can be of a nature to prove that she hath in reality had this communication; she hath consulted neither Bishop, Priest, nor Prelate, nor any ecclesiastical person whatsoever, to

---

[275] Cf. 4th Public Examination, February 27th; 5th Public Examination, March 1st; 6th Public Examination, March 3rd.

[276] Cf. 6th Public Examination, March 3rd.

[277] Cf. 6th Public Examination, March 3rd; 6th Private Examination, March 14th.

know whether she ought to have faith in such spirits; yet more, she saith that her Voices have forbidden her to reveal anything to any one whosoever it may be, save first to a captain of soldiers, then to Charles her King, and afterwards to other persons purely laic. By this, she admits that her belief on this point is audacious, her faith erroneous, her revelations doubtful, having always kept them from the knowledge of the clergy and never having been willing to reveal them save to seculars.

"What have you to say to this Article?"

"I have answered it already. I refer to what is written. And as to the signs, if those who asked for them were not worthy, I could not help it. Many a time did I pray that it might please God to reveal it to some of this party. It is true, that to believe in my revelations I asked neither Bishop, Priest, nor any one else. I believe it was Saint Michael, from the good teaching he shewed me."

"Did Saint Michael say to you: 'I am Saint Michael'?"

"I have answered before."

As to the concluding part of the Article, she answered: "I refer me to Our Lord.... As firmly as I believe Our Saviour Jesus Christ suffered death to redeem us from the pains of hell, so firmly do I believe that it was Saint Michael and Saint Gabriel, Saint Catherine and Saint Margaret whom Our Saviour sent to comfort and to counsel me."[278]

ARTICLE XLIX. On the foundation of this fancy alone Jeanne hath venerated spirits of this kind, kissing the ground on the which she said they had walked, bending the knee before them, embracing them, kissing them, paying all sorts of adoration to them, giving them thanks with clasped hands, taking the greatest familiarities with them; when she did not know if they were good or evil spirits, and when, by reason of all the circumstances revealed above, these spirits should have been rather considered by her as evil. This worship, this veneration, is idolatry: it is a compact with demons.

---

[278] Cf. 3rd Public Examination, February 24th; 6th Public Examination, March 3rd; 2nd Private Examination, March 12th.

"What have you to say on this Article?"

"I have already answered; for the conclusion, I refer me to Our Lord."[279]

ARTICLE L. Every day and many times daily Jeanne doth invoke these evil spirits and consult them on what she should do,—notably on the manner in which she should answer in court. This seems to constitute, and doth in effect constitute, an invocation of demons.

"What have you to say on this Article?"

"I have already answered it; I shall call them to my help as long as I live."

"In what way shall you call them?"

"I beseech Our Lord and Our Lady that they will send me counsel and comfort, and then They send it to me."

"In what words do you beseech this?"

"I say 'Most sweet Lord, in honour of Thy Holy Passion I beseech Thee, if Thou lovest me, that Thou wilt reveal to me how I should answer these Clergy. I know well, as regards this dress, the command by which I have taken it; but I do not know in what way I should leave it off: for this, may it please Thee to teach me.' And soon they come to me. I often by my Voices have news of my Lord of Beauvais."

*The Bishop*: "What do your Voices say of Us?"

"I will tell you apart.... To-day they came to me three times."

"In your chamber?"

"I have answered you; I hear them well. Saint Catherine and Saint Margaret have told me what I should say on the subject of my dress."[280]

ARTICLE LI. Jeanne hath not feared to proclaim that Saint Michael, the Archangel of God, did come to her with a great multitude of Angels in the house of a woman where she had stopped at Chinon; that he walked with

---

[279] Cf. 3rd Public Examination, February 24th; 1st Private Examination, March 10th; 2nd Private Examination, March 12th; 7th Private Examination, March 15th; 9th Private Examination, March 17th.

[280] Cf. 3rd Public Examination, February 24th; 4th Public Examination, February 27th; 2nd Private Examination, March 12th; 4th Private Examination, March 13th; 5th Private Examination, March 14th.

her, holding her by the hand; that they together mounted the stairs of the Castle and together gained the Chamber of the King; that the Angel did reverence to the King, bowing before him, surrounded by this multitude of Angels, of which some had crowns on their heads and others had wings. To say such things of Archangels and the Holy Angels is presumption, audacity, lying, as in the holy books we do not read that they did a like reverence, a like demonstration, to any saint—not even to the Blessed Virgin, Mother of God. Jeanne hath said that the Archangel Saint Gabriel hath often come to her with the blessed Michael, and sometimes even with thousands of Angels. She hath also proclaimed that the same Angel, at her prayer, did bring in this company of Angels a crown, the most precious possible, to place upon the head of her King—a crown which is to-day deposited in the treasury of the King; that the King would have been crowned at Rheims with this crown, if he had deferred his consecration some days: it was only because of the extreme haste of his coronation that he received another. All these are lies imagined by Jeanne at the instigation of the devil, or suggested by demons in deceitful apparitions, to make sport of her curiosity,—she who would search secrets beyond her capacity and condition.

"What have you to say on this Article?"

"On the subject of the Angel who brought the sign I have already answered. As to what the Promoter suggests on the subject of the thousands of Angels, I do not recollect having said it—that is to say, the number; I did certainly say that I had never been wounded without receiving great comfort and help from God and from the Saints Catherine and Margaret. As to the crown, on this also I have replied. Of the conclusion which the Promoter makes against my deeds, I refer me to God, Our Lord; and where the crown was made and forged, I leave to Our Lord."[281]

ARTICLE LII. By all these inventions, Jeanne hath so

---

[281] Cf. 4th Public Examination, February 27th; 5th Public Examination, March 1st; 1st Private Examination, March 10th; 2nd Private Examination, March 12th; 4th Private Examination, March 13th.

seduced Christian people that many have in her presence adored her as a Saint, and in her absence do adore her still, composing in her honour masses and collects; yet more, going so far as to call her the greatest of all the Saints after the Virgin Mary, raising statues and images to her in the Churches of the Saints, and bearing about them medals in lead or other metal representing her—exactly as the Church does to honour the memory and the recollection of the canonized Saints—publicly proclaiming that she is sent from God, and more Angel than woman. Such things are pernicious to the Christian religion, scandalous, and prejudicial to the salvation of souls.

"What have you to say to this Article?"

"As to the commencement of the Article, I have already answered; as to the conclusion, I refer to Our Lord."[282]

ARTICLE LIII. In contempt of the orders of God and the Saints, Jeanne, in her presumption and pride, hath gone so far as to take command over men; she hath made herself commander-in-chief and hath had under her orders nearly 16,000 men, among whom were Princes, Barons, and a number of Gentlemen: she hath made them all fight, being their principal captain.

"What have you to say on this Article?"

"As to the fact of being commander-in-chief, I have answered before; if I have been commander-in-chief, it was to fight the English. As to the conclusion of the Article I refer me to God."[283]

ARTICLE LIV. Jeanne doth behave in an unseemly manner with men, refuses the society of women, wishes to live with men only, to be waited upon by them, even in her own room and in the most private details: a like thing hath never been seen nor heard of a chaste and pious woman.

"What have you to say on this Article?"

"It is true that my command was over men; but as to

---

[282] Cf. 6th Public Examination, March 3rd.
[283] Cf. 4th Public Examination, February 27th.

my quarters and lodging, most often I had a woman with me. And when I was engaged in the war I slept fully dressed and armed, not being able always to find a woman. As to the conclusion of the Article, I refer me to God."

ARTICLE LV. Jeanne hath abused the revelations and prophecies that she saith she hath had from God, to procure for herself lucre and temporal profit; by means of these pretended revelations, she hath acquired great riches, a great show and great estate in officers, horses, and attire; she hath obtained great revenues for her brothers and relations, imitating in this the false prophets, who, to acquire temporal gain or to obtain the favour of kings, were accustomed to pretend that they had had revelations from God on things which they knew would be to the taste of their princes; abusing the divine oracles, she hath thus attributed her lies to God.

"What have you to say to this Article?"

"I have answered elsewhere. As to the gifts made to my brothers, that which the King gave to them was of his grace, without my asking. As to the charge made by the Promoter and the conclusion of the Article, I refer me to Our Lord."[284]

ARTICLE LVI. Jeanne hath many times proclaimed that she hath two counsellors whom she calls 'Counsellors of the Well,' and who have come to her since she hath been taken captive, as appears from the declaration made by Catherine de la Rochelle before the Officials in Paris.[285] This Catherine hath said that Jeanne, if she be not well guarded, will get out of prison, by the help of the Devil.

"What have you to say on this Article?"

"I hold by what I have already said; and as to the 'Counsellors of the Well,' I do not know what it means. I certainly believe that I overheard Saint Catherine and Saint Margaret there. The conclusion of the Article I deny."

[284] Cf. 1st Private Examination, March 10th.
[285] This is the only known reference to this declaration of Catherine de la Rochelle.

[And then she did swear by her oath[286] that she did not wish that the Devil should get her out of prison.[287]]

ARTICLE LVII. The day of the Nativity of the Blessed Virgin, Jeanne did assemble the whole army of Charles, to make an attack on the city of Paris; she did lead the army against the city, affirming that she would enter it on that day—that she knew it by revelation: she directed all the arrangements possible for the entry. And, nevertheless, she is not afraid to deny it before us here in court. And at other places also, at La Charité-sur-Loire, for example, at Pont L'Evêque, at Compiègne, when she attacked the army of the Duke of Burgundy, she affirmed and foretold that which, according to her, would take place, saying that she knew it by revelation: now, not only did the things predicted by her not come to pass, but the very contrary happened. Before you she hath denied having made these predictions, because they were not realized, as she had said; but many people worthy of trust report[288] to have heard her utter them. At the time of the assault on Paris, she said that thousands of angels were around her, ready to bear her to Paradise if she should be killed: now, when she was asked why, after the promises made to her, not only did she not enter Paris but that many of her men and she herself had been wounded in a horrible manner and some even killed, she answered "It was Jesus, who broke His word to me."

"What have you to say to this Article?"

"As to the beginning, I have answered it already. If I think of more later, I will willingly answer then. I never said that Jesus had failed me."[289]

ARTICLE LVIII. Jeanne did cause to be painted a standard whereon are two Angels, one on each side of God holding the world in His hand, with the words "*Jhésus Maria*" and other designs. She said that she caused this standard to be done by the order of God, who

---

[286] Her usual oath was 'En nom Dé' or 'Par mon martin' (bâton).

[287] Cf. 6th Public Examination, March 3rd.

[288] These reports do not appear in the official documents.

[289] Cf. 6th Public Examination, March 3rd; 4th Private Examination, March 13th.

had revealed it to her by the agency of His Angels and Saints. This standard she did place at Rheims near the Altar, during the consecration of Charles, wishing, in her pride and vain glory, that it should be peculiarly honoured. Also did she cause to be painted arms, in the which she placed two golden lilies on a field azure; between the lilies a sword argent, with a hilt and guard gilded, the point of the sword pointing upwards and surmounted with a crown, gilded. All this is display and vanity, it is not religion nor piety; to attribute such vanities to God and to the Angels, is to be wanting in respect to God and the Saints.

"What have you to say on this Article?"

"I have already answered it; for the conclusions drawn by the Promoter, I refer to Our Lord."[290]

ARTICLE LIX. At St. Denis in France Jeanne did offer and cause to be placed in the Church, in the most prominent place, the armour she wore when she was wounded while attacking the town of Paris; she desired that this armour should be honoured as relics. In this same town, she did cause to be lighted candles, for the melted wax to fall on the heads of little children, saying that this would bring them happiness, and making by such witchcrafts many divinations.

"What have you to say on this Article?"

"As to my armour, I have answered; as to the candles lighted and melted, I deny it."[291]

ARTICLE LX. In contempt of the laws and sanction of the Church, Jeanne hath several times before this tribunal refused to speak the truth: by this, she doth render suspect all she hath said or done in matters of faith and revelation, because she dares not reveal them to ecclesiastical judges; she dreads the just punishment she hath merited and of which she appears herself to be conscious, when, on this question, she did in court urge this proverb, that "for speaking the truth, one was often hanged." Also she hath

---

[290] 4th Public Examination, February 28th; 6th Public Examination, March 3rd; 1st Private Examination, March 10th; 8th Private Examination, March 17th; 9th Private Examination, March 17th.
[291] Cf. 8th Private Examination, March 17th.

often said: "You will not know all," and again, "I would rather have my head cut off than tell you all."

"What have you to say on this Article?"

"I never sought delay, except to answer more surely on what was asked me. When I am doubtful if I ought to answer, I ask delay to know if I ought to speak. As to the counsel of my King, because it does not touch on this case, I would not reveal it. Of the sign given to the King, I have told it, because the clergy did constrain me to do so."[292]

ARTICLE LXI. Admonished of having to submit all her words and actions to the Church Militant, after that the distinction between the Church Militant and the Church Triumphant had been shewn to her, Jeanne declared that she submitted herself to the Church Triumphant and refused to submit to the Church Militant, confessing by this that she doth not rightly understand the Article of the Faith 'I believe in the Church, One, Holy, Catholic,' and that she is in error on this point. She hath said she would reveal them only to God, and that she referred her acts to God and to His Saints and not to the judgment of the Church.

"What have you to say on this Article?"

"I wish with all my power to give honour and reverence to the Church Militant. For referring my acts to the Church Militant, I must refer to Our Lord Who caused me to do them."

"Will you refer to the Church Militant as to what you have done?"

"Send me the clerk on Saturday next, and I will answer."[293]

ARTICLE LXII. Jeanne hath laboured to scandalize the people, to induce them to believe in her talk, taking to herself the authority of God and His Angels, presumptuously seeking to seduce men from ecclesiastical

---

[292] Cf. 3rd Public Examination, February 24th; 4th Public Examination, February 27th; 5th Public Examination, March 1st; 6th Public Examination, March 3rd; 2nd Private Examination, March 12th.

[293] Cf. 7th Private Examination, March 15th; 9th Private Examination, March 17th.

authority, as do the false prophets who establish sects of error and perdition and separate themselves from the unity of the Church; a thing pernicious in the Christian religion, which, if the Bishops did not provide against it, might destroy ecclesiastical authority; on all sides, in fact, raising up men and women who, pretending to have revelations from God and the Angels, will sow untruth and error—as hath already happened to many since this woman hath arisen and hath begun to scandalize Christian people and to publish her knaveries.

"What have you to say to this Article?"

"I will answer next Saturday."

ARTICLE LXIII. Jeanne is not afraid to lie in court, and to violate her own oath when on the subject of her revelations; she doth affirm a number of contradictory things, and which imply contradiction among themselves: she doth not fear to hurl malediction against a whole nation, the rulers of that nation and its greatest people; she doth speak of them without respect, allowing herself a tone of mockery and derision such as no woman in a state of holiness would allow; which sheweth well that she is ruled and guided by evil spirits and not, as she hath boasted, by God and the Angels. Christ said of false prophets, "Ye shall know them by their fruits."

"What have you to say to this Article?"

"I refer to what I have said, and, for the conclusion, to God Our Lord."[294]

ARTICLE LXIV. Jeanne doth pretend to know that she hath obtained pardon of the sin committed when, in despair, driven by the evil spirits, she threw herself from the tower of the Castle at Beaurevoir: yet the Scriptures say that no one knoweth if he is worthy of love or hate, nor, in consequence, if he is purged of sin and justified.

"What have you to say on this Article?"

"I have answered you, and to that I refer. Of the charge and the conclusion, I refer me to Our Lord."

ARTICLE LXV. Many times Jeanne hath said that she

---

[294] Cf. 4th Public Examination, February 27th; 5th Public Examination, March 1st.

asked of God to send her special revelations by the
Angels and by the Saints Catherine and Margaret upon
what she ought to do: for example, in the matter of
learning if she ought to make known the truth in court on
certain points and certain facts which are personal to
herself. It is to tempt God, to ask Him that which ought
not to be asked of Him, because there is no need, and man
may himself suffice for it by his own research. Thus, by
the leap from the tower of Beaurevoir she doth seem
manifestly to have tempted God.

"What have you to say on this Article?"

"I have answered it, and will not, without the leave of
Our Lord, reveal what has been revealed to me. It is not
without need that I beseech God. I would He might send
me yet more, so that it might be discerned that I am come
from God and that it is He Who hath sent me."

ARTICLE LXVI. Of many of the deeds and words that
have just been noticed some are opposed to the Divine
Law, to Gospel Law, to Canon Law, to Civil Law, and to
the rules of General Councils; others are witchcrafts,
divinations, or superstitions; others breathe heresy and
errors in faith; others are attempts against peace and tend
to the effusion of human blood; others constitute
blasphemies against God and the Saints and are wounding
to pious ears. In all this, the Accused, by her audacious
temerity, at the instigation of the Devil, hath offended
God and sinned against Holy Church; she hath been a
cause of scandal; she is on all these points notoriously
defamed: she should be punished and corrected by you.

"What have you to say to this Article?"

"I am a good Christian; for all with which you charge
me I refer to Our Lord."

ARTICLE LXVII. All and each of these transgressions
the Accused hath committed, perpetrated, said, uttered,
recited, dogmatized, promulgated, put in action, as much
in your jurisdiction as elsewhere, in many and divers
places of this realm, not once only but many times, in
divers times, days and hours. She hath fallen again and
again into all these errors; she hath furnished counsel,
help, and favour to those who have committed them with

her.

"What have you to say to this Article?"

"I deny it."

ARTICLE LXVIII. Because a persistent clamour hath struck your ears not once only, but many times; because public rumour and an information based on what hath gone before hath made you recognize that the Accused is vehemently suspect and defamed; you have decreed that there is reason to bring an action against her, and to proceed therein, by you or one of you, by causing the said woman to be cited, and by setting her to answer—as hath been done.

"What have you to say to this Article?"

"This Article concerns the Judges."

ARTICLE LXIX. By all which precedes, the Accused is vehemently suspect, scandalized and as far as possible defamed by all honest and serious people. But by all that hath gone before she is neither corrected nor amended; she hath postponed and doth still postpone; she hath refused and doth still refuse to correct or amend herself; she hath continued and persevered, doth continue and persevere, in her errors, although by you the Judges, and by a great number of notable clergy, and other honest persons, she hath been charitably and otherwise duly and sufficiently warned, summoned and required.

"What have you to say to this Article?"

"The misdeeds brought forward against me by the Promoter, I have not done. For the rest, I refer me to God. Of all the misdeeds brought forward against me, I do not think I have committed any against the Christian faith."

"If you have done anything against the Christian faith, will you submit to the Church and to those to whom correction belongs?"

"On Saturday, after dinner, I will answer you."

ARTICLE LXX. All and each of these propositions contained in these Articles are true, notorious and manifest; the public voice and rumour hath occupied and doth occupy itself therewith; the Accused hath recognized and acknowledged these things as true, many times and sufficiently, before witnesses proved and worthy of belief, in and out of court.

"What have you to say on this Article?"

"I deny all that I have not recognized and confessed."

CONCLUSION.—Having attained conviction of the truth of all or part of the preceding Articles in a manner to justify the proposed end, which is that you may be enabled to pronounce in recognition of the cause, the Promoter doth conclude that it will be ultimately judged by you, upon the whole, according to law and right.

And the said Promoter humbly imploreth your offices on all these things, as may be suitable.

The Seventy Articles preceding which form the Act of Accusation for the Trial, were reduced to Twelve by Maître Nicolas Midi; the twelve Articles are here given.

## THE TWELVE ARTICLES OF ACCUSATION.
### ARTICLE I.

A woman doth say and affirm that when she was of the age of thirteen years or thereabouts, she did, with her bodily eyes, see Saint Michael come to comfort her, and from time to time also Saint Gabriel; that both the one and the other appeared to her in bodily form. Sometimes also she hath seen a great multitude of Angels; since then, Saint Catherine and Saint Margaret have shewn themselves to her in bodily form; every day she sees these two Saints and hears their voices; she hath often kissed and embraced them, and sometimes she hath touched them, in a physical and corporeal manner. She hath seen the heads of these Angels and these Saints, but of the rest of their persons and of their dress she will say nothing. The said Saint Catherine and Saint Margaret have also formerly spoken to her near a spring which flows at the foot of a great tree, called in the neighbourhood "The Fairies' Tree." This spring and this tree nevertheless have been, it is said, frequented by fairies; persons ill of fever have repaired there in great numbers to recover their health. This spring and this tree are nevertheless in a profane place. There and elsewhere she hath often venerated these two Saints, and hath done them obeisance.

Besides this, she doth say that Saint Catherine and Saint Margaret appear and shew themselves to her adorned with most beautiful and most precious crowns. At this time and very often since, they have announced to her, by the order of God, that she was to go in search of a certain secular Prince, promising that, by her help and succour, this same Prince should, by force of arms, recover a great temporal domain and the honour of this world, and should obtain victory over his adversaries: this same Prince received her, and furnished her with arms and soldiers for the carrying out of what has just been said. Further, Saint Catherine and Saint Margaret have ordered this same woman, by the command of God, to take and to wear a man's dress, which she hath borne and doth still bear, persisting in obeying this order, to the extent that she saith she would rather die than give up this dress, adding that she will only abandon it by the express order of God. She hath even preferred not to assist in the Office of the Mass and to deprive herself of the Holy Communion of the Eucharist, at the time when the Church commands the faithful to receive it, rather than to resume female dress and to quit this man's habit.

The said woman hath gone so far, under the inspiration of these two Saints, that without the knowledge and against the will of her parents, at the age of seventeen, she did quit the paternal roof and joined herself to a great troop of soldiers, with whom she lived night and day, having never had, or at least very rarely, another woman with her. These two Saints have said and prescribed to her many other things for the which she declares herself sent by the God of Heaven and the Church Victorious, composed of Saints who already enjoy celestial blessedness; it is to them that she submits as right all she hath done. As to the Church Militant, she hath deferred and refused to submit herself, her deeds, and her words to it, although many times required and admonished so to do, saying always that it is impossible to her to do contrary to what she hath, in her Trial, affirmed to have done by the order of God; and that for these things she will not refer to the decision or the judgment of any man alive, but to the judgment of God alone.

The said Saints have revealed to this woman that she will obtain the glory of the blessed and will gain the salvation of her soul if she doth preserve the virginity which she vowed to these Saints the first time she saw and recognized them. As a result of this revelation, she doth affirm that she is as assured of her salvation as if, now and in fact, she were already in the Kingdom of Heaven.

## ARTICLE II.

The same woman saith that the sign which was received by the Prince to whom she was sent—a sign which decided this Prince to believe in her and to aid her to carry on the war—was, that Saint Michael came to the said Prince, accompanied by a multitude of Angels, of which some had crowns and others had wings; with them also were Saint Catherine and Saint Margaret. She and the Angel proceeded together, their feet touching the ground, by the road, the staircase, and the Prince's chamber; the Angel was accompanied by other Angels and by the said two Saints; he gave to the Prince a crown, very precious and made of the purest gold, bowing before him and doing him reverence. Once she hath said that when her Prince received this sign, it seemed to her he was alone, although many other persons were close by; another time she hath said that it seemed to her that an Archbishop had received the sign of the crown and had given it to the Prince, in the presence of several temporal lords.

## ARTICLE III.

The same woman doth say and affirm that he who visits her is Saint Michael; that which makes her believe in him is the good counsel, the comfort, and the good teaching which he doth give her, and because he hath named himself to her, and hath told her that he was Saint Michael. She hath in the same way recognized Saint Catherine and Saint Margaret; she knoweth how to distinguish the one from the other, because they name themselves to her and greet her.

On the subject of the pretended Saint Michael who appeared to her, she believes that it is truly Saint Michael; and the sayings and deeds of this Michael she believes to be true and good as firmly as she believes that Our Lord Jesus suffered and died for our redemption.

## ARTICLE IV.

The same woman doth say and affirm that she is certain of what should happen on the subject of certain future things, as surely as she is certain of those which she sees passing under her eyes. On the subject of occult things she doth boast to know or to have known them by means of the revelations which have been made to her by the Voices of Saint Catherine and Saint Margaret: for example, that she will be delivered from her captivity, and that the French will do, under her guidance, the greatest exploits that they have ever done in all Christendom; for example, again, she saith she hath known by revelation without any one pointing them out to her, men whom she had never seen, and herself revealed and pointed out the existence of a sword which was hidden in the earth.

## ARTICLE V.

The same woman doth say and affirm that, by the command and good pleasure of God, she hath taken and borne and continueth still to bear a man's dress. Further, she doth say that, because she hath had God's command to bear this habit, it was necessary that she should have a short tunic, cap, jerkin, breeches, hose with many points, hair cut close above her ears, keeping no garment which might indicate her sex. She doth say and affirm that she hath, in this dress, several times received the Sacrament of the Eucharist. She hath not desired and doth still not desire to resume woman's dress, although many times required and charitably admonished so to do. At times she saith that she would rather die than leave off the dress which she bears; at times she saith that she will leave it off only by the command of God. She doth also say, that if she again found herself with this dress among those for whom she hath armed herself, she would act as she did before her capture; and this would be, she doth add, one of the greatest benefits that could happen to the whole kingdom of France. Also, for nothing in the world will she swear to wear this dress or to take arms no more. In all this she doth say that she hath done and doeth well, obeying God and His Commandments.

## ARTICLE VI.

The same woman doth avow and acknowledge that she hath caused to be written many letters and warnings on the which were placed these names "*Jhésus Maria*," with the sign of the Cross. Sometimes, she put a cross, and between her and her party this signified that she did not wish them to do what in this same letter she told them to do. At other times she caused it to be written that she would have those who did not obey her warnings killed, and "by the blows she would give they would see who had the true right from the God of Heaven." She hath often said that she hath done nothing but by the revelation and order of God.

## ARTICLE VII.

The same woman doth say and confess that, being of the age of seventeen, by revelation, as she saith, and spontaneously, she went to seek a Knight whom she had never seen, abandoning for this the paternal roof, against the will of her parents. These, when they had knowledge of her departure, were wild with grief. This same woman ordered the Knight to conduct her, or to have her conducted, to the Prince already mentioned. The said Knight, or Captain, furnished this woman, on her demand, with a man's dress and a sword, and appointed and commanded for her conduct a Knight, a Squire, and four servants. When they had come to the Prince, this woman told him that she wished to fight against his adversaries. She promised to establish him in great sovereignty and to vanquish his enemies; and for this she had been sent by the God of Heaven. She saith she hath acted well, having had revelation and the command of God.

## ARTICLE VIII.

The same woman doth say and affirm that she, of herself, no one compelling her, did throw herself down from a very high tower, wishing rather to die than to be placed in the hands of her enemies and to live after the destruction of the town of Compiègne. She saith also that she was not able to avoid this fall, although Saint Catherine and Saint Margaret had forbidden it to her. To offend them is, she herself saith, a great sin. But she knoweth that this sin was remitted to her after she had confessed it; she saith she received revelation of this.

## ARTICLE IX.

The same woman saith that Saint Catherine and Saint Margaret have promised to conduct her to Paradise, if she doth preserve with care the virginity of body and soul which she vowed to them. Of this she saith she is as assured as if she were already in the glory of the blessed. She doth not think she hath committed mortal sin; for, if she were in a state of mortal sin, she saith it seemeth to her that Saint Catherine and Saint Margaret would not visit her each day as they do.

## ARTICLE X.

The same woman doth say and affirm that God doth love sundry persons still living, designated by her and named, more than He doth this woman: this, she knoweth by revelation from Saint Catherine and Saint Margaret, who speak frequently to her, but in French and not in English, because these Saints are not on the side of the English. Since she hath known by revelation that their Voices were for the Prince aforesaid she hath ceased to love the Burgundians.

## ARTICLE XI.

The same woman doth say and confess that to the Voices and the Spirits now under consideration, whom she calls Michael, Gabriel, Catherine and Margaret, she doth often do reverence, uncovering, bending the knee, kissing the earth on which they walk, vowing to them her virginity, at times kissing and embracing Saint Catherine and Saint Margaret; she hath touched them with her own hands, corporeally and physically; she hath asked of them counsel and help; at times she doth call them, and they even come to her without being called; she accedes to and obeys their counsels and their commands; she hath always obeyed them, without having asked counsel thereon from whomsoever it be—father, mother, curé, prelate, or any ecclesiastic whatsoever. She doth believe no less firmly that the Voices and the revelations she receives by the medium of the Saints of whom she speaks come from God and by His order: she believes it as firmly as she believes the Christian Faith and that Our Lord Jesus Christ suffered for us Death and Passion. She doth add that, if it were an evil spirit who had come to her under the appearance and mask of Saint Michael she would quite well have known how to distinguish that it was not Saint Michael. Finally she saith, that of her own wish and without any one pressing her thereto, she hath sworn to Saint Catherine and Saint Margaret, who appeared to her, to reveal to no one the sign of the crown given to the Prince to whom she was sent, until she should have permission from God to reveal it.

## ARTICLE XII.

The same woman doth say and confess that if the Church wished that she should do anything contrary to the order she doth pretend to have received from God, she would not consent, whatsoever it might be. She doth affirm that she knows well, that all contained in her Trial has come to her by the order of God, and it would be impossible for her to do contrary to what she doth. Thereupon she doth not wish to refer to the decision of the Church Militant, nor to any one, whoever it be in the world, but to God alone, Our Lord, Whose commands she doth always execute, above all in what doth concern her revelations, and in what she doth in consequence. This answer and all the others are not from her own head, she saith, but she hath made and given them by order of her Voices and revelations: she doth persist [in this], although by the Judges and others of the Assessors, the Article of Faith, 'The Church, One, Holy, Catholic,' hath often been recalled to her, and it hath often been shewn to her that all the faithful are bound to obey the Church Militant and to submit to it their words and actions—above all in matters of faith and in all which concerns sacred Doctrine and Ecclesiastical sanction.

## INTRODUCTORY NOTE TO THE REHABILITATION.

It was not until nearly twenty years after the death of Jeanne d'Arc that any attempt was made by those in authority to vindicate her memory or even to acknowledge the services she had rendered to the kingdom of France.

In 1450, however, after the occupation of Normandy and the submission of the town of Rouen, the idea appeared to have occurred to Charles VII. that to suffer the stigma of heresy and witchcraft to rest on the name of the Maid of Orleans, who had "led him to his anointing," was to throw a doubt upon his own orthodoxy, and to justify the taunt of his enemies that he had been the mere tool of "a lyme of the Fiend." On February 13th, 1450, therefore, he issued a Declaration empowering one of his Counsellors, Guillaume Bouillé, to enquire into the conduct of the Trial undertaken against Jeanne by "our ancient enemies the English," who, "against reason, had cruelly put her to death," and to report the result of his investigations to the Council.

Bouillé was Rector of the University of Paris, Dean of the Theological Faculty, Dean of Noyon, a Member of the Great Council, and at one time Ambassador to Rome. It is very probable that he was the author of the first memorial issued in favour of Jeanne, throwing doubts upon the validity of the Rouen sentence—a memorial which, according to some, was prior to the Enquiry of 1450 with which we are now dealing.

It was to an able and competent person therefore, that Charles committed the Enquiry, which was held at Rouen on March 4th and 5th, less than three weeks after the issue of the Royal Mandate.

Seven witnesses were heard; namely, Toutmouillé, de la Pierre, Ladvenu, and Duval,—all Dominicans of Saint Jacques, Rouen; the Notary Manchon, the Usher Massieu, and Beaupère, one of the chief Examiners. But the Court took no further interest in the matter; and, although in the opinion of several legal authorities consulted by De Bouillé, the Process of Condemnation was held as null and void, the proceedings were carried no further: the Enquiry was forwarded to the King and Council, and the whole question once more fell into abeyance.

Two years later, the Cardinal-Bishop of Digne, Guillaume d'Estouteville, Legate in France for Pope Nicholas V. took up the Enquiry, at the formal request of Isabel d'Arc, mother of the Maid, who claimed, on Civil as well as on Ecclesiastical authority, the rehabilitation of her daughter, and the restoration of the family to the position they had lost by the imputation of heresy cast on them in the person of one of their number.

The failure of the former Enquiry was due, in great part, to the fear of arousing the hostility of the English, and also of meeting with opposition from the Ecclesiastical authorities, by bringing forward an action instituted by the Sovereign against proceedings which had received the unquestioned sanction of the Holy Office and the University of Paris, and which were also guaranteed by the protection of the English King. The expedient of shifting the entire responsibility on to the shoulders of the d'Arc family obviated these difficulties, and enabled the Case to be taken as a purely private one, an appeal against a judgment given on false premisses. The reversal of this verdict could offend no one, as the action was brought against Defendants none of whom were living to meet the charge, and who could therefore be represented only by their titular legal successors. Their innocence in the whole matter made the case a perfectly harmless one—a legal fiction which might satisfy many and could injure none.

The first act of the Cardinal d'Estouteville was to associate with himself the Prior of the Convent of the Jacobins at Paris, Jean Bréhal, Inquisitor of France; and, together, they proceeded to an Enquiry at Rouen in April, 1452, at which witnesses to the number of twenty-one, including some of those heard in 1450, gave their evidence. The Cardinal being obliged by his duties to leave Rouen, the Enquiry was left in the hands of Bréhal and of Philippe la Rose, the Treasurer of the Cathedral. There were still difficulties in the way. The Pope feared to wound English susceptibilities; and, in spite of the efforts of the Cardinal and of the petition presented to Rome by Isabel d'Arc and her two sons, the proceeding languished; and three more years passed without any definite step being taken.

In 1455, however, the Pope Nicholas V. died, and his successor Calixtus III. [Borgia], less timorous, acceded to the request of the d'Arc family, granting a Rescript authorizing the process of revision, and appointing as delegates for the Trial the Archbishop of Rheims (Jean Jouvenal des Ursins), the Bishop of Paris (Guillaume Chartier), and the Bishop of Coutances (Richard de Longueil), who afterwards associated with themselves the Inquisitor, Jean Bréhal.

The Case was solemnly opened on November 7th, 1455, in the Church of Notre Dame at Paris, when the mother and brothers of the Maid came before the Court to present their humble petition for a revision of her sentence, demanding only "the triumph of truth and justice." The Court heard the request with some emotion. When Isabel d'Arc threw herself at the feet of the Commissioners, shewing the Papal Rescript and weeping aloud, while her Advocate, Pierre Maugier, and his assistants prayed for justice for her and for the memory of her martyred daughter, so many of those present joined aloud in the petition, that at last, we are told, it seemed that one great cry for justice broke from the multitude.

The Commissioners formally received the petition, and appointed November 17th, ten days later, for its consideration, warning the Petitioners of the possible danger of a confirmation of the previous Trial, instead of the reversal they looked for, but promising careful consideration of the Case should they persist in their appeal.

On November 17th the Court met a second time at Notre Dame; the Papal Rescript was solemnly read, and the Advocate for the Petitioners brought his formal accusation against the Judges and Promoter of the late Trial—none of whom, as has been said, were then alive— carefully excluding the Assessors concerned in the case, who, he said, were led to wrong conclusions by false deductions. At the close of the Advocate's address, the Archbishop of Rheims and the Bishop of Paris declared themselves ready to act as Judges in the Appeal Case, in conjunction with the Inquisitor Bréhal, appointing the following December 12th for the inaugural sitting, and citing all those concerned in this Case to appear before them on that day.

The Trial opened on December 12th. The family of d'Arc were represented by the Procurator, Guillaume Prévosteau, who had formerly been appointed Promoter in the case instituted by Cardinal d'Estouteville: but the Plaintiffs alone were represented, no one appearing to answer for either of the accused Judges nor for the Promoter d'Estivet. The Case was adjourned until December 15th, in order that Advocates for the Defendants might be summoned to appear.

The Court met accordingly on the 15th December; but, in spite of mandates and citations placed on Church-doors and other public places, no one was found to come forward as representatives of the accused; and a further delay of five days was therefore granted. At the same time, the Commissioners formally constituted the Tribunal and appointed their Officers: Simon Chapitault as Promoter or Advocate-General, Ferrebouc and Lecomte as Registrars for the Court. The Registrars of the former Trial, being present, were asked if they wished in any way to defend the Process in which they had been concerned; but, on their replying in the negative, they were requested to lay before the Court any documents relating to the previous Trial which they might have in their possession. By this means the Commissioners were enabled to have before them the actual Minute of the Trial of 1431, written in Manchon's own hand and presented by him, and also to obtain his formal attestation of the authenticity of the Official Procès-Verbal, upon which their further enquiries were to be based.

The "Preliminary Enquiry" made in 1452, by command of the Cardinal d'Estouteville and his delegates, was formally annexed, by request of the Promoter, to the official documents of the Trial of Rehabilitation; but the earlier Enquiry of 1450, having been made under secular authority, was unfortunately treated as of no value, and not included in the authorized Case.

On December 18th the Promoter lodged his request on the part of the family of d'Arc, and prayed for a Judgment of Nullity on the previous sentence, on the ground that, both in form and substantiation, it was null and void, and that it should therefore be publicly and legally so declared.

On December 20th—the last day appointed for the appearance of any representatives of the accused—only the Advocate for the family of Cauchon presented himself. He made a declaration to the effect that the heirs of the late Bishop had no desire to maintain the validity of a Trial with which they had no concern, and which took place either before they were born or when they were very little children; that Jeanne had been the victim of the hatred of the English, and that therefore the responsibility fell rather upon them; finally they begged that the Rehabilitation of Jeanne might not be to their prejudice, invoking for themselves the benefits of the King's amnesty granted after the conquest of Normandy.

The Procurator having declared his willingness to agree, the heirs of Cauchon were put out of the question; and the other Defendants, not having appeared, were declared contumacious, and cited once more to appear on February 16th following. On the same day [Dec. 20th] the Promoter formulated his Accusation, and brought before the notice of the Court certain special points in the previous Trial which tended to vitiate the whole: 1st, the intervention of the hidden registrars and the alterations, additions, and omissions made in the Twelve Articles;

2nd, the suppression of the Preliminary Enquiry, and the obvious predisposition of the Judges; 3rd, the incompetence of the Court, and the unfairness of the treatment received throughout by the Accused, culminating in an illegal sentence and an irregular execution.

The Promoter then asked that enquiries might be instituted into the life and conduct of the Maid, and as to the manner in which she had undertaken the reconquest of the country. Orders were accordingly given, that information should at once be taken at Domremy and Vaucouleurs, under the direction of Reginald de Chichery, Dean of Vaucouleurs, and of Wautrin Thierry, Canon of Toul.

While these enquiries were being made, a document containing 101 Articles was drawn up,[295] setting forth the case of the Plaintiffs for the consideration of the still-absent Defendants, and stating at great length the grounds, both in fact and reason, for the demand of a revision of sentence.

On the day fixed for the final citation of the Defendants—Feb. 16th, 1456,—the Court again assembled; and on this occasion the accused were represented by their legal successors: the Promoter of the Diocese of Beauvais, Brédouille, as representative of the authority of the Bishop, Guillaume de Hellande; and Chaussetier, the Prior of the Convent of Evreux, as representing the Dominicans of Beauvais, to whose Order Jean Lemaître, the other Judge of the Maid, belonged. Both of these disclaimed any responsibility for the former Trial, but submitted themselves to the mandate of the Court; and, no objection being offered to the 101 Articles, these were accepted by the Judges, and the case was proceeded with.

The Enquiry of 1456 extended over several months. Thirty-four witnesses were heard, in January and February, at Domremy and Vaucouleurs; forty-one, in

---

[295] Of these 101 Articles, the first thirty-three form the basis of the succeeding enquiries made at Paris, Orleans, and Rouen.

February and March, at Orleans; twenty at Paris, in April and May; nineteen at Rouen, in December and May; and on May 28th, at Lyons, the Vice-Inquisitor of the province received the deposition of Jean d'Aulon, whose evidence is specially important, as being that of the Steward of the Maid's household, and the most devoted of her followers.

After the close of these Enquiries and their formal reception as part of the Process, the Advocate of the d'Arc family petitioned the Judges to give their attention to certain Memorials drawn up on the Case by learned men, which documents he prayed might also be inserted among the formal proceedings of the Trial. The request being granted, Eight Memorials were presented and formally annexed to the Authentic Documents of the Process. The whole case was then admirably summed up, for the guidance of the Judges, in the 'Recollectio' of the Inquisitor, Jean Bréhal, and on this document the final Sentence of Rehabilitation was subsequently based.

On the 18th of June, Jean d'Arc and the Promoter, Chapitault in the name of the Plaintiffs, appeared at the Palace of the Bishop of Paris, and prayed that a day might be fixed for the conclusion of the Case. In answer to this request the following 1st of July was appointed for the purpose, and an announcement to that effect was ordered to be placed on all the doors of the Cathedral at Rouen.

On July 2nd the Pontifical Delegates met and appointed the following Wednesday, July 7th, for the pronouncement of the final Sentence; and on that day, at 8 a.m., the Court assembled in the Hall of the Archiepiscopal Palace, and the formal Sentence of Rehabilitation was solemnly read by the Archbishop of Rheims. This was followed by a procession and sermon on the same day in the Place St. Ouen, and by a second sermon on the day following in the Old Market Place, where a Cross to perpetuate the memory of the martyrdom was then erected, "for the salvation of her soul." This Cross remained until the end of the following century, when it was replaced by a fountain, with a statue of the Maid under an arcade surmounted by a Cross; the

*Jeanne D'Arc*

fountain now standing was erected in 1756.

# CHRONOLOGICAL TABLE OF PRINCIPAL EVENTS IN THE LIFE OF JEANNE D'ARC.

| | | |
|---|---|---|
| 1411-12 | January 6 | Birth at Domremy |
| 1424 | Summer | First Visions |
| | | Sojourn at Neufchâteau |
| 1428 | | Call to mission in France |
| | May | Visit to Vaucouleurs |
| | May 13 | Ascension Day |
| 1428-9 | February | Second visit to Vaucouleurs |
| | | Visit to Duke of Lorraine |
| | | Pilgrimage to Saint Nicolas |
| | February 12 | Battle of the Herrings |
| | February 13 | Return to Vaucouleurs |
| | First Sunday of Lent | |
| | February 23, Wed. | Vaucouleurs, with Jean de Metz & others |
| | March 5, Sat. | Fierbois |
| | March 6, Sun. | Arrival at Chinon |
| | March 8, Tues. | Interview with the King |
| | March 22, Tues. in Holy Week | First letter to the English |
| 1429 | March 27, Easter Day | |

*Note.* The year, in the fifteenth century, is computed from Easter.

| | |
|---|---|
| April | Stay at Tours |
| | Household appointed. |
| | Banner painted. |
| | Joins the army at Blois. |
| April 27, Wed. | Start for Orleans. |
| April 29, Fri. | Arrival at Orleans. |
| May 4, Wed. | Fort of Saint Loup taken. |
| May 5, Ascension Day | Third letter to the English. |
| May 5, Fri. | Fort of the Augustins taken. |
| May 7, Sat. | Jeanne wounded. |
| May 8, Sun. | Siege of Orleans raised. |
| May 10, Tues. | Leaves for Blois. |
| May 12, Thurs. | Tours. |
| May 13, Fri. | Meeting with King Charles. |
| May 23, Mon. | Loches. |
| June 2, Thurs. | Selles: grant of arms to Jeanne and her family. |
| June 6, Mon. | Selles: Incident of the horse. |
| June 9, Thurs. | Return to Orleans. |
| June 11-12 | Siege of Jargeau. |
| June 14 | Attack on Meung. |
| June 16 | Siege of Beaugency. |

| | |
|---|---|
| June 17, Fri. | Arrival of the Constable of France. |
| June 18, Sat. | Battle of Patay. |
| June 19, Sun. | Return to Orleans. |
| June 24, Fri. | Jeanne encamps at Given. |
| June 29, Wed. | Start for Rheims. |
| July 1, Fri. | Arrival before Auxerre. |
| July 5, Tues. | Arrival before Troyes. |
| July | Meeting with Brother Richard. |
| July 9, Sat. | Surrender of Troyes. |
| July 10, Sun. | Entry into Troyes. |
| July 12, Tues. | Departure from Troyes. |
| July 14, Thurs. | Chalons. |
| July 15, Fri. | Departure from Chalons. |
| July 16, Sat. | Charles enters Rheims. |
| July 17, Sun. | Coronation of Charles. |
| July 21, Thurs. | Charles touches for "the Evil" at Saint Marcoul. |
| July 22, Fri. | Charles receives keys of Soissons and Laon at Vailly, |
| July 23, Sat. | and of four other towns. |
| July 29, Fri. | Skirmish at Château Thierry. |
| August 4, Thurs. | Charles signs fifteen days' truce with the Duke of Burgundy. |
| August 13, Sat. | Skirmish at Dammartin. |
| August 18, Thurs. | Compiègne entered. |
| August | Senlis and Beauvais surrender; flight of Bishop. |
| August 23, Tues. | Jeanne leaves Compiègne for Saint Denis; letter from the Count of Armagnac received when starting. |
| August 26, Fri. | Jeanne at Saint Denis. |
| August 28, Sun. | Secret treaty of Charles VII. With the Duke of Burgundy, to Christmas. |
| Sept. 8, Thurs. Nativity of the B.V.M. | Attack on Paris. Jeanne wounded. |
| Sept. 10, Sat. | Retreat ordered by Charles. |
| Sept. | Jeanne's armour hung up in the church at Saint Denis. |
| Sept. 13, Tues. | Charles leaves Saint Denis. |
| Sept. 18, Sun. | Second treaty of Charles VII. with the Duke of Burgundy. |
| October | Jeanne at Bourges. |
| November | Saint Pierre-le-Moustier assailed and taken. |
| Nov. 9, Wed. | Siege of La Charité |
| November | Truce with Burgundy til Easter. |
| 1429-30 December | Passed in visiting the towns she had |
| January | freed. Orleans visited for the last |
| February | time on January 19th. |
| March 3 | At Sully with the King. Leaves |

|      |                     | Sully, accompanied by D'Aulon Pasquerel, and goes to Lagny. |
|------|---------------------|-----------------------------------------------------------|
|      | April               | Franquet d'Arras taken and executed at Lagny. Alleged miracle. |
| 1430 | April 16            | Easter Sunday                                             |
|      | April               | Melun-warning of capture.                                 |
|      | April 23, Sun.      | Henry VI. Lands at Calais.                                |
|      | May 13, Sat.        | Jeanne at Compiègne (Archbishop of Rheims then in the city). During this month she visits Senlis, Soissons, and other towns. |
|      | May                 | Jeanne repulsed on the Oise whilst trying to relieve Choisy, then besieged by the Duke of Burgundy. Jeanne in Compiègne; prediction in the church of Saint Jacques. |
|      | May 22, Mon.        | Jeanne goes to Crespy for reinforcements.                 |
|      | May 23, Tues.       | Jeanne's return to Compiègne, and capture. Letter of Duke of Burgundy to the people of Saint-Quentin, announcing the capture. |
|      | May 25, Ascension Day | News of capture reaches Paris.                          |
|      | May                 | Jeanne a prisoner for several days at Marigny.            |
|      | May                 | In prison at Beaulieu.                                    |
| 1430 | June 6              | At Noyon.                                                 |
|      | July 14, Fri.       | Cauchon's mission to the Duke of Burgundy.                |
|      | July 29, Sat.       | Henry VI. arrives at Rouen.                               |
|      | August              | In prison at Beaurevoir.                                  |
|      | October             | Leap from the Tower of Beaurevoir. Prophecy of the relief of Compiègne "before Martinmas." |
|      | October 25          | Relief of Compiègne.                                      |
|      | Nov. (about the middle) | Jeanne sold by Jean de Luxembourg. Jeanne taken to Arras, then Crotoy. |
|      | December (late)     | Brought to Rouen.                                         |
| 1430-1 | January 3, Wed.   | Order of surrender of Jeanne as "suspect of heresy," from Henry VI. to the judges. |

### I. CAUSE DE LAPSE.

*Trial Ex Officio.*

|      | January 9, Tues. | First day of the trial. Preliminary meeting in the Bishop's house. Appointment of officers. |
|------|------------------|----------------------------------------------------------------------------------------------|

| | January 13, Sat. | First consultation of the Bishop with the Doctors; the result of the Domremy enquiry discussed (?) Articles of Accusation to be prepared. |
| | January 23, Tues. | Second consultation with the six Doctors. Articles approved. Delafontaine appointed to make further enquiries. |
| | Feb. 13-17 Tues. – Sat. | Officers make oath of fidelity. |
| 1430-1 | Feb. 19, Mon | Consultation of the Bishop with twelve Doctors. Decision that the Case shall be proceeded with, and the Inquisitor or his Deputy invited to attend. The Deputy Inquisitor, being summoned, pleads inability. |
| | Feb. 20, Tues. | The Deputy Inquisitor again appears, But still refuses to act as Judge without Commission from his Superior. It is decided to write to the Chief Inquisitor. Jeanne is cited to appear the next day. |
| | Feb. 21, Wed. | First Public Examination, in the Chapel-Royal. Jeanne's guardians appointed from the King's Body Guard. (42 Assessors.) |
| | Feb. 22, Thurs. | Second Public Examination in the Ornament Room. The Deputy Inquisitor declares his assent to the trial. Beaupère charged with the examination. (48 Assessors.) |
| | Feb. 24, Sat. | Third Public Examination, in the Ornament Room. (52 Assessors.) |
| | Feb. 27, Tues. | Fourth Public Examination, in the Ornament Room. (54 Assessors.) |
| | March 1, Thurs. | Fifth Public Examination, in the Ornament Room. (58 Assessors.) |
| | March 3, Sat. | Sixth Public Examination, in the Ornament Room. (41 Assessors.) The Bishop decides to continue the Examination privately. |
| | March 4-9, Sun.-Fri. | The Examinations are considered by the Bishop and some of the Doctors, and it is decided to question Jeanne on sundry doubtful points. |
| | March 10, Sat. | First Private Examination, in prison, conducted by Delafontaine, assisted by two Assessors and two witnesses. |
| | March 12, Mon. | Second Private Examination, in |

|  |  | Prison, in the morning. |
|---|---|---|
|  |  | Third Private Examination, in prison, in the afternoon, the Bishop not present. |
|  |  | In the Bishop's house, on the same day, the letter from the Inquisitor, appointing his Vicar to act as his deputy, is read; and the Vicar is appointed to act as Judge. |
|  | March 13, Tues. | The Vicar joins with the Bishop and appoints his officers. |
|  |  | Fourth Private Examination, the first at which the Inquisitor is present as Judge. |
|  | March 14, Wed. | Fifth Private Examination, in prison, in the morning. |
|  |  | Sixth Private Examination, in prison, in the afternoon. |
| 1430 | March 15, Thurs. | Seventh Private Examination in prison. |
|  | March 17, Sat. | Eighth Private Examination, in prison, in the morning. |
|  |  | Ninth Private Examination, in prison, in the afternoon. |
|  | March 18, Passion Sunday | Consultation of the Bishop with twelve Assessors, in the Bishop's House. They adjourn til March 22$^{nd}$ to deliberate over the examinations already held. |
|  | March 22, Thurs. | Consultation at the Bishop's house. Résumé of the answers of Jeanne read to twenty-two Assessors. |
|  | March 24, Sat. | The Judges, Delafontaine, and six Assessors visit Jeanne in prison, And the examinations are read over To her in French by Manchon. |
|  | March 25, Palm Sunday | The Bishop and four Assessors visit Jeanne in prison. |
|  |  | The complete papers of the Process *ex officio* are given to the Promoter that he may prepare the Articles of Accusation for the Trial in Ordinary. |
|  | March 26, Mon. | At a meeting at the Bishop's house, Twelve Assessors and the two Judges being present, it is decided to proceed on the following day to the Trial in Ordinary, to be conducted by the Promoter. |

*Trial in Ordinary.*

| | | |
|---|---|---|
| 1430-1 | March 27, Tues. | Solemn sitting in the Great Hall of the Castle; the two Judges and 38 Assessors present. The Act of Accusation, in Seventy Articles, is produced by the Promoter, and read to Jeanne by Thomas de Courcelles. questions are put to her on each Article. |
| | March 28, Wed. | The same continued – 35 Assessors Present. |
| | March 31, Easter Eve | The Judges and 9 Assessors visit Jeanne in prison, to question her on Sundry points upon which she had Asked for delay. |
| 1431 | April 1, Easter Day | |
| | April 2-4, Mon.-Wed. | The Judges and certain of the Assessors employ themselves in reducing the Seventy Articles to Twelve; these are finally drawn up by Nicholas Midi. |
| | April 5, Thurs. | The Twelve Articles are sent to the Assessors for their opinion, which they are asked to send in by April 10$^{th}$. |
| | April 12, Thurs. | Consultation of 22 Assessors, who decide that Jeanne must be condemned. During the following week many other opinions, all more or less in accordance with this, are sent in. |
| | April 28, Wed. | Jeanne is ill. The two Judges and 7 Assessors visit her in prison; and the Bishop addresses to her a charitable exhortation. |
| | April 19, Thurs. | The Twelve Articles are sent to the University of Paris. |
| | May 14 | These are discussed in full assembly on April 29$^{th}$; then by the Faculties of Theology and Decrees, separately; and finally, the Resolutions of these Faculties are adopted by the University and forwarded to Rouen. |
| | May 2, Wed. | Solemn assembly in the Ornament Room; the two Judges and 63 Assessors present. Jeanne is summoned and admonished by the Bishop; and a solemn preachment is made to her by the Archdeacon of |

|                  | Eu. |
|------------------|-----|
| May 9, Wed.      | The Judges and 9 Assessors summon Jeanne to the Torture Chamber in the Great Tower, and threaten her with Torture. |
| May 10           | Ascension Day. |
| May 12, Sat.     | Consultation in the Bishop's house; the Judges and 12 Assessors present. It is decided not to torture Jeanne. |
| May 19, Sat.     | Solemn assembly in the Chapel of the Archiepiscopal Manor – 51 Assessors present. The Resolutions of the University of Paris are read, and the opinions of the Assessors taken. |
| May 23, Wed.     | Solemn meeting in a room near the Prison. The Judges and 7 Assessors Are accompanied by the Bishops of Noyon and Thérouanne. Jeanne is summoned, and solemnly admonished by Pierre Maurice. The Final Sentence is appointed for the next day. |
| May 24, Thurs.   | Public assembly in the Cemetery of Saint Ouen; the Cardinal of England And the Bishop of Norwich present. Exhortation from Érard. Abjuration Of Jeanne. Sentence of perpetual Imprisonment. In the afternoon, the Deputy Inquisitor and sundry Assessors visit Jeanne in prison. |

## II. CAUSE DE RELAPSE.

|                  |     |
|------------------|-----|
| May 28, Mon.     | The Judges and 4 Assessors visit Jeanne in prison, having been informed of her relapse. |
| May 29, Tues.    | Solemn meeting in the Chapel of the Archiepiscopal Manor, 40 Assessors present. Consultation on the relapse of Jeanne. Decision of the Assessors that she must be delivered up to the secular arm as a relapsed heretic. |
| May 30, Wed.     | Massieu delivers the order of execution to Jeanne. Visit of sundry Assessors and of the Bishop to the prison. Jeanne receives the Holy Communion. Final exhortation from Nicholas Midi at the public assembly |

|                |                                                                                           |
| -------------- | ----------------------------------------------------------------------------------------- |
|                | in the Old Market Place. Sentence pronounced against Jeanne. Her death.                   |
| June 7, Wed.   | Information taken after the death of Jeanne by certain persons who visited her in prison on May 30. |
| June 8, Thurs. | (1) Letter from the King, Henry VI., to the Emperor, announcing the trial, sentence, and execution of Jeanne. |
| June 12, Mon.  | Letter of Guarantee for those concerned in the Trial, from Henry VI.                      |
| June 28        | (2) Letter from Henry VI. to the same effect as (1), to prelates and nobles. Letter of the University of Paris to the Pope. |
| August 8       | Sentence pronounced against a monk who had spoken ill of the Judges.                      |

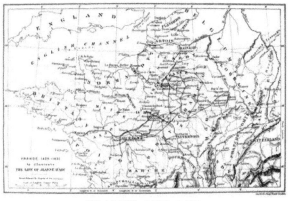

FRANCE, 1429–1431
to illustrate
THE LIFE OF JEANNE D'ARC
*Route followed by Jeanne d'Arc*
*Stanford's Geog^l Estab^t. London.*

Printed in the USA
CPSIA information can be obtained
at www.ICGtesting.com
CBHW031456271124
18025CB00045B/547

9 798330 219483